"Many are familiar with early stage investing. Many are familiar with technology. Many are familiar with disruption and innovation. Yet, few truly understand how different an animal is the financial services industry. Such vectors as regulation, compliance, risk, handling other people's money, the psychological behaviours around money and capital ensure that our financial services industry is full of quirks and complexities. As such *The FinTech Book* offers a refreshing take and knowledge expertise, which neophytes as well as experts will be well advised to read."

Pascal Bouvier, Venture Partner, Santander InnoVentures

"This first ever crowd-sourced book on the broad FinTech ecosystem is an extremely worthwhile read for anyone trying to understand why and how technology will impact most, if not all, of the financial services industry. It captures and highlights the disruptive forces at play. Start-up FinTech firms across the globe will have a profound impact on the future delivery of services to both institutions and individuals. This book is a terrific compilation of information and prescient thought that should prove useful to both financial services practitioners and users."

R. Todd Ruppert, retired CEO and President of T. Rowe Price Global Investment Services and serial FinTech investor and advisor

"Sometimes a book explains how the world has changed. Rarely, a book comes along that explains how the world is going to change in the future. This is one of those rare compilations that describe the fundamental changes taking place in how people live their lives. It portrays a world where, through a potent potion of technology and entrepreneurialism, power moves away from central banking institutions to local communities and the people within them. This book helps explain why London is the global hotspot for innovation in financial and payment technology. You won't be able to put it down."

Tony Craddock, Director General, Emerging Payments Association

"Finally FinTech is entering the mainstream vernacular such that more than just we finance, banking and payments geeks and innovators are aware of the revolution underway. If you're looking for a 'crash-course' on the FinTech industry, and the explosion of innovation that it's creating across the globe, look no further. The depth and diversity of views herein is staggering; a phenomenal compilation that will get you up-to-speed fast. Definitely worth a read."

Roy Vella, FinTech Expert, Public Speaker and Managing Director of Vella Ventures Ltd

"Fantastic to see a book on FinTech brought together by the community and written by the community. It will be valuable to anyone starting off in FinTech".

Nigel Verdon, Founder, Currency Cloud, Partner, Digital Change

"FinTech is about all of us – it's the future intersection of people, technology and money, and it's happening now there is an  *The FinTech Book* paint a visual pi A must-read for every disruptor, in

De

"FinTech is reshaping the financial the world today, and has the potential to dramatically alter our understanding of financial services tomorrow. We're in the thick of the development of an Internet of Value that will deliver sweeping, positive change around the world just as the internet itself did a few short decades ago. *The FinTech Book* captures the unique ecosystem that has coalesced around this sector, bringing together visionary entrepreneurs, innovative finance leaders, and forward-thinking policymakers to comment on the exciting changes taking place."

Chris Larsen, Co-Founder and CEO of Ripple

"There are few books out there that capture the pulse of how the internet is changing finance, but *The FinTech Book* has captured the views of many of the key players building the ValueWeb. It will prove an essential read to anyone wanting to know more about the next generation of banking, insurance and finance."

Chris Skinner, Author of *ValueWeb* and Chair of the Financial Services Club

"Over the next decade, the notion of what a bank is will be turned on its head – where bricks and mortar give way to apps, artificial intelligence, and decentralized ledgers. *The FinTech Book* comes at a perfect time when incumbents, start-ups, and investors alike are trying to grasp what this future holds, for the stakes of getting it right or wrong are truly enormous."

Greg Rogers, Executive Director, Techstars

"*The FinTech Book* provides an excellent open platform to hear from a wide variety of thought-provoking voices. True innovative change only happens with the support of collaborative ecosystems. *The FinTech Book* allows readers to hold this ecosystem in the palm of their hands,"

Liz Lumley, Director of Global Ecosystem Development, Startupbootcamp FinTech and InsurTech

"A truly indispensable guide for anyone who wants to understand the market dynamics of the FinTech revolution and the disruption behind it. Intelligent and thought provoking, you'll either be exhilarated by the scale of the growth opportunities or horrified that your world is going to change so fundamentally."

Dr Louise Beaumont, Head of Public Affairs and Marketing, GLI Finance Limited

"London has established itself firmly as a global powerhouse for FinTech. With the world's leading international financial centre and Europe's fastest growing technology hub, London is at the forefront of the latest innovations in financial technology and we are changing the way governments, businesses and consumers manage their financial affairs. We are also a city of great creativity, where new ideas thrive and disruption is welcome. All these ingredients will help London to become the FinTech capital of the world. It is important that we continue to promote the sector and shout about our successes. *The FinTech Book* not only provides valuable insight into the industry from some of the leading experts in London, but also shines a spotlight on what makes London an ideal destination for FinTech companies."

David Slater, Director of International Trade and Investment, London & Partners

"With many of the contributors to this book we shared the very first FinTech days, back to 2008. In the middle of the hype now, where often noise and relevance are intertwined, I am really happy to see so many meaningful thoughts and opinion pieces about what is certainly one of the biggest pivotal shifts in financial services."

Matteo Rizzi, FinTech Investor and Co-Founder, FinTechStage

"FINTECH Circle are at the forefront of the latest FinTech developments and innovation, and *The FinTech Book* reflects their open, collaborative and inclusive approach. It offers a unique insight into key trends in this industry to each part of the ecosystem – entrepreneurs, investors and service providers alike will connect with the dynamics captured here. Reaching out to such a wide range of experts provides unprecedented insight into FinTech, making this an interesting read for anyone interested in this space."

Axel Coustere, Founding Partner, The Hub Exchange

"The FinTech book is a great jumping off point for anyone looking to understand FinTech, especially in Asia. As this new kind of technology becomes more ubiquitous, resources like this book will become more and more valuable to both newbies and experienced hands."

Vladislav Solodkiy, CEO, Life.Sreda

"This book is a brilliant kaleidoscope of themes, success stories, and current and future trends in the financial technology space. A must-read for anyone who is interested in FinTech, it provides a solid overview of the various ways digital innovation can transform banking and finance."

Dr Markos Zachariadis, Assistant Professor, Warwick Business School; FinTech Research Fellow at Cambridge Digital Innovation, University of Cambridge

"There is a lot of confusion around what FinTech really is and how it could be deployed by existing financial services companies. This book is well timed as it cuts through the hype and allows the reader to review practical approaches from actual exponents and thereby educate themselves on where different technologies can be applied to their businesses."

Brendan Bradley, Chief Innovation Officer and Member of the Eurex Executive Board; Chairman of the Executive Board, Deutsche Boerse Asia Holdings Ltd

"*The FinTech Book* really lives up to its title. Janos and Susanne have not just succeeded in explaining the key trends, drivers and implications across a wide spectrum of FinTech themes (including payments, crowdfunding, advisory and cryptocurrencies), but have also clearly laid out the path forward, pragmatically detailing enablers such as regulatory / compliance management, analytic capabilities, and technical competency that are required to effectively capture and monetize the different FinTech disruptions. This is a truly cross-discipline, hands-on and comprehensive FinTech bible, which all players in the FinTech space, including investors, entrepreneurs, incumbent institutions and regulators, can benefit from."

Robin J. Loh, General Manager, Ping'an FinTech

"FinTech innovation is an important component of economic development, especially for emerging economies. There are few books that summarize the FinTech movement more completely than The FinTech Book. It provides a wonderful summary of the global innovation in the industry to date."

Melissa Guzy, Managing Partner and Founder, Arbor Ventures

"I have a passion for helping businesses invest and grow, and often the key to this is education. At a stroke here is a book that opens up the FinTech world to all who are curious, ambitious and entrepreneurial. FinTech is moving at a tremendous pace and this truly excellent book enables the reader to keep up and even get ahead of how global innovation in financial and payment technology will change and shape the world we live in. The joint editors, Susanne Chishti and Janos Barberis, have done an outstanding job."

John Davies, CEO, The Just Loans Group PLC

"London is rapidly becoming known as a leading FinTech centre internationally. The development of *The FinTech Book* is timely and innovative, capturing the knowledge of the City's ecosystem players. It will be a valuable resource for those seeking to understand the implications of these disruptive technologies for the finance landscape."

Professor Michael Barrett, Cambridge Judge Business School, Academic Director, Cambridge Digital Innovation

The FinTech Book

This edition first published 2016

© 2016 Susanne Chishti and Janos Barberis

Registered office

John Wiley & Sons Ltd, The Atrium, Southern Gate, Chichester, West Sussex, PO19 8SQ, United Kingdom

For details of our global editorial offices, for customer services and for information about how to apply for permission to reuse the copyright material in this book please see our website at www.wiley.com.

All rights reserved. No part of this publication may be reproduced, stored in a retrieval system, or transmitted, in any form or by any means, electronic, mechanical, photocopying, recording or otherwise, except as permitted by the UK Copyright, Designs and Patents Act 1988, without the prior permission of the publisher.

Wiley publishes in a variety of print and electronic formats and by print-on-demand. Some material included with standard print versions of this book may not be included in e-books or in print-on-demand. If this book refers to media such as a CD or DVD that is not included in the version you purchased, you may download this material at http://booksupport.wiley.com. For more information about Wiley products, visit www.wiley.com.

Designations used by companies to distinguish their products are often claimed as trademarks. All brand names and product names used in this book are trade names, service marks, trademarks or registered trademarks of their respective owners. The publisher is not associated with any product or vendor mentioned in this book.

Limit of Liability/Disclaimer of Warranty: While the publisher and author have used their best efforts in preparing this book, they make no representations or warranties with respect to the accuracy or completeness of the contents of this book and specifically disclaim any implied warranties of merchantability or fitness for a particular purpose. It is sold on the understanding that the publisher is not engaged in rendering professional services and neither the publisher nor the author shall be liable for damages arising herefrom. If professional advice or other expert assistance is required, the services of a competent professional should be sought.

Library of Congress Cataloging-in-Publication Data

Names: Chishti, Susanne, author. | Barberis, Janos, author.
Title: The FinTech Book / Susanne Chishti, Janos Barberis.
Description: Hoboken : Wiley, 2016. | Includes index.
Identifiers: LCCN 2016000567| ISBN 9781119218876 (paperback)
Subjects: LCSH: Banks and banking. | Bank loans. | Credit. | Financial
services industry—Information technology. | BISAC: BUSINESS & ECONOMICS /
Finance.
Classification: LCC HG1601 .C47 2016 | DDC 332.1028/4—dc23 LC record available at http://lccn.loc.gov/2016000567
A catalogue record for this book is available from the British Library.
ISBN 978-1-119-21887-6 (pbk) ISBN 978-1-119-21893-7 (ebk)
ISBN 978-1-119-21888-3 (ebk) ISBN 978-1-119-21890-6 (ebk)

Cover Design: Wiley
Cover Image: © pkproject/Shutterstock

Set in 8/13 Helvetica LT Std by Aptara, New Delhi, India
Printed in Great Britain by TJ International Ltd, Padstow, Cornwall, UK

The FinTech Book

The Financial Technology Handbook for Investors, Entrepreneurs and Visionaries

Edited by
Susanne Chishti
Janos Barberis

Contents

7. Enterprise Innovation

8. More Success Stories

9. Crypto-currencies and Blockchains

10. The Future of FinTech

Preface

We both started off delving into the field of FinTech at roughly the same point in time. Eager to learn more, we quickly discovered that there existed no single, consolidated, and authoritative source on the subject. On a remarkably sunny London day, we met up in a local café, ascertaining our mutual passion for FinTech and our desire to find out more. Typically of entrepreneurs, we decided to fill the currently existing gap in FinTech knowledge and produce a FinTech book ourselves, a book that would provide food for thought to FinTech newbies, pioneers, and well-seasoned experts alike. This is how *The FinTech Book* was born.

The reader will notice that this is the first "globally crowdsourced" treatment of the subject. The reason we decided to reach out to the global FinTech community in sourcing contributors for the book lies in the inherently fragmented nature of the field of Financial Technology. There was no single author, organization, or indeed region in the world that could exhaustively cover all the facets and nuances of FinTech. What is more, by being able to call upon a truly global contributor base, we not only stayed true to the spirit of FinTech, making

use of technological channels of communication in reaching out to, selecting, and reviewing our would-be contributors, we also made sure that every corner of the globe had the chance to have its say. Thus, we aimed to fulfil one of the most important purposes of *The FinTech Book*, namely to give a voice to those that would remain unheard, those that did not belong to a true FinTech community in their local areas, and spread that voice to an international audience. We have immensely enjoyed the journey of editing *The FinTech Book* and sincerely hope that you will enjoy the journey of reading it, at least as much.

More than 160 authors from 27 countries submitted 189 abstracts to be part of the book. We asked our global FinTech community for their views regarding which abstracts they would like to have fully expanded for *The FinTech Book*. From all these potential contributors, we selected 86 authors who have been asked to write full chapters, which have now been included in this book. We conducted a questionnaire among all our selected authors to further understand their background and expertise.

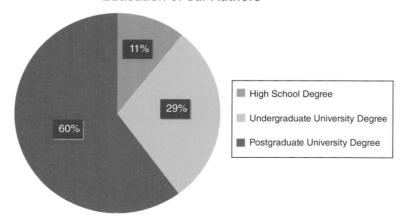

Figure 1: **What is the highest educational qualification of our authors?**

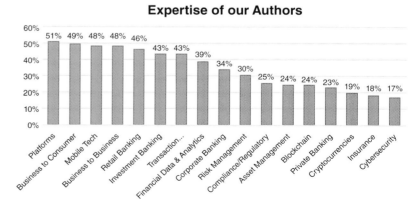

Figure 2: **Areas in which our authors have domain expertise (multiple choices were possible)**

Where do our Authors work?

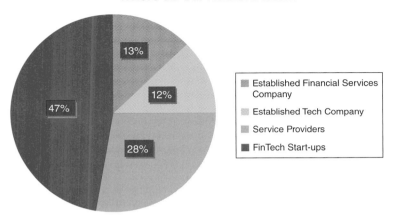

Legend:
- Established Financial Services Company
- Established Tech Company
- Service Providers
- FinTech Start-ups

13%
12%
47%
28%

Figure 3: Type of company in which our authors were working

Size of Companies where our Authors work

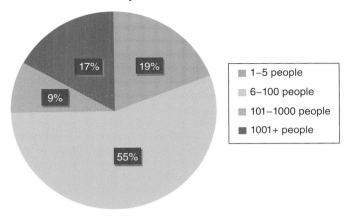

Legend:
- 1–5 people
- 6–100 people
- 101–1000 people
- 1001+ people

17%
19%
9%
55%

Figure 4: Size of companies for which our authors work

Our selected final authors come from 20 countries. The majority have postgraduate university degrees (60%) (Figure 1), strong domain expertise across many fields (Figure 2), and 93% of our finalist authors have had articles published before.

Figures 3 and 4 show that almost half our finalist authors are entrepreneurs working for FinTech start-ups (many of them part of the founding team), a quarter come from established financial and technology companies, and another quarter from service providers such as consulting firms or law firms servicing the FinTech sector.

Almost a fifth of our authors work for start-ups with up to five people and another 55% for start-ups/small and medium-sized enterprises (SMEs) of up to 100 people. 17% of our contributors are employed by a large organization of more than 1,000 employees.

In summary, we are very proud of our highly qualified authors, their strong expertise, and passion for FinTech through being either entrepreneurs or often

"intrapreneurs" in large established organizations who all are committed to play a significant role in the global FinTech revolution. These remarkable people are willing to share their insights with all of us in these pages.

Firstly, this project would not have been possible without the dedication and efforts of all contributors to *The FinTech Book* (both those who submitted their initial abstracts for consideration by the global FinTech community, as well as the final authors whose insights you will be reading shortly). In addition, we would like to thank Inna Amesheva, Suki Jutla, and Maya Petersohn for their invaluable help in the final stages of the editing process. Last, but certainly not least, we would like to thank our editors at Wiley whose guidance and help ensured that the project which started off as an idea in a London café has become the book which you are now holding in your hands.

Susanne Chishti and Janos Barberis
The FinTech Book Editors
2016

About the Editors

Susanne Chishti

Susanne Chishti is the CEO of FINTECH Circle, Europe's 1st Angel Network focused on FinTech investments, founder of London FINTECH Tours, and Chairman of FINTECH Circle Innovate. Selected as one of the 100 leading Women in FinTech and top 15 FinTech UK Twitter influencers, she was recognized in the European Digital Financial Services 'Power 50' 2015, an independent ranking of the most influential people in digital financial services in Europe.

Susanne is a senior capital markets manager, entrepreneur, and investor with strong FinTech expertise. She is a mentor, judge, and coach at FinTech events such as SWIFT Innotribe, Barclays TechStars Accelerator, Cambridge Judge Business School, and Startupbootcamp FinTech Accelerators. She has more than 14 years' experience across Deutsche Bank, Lloyds Banking Group, Morgan Stanley, and Accenture in London and Hong Kong. Selected among top UK FinTech Influencers by City A.M. Susanne is also the author of FinTech articles and an international keynote speaker at FinTech conferences. She runs one of the leading online FinTech communities of FinTech entrepreneurs, investors, senior management from established financial and tech firms, and thought leaders – FINTECH Circle's LinkedIn Group with more than 10,000 members worldwide.

You can follow Susanne on Twitter via her account @SusanneChishti.

About FINTECH Circle

Founded by Susanne Chishti, FINTECH Circle is an international brand linking the FinTech ecosystem of investors, entrepreneurs, business leaders, and influencers who all are enthusiastic about the growing FinTech sector globally. In addition to accessing top FinTech investment opportunities via the Angel Network, members also enjoy knowledge sharing amongst peers, access to board and non-exec positions in FinTech companies, and the opportunity to attend exclusive FinTech and angel investment educational seminars (www.fintechcircle.com). In addition, London FINTECH Tours (www.fintechtours.com) provide non-UK FinTech entrepreneurs with the opportunity to visit London to leverage London's FinTech ecosystem of investors and clients to help them grow their business. FINTECH Circle Innovate (www.fintechcircleinnovate.com) was set up in response to demand from growing numbers of banks and large institutions who needed help to close the gap between corporate strategy and sustainable innovation in FinTech. We guide them through the global FinTech landscape and are able to source the best targets for partnership, incubation, investment and acquisition purposes. You can follow FINTECH Circle on Twitter via @FINTECHCircle and @FINTECHTours, and FINTECH Circle Innovate via @FTCInnovate.

Janos Barberis

Janos Barberis is a Millennial in FinTech, recognized as a top-35 global FinTech leader. His expertise is focused on the new regulatory considerations raised by the development of FinTech. With a passion to drive change, he founded FinTech HK, a thought leadership platform, and the SuperCharger – a FinTech Accelerator that strategically leverages Hong Kong as a gateway to Asia.

In parallel, he sits on the advisory board of the World Economic Forum's FinTech Committee and is a PhD Candidate at Hong Kong University Law School. Janos regularly delivers Keynote speeches and has been featured in *Forbes, The Financial Times* and *Business Insider,* among others. He is also the Co-Founder and Editor of *The FinTech Book.*

Previously, Janos was the first hire at a prospective UK challenger bank, Lintel, helping it to secure a banking license from the PRA and FCA. This role followed a specialist interest, developed over 7 years, in financial systems and their stability. Notably, in 2012 Janos proposed to reform the Chinese shadow banking sector by developing P2P lending channels. He also introduced a framework of developing real-time and dynamic regulatory supervision models for financial networks, paving the way towards what is now regarded as RegTech.

Janos holds an LLM in Corporate and Financial Law (HKU) as well as a BSc in Economics & Finance and an LLB in Law (UK). He has been awarded a Research Postgraduate Scholarship from Hong Kong University Law School. He co-authored the academic paper, "The Evolution of FinTech" which ranked within the Top 10 of SSRN globally.

You can follow Janos on Twitter via his account @JNBarberis

About FinTech HK

Founded by Janos Barberis in July 2014, FinTech HK is a thought leadership platform that has the objective of catalysing Hong Kong's position as a world-leading FinTech Hub. FinTech HK produced Hong Kong's first FinTech Report: "The Rise of FinTech: Getting Hong Kong to Lead the Digital Financial Transition in APAC."* Since then, the platform has hosted and supported a number of local and international FinTech events. FinTech HK is a main supporting organization of the SuperCharger, Hong Kong's first home-grown FinTech accelerator dedicated to both early- and late-stage companies that are scaling within Asia.

---

* The report is available on: http://www.slideshare.net/FinTechHk/fintech-hong-kong-report.

Acknowledgements

When we started discussing our desire for a book which would summarize the global FinTech sector in an easy way, it was just an idea between two people. From that moment onwards we spoke to hundreds of our FinTech friends globally and everybody supported the idea. FinTech entrepreneurs across all continents were eager to share their powerful insights. They wanted to explain the new business models and technologies they were working on to change the world of finance. FinTech investors, "intrapreneurs", innovation leaders at leading financial institutions and thought leaders were keen to describe their embrace of the FinTech revolution. Finally, many FinTech visionaries wanted to share their vision for the future.

This global effort of crowdsourcing such insights is a world first. We are aware that this would not have been possible without the FINTECH Circle and FinTech HK global communities. We are very grateful to our members who have been with us since 2014 when both groups were created. Our FINTECH Circle Group on LinkedIn has more than 10,000 members globally and all readers of the book are invited to join and continue the conversation online. We also want to thank our 20,000 Twitter followers across our Twitter accounts @FINTECHCircle; @FinTechHK; @FTCInnovate; @FINTECHTours; @SuperChargerFT; and of course our dedicated Twitter account @TheFINTECHBook. Without the public support and engagement of our global FinTech community this book would not have been possible.

The authors you will read about have been chosen by our global FinTech community purely on merit, thus no matter how big or small their organization,

no matter in which country they work in, no matter if they were well known or still undiscovered, everybody had the same chance. We are proud of that because we believe that FinTech will change the world of finance forever and the global FinTech community is made up of the smartest, most innovative and nicest people we know. Thank you for being part of our Journey. It is difficult to name you all here, but you are all listed in the directory at the end of this book.

We also wanted to select the best publisher for the book and we have chosen Wiley to allow readers globally to buy their hardcopies or order online. A special thanks goes to our fantastic editor Thomas Hyrkiel who saw the vision for the book from the moment we met. Thank you and to your team – we could not have done it without your amazing support!

We look forward to hearing from you. Please visit our website www.TheFINTECHBook.com for additional bonus content from our global FinTech community, consisting of the top FinTech entrepreneurs, investors, intrapreneurs and FinTech visionaries!

Please send us your comments on *The FinTech Book* and let us know how you wish to be engaged by dropping us a line at info@thefintechbook.com

Susanne Chishti
Twitter @susannechishti

Janos Barberis
Twitter @JNBarberis

Introduction

Financial Technology or FinTech is one of the most promising industries in 2016. The FinTech revolution, driven by a wave of start-ups with innovative new business and revenue models, new products and services, is changing finance for the better globally. These FinTech firms offer users a range of financial services that were once almost exclusively the business of banks. Should banks be afraid of the FinTech boom?

At the end of 2015 *Forbes* concluded:

> The banking industry is ripe for change with the rise of fintech startups, the growing popularity of blockchain technology, and the dominance of millennials. The industry is evolving and the ever-increasing need to prepare for cybersecurity threats remains top of mind, as banks continue evaluating new threats and potential fraud risks.[1]

This introduction provides a broad overview of the Financial Technology sector by setting the scene and explaining what is actually meant by "FinTech". These chapters serve as stepping stones paving the way towards the more specific topics that are covered in greater detail in *The FinTech Book*.

---

[1] *Forbes*, 20 November 2015: "Millennials and FinTech are Top of Mind for Traditional Banks",<http://www.forbes.com/sites/franksorrentino/2015/11/20/heard-at-the=2015-ABA-national-convention/>.

Banking and the E-Book Moment

By Warren Mead

Partner, Head of Challenger Banks and Global Co-Lead FinTech, KPMG

Cast your mind back to 2007, the year that saw the launch of the first-generation Kindle. At that time e-readers were widely available in electronics stores but there was no real indication that a revolution was about to sweep the publishing industry. The merits of the e-book were widely discussed by book buyers, but the printed word still reigned supreme – digital consumption was very much a minority sport.

Fast-forward to the present day and both readers and publishers are in a very different place, and sales of e-books have rocketed. According to figures published by Statista,[1] the US digital book market was worth just US$0.27 billion in 2008, but by 2015 that figure had risen to $5.69 billion. Physical book sales haven't collapsed; what we have seen is digital publishing taking a rapid route from the periphery of public consciousness to the mainstream in less than 10 years. The e-book is now part of our lives. It's a journey that reflects the willingness – and eagerness – of consumers to embrace convenience even where this is made possible by complex new technologies, delivery channels, and business models. And this journey is currently being echoed in the financial services industry.

The Shifting Financial Landscape

The world's major retail banks still dominate the financial services landscape, providing the deposit, payment, and credit facilities that we all use and take for granted, but they are no longer the only players in town. Today's online shopper might pay with a debit card but equally they might choose PayPal. The business that would once have relied on its bank for credit can now borrow from peer-to-peer (P2P) platforms or specialist lenders. And digital banks are vying with their bricks-and-mortar counterparts for customer deposits. It's all about access and convenience.

As alternative finance gains traction with customers, FinTech is approaching its e-book moment – the point at which a critical mass of consumers and business customers see the technology-driven solutions offered by new players in the marketplace as a viable – and often preferable – alternative to the services offered by incumbent banks.

The implications for the traditional banking industry are immense. Developments in FinTech have the potential to erode the brand equity of the incumbent players and eat into market share. But banks also have an opportunity to embrace FinTech innovation and offer new solutions to their customers.

An Unfinished Revolution

Anyone seeking evidence of the potential market power and reach of technology-driven finance providers need look no further than the now venerable PayPal. Launched in 1998, the company was taken over by eBay in 2002 and became the default payment system across all of the online auction operator's international sites. Since then PayPal has expanded its offering and it now sits alongside debit and credit cards as a payment option on an ever-increasing number of e-commerce sites. Whether that online performance will translate to dominance in face-to-face transactions remains to be seen. Today, the company boasts more than 100 million active accounts and processes an average of US$315 million in payments every day.[2]

The payments market is evolving fast and this evolution will chase convenience, speed, and data collation. Witness the initial success of Apple's contactless payment system Apple Pay, which allows consumers to purchase and pay for goods and services simply by placing an iPhone 6 in proximity to a point-of-sale terminal. Apple Pay is just launching in the UK, but it currently accounts for US$2 out of every $3 processed by contactless systems in the US.[3]

One of the single greatest obstacles is ubiquity – the consumer can be faced with a myriad ways to pay. We are now witnessing a global wave to introduce 24/7

---

[1] Revenue from e-book sales in the United States from 2008 to 2018 (in billion US dollars), http://www.statista.com/statistics/190800/ebook-sales-revenue-forecast-for-the-us-market/.

[2] Paypal Company Statistics, http://www.statisticbrain.com/paypal-statistics/.

[3] Bloomberg, "Apple Sees Mobile-Payment Service Gaining in Challenge to PayPal", 28 January 2015, http://www.bloomberg.com/news/articles/2015-01-27/apple-sees-mobile-payment-service-gaining-in-challenge-to-paypal.

real-time bank account-to-account transfers in all the major jurisdictions. This shift, coupled with regulatory reform, will create opportunities for new players to enter the market and provide data aggregation services and payment initiation options to give life to the Internet of Things revolution.

The use of pre-paid cards is also on the rise. A 2012 report from MasterCard[4] predicts that the market for so-called e-money (cards pre-loaded with cash) will be worth around £822 billion by 2017. If these numbers are impressive, they represent only the tip of the FinTech iceberg.

Borrowing and depositing is also undergoing something of a revolution, thanks in no small part to the emergence of P2P lending platforms. In the UK P2P lending emerged shortly before the financial crisis with the launch of Zopa in 2005. Other platforms such as Funding Circle and RateSetter followed. To date, the industry has lent a cumulative figure of £2.6 billion and the market is growing. Lending in the first quarter of 2015 came in at £459 million, an increase of one-third on the previous three months.[5] These figures are small when compared to the sums advanced by the big banks but it is a young and rapidly growing market.

Importantly, the P2P market not only provides businesses and private borrowers with a source of cash, it also offers investors and savers a place to deposit cash and earn higher interest rates than in a conventional bank account. Elsewhere, challenger banks – some of them digital only – are also moving in on the deposits market.

Some aspects of FinTech innovation remain well outside the mainstream. Digital currencies, such as bitcoin,[6] potentially offer an opportunity and means to exchange value, but most would agree that the real value will emerge from the application of the supporting distributed ledger technology. The use of the distributed ledger brings additional value in the recording of non-financial asset ownership and, coupled with digital currency, could provide a platform for future

innovation to reduce costs and speed up transactions. Effective regulation of this environment is required to reduce risk for all participants.

Move away from the corporate face of FinTech innovation – PayPal, Apple, Google, et al. – and thousands of companies are working in technology hubs around the world on ways to make familiar activities such as stock trading or money transfers not only more convenient, but also more attuned to the way consumers use their smartphones, tablets, PCs, and smart watches. This wave of innovation is not only coming from established FinTech centres but also from emerging hubs. For example, Johannesburg has become a centre for bitcoin development, while across Africa entrepreneurs are developing mobile-based banking and payment systems appropriate to the local telecoms and financial services infrastructures.[7]

The Challenge to the Banks

So how will financial institutions – and particularly the big banks – respond to this wave of FinTech innovation? The banking sector is vulnerable to disruption, partly as a result of recent history. Until the onset of the financial crisis, banks enjoyed a degree of public trust that was crucial to their brands. Although that trust hasn't been entirely eliminated, it has certainly been eroded. As a study by the CCP Research Foundation revealed in June 2015, the world's top sixteen global banks have, between them, incurred US$306 billion in conduct-related costs since 2010.[8]

In contrast, the leading lights of the digital era tend to be viewed positively. Research carried out for the Millennial Disruption Index report found that 73% of respondents (teens to mid-thirties) would be much more excited about a new financial service delivered by Google or Apple than one announced by their incumbent bank.[9] In that respect, traditional financial service providers are at risk. Customers no longer necessarily see the bank as the default provider or first port of call – what's out there in the market is more exciting. And what's out there in the market is treading heavily on the toes of incumbents. So, while individuals and businesses will always need banking services, will they still need banks?

---

[4] 2012 Global Prepaid Sizing Study, commissioned by Mastercard: A look at the potential for global prepaid growth by 2017, https://www.partnersinprepaid.com/pdf/a-look-at-the-potential-for-global-prepaid-growth-by-2017.pdf.

[5] P2P Finance Association, "Strong Growth Continues in Peer-toPeer Lending Market", 30 April 2015, http://p2pfa.info/strong-growth-continues-in-peer-to-peer-lending-market.

[6] For more information on crypto-currencies, blockchain technology, and bitcoin, see Part 9.

---

[7] For further insights regarding emerging and established FinTech hubs, see Part 3.

[8] Financial Times, "Banks' Post-Crisis Legal Costs Hit $300bn", 8 June 2015, http://www.ft.com/cms/s/0/debe3f58-0bd8-11e5-a06e-00144feabdc0.html#axzz3eT1XUB4B.

[9] Millennial Disruption Index, http://www.ritholtz.com/blog/2015/04/millennial-disruption-index/.

At the most simple level, retail banks provide three crucial functions, namely:

- They take deposits and provide customers with a secure place to store cash and earn interest, backed by deposit insurance and significant regulation.
- They facilitate payments through a range of systems, including cash, cards, and transfers.
- They lend money.

To a financial services agnostic the same services can be provided by the new generation of technology-driven challengers. In terms of retail banking, money can be deposited with challenger banks, placed in pre-paid cards, stored in PayPal accounts, invested in bitcoins, or invested through P2P lending sites.

Credit is available from challenger banks and alternative lenders (including P2P), and customers have an increasing choice of payment options, including PayPal, e-wallets, and phone-based systems. While many of these options still use the plumbing of the banking system, in the medium term we may see payment and foreign exchange mechanisms that completely bypass the incumbent banking systems.

The Utilities Risk

So the major risk for the incumbents is that they come to be perceived as utilities that do little more than supply the infrastructure while the FinTech companies take the credit for providing innovative consumer-friendly services – and ultimately own the customer relationship. When this happens, the brand equity of banks will surely take a hit.

Unlike the major banks who are often constrained by legacy IT systems and operating models, the new players have designed their digital services from the ground up to meet the needs of specific customer groups. FinTech challengers can be both agile and completely focused on positive customer outcomes.

While traditional banks are dealing with increasing layers of compliance, consumer protection, and their own bureaucratic structures, P2Ps have a transparent approach to borrowing and lending, based on disclosure by the company seeking credit, and assessment by the community of lenders (rather than faceless credit

committees). This approach speaks to a generation raised on social media and these lenders regularly score high on customer satisfaction. Equally important, P2P sites have lower operating costs than banks and the capital requirements they face are also lower.

The Future for the Banking Sector

BBVA chairman and CEO Francisco González forecast in early 2015 that up to half of the world's banks will disappear through the cracks opened up by digital disruption of the industry.[10] That may be so, but I would argue that the most forward-looking banks will not just survive the wave of digital disruption, but will thrive, as these FinTech-driven challengers gain momentum. The world's major retail banks enjoy huge advantages, not least in terms of their collective customer base and the data they hold on their clients. These "thriver banks" will migrate the majority of their customers to their own digital banking services. They will reposition themselves in the value chain from being a provider of infrastructure and product, to being at the heart of the customer relationship in a secure and holistic digital environment. In effect, they will become financial app stores showcasing a range of financial solutions from different providers. In doing so, they remain relevant to customers as a single source for the best global financial solutions.

So, in the future, once I have logged into my mobile bank (presumably using heart biometrics or face recognition) I will be able to borrow money P2P via Ratesetter, make an international payment using Transferwise, top up my Starbucks e-wallet, or make a deposit into my Alibaba money market fund. In order to achieve such a goal, collaboration will have to become the norm. Corporate incumbents can't match the speed to market and the ability to innovate that the best FinTech developers bring to the table. So, rather than trying to reinvent the wheel by developing their own solutions, banks will have to work with innovators to bring new services to their consumers.

From start-ups working in shared spaces in London's Tech City or Johannesburg, to the corporate giants such as Apple and Google, FinTech is a dynamic sector. But while market leaders have emerged, no one really knows where the next successful payment system or bitcoin wallet will come from. And for all those ideas that make it to the market, many others will fail. The services that succeed will be those that

---

[10] Half of the world's banks set to fall by the digital wayside – BBVA, http://www.finextra.com/news/fullstory.aspx?newsitemid=26965.

genuinely make life easier, perhaps by mixing FinTech with other technologies. The bank of the future could be a place to deposit not just your money, but other valuables – for example, your medical records, your will, or the biometric data used to start your car.

With their customer base and experience in securely handling data, banks are in an ideal position to create holistic customer solutions that combine financial services with a wider range of digital offers. It could be the key to their future prosperity.

Why We're so Excited About FinTech

By Rébecca Menat

Director of Communications, The Assets

Banks are not exciting – FinTech is. Why should we be excited about the global FinTech sector?

Here is some background information for novice readers: FinTech means "financial technology". It encompasses a new wave of companies changing the way people pay, send money, borrow, lend, and invest. The most disrupted sectors – or at least the ones that we hear the most about – are payments and money transfer, with TransferWise (money transfer), Square (mobile payments), crowdfunding (Kickstarter, Crowdcube, Smart Angels …), and peer-to-peer lending (LendingClub, Zopa, Prêt d'Union …) increasingly becoming household names and products. So where is all this exciting activity taking place? London is clearly the leading FinTech hub, followed by New York, and other cities fighting to get to the top: Paris, Hong Kong, Singapore, Tel Aviv … Just to give you an idea, FinTech investments reached $22 billion (including $4 billion insurance) in 2015 and are expected to increase significantly, so there is room for new players!

How Did it all Begin?

The birth and rise of FinTech is deeply rooted in the financial crisis, and the erosion of trust it generated. People's anger at the banking system was the perfect breeding ground for financial innovation. Good timing, because digital natives (a.k.a. millennials) were becoming old enough to be potential customers and their preferences pointed to the mobile services they understood and mastered, instead of bankers they could not relate to. In this favourable landscape, FinTech providers came in, offering new and fresh services at lower costs, through well-designed platforms or mobile apps.

To sum it up, FinTech companies offer trust, transparency, and technology. Responding to a trust crisis towards banks, start-ups are able to offer services at a lower cost in a more transparent way, through easy-to-use interfaces. The customer is king and there is no one who knows their customers better than youthful, edgy start-ups, often drawn from the ranks of the millennial generation itself.

More than a Fuss: What Does FinTech Bring?

In four simple words, FinTech means: "Power to the People!" Take money transfers for instance. By allowing transparency and cutting middlemen fees, FinTech start-ups enable individuals to have control over their own money. End-users know how much they pay, and incidentally, this is less than what they used to pay. This innovation is actually having a really big social impact,[1] as there are start-ups specializing in a certain kind of money transfers: remittances (money sent by foreign workers to their home country). WorldRemit and Remitly are attracting serious attention, having respectively raised $100 million and $12.5 million in funding. This is not surprising, as they are entering a market worth more than $600 billion a year.

Another way of empowering people is to provide them with … money. The financial crisis not only resulted in a lack of trust towards banks – it also made it more difficult for people to take out loans. Peer-to-peer lending has broadened the availability of financing, enabling people and businesses to borrow money more easily, faster, and in a more transparent way. These FinTech start-ups have applied disintermediation to credit, connecting buyers and sellers through marketplaces. At the forefront of this trend stands Lending Club which raised almost $900 million in one of the largest IPOs of 2014.

FinTech is also widening access to investment opportunities, through crowdfunding.[2] Let us not forget that equity investment was once restricted to wealthy individuals. It is now accessible to all! If you have a small amount to invest, you can still have an impact and potentially reap some benefits. Kickstarter, Indiegogo, Crowdcube … just scroll down and choose your project. We already seem to be accustomed to this sector of FinTech, and tend to forget how revolutionary it is. Robo advisors are also shaking up the investment world, extending financial advice to just everybody.[3] According to a report by consulting firm A.T. Kearney, these automated investment services will manage about $2 trillion in the US by 2020, accounting for 5.6% of Americans' investment assets.[4]

---

[1] For additional insights on the social impact of FinTech, see Part 4.

[2] For further information on crowdfunding and the impact of FinTech on other sectors, see Part 6.

[3] See Part 6 for more information of FinTech influencing investment and capital trends.

[4] See http://money.cnn.com/2015/06/18/investing/robo-advisor-millennials-wealthfront/.

Generally – and I think this is the biggest revolution – FinTech is providing access to information, that once belonged to a select few, to an ever-increasing pool of people. In our "information economy" age, that is a big democratic move.

FinTech in the Developing World: Starting from Scratch[5]

John Chaplin, a payments industry veteran, gathered a bunch of experts to generate insights into the state of the FinTech industry: their conclusions are assembled in *The Payments Innovation Jury Report*.[6] Among various questions they asked themselves: which region will show the most payments innovation over the next 24 months? Verdict: FinTech innovation will come from Asia for the most part, followed by Africa, North America, Latin America, and eventually Europe. The reason is quite intuitive: the lack of infrastructure in developing countries leaves room for innovation that would not find success in over-banked and heavily entrenched economies in the West. As one of the report's contributors perfectly sums up, "the developing world is not bound by existing legacy systems, business models or customer behaviors and as such offers a fresher perspective that can often see beyond the scope of established business models."[7]

In addition, whereas FinTech services in developed countries are focused on online customers, start-ups in developing countries are addressing a broader market: cell phone users. According to the International Telecommunications Union, an estimated 95.5% of the world's population have access to a cell phone – which gives SMS a greater impact than the internet. Mobile money transfer services such as M-Pesa have made major contributions in changing the economic situation of underbanked populations in Bangladesh and Kenya. In Bangladesh the M-Pesa equivalent is bKash which is focused on mass-market mobile financial services. While Bangladesh offers a strong micro-finance industry (small-scale unsecured credit), bKash works like M-Pesa, sending payments quickly and easily to others.[8]

---

[5] For further information of the applicability of FinTech solutions to emerging markets and their social impact, see Part 4.

[6] Currency Cloud, "The Insider's View to Payments and Fintech", 2015, https://www.currency-cloud.com/payments-innovation-2015.

[7] Ibid.

[8] Source: http://www.totalpayments.org/2014/08/05/bkash-bangladeshs-m-pesa/.

In 2013, International Finance Corporation (IFC), a member of the World Bank Group, became an equity partner in bKash and in 2014, Bill & Melinda Gates Foundation also invested in bKash to ensure access to a broader range of financial services for the low-income masses of Bangladesh to achieve broader financial inclusion.[9]

Looking at the impact of FinTech solutions in Africa it is important to keep in mind that in sixteen African markets, there are now more mobile money accounts than bank accounts.

Thus, FinTech in developing countries is not only about making existing services more convenient: it is creating new infrastructure, and providing for greater inclusion of millions of people in the real economy. Since the markets addressed are enormous – and admittedly represent huge potential opportunities – one can truly say that FinTech is "changing the world for the better".

Banks, Beware!

FinTech has already unveiled many "disruptions", and is probably keeping many more under its belt. Is there enough space for these innovative new entrants and traditional institutions alike? What are the concrete threats to the latter?

"People need banking, but they don't necessarily need banks," Heather Cox, Citi's Chief Client Experience, Digital, and Marketing Officer said during IBM InterConnect 2015. New and more convenient and customer-centric services are changing the landscape, while customers are becoming more demanding. No bank can deny this: the proliferation of niche players focusing on certain services makes it more and more difficult for traditional financial institutions to keep ownership of their customers. The time when financial institutions could bundle their services together without transparency and still enjoy full loyalty from their customers, is coming to an end. Admittedly, this phenomenon only applies to a certain generation in certain areas, and even most of my "millennial" peers are still using their bank's services for all of their financial operations. We are not there yet. Actually, this is probably just the beginning of what is forecast to be a financial revolution.

---

[9] Source: http://www.bkash.com/about/company-profile.

In his annual letter to shareholders in April 2015, JP Morgan's CEO Jamie Dimon raised the alarm: "There are hundreds of start-ups with a lot of brains and money working on various alternatives to traditional banking." In spite of the apparent hegemony of these large establishments, more and more traditional institutions are becoming conscious of the threat innovative players represent. Would it be a smart move to try and beat them? Nothing is less certain. Start-ups have certain advantages over financial behemoths. Their small size, lean culture, technological progress, and ability to attract top talent give them a competitive advantage that is inherent in their very nature.

Disrupted, Reimagined

You know what they say: if you can't beat them, join them. The smartest move is to collaborate, not to compete – and many banks have understood this. They are creating incubators (Barclays' accelerator), setting up specialized venture funds (Santander's Innoventures), creating partnerships (Metro Bank and Zopa), or simply acquiring start-ups. Strategies differ but the goal remains the same: survive, and even profit from the digital disruption.

Yes, the big players will need to abide by start-ups' rules, in some ways. But this may actually be beneficial. What is better than having someone inventing everything right in front of you, and allowing you to just buy it? This is a once-in-a-lifetime opportunity for banks to obtain advanced capabilities and modernize inefficient infrastructure without having to develop it in-house. In other words, it only requires an open innovation mind-set for banks to join the game.

In this context, different scenarios can be imagined. In its report entitled *The Future of Fintech and Banking: Digitally disrupted or reimagined?*[10] Accenture details what it considers to be the most probable ones. Scenario 1: banks continue to believe in the supremacy of their business model and fail to adapt, hence losing out to new players. Scenario 2: they understand the importance of customer experience and embrace innovation within their business model, mainly collaborating with new entrants. The second option seems far more likely, now that banks are expressing their awareness and laying their cards on the table. Let us hope this will result in many win-win situations for the financial service sector and its global customers.

---

[10] Accenture, "The Future of Fintech and Banking: Digitally disrupted or reimagined?" http://www.fintechinnovationlablondon.net/media/730274/Accenture-The-Future-of-Fintech-and-Banking-digitallydisrupted-or-reima-.pdf.

12

Current Trends in Financial Technology

By Alexandre Glas
Co-Founder and CMO, The Assets

and Marcin Truszel
CEO, Kontomatik

For a very long time now banks have had to compete primarily with other banks. These were the times of mass branch openings, bold marketing campaigns, and ongoing competition for the highest interest paying accounts. In 2015 FinTech became not just "a" buzzword but, arguably, "*the*" buzzword and this shows no signs of changing. Now direct competitive pressure for banks is not only coming from other banks, but from thousands of FinTech start-ups and powerful tech giants with enough capital to cherry pick the most interesting areas of banking to leverage their own business models and millions of customers.

For decades, universal banks have been serving the full scope of financial services. In most countries, competition in the banking sector was moderate, since the bulk of jurisdictions had just a few large banks that accounted for quite a large share of the market. It was thus rarely possible to see a bank that had grown from a small one to a large industry player. While banks try to offer a wide scope of services, there are many innovative FinTech companies that just focus on the development of one simple service with great user experience. This certainly makes the lives of banks harder, as it is simply impossible for a large organization to achieve sustainable growth in every niche of the financial services sector. This development refers to the "unbundling" trend, meaning that FinTech firms focus on distinct areas of banking with the goal to become the "best of breed" providers in these areas. Therefore on an aggregate level there is a danger that the banking service offering overall is "unbundled" by the best FinTech providers in each category.

While the residents of developed countries certainly enjoy doing their banking activities from the comfort of their homes with the benefit of online banking, we can still see that online banking is not widely present or not present at all in emerging markets. However emerging markets will experience quite rapid growth

and substantial improvement in financial services provision. This process should take substantially less time than it took developed markets to achieve. This will be quite a similar scenario to what has already happened with the development of internet networks in such countries. While residents of developed countries have been steadily moving from one type of connection to another, it is not at all unusual to see developing countries quickly jump from a common 56k modem to high-speed wireless connections straight away. In other words, developing countries tend to start and stay on the low-end technology for longer than developed countries; however, they then skip many stages and quickly adopt the most developed product.

Regulation Supporting the FinTech Sector

2015 began with exciting news coming from the United Kingdom, where the government announced the initiation of a data sharing and open data initiative in banking (open Application Programming Interface (API) initiative).[1] UK officials are planning to implement a detailed framework for an open banking data environment that can be used by banks and FinTech companies to collaborate more for the benefit of their customers. The objective is to boost competition for the benefit of consumers. This is an important step, as thanks to the influence from the UK government many innovative organizations could get access to financial data going forward.

Another important piece of legislation in Europe is the Payment Services Directive 2 (PSD II). Although the whole analysis of PSD II is rather complex and beyond the scope of this chapter, in summary the European Parliament also wants to see easier access to banking data to enable innovation while at the same time preventing any data misuse and security breaches.

---

[1] Source: https://www.gov.uk/government/consultations/data-sharing-and-open-data-in-banking-call-for-evidence/call-for-evidence-on-data-sharing-and-open-data-in-banking. The application program interface is a set of routines, protocols, and tools for building software applications. The API specifies how software components should interact. See the chapter entitled "Embracing the Connected API Economy" for further detail about APIs.

Wearables, Foreign Exchange (FX), Bitcoin, and Blockchain Trends

Having reviewed regulation trends, we now want to highlight key applications of FinTech. In the foreign exchange sector, services like WeSwap[2] are entrants into the currency exchange market, but they are doing things quite differently from the traditional money exchanges – WeSwap actually allows people from different countries to interact and exchange local currency at a pre-determined local rate, far cheaper than the commission traditional money exchange businesses place on exchanges. WeSwap is backed by MasterCard[3] and is expected to grow exponentially over the next 18 months.

Although not yet commonplace, smart wearables are set to revolutionize the banking industry. The forecast for shipping wearables in 2015 is 45.7m units[4] and this is only going to increase. The Apple watch already allows the wearer to check their banking balance, track their transaction history, and find a nearby branch – once the mobile banking transaction systems are expanded and improved, the functionality of these smart wearables will only increase further. Jeremy Mugridge, Marketing Director at Instinct Studios is quoted as saying, "wearables have been around for a while now, but we're likely to see this gain momentum after the release of Apple Watch. 2015 will be the year where we'll see a shift in focus from health and fitness towards other areas like people's financial health."[5] For those of you who doubt that smart wearables will become that popular, take a glance at your smartphone and think back 10 years.

It is perhaps no coincidence that after the economic crisis, driven in part by banks, consumers are now paying closer attention to their own finances than ever before. Indeed, several apps have been created to allow consumers to do just that – one app, called Spendific, connects to a user's bank account and, after taking into account all of their outgoings, states what is left to spend. This is updated in real time as purchases and payments are made from that account. This innovation, though, is comparatively basic when compared to MoneyHub, who have developed an app that does something similar, but also includes long-term savings in the financial planning process. Things like buying a house and desired retirement age are included and different scenarios can be created to see what impact the consumer's decisions will have on their financial outlook.

More and more financial services provision is being conducted online and as Generation Z (the demographic segment born after millennials) will only ever know "mobile", it should come as no surprise that this is and will continue to be the case. Smart wearables, specifically technologically advanced financial apps and an increase in mobile payment opportunities, are the result of consumer demand.

Although they are taking a somewhat slow foothold, there are clear signs that crypto-currencies are here to stay – for example, California made them legal tender in 2015.[6] In Europe some countries are already seeing bitcoin – an example of a crypto-currency – take hold in bartering-type exchange systems. Arguably, there is not yet a bitcoin usage model quite where the industry needs it to be, but this will be developed over time. However, the development of all of this could be hindered by regulations and national laws. Seen from an idealistic viewpoint, people would be able to use bitcoin, or other crypto-currencies, anywhere in the world, instantaneously. Yet, with different rules and regulations governing states and the different financial institutions involved, getting unanimous agreement on how crypto-currencies should work could prove difficult.

In this respect, blockchain (the technology on which bitcoin is based) is a distributed data store that holds a public ledger of transactions for crypto-currencies, such as bitcoin itself. A dedicated chapter in the book covers crypto-currencies and blockchain technology.

It is clear that FinTech has already made huge inroads into many aspects of our daily lives. What is perhaps even clearer is that the surface has barely been scratched in relation to what FinTech can do for us all in the future. As we consumers become ever more demanding and discerning in our choices, you can

---

[2] See https://www.weswap.com/en/.

[3] See https://www.weswap.com/en/learn-more/.

[4] Ibid., and see http://www.idc.com/getdoc.jsp?containerId=prUS25519615.

[5] "FinTech Trends and Predictions for 2015", 14 January 2015, http://www.bobsguide.com/guide/news/2015/Jan/14/fintech-trends-and-predictions-for-2015.html.

[6] "Cryptocurrencies made legal in California", 8 January 2015, http://www.bobsguide.com/guide/news/2015/Jan/8/cryptocurrencies-made-legal-in-california.html.

expect to see financial institutions rely increasingly on FinTech developments to provide the solutions to keep us happy and meet our needs.

In summary, we are now living in times of significant transformation of the banking sector. We can probably assume that banking over the next 10 years will experience a higher degree of change than in the last 100 years. Financial technology innovation has started a global shake-up of the sector. Now the most important question remains: will banks be able to successfully embrace FinTech innovation or not? FinTech is set to play a bigger role in your life than you might have ever expected.

FinTech Themes

2

After the introduction to the financial technology sector in the previous part, this second part focuses on some key general themes. The chapters highlight the importance of collaboration between the established players and the FinTech start-ups while providing a global overview on regulatory frameworks impacting FinTech. Regulatory compliance is a prerequisite for success for FinTech companies worldwide. Marketplace lending – one of the key disruptive FinTech business models is also explained in more detail here.

As we all tend to live increasingly digital lives, we have several identities online. The topic of identity management, particularly important for FinTech, is covered here. The threat of tech giants to incumbents, as companies such as Apple and Facebook have entered the global payments arena, is also highlighted.

Finally, principles and the importance of good design are discussed to ensure that the user experience of financial products and services is what the customer expects, based on their interaction with the leading consumer and technology solutions.

Banks Need to Think Collaboration Rather Than Competition

By Rachel Nienaber

VP Engineering, Currency Cloud

Historically, banks have been responsible for most innovations in the financial industry. The inception of the credit card in the 1950s and ATMs in the 1970s completely revolutionized the way we access and pay for goods. Jump forward to 2016 and it is a very different story. Those developments came decades apart, but following the significant growth and accessibility of the internet and the technology that advances in its wake – including smart phones, big data, social media, and cloud computing – demand has come from consumers to make it even easier to manage their finances. As such, financial innovation is no longer restricted to those institutions, allowing outside players to creep in to shake up the industry.

The financial sector has continued to witness many impressive innovations and technological advancements such as contactless technology, digital wallets, and crypto-currencies. However the innovators are now rarely banks but small FinTech firms. These are often led by former bank employees who have identified a gap in an existing offering or service.

Application Programming Interface (API) is the term used to describe a set of tools that enable different software components or systems to effectively communicate with one another.[1] Using an API, banks or challenger financial services providers can incorporate the technology from FinTech firms into the key areas in which support is required – simplifying the process of adding innovative technology services by piecing together building blocks of flexible services, much like financial lego.

With financial lego APIs, IT leaders within businesses can create their own financial IT solution or support other internal processes without having to build every piece of the technology from scratch. Instead, they can mix and match a portfolio of financial technology APIs to create a bespoke solution where the development team can integrate the functionality of the APIs as part of their technology. For example, banks and payments firms can send money internationally through Currency Cloud's API, rather than having to develop proprietary technology.

The flexibility of APIs means that it is also easier to create experiences that users will enjoy because the experience can be easily decoupled from the system behind it. Barclays' development of mobile payment service Pingit is a great example of this where opening their API has helped in bringing a successful new service to market. Pingit has experienced extraordinary growth since launch in 2012, with users in London alone sending more than £60 million via Pingit in the first six months of 2014.

Despite the scale of innovation sweeping across the financial services industry, many banks still retain their R&D behind closed doors. Understandably, security is one of their top priorities and rather than risk sharing information with another party, banks tend to only trust themselves. While this means that the threat from the outside is limited, it also means that there can be no external development. And we just need to look as far as the success stories from Apple and Google, who routinely open up their APIs to outside creative minds, to understand just how valuable and exciting the results of the latter can be.

Developed in a pre-internet era, banks' business models and technology infrastructure has largely been constructed around product sets and delivered through the branch. In other words, banks were not built to serve today's fast-paced and digitally savvy customers. As such, a whole host of technology players have taken the opportunity to develop innovative alternatives, built on flexible platforms that can adapt to this changing environment. PayPal is one of the first notable examples of a successful solution that provided great benefit for the customer and since then has paved the way for an explosion of alternative services, offering everything from investments to international payments, loans, and bank accounts. From the likes of Kickstarter and Seedr, which have been leading the crowdfunding market for some time, to Amigo which provides personalized credit approval, and Transferwise which offers consumers cheaper access to overseas transfers, these firms are redefining old verticals or creating entirely new ones.

Yet, the rise of FinTech newcomers in the industry does not need to send banks panicking about the challenges involved with overhauling their entire IT

---

[1] See the chapter entitled "Embracing the Connected API Economy" for further details.

infrastructure in order to compete. The "us versus them" debate that has gained perpetual popularity does not provide an accurate picture of the relationship between FinTech innovators and banks. Let us be very clear, the banks are the cornerstone on which our economies are built, they are the rails on which most FinTech firms operate and they are not going away in the near or even the distant future. However, we are creating a fundamentally different way of viewing and approaching the industry.

Tech start-ups look at this financial services landscape and using the rationality of the internet, see poor customer service and room for tremendous efficiencies. The same logic has been applied in other industries such as music and telecommunications, which have also been completely transformed by the power of new technologies and the internet. What a traditional bank might view as a threat in the digital age, their more nimble counterparts might see as an opportunity. The result is a wave of FinTech firms that look to optimize particular segments of the financial value chain (whether that be international money transfers, loans, or payment processing) and offer their specialist services to other businesses and banks, via APIs. A company that wanted to support musicians could, for example, use one technology firm such as Kickstarter to provide loans, and another firm such as Currency Cloud to make the payment. The success of these players is in part due to their ability to focus on a very niche segment of the industry, rather than trying to compete on all levels. Banks on the other hand, have always tried to own every aspect of the financial services spectrum, yet this is where they are now struggling as alternative players offer up more sophisticated services for customers within a specific niche.

Despite their differences, both FinTech players and banks have much to gain from working together. FinTech firms can benefit from the long history of banking operations and the foundation that banks provide. They are a vital part of the puzzle as the banks provide the financial instruments that FinTech firms package up in different ways, at the same time concentrating on one specific use case at a time. Banks can simultaneously gain value in new players – whether that means looking

to partner with them or acquire their advanced technology offerings. Using API capabilities delivered in this way can help banks to expand services internationally, reduce development costs, and unlock fresh revenue without having to invest in and build new architecture.

The growth of FinTech and push for open access to financial data has been noted industry-wide as the government continues its support of FinTech firms and the development of the UK as the world's most exciting financial hub. It is not all that surprising that they have recently announced plans to create a consolidated, open API standard for banks. The government has committed to launch a call for evidence on how best to deliver an open standard for APIs in UK banking and to ask whether more open data in banking could benefit consumers. While the start of this process has been to discuss the product banks offer, what FinTech firms are really interested in is the next step: opening up the transactional data from within a bank. Banks, however, are still very cautious about giving outside developers access to this type of data and it will take many more discussions before such a move becomes a reality. It may not have been the strides that we had all originally hoped for when we heard about the open standard but at least it is a very good start. This is an encouraging step forward for the industry. We have already seen how nurturing the API economy can provide the industry with a large dose of innovation, and with further support it will undoubtedly continue to produce new opportunities for both banks and the up-and-coming alternative players in this industry. With the UK government putting their faith in these successful newcomers to take the industry forward into the 21st century, this further indicates that alternative players have done a successful job of proving their value to the industry – and such credibility will continue to grow.

There is much to gain from FinTech firms and traditional banks embarking on a collaborative relationship to discover and define the future growth potential within the industry. We strongly believe in working with, rather than against, the banks and we are in no doubt that collaboration with forward-thinking technology firms will ensure that the finance industry continues to innovate.

Global Compliance is Key

By Jan C. Wendenburg

Member, Executive Board, XCOMpetence AG

We love great FinTechs, like PayPal, Apple Pay, and Stripe. We love to see them rise. We love using them. But we would all dump them within a second if they were to fail – fail to be trusted, fail to be secure, or fail to comply with local financial regulations. Compliance with legal financial regulations is not optional, but mandatory. It is mandatory for each FinTech to build a secure, trustworthy service, regardless of geography and legislation. Almost every nation has its own individual financial regulation based on its distinct culture, financial system, and historical experiences.

If you have launched your FinTech company but disregarded compliance for your service, you may well be shut down by supervisory authorities, resulting in potential reputational damage and associated costs needed to rectify them. If you over-comply with regulations, you will not move forward fast enough and be ousted by the competition. Are there any shortcuts to compliance?

FinTechs Must Understand Each Local Regulatory Stack!

If you want to bypass industry incumbents, you must understand the rules of the game. While FinTechs are trying to bypass major players, they cannot begin attacking them unless they understand the regulatory landscape and quickly learn how to use regulation and legal specialties to their advantage.

A key rule is that you should never try to bypass regulation. It's much better to embrace it as a core function of your organization. If you take care of regulation and compliance from the start, you will be in a stronger position from the very beginning instead of having to play catch up. It's like customer acquisition: it pays big dividends down the line. Think twice about what your organization does and how you intend to structure your compliance. Do you really see regulation and compliance as part of your organization, your life, and the DNA of your start-up? What are you doing today regarding regulatory compliance? Do you know how financial regulation works throughout the most important regions around the world?

The United States: A Single Market with Complex, Multi-level Regulations

Let us first take a look at financial regulation in the United States, which is highly fragmented compared to European and Asian countries, where most jurisdictions have only one bank regulator. In the US, banking is regulated at both the federal and the state level. Depending on the type of charter a banking organization has, and on its organizational structure, it may be subject to numerous federal and state banking regulations.

This structure makes life complex for FinTechs in the United States. For example, if you want to provide investment management and advice, like Wealthfront in Palo Alto, CA, you will have to specify first which state law may apply to a particular client. Beyond that, you will not be allowed to serve international clients, unless you implement international anti-money laundering procedures and handle cross-border tax issues properly. As a result it may be easier to open international offices within other countries instead and serve local clients within the regulatory framework.

If you want to launch something in the lending space, like Lending Club in San Francisco, CA, you will have your marketplace of lenders and investors at the bottom. On top of that, in increasing order of difficulty and market breadth, you will have US state-level legislators, then US federal regulators, NASAA, then the Securities Exchange Commission (SEC). Once you succeed here, and want to serve European lenders and investors, you will have to open European or Asian offices and must follow their local regulations.

Europe: Still Complex but with Some Harmonized Regulations

In 2014 Europe implemented the Single Supervisory Mechanism (SSM), which is intended to harmonize the different national financial regulations within the 27 European member states. Within each country, a National Competent Authority (NCA) supervises national banks and financial service providers. If you want to expand into other European countries, you will have to work with the local NCAs and their respective regulations, i.e. in the UK the Prudential Regulation Authority

(PRA), which oversees about 1,700 banks and financial service providers, and in France the Autorité de contrôle prudentiel et de résolution (ACPR), both based on a similar regulatory and legal stack as Germany.

Asia: Remains Very Fragmented

Going to Asia, you may want to focus only on China and India – the rest of Asia is very fragmented and mainly focuses on what the two major Asian countries are doing. China's financial system is highly regulated and has recently started to liberalize itself as China's financial policy becomes more significant to its overall economic strategy. As a result, banks and financial service providers are becoming more important to China's economy by providing increasing amounts of finance to enterprises for investment, seeking deposits, and lending money to the government. The People's Bank of China is the largest bank in China and acts as the Treasury. It also issues currency, monitors money supply, regulates monetary organizations, and formulates monetary policy for the State Council. The Bank of China manages foreign exchange transactions and foreign exchange reserves. The China Development Bank distributes foreign capital from a variety of sources, and the China International Trust and Investment Corporation (CITIC), previously a financial organization that smoothed the inflow of foreign funds, is now a full-fledged bank, allowed to compete for foreign investment funds with the Bank of China. The China Construction Bank lends funds for capital construction projects from the state budget, and finally the Agricultural Bank of China functions as a lending and deposit-taking institution for the agricultural sector.

By the end of 2014, the Chinese government had adopted new regulations requiring 75% of all technology products used by Chinese financial institutions to be classified as "secure and controllable" by 2019. This means suppliers and service providers will be forced to turn over their secret source code to Chinese auditors to enable invasive governmental audits to detect back doors into hardware and software. This rule applies to all financial institutions and their suppliers providing financial services in China, making competition pretty hard for foreign companies.

In India the regulation and supervision of the financial system has a complex multi-level architecture undertaken by different regulatory authorities. The Reserve Bank of India (RBI) regulates and supervises the major part of the financial system. The supervisory role of the RBI covers commercial banks, urban co-operative banks (UCBs), some financial institutions, and non-banking finance companies (NBFCs).

Regional Rural Banks, the co-operative banks, and housing finance companies are supervised by the National Housing Bank (NHB). Through the Department of Company Affairs (DCA), the Government of India regulates deposit-taking activities of corporates, other than NBFCs. The Indian capital market, mutual funds, and other capital market intermediaries are regulated by the Securities and Exchange Board of India (SEBI); the Insurance Regulatory and Development Authority (IRDA) regulates the insurance sector; and the Pension Funds Regulatory and Development Authority (PFRDA) regulates pension funds.

In 2011 only about 35% of Indians over the age of 15 held an account at a formal financial institution.[1] After a failed initiative to connect each household with a bank account, the ADHAR initiative issued 770 unique identities (UID), a cornerstone for easy mobile SIM card registration and mobile money. Promoted by the PMJDY campaign, today about 99.7% of households are connected to a bank account. Driven by this huge success, the Indian RBI committee started to accept applications from companies for a specialized banking licence – a payment-only bank licence, subject to regulatory scrutiny and clearance, it was granted to first applicants in late 2015.

Payment Services are Globally Regulated

Adding payment services to your portfolio will trigger another set of strict regulations. To prevent money laundering, payment services in general, including P2P, P2B, and B2B services, are heavily regulated by governments almost everywhere. The FATF (Financial Action Task Force on Money Laundering), an international joint organization of more than 34 member countries located at the global OECD offices in Belgium, issued in 2012 a comprehensive framework against money laundering and the financing of terrorism. This internationally accepted framework has been converted into very specific national money transfer regulations, which are essential when operating an international or global money transfer or payment service.

---

[1] Source: The World Bank; See also Raymond Zhong, "India Launches Program Giving Poor Access to Bank Accounts", *The Wall Street Journal*, 28 April 2014, available at http://www.wsj.com/articles/india-government-launches-program-giving-poor-access-to-bank-accounts-1409234530.

Europe implemented the Directive on Payment Services (PSD), to provide the legal framework for the creation of an EU-wide single market for payments. The PSD, recently updated to PSD2, aims to establish a modern and comprehensive set of rules applicable to all payment services in the European Union. The target is to make cross-border payments as easy, efficient, and secure as "national" payments within a Member State. The PSD also seeks to improve competition by opening up payment markets to new entrants, thus fostering greater efficiency and cost reduction. At the same time, the Directive provides the necessary legal platform for the Single Euro Payments Area (SEPA).

In the US, on 26 January 2015 the Federal Reserve System issued the federal "Strategies for Improving the U.S. Payment System", which represents a multi-faceted plan for collaborating with payment system stakeholders including large and small businesses, emerging payments firms, card networks, payment processors, consumers, and financial institutions to enhance the speed, safety and efficiency of the US payment system. This document includes multi-level regulations and comments to ISO 20022 to improve the efficiency and security of national and cross-border payments.

Local and Global Compliance – Make, Buy, or Partner?

Each FinTech, each service, each level, and each geography has its own set of rules and you must implement a strategy for how you might use regulation to your advantage at every stage of your FinTech's expansion and development. The way you manage the process at each stage will have substantial implications for later stages. You may need to exchange a suboptimal customer experience or fast growth, for example, to gain regulatory approval en route to providing a better customer experience and faster growth later.

Even something as simple as regulation in a specific geography must be carefully considered. For example, where you choose to base your start-up is one of the most important decisions that you will make. There may be local, national, and international laws that can support (or damage) your business model and it is up to you to find them. Global examples of problems abound, like Uber entering a market regardless of legal and industry-specific regulations, resulting in many regulatory and union challenges at a local level in several countries and cities around the world. Others, like PayPal, first carefully investigated the regulatory ecosystem in each region, launched a very basic "ebay payment service", and then expanded into other areas, i.e. P2P payments, after knowing exactly how to comply with each regulation for each service in each jurisdiction. Having a revenue stream originating in the jurisdiction also helped.

If you have got multi-million or billion-dollar funding for a global business, you may have the funds to buy any advice that you may need from local or global consultant firms. For FinTech start-ups, it might not be a bad idea partnering with medium-sized, flexible local bank heroes, and be guided by some experienced experts. Throughout all geographies (China is a more complex story), there are some great and powerful banks specializing in FinTech backbone services, e.g. Barclays (UK), biw-Bank & Fidor (Germany), mBank (Poland), Santander (Spain), Toronto-Domion (Canada), Westpac Banking Corp. (Australia), and many others. For a fee they will take care of much of the relevant regulatory stuff so that you can concentrate on your core business.

Regardless of any purchased advice or great partnership, please keep in mind that you will never be able to outsource or delegate regulatory compliance. If compliance becomes part of your company, your life, and your DNA, it will be one of your key success factors.

Lending (Capital) in the 21st Century

By Rodolfo Gonzalez
Partner, Foundation Capital

Finance seems too big. Certainly, some banks are still too big to fail. But what if finance is not big enough yet? Financial services are highly concentrated. Much as the wealthiest 1% of households control 20% of income in the United States, the distribution of consumer financial services can be viewed in the same way — but on a global scale. Right now, only 50% of people worldwide have a savings account[1] and just 20% have access to a loan product from a financial institution. There are roughly five billion people that banks do not serve today. More than anything, finance is poorly distributed.

It is staggering to think how banking – one of the oldest, most powerful, and most globalized industries – remains elusive for four-fifths of humankind. It is also telling that banks have not figured out how to profit from lending to those other five billion people (while still alienating plenty of their actual customers by way of poor service). Last year, in Foundation Capital's white paper, it was predicted that new marketplace lending platforms would originate $1 trillion in loans within the decade[2] – but what if the actual potential is even larger? Lending holds the highest transformative potential for those excluded from banking services. After all, it is through credit that money is created in the modern economy.

Data and New Technologies are the Key to Unlocking Credit Globally

In the US, the ability to open a bank account, get a credit card, or obtain a loan to start building a life or business all hinge upon the approval of credit bureau data. Lending Club has built a multibillion-dollar business by accurately pricing the risk of borrowers that were overcharged by credit card operators. Emerging lending platforms are finding new ways to bypass and best FICO – the "gold standard"

of credit bureaus. In the developed world, banks have been sitting on (and not utilizing) a wealth of available data that would improve their loan origination decisions. Banks need to become smarter just to catch up with the underwriting capabilities of new marketplace lending platforms. The very same data problem also hurts non-bank lenders. At the lower end of the spectrum, most payday lenders refuse to report the repayment history of their clients to bureaus, as they fear graduating them into lower interest loans.

Even when you have a privately owned repository of repayment data, as you do with credit bureaus in the US, it is incredibly expensive to access it. A hard pull from a single US credit bureau costs a lender between $1 and $2 at scale, depending on their size. While that works fine for an auto loan or mortgage where underwriting is done only a few times within a consumer's lifetime, it is entirely uneconomical to do so on a regular basis – like an adjustable rate revolving loan or for small loan amounts ("Can you lend me a few dollars? This 6-month old printout shows I have a good FICO score!").

Across the world, the challenge is that most countries have no credit bureaus, and of those who have them, they only tend to report negative payment behaviour (as opposed to positive and negative behaviour and a numerical score). Even then, coverage is patchy, as most of the population is not even listed in the credit bureau databases. Most utility and bill payments are not captured or reported. Many organizations still carry out a lot of the data collection by hand.

Underwriting based on behavioural data, using machine learning, neural networks, and other advanced statistical techniques, will provide the scalability required for financial institutions to offer more to those still without access. Mobile phones are making most of the world's people electronically accessible for the first time, and are providing a wealth of data that a stale stack of stamped bill receipts simply cannot compare with. Unless banks and traditional lenders think of themselves primarily as data and technology companies, they will become increasingly irrelevant.

Non-credit bureau-based underwriting is an area that shows great promise in the developing world. Indeed, in China, Social Credit Scoring performed by Sesame Credit (part of Alibaba), is due to credit score 900 million people before 2020. In the US and a few other developing countries, fair lending laws limit the use of many pieces of behavioural and demographic data to make credit decisions. I believe the worldwide transition from feature phones to smartphones will mostly be completed within one or two replacement cycles (maximum 5–10 years), and at that point the comprehensive use of mobile phone data to make consumer underwriting decisions will be the norm.

[1] See http://elibrary.worldbank.org/doi/pdf/10.1596/1813-9450-6025.

[2] See http://www.foundationcapital.com/admin/resources/whitepapers/p2p-lending-print-h-v20.pdf.

There are great opportunities ahead, and a new notion of identity can emerge via new technologies. The bitcoin blockchain holds enormous potential here. I will not get into the weeds of bitcoin, but given the distributed nature of the blockchain, the emergence of a decentralized credit bureau with global reach is now a real possibility. Using the blockchain ledger to create a global repository of the world's credit transactions will establish a new way to assess underwriting and risk with data that was previously unavailable. The notion of a thin-file or no-file borrower can become irrelevant – people and companies will have full, instant access to their complete credit history, and make use of it to access loans in any country, regardless of how long these potential borrowers have been there. The notion of data portability across credit bureaus has so far been unheard of. For consumers, the costs to switch financial institutions (monetary and convenience) will reduce drastically. To keep a client, banks will have to compete on service levels as well as on price.

Lowering Costs, Increasing Transaction Frequency

Every day most Americans swipe their credit cards for groceries, utility bills, or a night out on the town. Charges are applied – merchants pay roughly 30 cents plus 3% of the value of the transaction – and while expensive, merchants oblige because of the convenience credit cards offer to their customers. Given that most retailers have 5–10% net margins, taking credit card payments often wipes out half or more of their profits! Furthermore, imagine that you are a merchant who is also a part of the three billion people (50% of the world's population) living on less than $2.50 a day. The 30-cent credit card fixed fee just does not add up. Who would pay a third of their income (plus taxes, which often do not get collected on cash transactions) just to swipe a card?

In this case, bitcoin – the internet of money – holds promising potential to bring transaction costs down. Anyone can send thousands of bitcoins across the world just as easily as sending one hundredth of a bitcoin, without incurring transaction or remittance fees. Moreover, unlike cash, full information details on the transaction can be attached to it, and be programmed to disburse only after whatever condition has been agreed upon is met— all without any extra cost. Talk about reducing the costs of moving money around!

Most of the costs of holding and moving small balances will be stripped out of such a system (eventually including deposit insurance). Electronic delivery and instant disbursement of funds will take place via mobile phone. Daily amortization would be possible for microloans. Pay as you go financial services are on the horizon. As the frequency of transactions increases, across all financial services, the ability for all participants (both customers and lenders) to better react and prevent financial shocks will improve dramatically.

Non-banks, all while still turning a profit and serving more clients, will perform many of the banks' functions better. It is natural that service providers that interact more frequently with clients (mobile phone, retailers, internet providers) perform many of the consumer relationship functions. In many scenarios, banks will need to partner with such lower cost providers in order to remain competitive and relevant to the consumers who are experiencing financial services for the first time. One really wonders what banks will use their branches for 20 years from now!

Change is Coming, Past a Bank Near You

The current banking system is not equipped to carry out the challenging task of adapting to the new digital landscape. Banks use mostly centralized legacy technology infrastructure, and rely heavily on expensive branches and manual processes. Moreover, given their role in the recent financial crisis, they will keep facing increasing capital and regulatory constraints. Banks will continue to pull away from lending to "risky" clients. Given their high cost base, banks cannot afford to underwrite and lend money in small amounts, as would be convenient for clients.

Under this cost structure, banks rely heavily on fees and tricky penalties to make money – no need to hold capital reserves to earn those. Take the overdraft, which generates $30bn+ in fees per year,[3] on automatic overdraft loans of less than $30bn+ annually. One FDIC study found that the average consumer would pay an implied APR of 3520% on a $24 ATM overdraft (at the median overdraft fee of $34) – if the overdraft loan were paid back in two weeks.[4] By the way, in 2007, total overdraft charges were $17.5bn, so this line item has grown at a "healthy" 9% CAGR since.

---

[3] See http://www.bloomberg.com/news/articles/2014-07-31/banks-face-hit-on-30-billion-in-overdraft-fees-from-cfpb-rules.

[4] See http://www.bankrate.com/finance/investing/fdic-study-outrageous-overdraft-fees-1.aspx.

Marketplace lending platforms hold the key to making finance as significant and well-distributed as it should be. Embracing new data sources and underwriting techniques, as well as using cost-reducing and feature-enabling technologies like bitcoin and the blockchain, is where the next mass-scale opportunities will be unlocked. Lending in the 21st century comes with the promise of transforming the world. The addressable market is immense – five billion people strong. There are plenty of loans yet to be made, and one trillion of them might just be the beginning.

The Next Big Innovation in FinTech – Identity

By Benjamin Wakeham
Founder & CEO, Pollen

Identity is changing. Where historically it was based around family, clan, and reputation, it is now governed by the state – incumbents in the truest form. A plastic card is supposed to be a mechanism for who we are, where we come from, and whether this information is legitimate. Something which companies and individuals risk their future and their history on.

Identity is a key piece of global infrastructure which underpins every element of our lives. We now reside in a world too advanced for our current identification infrastructure. As we move from a physical world to a digital world, identity has yet to foster any transformative innovation.

However, it is not just identity that is changing. The concept of money is also being morphed just as profoundly – 2015 was predicted to be the landmark year when digital transactions overtook cash. With the two trends converging, potentially all we will need for transacting will be our identities. Isn't the concept of payment just two entities exchanging value anyway? If you look at a £10 note, "I promise to pay the bearer", it is a trust mechanism, except that with physical cash the trust is put in the government bank.

In America, in the early 1950s, because of a lack of cross-country travel infrastructure, transactions took place within villages and towns. Most merchants knew their customers by name, and would therefore keep a credit book for each customer, who would pay off their debts each month, for fear of being banned from the store. However with the growth of train networks and roads, people began to move interstate. Judging a person's creditworthiness became nigh on impossible.

Then, in 1960, an IBM engineer named Forrest Parry, who was developing a new type of ID card for the CIA, had an epiphany: Why not make each card a tiny data storage device in and of itself? He cut a short length of half-inch wide magnetic tape from a reel and wrapped it around a blank plastic card, secured it with Scotch tape, and then, at his wife's suggestion, pressed it on with a warm iron. The magnetic strip was born. When making a payment, this alongside your signature has been the de facto identity check for over 50 years.

If it Ain't Broke, Don't Fix it, Right?

However, payment data hacking was at an all-time high in 2014, with an increase of 21% on the year before. Home Depot believes that a cyberattack earlier that year affected 56 million unique payment cards as part of the largest retail security breach in history.

Javelin Strategy & Research found that $16 billion was stolen from 12.7 million US consumers in 2014, or put another way there is a new identity fraud victim every two seconds in 2014.

Identity however, reaches far beyond just payments. The writer of a *New York Times* article detailed how a recent healthcare data breach exposed his child to identity theft that could hinder her for the rest of her life, because her Social Security number was stolen. Since 2005, more than 675 million data records have been involved in data breaches in the US alone, according to the Identity Theft Resource Center. With this level of information, fraudsters can create new bank accounts or take out loans under an actual person's name. The opportunities for fraudsters are largely due to the sheer number of online accounts that people have these days. Experian found that on average, UK residents will have around 26 accounts, while 25–34-year-olds are more likely to have 40, and around 25% just use the same password for most of their accounts, rather than coming up with a unique password per site.

Some people argue that linking identity and payments leads to the loss of data protection and anonymity. My rebuttal consists of the fact that there is a difference between privacy and anonymity. The use of Amazon gift cards in the adult webcam services industry (I found this out through research, not first-hand knowledge) means that users need only share an identifier such as an email address in order to create transactions, therefore protecting their privacy. Those hanging on to the notion of anonymity through cash transactions don't have much of a choice. Eric Karson, Professor of Marketing and Business Law at the Villanova School of Business, believes that 20 years from now, paper money and coins will be close to extinction, in part because the cost of producing currency will continue to climb, and customer resistance is bound to weaken eventually. "As time passes, more and more consumers will be more comfortable with all things digital. Today's kids will grow up. There will be less and less separation between their digital life and their life in general."

So let's all jump aboard and set sail for a new world of digital identity and trust – there are certain companies in existence trying to steady this ship:

Social Login

This has been widely adopted by both businesses and consumers, allowing users to verify their identities and log in to websites and mobile applications using existing profiles from networks such as Facebook and LinkedIn. This not only creates a more streamlined experience for consumers, it also enables marketers to capture and leverage rich, first-party social identity data – scary, although users clearly don't mind – Facebook Login was used more than 10 billion times in 2013 alone.

Twitter Digits

In late 2014, social networking company Twitter introduced Digits, a tool that allows users to sign up for mobile apps and authenticate their identities without the need to create new login credentials. Rather than creating new usernames and passwords, consumers can log in using their cell phone numbers – an identification mechanism they already use every day, eliminating password fatigue for users, and reducing the amount of spam or inactive accounts businesses have to deal with. An individual signs up using his or her phone number, receives an SMS code, enters the code into the verification field, and the process is complete.

Apple Touch ID

Introduced for the Apple 5S, this is a combination of biometric fingerprint, GPS location, and tokenization. Natwest and RBS in the UK are currently using it instead of passwords for account login, and it is a focal point for security for Apple Pay, taking it beyond debit/credit cards in terms of security. One to watch in the next few years.

Trulio

Trulio is the world's first, social-driven "identity bureau" providing online businesses with an API[1] featuring bank grade levels of security, to instantly verify users across the globe. Trulio has created an identity verification product that fuses both

traditional and cyber identity data, enabling organizations to verify people online regardless of location, race, creed, colour, situation, circumstance, or environment – anywhere and anytime.

Whilst these applications attempt to create a solution to the password problem, I think we need to look deeper and think bigger. Identity management has been identified as one of the most important challenges to overcome – if we know exactly who makes/receives payments globally, the financial systems will be more secure (avoiding fraud, black market economies etc.) and therefore lead to further economic development.

"Identity" is not a simple notion. People can have many different overlapping identities which are fundamental to their individuality. Identities can exercise a powerful influence on the health and wellbeing of communities, and the degree to which they can build up social capital.

> The chief principle of a well-regulated police state is this: That each person shall be at all times and places … recognised as this or the particular person.
>
> *Johann Gottlieb Fichte (1796)*

Identity is not about control though, it is about honesty.

The internet is currently something reminiscent of the Wild West. Except instead of outlaws, there are hackers and fraudsters. Currently the degree to which these black hat entities operate is mainly in causing digital harm. But our digital and physical worlds are becoming blurred – much like payments, they are one, it is all about connectivity and interaction. With the advent of robotics, the internet of things, and artificial intelligence, it may not be our bank accounts that are hacked, but potentially our airplanes or elderly relative helper robots. I'm very bullish on AI. In the right hands it could do more for humanity than any other innovation to date. However in the wrong hands it could be catastrophic, and whose hands those are relates back to identity.

My vision is for "White Space" on the internet. A concept built on networks, rather than index cards in a filing cabinet. Data being shared between entities to create a more holistic view of an individual or entity. It will be reputation rather than regulation that will animate trust in economic exchange. Politician Edmund Bohun in 1696 stated that there was no cash in England with the result that "no trade is managed but by trust".

---

[1] API stands for application program interface, a set of routines, protocols, and tools for building software applications. The API specifies how software components should interact. See the chapter entitled "Embracing the Connected API Economy" for further details.

Due to advances in decentralized ledger technology it is now possible for a record, be it a passport or a bank account, to be encrypted and validated amongst all participants in the network. I am talking about the blockchain, the infrastructure on which bitcoin sits. It is currently the biggest decentralized ledger in 2015, and therefore the most failsafe – as with networks, size matters. To all of those involved in blockchain technology, it sounds unscalable, and it is. There will have to be efficiencies created around this – as the network grows, not every record will need to be hashed on every node. The key is in the power of the network making the information stored in such a way that unauthorized alterations are impossible, and therefore the network can be trusted.

We can then create a safe harbour where only "validated identities" can interact and transact, where people are permanently connected to the network. But it has to go deeper than just being logged in biometrically to a phone, it has to be a web of connectivity with regular touch points confirming or questioning identity. This web of information would essentially create a self-policing network that does not need to be snooped on or monitored in ways it currently is. It would therefore take us back to something reminiscent of the 17th century, and the importance of reputation. A time where individuals took pride in how they conducted themselves in all aspects of their business, social, and personal life. Something which, I think everyone would agree, could only help civilization at present.

Tech Giants Becoming Non-Bank Banks

By Eric van der Kleij

Former Head of Level 39 Technology Accelerator;
Managing Director, ENTIQ

In March 2015, Level39, Europe's largest accelerator space for financial, retail, cyber security, and future city technologies based at Canary Wharf in London, celebrated its second birthday. This gave us a great opportunity to take what we had learned over the previous two years and look forward to the future of FinTech. We made several predictions and the most tantalizing was that social media giant Facebook, should it choose to do so, could become the non-bank bank. Just two weeks later, Facebook announced Facebook Pay. Such is the exciting pace of change affecting the industry. It is also the biggest opportunity.

To some, Facebook becoming a major financial service player capable of rivalling the current giants might be an outlandish assertion. But if we explore some of the reasoning behind it, some compelling and wholly disruptive possibilities for the FinTech sector as a whole start to emerge.

The big question facing established financial services organizations, from banks to insurers and beyond, is whether they can regain the trust of the consumer in order to safeguard their retail and private banking, and consumer-facing businesses. The financial crisis has had many victims, and banking and insurance brands are among them. The additional uncertainty to all of this is whether consumers can trust governments, and this is currently being played out in places like Greece – with even more uncertainty to come. Distrust in anything that can be lumped together by the consumer as traditional financial services is running at uncomfortable levels, if not becoming endemic. But the more fascinating question I would ask is not whether banks can regain trust, but rather, perhaps, whether they should even try. Instead, should we be rethinking financial services models to allow a new wave of consumer-facing brands to emerge, with traditional banks becoming the banks of service behind these new brands?

The erosion of trust in retail banking is of course partly a function of banks' departure from their original purpose of keeping our money safe, in return for a promissory note. The promise to pay the bearer on demand remains on the banknotes, but it is the stuff of history. Arguably, the departure from this early promise is a contributory factor in customer disappointment at what their bank's brand has ultimately come to represent.

You can see interesting signs of this in fluctuations in the value of bitcoin (effectively a non-sovereign currency, with only the confidence of its users underpinning its value), which tends to rise when there is negative sentiment or distrust of traditional banking and finance. If, for example, Greeks find they cannot withdraw cash from a bank, but that they can receive payment for their produce in bitcoin, and if they can buy a growing number of things with those bitcoins (instantly and without bank charges), then who could blame them for switching over?

But consider this: if traditional financial services providers reposition themselves as "infrastructure" or banks of service, or insurers of service behind new, trusted, non-financial brands, they may no longer need to fight to remain costly retail brands. This would create an opportunity for brands with better consumer trust to emerge as potentially very strong financial services players, as markets open up to competition from entirely new platforms. These online challengers would enjoy the privilege of building highly efficient platforms from scratch without the financial or reputational overhead of supporting a legacy. As such, they may find it easier to meet the new regulatory requirements demanded from the industry. They will certainly be well placed to achieve a single customer view which is something that has eluded legacy banks for years.

But is this really going to happen? The early signs suggest yes and the pace of change is fast. In just one year we have seen Facebook launch free friend-to-friend payments, Atom launched its app-based challenger bank, Alibaba, China's largest e-commerce platform, opened the online Mybank, and Amazon offered loans to SMEs which sell through its platform. The potential for Facebook in this context is phenomenal. More than any other social media platform, Facebook is the custodian of the narrative of our lives. While the ongoing debate on privacy rages and commentators grapple with policy imperatives, one fact remains: Facebook knows things about us that no other company does. Ergo, they are in an unrivalled position to offer financial services products to us because they can evaluate demand, risk, and potentially character, in a richer and deeper way than has ever been possible previously. Unlike the traditional credit rating houses, Facebook's trove of personal insight adds more layers to risk assessment than conventional trawls though legacy data, transactional histories, and the electoral roll. Therefore, it moves the process from a largely one-dimensional, numerical footing onto an altogether more behavioural and thematic dimension.

A key contributor to the financial crisis was the poor origination and underwriting process of mortgage companies. If those lenders had an additional signal, such as a simple traffic light system based on a life-narrative-based profile and only lent to the "greens" and "ambers", do you think that their mortgage-backed securities would have been more secure? My hunch is absolutely yes, especially if the ultimate, true value and risk of those "packaged" securities were made instantly transparent through FinTech innovation such as the truth embodied in an indelible blockchain.

The full extent of Facebook's ambitions in financial services is only just starting to become apparent, but what is obvious is the phenomenal disruptive advantage Facebook would have if it chose to enter the sector fully. If handled well, and with reassuring transparency, a serious move into financial services could utterly delight their community.

If, for the sake of argument, we consider Facebook to be a somewhat more trusted brand than many banks are right now, the fact that they can compete very aggressively by offering free payment services is a good thing for the consumer. It reduces consumer cost and provides better choice. For the under-banked on tight household budgets, a few pounds' saving on bill payments over a year can be significant.

But this model throws up the need for a whole new relationship of trust. The consumer must be satisfied that they trust their new "non-bank bank" with their data. So there needs to be a new promise. Where previously the bank promised to pay the bearer in silver, the new promise might be a guarantee not to share your data, in effect to be the bank of your data and keep it safe. Or do they actually go a step further? The new promise to the bearer could in fact be: "If you trust me to keep your data safe, I will optimize its value by helping you to monetize it." Plus, of course, free financial services as a given.

There is a potentially huge volume of continuous data to be drawn from consenting customers' financial narratives. The world's best data monetizers like Facebook, Google, and Twitter could quite naturally promise to pay you, the bearer, in some

form of financial credit. In essence, the non-bank bank could pay you "interest" on your data deposits. This is an entirely new form of promise that the industry might propagate.

But things are never that simple and it is not all rosy for new entrants to the well-established financial services sector. Because they are new to the market, there is the risk of significantly under-estimating the technical scale and regulatory requirements for delivering the services we are currently used to from the established banks. While the new entrants may be enjoying their honeymoon period, this could easily be soured if the sophisticated digital consumer encounters second-rate user interfaces or latency in transactions.

Worse still, any failure to protect customer data in the way that financial services customers have come to expect could be devastating. And of course, the new players also present a wider canvas of vulnerability for hackers. The more systems there are with more data to hack, the greater the vulnerability. New entrants to the market will need to play serious catch-up to understand, replicate, or indeed improve the established proprietary systems for protecting customers.

But one thing is certain – technology will succeed. Technologists will learn quickly what they need to do to provide competitive, secure services to the required quality, standard, and regulatory rigour. And when they do, the full potential of the non-bank banks will become clearer.

What, for example, if a single (or a collaboration of) new financial services brands create sufficient volume of transactions to allow "netting"? It is a concept from the telecommunications sector, where operators allowed each other to originate and terminate calls on their respective infrastructure and net the charges at the end of each month. If applied to new retail banking platforms, digital netting would allow a huge volume of transactions to side-step the need for the transfer of value through established networks. The regulators and tax authorities would need to be happy, but if they were, then netting could save substantial transmission costs with a commensurate impact on margins. Of course, netting would only be feasible for new brands with sufficient scale. Clearly, the opportunity for a Facebook or an Alibaba in this context is significant.

Sceptics might ask one simple but pertinent question; can a new brand with absolutely no experience in financial services succeed as a bank, insurer, or other provider of service to the financial consumer? From a purely branding perspective, there are some affirmative precedents. As a brand, Virgin was a record label before it was a bank (albeit a bank which now offers Sex Pistols credit cards). And Russian Standard Bank, with its 28 million customers and 53,000 points of sale in 1,800 cities, was a leading brand of vodka when its entrepreneurial owners made the move into banking. Today, the vodka and the bank co-exist quite successfully under a single brand identity and consumer loyalty. So, from a brand perspective, the rise of the non-bank bank is entirely possible. Especially so with the phenomenal work being done by entrepreneurs to improve access control, to develop unimpeachable authentication and, with support from the regulator and Treasury, to encourage banks to safely open up their platforms through APIs.[1]

---

[1] See the chapter entitled "Embracing the Connected API Economy" for further details.

Design is No Longer an Option – User Experience (UX) in FinTech

By Terry Cordeiro
FinTech Thought Leader

and Ivo Weevers
Co-Founder, Albert – Mobile Invoicing App

Design was previously an afterthought in the financial services sector. However this has changed completely as financial services compete with the most famous consumer brands for customers. Good design is strategically important and also provides guidelines for good user experience (UX) in FinTech.

If a stranger on the street asked you for your bank details, would you give them to him? And if he said he would use them to help you with financial planning would you share them? And finally, if you found out he worked for a trusted organization, authorized by the Financial Conduct Authority, would that persuade you to divulge your financial details?

These types of conversations are not uncommon in the world of FinTech. In both the real and digital worlds, the customer decides based on his first impression and typically relies on trust and the perceived integrity of the relationship. Designing UX for FinTech is all about these interactions and building trusted relationships between the end user and the product.

UX DESIGN = Big Bucks

The design change of a button increased a large online retailer's annual revenue by $300 million.[1] Expedia increased profits by $12M by changing the design of their registration process.[2] And a recent report from venture capital firm Kleiner Perkin in San Francisco demonstrates the important role design plays in the success of new start-ups and technologies.[3] Today, new solutions are less about the actual technology and more about the experience and value they create for the user. Many FinTech companies have not yet fully embraced UX which can be a risk for product success. This chapter gives a brief introduction to UX in FinTech alongside guidelines from our own experiences which will hopefully push the thinking around the topic forward.

A Definition for UX

Let's start with a formal definition. "User experience encompasses all aspects of the end-user's interaction with the company, its services, and its products."[4] Its goal is to enhance user satisfaction by improving the usability, accessibility, and pleasure provided by the interaction between the user and the product (often digital). UX design includes interaction design, visual design, motion design, user research and more. It is a critical ingredient in a successful product development approach.

UX and FinTech

Over 15 million banking apps have been downloaded in the UK and almost 80% of bank customers use online or mobile banking at least once a month. Financial services are embracing the digital revolution. Financial organizations are starting to understand the crucial role of UX in the overall customer experience and brand loyalty. More and more have established internal design teams by hiring talent and acquiring UX agencies or UX-led tech companies. Capital One bank for instance has acquired top UX design agency Adaptive Path and UX-led personal finance app Level Money to quickly create an exceptional pool of internal design talents.

The nature of financial services however imposes specific challenges to designing great experiences. Its highly regulated environment needs security and data protection, strong identification, and authentication procedures and depends on existing, old-fashioned, but critical infrastructures. These conditions often threaten optimal interactions.

---

[1] The $300 million button: http://www.uie.com/articles/three_hund_million_button.

[2] Expedia deletes one field from their registration process, increases profit $12m http://www.conversionvoodoo.com/blog/2011/11/expedia-deletes-one-field-from-their-registration-process-increases-profit-12m/.

[3] Design In Tech Report, John Maeda, Design partner, Kleiner Perkins Caufield & Byers. http://www.kpcb.com/blog/design-in-tech-report-2015.

[4] User Experience: http://www.nngroup.com/articles/definition-user-experience/.

An Example: Password Fatigue

In order to protect our data and money, services check that we are who we say we are. This authentication often relies heavily on usernames and passwords. The problem is that secure passwords are both hard to create and hard to remember. On top of that we have multiple passwords and usernames.

To give an indication the average person:

- Logs into different 10 sites/ mobile apps per day

- Holds passwords to 30–40 sites.

To cope with this cognitive burden people make passwords easy to remember, like the first girlfriend's name with her year of birth (laura1980). Easy to remember? Yes. Secure? No. The most secure would be to create a unique password for each site consisting of a long random combination of alphanumerics and symbols (KJ76RTnns!). Secure? Yes. Easy to remember? No. Poor UX? Definitely.

Mobile banking login screens have chosen different authentication mechanisms, resulting in different product engagement. With the first one, the user needs to count in his head the required characters, which is a huge cognitive burden. The second one uses iPhone's fingerprint recognition, which consumes much less cognitive power. Recent mechanisms are exploring emotional alternatives, such as using emojis to find secure and much easier ways of interacting. Design choices on registration processes and buttons have a huge impact on adoption and revenue. They should not be taken lightly.

Seven Guidelines

The last few years have seen dramatic changes in how people engage with brands. New smart devices, with varying interaction mechanisms and with the power of desktop computers, are revolutionizing the immediate needs of people. And this is happening in a world that is moving faster every day.

With these shifting paradigms, and the need for building trusted interactions between users and products, FinTech organizations need to put UX design central in their organization. This is not a matter of spraying some colour on the products.

Design decisions made at the various stages of the development process will have significant impact on product success.

Based on our own years of experience in large and small FinTech organizations, we have defined seven guidelines that have proven to be helpful in designing financial experiences.

1. Invest in design from the start and from the top
   The twentieth-century marketing perspective of "making people want things" has transitioned to a twenty-first-century approach of "making things people want".[5] Design – with its focus on users – is the route through which brands will either succeed or fail. Imagine the creation of a new mobile payment product. Its success depends on whether customers get a positive first impression, trust it, sign up for it, understand it, and come back next time to make another payment. UX design influences all these steps and therefore should be top-of-mind from the start. It needs to integrate closely with most business decisions. To achieve this, any organization needs to:

   a. Dedicate money and time to design from the start;
   b. Build an empowered, talented, and preferably internal design team;
   c. Define clear business design objectives.

   The fourth employee of Square, the US-based payments company, was a creative director. Many new successful tech companies such as AirBnB and Pinterest have designers as founders.

2. Understand all steps in the end-to-end experience
   When we conducted a mobile payment pilot for a large UK bank, we found that its potential relied mostly on the compatibility of third-party point-of-sale systems. Users understood how to use the payments app, they would initiate the payment, and they even remembered to pull out their mobile phone to do so. However, as point-of-sale systems communicate differently (even within the same shops), they caused payment failures and as a consequence users lost trust.

   Financial services often, more than many other industries, depend on third-party systems to complete the end-to-end experience. These can include purchase systems, security and credit checks, bank connections, and many more. Strategic choices on which systems to partner with will have a huge impact on the adoption

---

[5] The secrets of the Chief Design Officer http://www.designcouncil.org.uk/news-opinion/secrets-chief-design-officer-0.

of the product. For example, the data required, the support needed, or the way these systems integrate in mobile experiences, are all important influencers for the user's experience. Any strategic choice on infrastructure and technology should be considered and tested in light of the expected end-user experience.

3. Marry design and engineering

Great UX is not just about what is happening on the screen. Close collaboration with engineering is an underestimated but crucial factor. Code and its performance directly impact the user's perception of the product's quality. This perception is formed by things such as start-up time, page-loading behaviour, smoothness of transitions and animations, errors, and waiting times. Instagram is a great example of how to achieve a lightning-fast mobile experience by close collaboration between engineering and design.[6] Some examples:

a. Their software starts uploading the picture after the user has taken it, but *before* he has confirmed the details, providing the customer with a sense of speed and contributing to their ease-of-use.
b. The local fast processing of photo filters to the image became the killer feature, setting the app apart from all others.

The best digital experiences are created by a happy marriage between design and engineering. We have seen many initiatives first hand struggling with this because of outsourcing one or the other, or misunderstanding and miscommunication between the two. Choices about how to organize design and engineering are crucial to make the marriage work.

4. Use design to speed up decision-making

Design techniques such as rapid prototyping maximize fast learning. They are used by Google Ventures's Design Sprint[7] and the Build-Measure-Learn[8] method. Design makes ideas tangible, which allows them to be tested quickly with potential end-users, and importantly for FinTech, they can be quickly evaluated in light of other finance factors, such as risk and compliance. It shortcuts the usual endless-debate cycles and compresses months into a week.

An example: At a previous start-up we had to build the sign-up flow for a payment service. The team had endless debates about whether the user should use a numeric pin code, a character-based password, or a Facebook login. A simple prototype built in half a day revealed that (by that time) Facebook login was not trusted with financial services, and a password slowed down the user much more than a pin code. A decision was made. Rapid prototyping techniques help to understand problems by all disciplines and make decisions much quicker.

5. Save costly development time

The designers and engineers at the London-based mobile FinTech start-up Albert iterated several times on the design of sign-up flow for our mobile app. They designed screens, put them together in a prototype, and tested these with several people. And then, they incorporated the feedback, updated the designs, and started again. Until the ultimate user experience was found.

What started as a flow of 11 screens was simplified to six screens. Most screens followed a similar layout. This not only resulted in a much simpler experience (a 100% sign-up success was achieved in beta test) but also in a much quicker development cycle:

a. The development team needed to implement and fewer screens and error cases.
b. The screens followed similar screen layouts, which allowed for code re-use.

Hours of design iterations saved weeks of development work. Instilling design practices from the start will save a lot of development work.

6. Aim at Uber-like simplicity with a high trust level

Mobile finance apps reside on the same phone as Uber and Instagram-like apps. Users compare finance apps with these consumer apps (rather than with other financial services). On top of that, the financial app needs to build extra trust. Losing a photograph is annoying, but leaking finance data is disastrous. FinTech experiences should have the simplicity of other consumer experiences but with the extra care devoted to security and building trust. There are many ways to do that. These are some examples that proved to be very helpful:

• Explain security measures: Personal finance tool Mint was one of the first to start by explaining clearly and upfront to users the encryption mechanisms it had put in place to guarantee data security.

• People forget passwords: This happens. Ensure the journey to reset their password is an integrated and simple part of the overall experience; this should never be an afterthought.

6 The 3 White Lies Behind Instagram's Lightning Speed http://www.fastcodesign.com/1669788/the-3-white-lies-behind-instagrams-lightning-speed.

7 Google Venture's Design Sprint http://www.gv.com/sprint/.

8 Build-Measure-Learn method in "The Lean Startup" http://theleanstartup.com/.

- Let users control when sensitive data is displayed: A great new mobile payment feature we developed generated an access code for the user to enter into an ATM. Rapid user testing showed that people were worried that others could read the code on the mobile screen. We ensured the code was masked initially, letting the user decide when he felt comfortable to reveal it.

- MAYA (Most Advanced, Yet Acceptable): New technologies often introduce new ways of interacting with data. This can be cool and unique but also unsettling. The more closely a design resonates with what a user knows, the easier it is to build trust. FinTech solutions should keep the current users' expectations of interacting with technologies in mind when designing new experiences.

7. Attractive things reduce errors

Good aesthetics will not only have a higher appeal, but also a functional and cost benefit. Japanese and Israeli researchers[9] developed two forms of automated teller machines, the ATM machines that allow us to get money and do simple banking tasks. Both forms were identical in function, the number of buttons, and how they worked, but one had the buttons and screens arranged attractively, the other unattractively. The researchers found that the attractive ones were easier to use.

And easier-to-use ATMs meant:

a. Fewer errors
b. Faster throughput
c. Fewer customer service requests
d. Fewer card blockages
e. And ultimately, happier customers.

Despite ATMs not being the latest advance in FinTech, this demonstrates the impact well-designed interfaces have on financial products and their customers.

Conclusion

We've gone over seven guidelines that address UX in relation to FinTech. Design choices on different levels affect user adoption, trust, customer satisfaction, and ultimately revenue. We have successfully adopted these guidelines to create trusted relationships between the user and the product, and hope they spark conversation to advance the role of UX in FinTech.

[9] Donald Norman (2005) *Emotional Design: Why We Love (or Hate) Everyday Things.*

FinTech Hubs

3

This part provides an overview of current and aspiring FinTech "hubs" – the places where FinTech ecosystems are catalysed and growing. It gives real-world examples of the essential prerequisites for the establishment of FinTech centres around the world. It is a success story and checklist of what FinTech players have done right for their city (or country) to thrive in a globally competitive FinTech environment.

We will explore established FinTech centres like London, discuss France's FinTech-favourable conditions, and examine the Netherlands as an integrated FinTech ecosystem. In addition, we review buzzing FinTech scenes, ranging from Luxembourg, to Austria, India, and Singapore, each having its own unique characteristics that set it apart as a potential frontrunner in FinTech.

Nurturing New FinTech Communities

By Claire Cockerton

CEO & Chairwoman, ENTIQ

Entrepreneurs, computer scientists, coders, investors, governments, and consumers are turning to FinTech innovations to drive forward the reinvention of banking, finance, and commerce. Financial services technology has been around for decades of course, but we are now seeing the emergence of entirely new business models, technical innovation, and customer experiences that are, thankfully, constructively and creatively disrupting the status quo.

In the UK, we have called it a great movement of tech-driven transformation. Similarly to what happened in the music, travel, and media industries, FinTech is bringing the digital revolution to finance, and in the process, creating high-growth SMEs, jobs, and broader economic development. FinTech clusters and start-up density can help accelerate this transformation and growth in the finance sector, as well as helping overcome common challenges. Identifying the ingredients and the best ways to stimulate these FinTech clusters will be vital for the industry going forward, and I consider it one of the most important agendas a government can pursue.

The global FinTech sector is growing at an incredible rate, enjoying 200% year-on-year growth in funding and, according to data from CB Insights, attracting $12.2 billion in growth capital in 2014. In 2014, in the UK alone the FinTech sector generated more than £20 billion in revenue. Clusters are emerging all over the world and offering innovators (big banks and start-ups alike) access to engaged communities of serial entrepreneurs, investors, academics, technologists, and industry experts, all of whom, combined, can provide accelerated learning, product iteration, and opportunities to collaborate and grow.

Regulation, its constraints and forthcoming changes, as well as the ongoing complexities and requirements in protecting the general consumer from another crisis, requires a new kind of engagement between stakeholders.

Large incumbents provide historical insight, a powerful resource pool (from human capital to venture funds), global market access, and infrastructure and are perfect clients in need of this community of FinTech innovators. Investors, from FinTech angels to specialist venture capitalists (VCs), are taking the calculated risk around the world, with particular interests and knowledge in payments, cloud computing, blockchain, enterprise software, cyber security, and data analytics – major challenges, major opportunities. Regulators are forging innovation hubs to increase accessibility to start-ups, clarity around the authorization process, and to help inform reform. Universities are revising curricula to focus on digital languages and applied learning, and they are creating channels to these FinTech hubs for students to do their part directly after graduation. After-school and "hobby" coders are enlisting in financial services hackathons, showcasing that talent does not necessarily come from the ivory tower or corporate metropolis. Policy-makers are opening their doors to these FinTech communities, inviting feedback from innovators and being present at tech demos and roundtables in accelerators. Real estate developers, like Canary Wharf Group, also play an important role in providing the office space, which leverages the proximity of these powerful industry actors and creates a growth proposition for these rapidly scaling companies. Despite the diverse and dynamic agendas and the big challenges of doing so, the strongest FinTech clusters are managing to facilitate conversations between these stakeholders, driven by the potential outcome for the industry.

London and New York are already well established as global FinTech hubs, but what can emerging FinTech start-up communities, like those in Sydney, Leeds, Singapore, Dublin, Tel Aviv, and Seoul, learn from the success of existing FinTech hubs?

Moving beyond Michael Porter's top-down approach to business clusters, and with a hat tip to Brad Feld's seminal book *Start-up Communities*, let us explore a couple of case studies from successful FinTech hubs and consider how new FinTech hubs can be created. How might another cluster emerge with its own unique composition of entrepreneurs, technologists, industry experts, and incumbents and how can these communities come together, to form constructive interactions and a cohesive narrative to thrive and grow on the global stage?

Lessons from a Leader

London was named as Europe's most successful FinTech hub in 2015, and serves as a prime example for future development in the sector. So what sets London apart from the competition?

London has been at the heart of global trade for centuries and has a well-established financial services industry to match. As you would expect, there are large established banks with new venture funds, FinTech-focused angels, and VCs, as well as alternative finance options, like crowdfunding and peer-to-peer lending, which are all-important in providing early-stage working capital for FinTech start-ups. Low corporate tax rates, labour laws, entrepreneur's relief, enterprise investment schemes, research and development tax recovery (like patent box), and the ease with which businesses can be set up, are all significant governmental measures which make the UK a favourable place for entrepreneurs and innovators. Close proximity to investors through a host of pitching and matchmaking events, government-initiated roundtable events, and in-depth consultations with SMEs as part of regulatory reform, are all fostering deep engagement with the sector. These features all make London a place where you have a seat at the table, regardless of background or size of business.

Proximity and the creation of convening points provide an important focus for the FinTech community. Stakeholders can minimize travel to meet with many companies and they can maximize exposure to the ecosystem. A flying visit to Silicon Valley, for example, is worth it for investors because they know they can visit dozens of companies in a couple of days, with hundreds of tech firms located within just 30 miles of each other. This proximity creates a natural knowledge-share and network effect, where one meeting leads to another complementary introduction, which can lead to a merger, joint venture, or partnership. This cluster also breeds competition, as one company spurs another one to refine the industry's products and services.

The multidisciplinary and multinational talent, which exists in the City, is another reason behind London's success. There is a deep pool of talent available, not only provided by experienced bankers who are looking to move into the "emergent" FinTech cluster, but also a thriving culture of technology innovation delivered by code clubs and basement developers. This is coupled with some of the world's leading educational institutions, like University College London and Imperial College, which serve as hotbeds of academic and specialist technological study. The Open Data institute and computer science programmes are linked with internships and apprenticeships within the start-up community. Businesses are desperate for talent and talent is a powerful catalyst for growth and innovation. It is our responsibility as an industry to identify and nurture these talents and bring them into FinTech – show them the career development opportunities, the skills which can be developed on the ground at a growing business. And we are not just speaking about tech or finance talent – the FinTech industry needs designers, communicators, marketers, human factors experts, and commercialization skills. Multiculturalism and diversity are also key to long-term and scalable success. Newcomers to London bring with them an understanding of foreign markets and diversity brings a healthier business and better products for all consumers. London has this in its roots, and must continue to cultivate it as it is so central to our competitive edge.

London is also a beneficiary of negative circumstance. If necessity is the mother of invention, London surely had a burning platform for change. The 2008 financial crisis caused a huge contraction of large incumbents, instigated rapid regulatory change, shifted public sentiment towards banking, and promoted a surge in entrepreneurship. The credit crisis gave rise to alternative forms of lending, consumers had a new desire to change service providers, and many ex-corporate employees looked to use their market insights to create new products and services for the banks now under new pressures to reform. The banking industry underwent restructuring, and it is this change, preceded by crisis, which laid the foundation for a more diverse and dynamic market to emerge.

To embrace and accelerate this change, the UK has also seen the rise of a new industry body for FinTech called Innovate Finance, a cross-sector, member-driven organization that aims to anchor and develop the UK's leading position in global financial services by serving as a single access point to the full financial services and technology ecosystem. Innovate Finance's role was designed to be a neutral voice for this FinTech revolution. The member organization serves large and small companies, works with the Treasury and aims to drive forward the agenda of competition, diversity, and consumer choice. It plays a key role in delivering a convening voice for all parties in a non-biased way, and creates channels to the stakeholder map discussed above.

These factors have all combined to create what is Europe's most successful FinTech hub to date, therefore learning the lessons of London will be vital in developing similar clusters across the globe. If firms can access talent, technology, and capital in a close-knit physical environment conducive to communication, innovation, and trade, they have an excellent chance of success. Let us pick up on these two threads of location and company culture to investigate the impact on developing FinTech clusters around the world today.

Location, Location, Location

Turning to other emerging clusters, we are seeing Sydney's FinTech community gather around tech hubs like Tyro and Stone & Chalk, which aim to encourage creativity and innovation in the sector. Tim Williams, chief executive of the Committee of Sydney, stated that this was "an absolute necessity if Sydney wants to stay ahead of the financial services game", going on to describe it as "a once-in-a-decade opportunity, to bring the ICT, banking, and start-up sectors together".

Like London, Sydney already has a respected and robust financial services sector. It is currently estimated that, as of June 2015, there are more than 100 companies which can be classified as FinTech start-ups based in the city, including players in data, payments, wealth, and capital markets, with Sydney's banks being among the most profitable in the world.

Likewise, Leeds, another emerging FinTech hub in the UK, has an extraordinary wealth of back office and operational functional outposts for big banks, so it continues to attract interest and investment in these areas. Identifying a city's strengths is therefore key to creating a lasting, high-quality, specialized ecosystem which is recognized globally.

The location of a FinTech hub cannot be underestimated. Historical and local assets must be engaged and leveraged to build a hub with its own specialisms. For these hubs to be successful, a wide range of industries and organizations need to participate – designers, writers, commercial teams – and we need to connect these hubs to universities, laboratories, trade bodies, data centres, professional service providers, and expert mentor communities.

Swedish FinTech hubs cite the Nordic "Law of Jante" – the idea of placing emphasis on collective benefit, rather than individual success. This means creating a collaborative, open culture, one which embraces potential and newness, rather than familiarity and hierarchy.

Actively encouraging employees to generate new concepts is not only great for boosting morale and keeping everyone on an even footing, but can act as a powerful catalyst – awakening the latent talent and expertise within an existing team. Some of the best ideas come from the "shop-floor", from the front lines of business delivery; so a corporate's innovation strategy should also start with its own assets – its employees.

In addition to the spirit of collaboration and partnership, competition is also a very healthy force in accelerating the growth of FinTech communities globally. This is a critical mandate for regulators, governments, and the academic community. Competition forces the incumbents to consistently re-examine their proposition to customers, not getting too comfortable, and investing in a process of continuous improvement.

It is with these dynamics in mind that we have mapped out the ingredients of thriving FinTech hubs. We can see that nurturing specialist FinTech communities has the potential to deliver a much bigger transformation in tech. It is not just about the start-ups, innovators, and entrepreneurs, but about bringing their vision, agility, and power together with the other necessary stakeholders to deliver lasting change.

La (French) FinTech Connection

By Alain Clot
CEO, Dexia Credit Local; President, France FinTech

and Jean-Michel Pailhon
FinTech Thought Leader

Over recent years, FinTech has begun to attract media visibility, partly given the massive amounts of new funding raised by some of its most pre-eminent representatives, either through IPO (Lending Club, Yodlee, On Deck), or through late-stage funding rounds of $100m and above (Stripe, Funding Circle, Transferwise, SoFi, Klarna, Square, Adyen, to name just a few). Among all these new "digital champions of financial services" that have successfully raised hundreds of millions of dollars – sometimes called "FinTech unicorns" – the majority are US and UK companies, some are Scandinavian, one Dutch, but so far there is not a single French one.

Are French entrepreneurs bad at creating successful FinTech companies? Renaud Laplanche[1] (CEO/founder of Lending Club), Stephane Dubois[2] (CEO/founder of Xignite), Philippe Gelis[3] (CEO and co-founder of Kantox), and even David Marcus[4] (Head of Messaging Products at Facebook, which entered the mobile payments battle in March 2015 with Facebook Messenger's new money transfer feature) were all born in France. Unfortunately (from a purely French perspective), they have all migrated elsewhere to launch or scale their successful venture (either to the US or the UK). Would their ventures have been less successful if they had decided to stay in, or return to, France to launch their FinTech projects back in the mid/late-2000s? Maybe … probably … certainly.

What happened in the past is in the past. Today's question should be: will the newly emerging French-born FinTech entrepreneurs have to migrate out of France to succeed in the FinTech space during the second half of the 2010s?

---

[1] https://www.lendingclub.com/public/renaud-laplanche.action.

[2] http://www.xignite.com/market-data/about/people/stephane-dubois/.

[3] http://www.fintechprofile.com/2015/04/15/philippe-gelis-kantox/.

[4] http://www.bloomberg.com/research/stocks/people/person.asp?personId=23246193&ticker=EBAY&previousCapId=27862&previousTitle=EBAY%2520INC.

France's International Centre of Excellence in Science and Technology

First of all France is widely known for the quality of its academic programmes in science, technology, engineering, and mathematics. France is the world's fourth Nobel Prize-winning country in the sciences (with awards for chemistry, physics, physiology, and medicine, plus the Nobel Memorial Prize in economics), with 36 laureates.[5] French research laboratories in applied mathematics, statistics, and economic sciences are widely recognized as among the best in the world: the Institute of Advanced Scientific Studies (IHES), the Ecole Normale Supérieure (ENS, Paris), the Toulouse School of Economics (TSE) and the Paris School of Economics (PSE), among others. Some French researchers have recently earned the highest international distinctions in mathematics (Fields Medal for Cédric Villani in 2010) and economic sciences (Nobel Prize in Economic Sciences for Jean Tirole in 2014). Not to mention the most highly sought-after engineers in cryptology and coding, graduating from French Computer Science schools such as the National Institute for Research in Computer Science and Automation (INRIA) or the Ecole Polytechnique (X).

At a more down-to-earth level (e.g., business-wise), several bankers, private equity investors, hedge fund managers, and quants currently working for the most powerful and prestigious financial services companies (e.g., banks, hedge funds, and private equity firms) in London, New York, Hong Kong, or Singapore graduated from top French business and engineering schools.

It is generally expected that FinTech start-ups that will succeed will do so thanks to their ability to innovate and leverage their own technology and business model. In that context, being able to source and attract highly qualified human capital is a key factor of success for a newly incorporated FinTech start-up. And being close to some of the most developed talent management clusters in computer science, economics, and cryptology is definitely a positively skewed key differentiator. It is no coincidence that Paris was ranked the World's Best Capital of Intellectual Capital and Innovation by PwC in May 2014[6] and that Facebook launched its first Artificial

---

[5] http://people.idsia.ch/~juergen/all.html.

[6] Source: "PwC Cities of Opportunity 6", http://www.pwccn.com/home/eng/cities_of_opportunity_6.html.

Intelligence (AI) Lab in Paris (first one outside of the US after those in Menlo Park and New York).[7]

France's Entrepreneurial, Investment, and Tax Environments

Secondly, France has become a (much more) favourable country for entrepreneurs and investors over the last couple of years. The French government has launched several public initiatives to support entrepreneurship, providing start-ups with highly competitive funding capacities for R&D activities through public grants, subsidies, and research tax credit ("CIR"), enhanced and facilitated equity and debt financing for tech and innovative companies through the French public investment bank ("BPI"), specific tax regime on capital gains for retail investors ("PEA" and "PEA/PME"), a 50% discount on investment in SMEs for high net worth individuals ("ISF"), and five years' amortization of corporate venture investments in SMEs, among (many) other initiatives.

KPMG's *Competitive Alternatives* report (2014) compared effective corporate tax rates in 10 different countries and ranked France first for R&D services and third for digital services, two highly FinTech-related topics.[8]

Since the beginning of the 2010s, the French capital, Paris, has shown buoyant entrepreneurial activity, with over 40 business incubators being created, hundreds of co-working spaces, several fab labs, between 1,000 and 1,500 start-ups being set up annually, and a growing number of Tech success stories (Criteo, BlaBlaCar, Deezer, SigFox, to name just a few).

France also aims to attract international entrepreneurial talent. In achieving that goal, France benefits from an inherent advantage: its quality of life is praised internationally, making it the best place in the world to live according to several international studies. France performs well in many measures of wellbeing relative to most other countries in the OECD's Better Life Index: France ranks above average in environmental quality, housing, work-life balance, and health

status.[9] In addition, the French government has created a dedicated programme designed for non-French entrepreneurs from all over the world who want to establish their start-up in Paris: The French Tech Ticket.[10] Through this competitive programme, the founding team will be helped to set up in France, with a dedicated contact to help them deal with administrative procedures. Prize money of up €25,000 will be awarded to each founder selected, and the start-up will also get free office space in the heart of Paris at one of the leading local incubators.

France's Regulatory Environment for Innovative Financial Services

France has also been rather quick to adapt to the "new deal of FinTech" from a regulatory and legislative standpoint. Indeed, France created a specific regulatory regime for crowdfunding activities in October 2014 (with the creation of a specific Crowdfunding Investment Adviser status: the "CIP" in French), and has responded positively to innovation in financial services with lighter regulation for non-banking activities.[11]

And if France is not (yet?) in the same situation as the UK, where the Financial Conduct Authority (FCA) launched an initiative dedicated to advise and assist FinTech start-ups with their regulatory duties in October 2014,[12] the latter initiative provides a very interesting model which may potentially be replicated in France to further enhance growth in the financial services sector, whilst maintaining an appropriate level of understanding and regulatory monitoring on the French FinTech sector.

France's Strategic Business and Geographic Positioning

France has a strong and highly diversified economy. Located at the heart of Europe, the world's largest market, it is also an ideal springboard for markets in other European countries, as well as Africa and the Middle East. From a business

---

[7] http://newsroom.fb.comf/news/2015/06/introducing-facebook-ai-research-paris/.

[8] http://www.gouvernement.fr/en/attractiveness-productivity-taxes-10-cliches-about-france-proved-wrong-once-and-for-all.

[9] http://www.oecdbetterlifeindex.org/countries/france/.

[10] http://www.frenchtechticket.paris/.

[11] http://www.amf-france.org/en_US/Acteurs-et-produits/Prestataires-financiers/Financement-participatif—crowdfunding/Cadre-reglementaire.html?langSwitch=true.

[12] http://www.fca.org.uk/news/innovation-the-regulatory-opportunity.

standpoint, France is a country of 67 million consumers, showing a potentially massive demand for innovative financial services in banking, insurance, investment/asset management, financing, and payment, whether supplied by domestic or international ventures.

France's FinTech Start-ups Association

On the basis of all these positive factors, and being keen to show the world that FinTech is thriving in France, 45 (as of end June 2015, and still growing) French FinTech entrepreneurs joined forces to create a lobbying body called "France FinTech".[13]

This newly created association (launched in 2015) is designed to welcome all start-ups using innovative business and technological models that aim to address currently existing or emerging issues in the financial services industry. France FinTech plans to share experience, knowledge, and information with its members, to commission and coordinate market research studies and reports, as well as to build relationships with other digital associations in France and abroad. It will also make sure that its members' rights and expectations are taken into consideration by the government, legislators, regulatory bodies, the media, and other types of market organizations.

Showing that FinTech has become a key topic in the French political agenda, France FinTech's launch benefited from the dual support of the French National Secretary for the Digital Economy (Ms Axelle Lemaire) and the French Minister of Finance and Economy (Mr Michel Sapin). Ms Axelle Lemaire commented:

> The challenges facing the financial industry are those of our entire economy. For this industry to be a key player in the digital revolution, it takes simplicity, trust and strong support to French start-ups and innovation. The French government also needs the (FinTech) industry to structure itself. This is the rationale for the creation of the FinTech France association, which I welcome.

And Mr Michel Sapin, reinforcing the previous message:

> FinTech is a major challenge for the development of innovative financial services for all; consumers have a stake in that new players jostle established players from the financial sector.

In conclusion, France has some strengths to build on when dealing with FinTech: a strong base of financial and tech skills, a "decent" and rapidly growing financing infrastructure, and noteworthy French state tax incentives. Entrepreneurs and investors in the FinTech sector should keep France on their radar screen. Who knows? The Lending Club of 2020 could well have been founded by a French guy, but this time in France.

---

[13] See www.francefintech.org/.

The Journey Towards an Integrated FinTech Ecosystem – The Netherlands

By Don Ginsel

Founder, Holland FinTech

Holland FinTech was launched in 2014 with the goal to build a FinTech ecosystem with a base in Amsterdam. Holland FinTech brings together the different players in the Dutch FinTech space, linking them to global developments via our newsletter, research, and international trips. As a local hub, we are well on our way with over 65 members on board, ranging from FinTech start-ups to banks, and from investors to government agencies. Increasingly we are expanding our international reach.

But we are not there yet. There are still many hurdles to overcome for FinTech in general. We do not consider ourselves experts in building FinTech ecosystems yet but think that sharing our journey may help others on a similar quest.

Netherlands in 2014

Back in 2014, FinTech in the Netherlands was about as dormant as in most other countries in continental Europe. Only a very small group of internationally well-connected financial professionals knew about this new thing called FinTech, a term being used in Silicon Valley, New York, and London. FinTech was only used to address the main IT suppliers of the financial industry. But FinTech start-ups were something nobody had ever heard of or thought about. Given the quite innovative financial landscape, this was a missed opportunity, especially since the Netherlands have been competing on a global scale for some time in the payments and security arena. So what caused this disconnect?

For the relatively large financial industry in the Netherlands, the financial crisis was still not over. Dealing with a lagging economy, staff reductions, increasing compliance regulation, and finalizing governmental bailout measures were top priorities. Combined with public and political scrutiny around bonuses and non-transparent financial products, financial institutions just had different things on their minds.

Not only was there a lack of serious competition to drive innovation in the first place, but also there was a lack of political awareness about financial innovation. Moreover, with the financial crisis being caused by "innovative" financial products, the topic of innovation in this sector was highly sensitive. In addition, Holland Financial Centre, the Dutch organization that had as one of its tasks to promote innovation in the financial industry, was forced to close due to the negative sentiment towards the financial industry. Basically the Dutch financial industry was innovation-disabled and had nowhere to turn for support.

So how about start-ups and tech companies? Were there really no companies in the Netherlands? Apparently the term FinTech had not really hit the ground before 2014. Most of the relevant companies simply considered themselves IT companies, like thousands of others. Many of them were either unaware of the opportunity that the international rise of FinTech offered or else they didn't know how to be associated with it. And the local venture capitalists were not picking up on the FinTech opportunity either, except for a few that were already active in London or beyond.

But there was one area where the Netherlands was already ahead of the FinTech competition: payments. The Dutch have had some great payment solutions both via banks (iDeal) and young tech companies like Global Collect and Adyen. For a trader nation like the Netherlands, it was obvious e-commerce developments were driving new solutions forward, especially those related to financial processes.

Seizing the Opportunity

Given the large potential of innovative payments from the Netherlands and the strong enterprise IT capabilities (infrastructure, security, ERP & Trade software), the FinTech potential of the Netherlands is quite considerable. This, combined with an excellent infrastructure (one of the busiest internet nodes worldwide), a well-educated population (best country in Europe to do business in English after the UK and Ireland), and a great international network, makes the Netherlands a great place to do business. So, how to set this in motion?

After confirming that there is an opportunity with FinTech to drive competition and bring new solutions that matter to entrepreneurs and consumers, the next step is closing the knowledge gap between financial institutions and their customers. This will financially empower entrepreneurs and consumers to deliver economic growth and prosperity.

The First Step

Leveraging my network: how to align the various stakeholders in my network, at banks, start-ups, investors, and service providers and make them enthusiastic about the idea of doing "something" with FinTech in the Netherlands. This took a lot of explaining to the industry. At first I focused on blogging part time, but as enthusiasm rose with each interview and discussion on the topic, it seemed that there was perhaps momentum for something bigger. KPMG's team for Innovative Start-ups was the first to bite, a good fit given their current focus on start-ups in combination with having many clients in the Financial Services industry. Their team was a big help in structuring the concept and promoting it. Innopay, an advanced payment consulting firm, was the next to give verbal commitment, as this initiative was well suited to complement their payment expertise. They were very helpful in sharing the history of FinTech in Europe, before the term FinTech was widely recognized. Soon after Van Doorne, an innovative Dutch law firm, and IBM joined the group of supporters and the concept started to take shape. On 23 October 2014, we had our first meetup, with over 100 people attending, and Holland FinTech was born.

Early Choices

We called the supporters founding members and started setting goals and structuring the organization. It seemed like a logical step to form a bridge between the world of FinTech, as found predominantly outside of the Netherlands, and the local FinTech ecosystem that we were building. Therefore we determined that an international focus was paramount and decided to communicate only in English. The main tasks then were to get the FinTech players together, and to make connections to developments and FinTech hubs worldwide. This meant telling people about FinTech, reaching out to (potential) FinTech companies, organizing events, and setting up structured communication about global FinTech developments.

Since we had to convert so many people to start with, we had to get easy access to them. Providing free information through our website, a free global FinTech newsletter, and free meetups enabled us to garner the interest of the relevant parties. Besides this we took every (self-created) opportunity to speak about FinTech and our cause when we thought relevant people would be there. While this meant our agenda was overloaded, being willing to go on stage and speak about FinTech remains a great way to get noticed.

One of the great things about working with (among others) start-ups is their energy and resourcefulness. Their capacity to go a long way with limited resources was also required for this self-funded initiative, very much a start-up itself. So just rolling up our sleeves and getting this going, even when not all partners were on board yet, was important. This agility is key to the success of a start-up, certainly in the fast changing FinTech landscape. Keeping stakeholders happy is also key, but not at the cost of inertia. This approach does however have its financial consequences and requires solid financial commitment from at least one shareholder. We have not been funded by grants or subsidies (so far).

As a privately started and funded initiative, it made sense to become a limited liability company. However, given the partly social goals and drive to tackle what is also a public cause, financial empowerment, many people also considered a foundation to be a good form to use. We have not yet done so, due to potential additional administrative hassle and perhaps even less transparency. Looking forward to when a foundation might help us to reach our goals, we may consider changing our legal structure.

Business Model

One of the things that I have learned is that asking for a success fee per transaction, which is the norm for M&A deals, makes it difficult to advise people objectively. But since we're building a marketplace for FinTech, we needed to find a way to fund our activities. The membership fees are relatively low (up to a maximum of EUR 15k for billion-plus companies) and free for start-ups for the first year. This model should lower the barriers to entry thereby maximizing the number of members, increasing knowledge sharing and the number of business opportunities available at our marketplace.

This model allows us to do more for the network and community, since marketing and distribution are already covered. That means that setting up a co-working space for FinTech companies, organizing hackathons, and/or running accelerators are all natural extensions since the sponsors, investors, and participants are already part of the organization. And the programmes can be run more cheaply due to overlapping resources. That makes a win-win for all parties involved. It also enables us to listen very carefully to our members and to tailor programmes to their current needs efficiently.

Governmental Relations

Given the potential pull Holland FinTech might have on companies from abroad and the contribution to the financial ecosystem, we started co-operating with the government at a very early stage. We maintain great relationships with our Ministries of Foreign Affairs, Economic Affairs, the Dutch regulators, the Dutch Central Bank (DNB), as well as the Authority on Financial Markets (AFM). These parties play such an important role in making or breaking the FinTech landscape, that we want them to know about and to support our objectives. Our discussions have been very constructive and there is a sense of urgency with all of the stakeholders that we cannot miss this window of opportunity.

One very important development at the beginning of 2015 was the creation of StartupDelta, simply put the "Ministry of Start-ups", led by former EU commissioner Neelie Kroes. This organization combines the forces of all start-ups and service providers in the Netherlands, connecting them internationally. It creates a great momentum for start-ups and attracts venture capital to the Netherlands. In particular, StartupDelta strengthens cooperation between start-ups and large corporates.

Execution Challenge

So now we are well on our way with a staff of eight. We have organized ten events since October 2014, have 65+ member companies (90% Dutch), 1500+ newsletter readers, and 2500+ Twitter followers. Recently the top three Dutch banks joined Holland FinTech as members. We have identified more than 250 FinTech companies in the Netherlands and are expanding our geographical mapping. Since the city of Amsterdam has also embraced our initiative, we will soon unveil a space for our physical FinTech hub in Amsterdam, that will be a "must visit" for those active in FinTech worldwide, similar to Level39 in London.

But of course our organization is still at the beginning stages. Bringing in sufficient revenue remains a challenge when working with corporate partners. This also means that we work with a limited number of staff members and that we rely on part-time and volunteer staff. Our team is extremely committed to building a vibrant FinTech community and has done a great job so far!

International Relevance

Setting up an organization that aims to manage the whole FinTech ecosystem in a region requires dedicated resources and the room to manoeuvre. The time must be right and you may be faced with extensive competition but that doesn't mean that you should avoid activity around FinTech – rather it requires finding a particular niche. In London you see massive competition between organizations that facilitate FinTech and everyone, including the Mayor of London, is calling London the FinTech capital of the world. That alignment sends out a very strong message, one that most regions can learn from.

This story shares our journey in the FinTech landscape so far and our aim to connect to other people and organizations who want to be a part of shaping the FinTech ecosystem worldwide. We hope this vision will give direction for an integrated ecosystem approach.

Luxembourg, a Future FinTech Hub?

By Nazim Faid

Corporate, Banking and Finance Lawyer, Kaufhold & Reveillaud

In May 2015, the ICT Spring Europe Conference was held in Luxembourg. This conference focused primarily on the FinTech sector. With more than five thousand people participating in this sixth edition of the ICT Spring Europe, Luxembourg has clearly announced itself as a contender to become a world-class FinTech hub with its unique ecosystem for growth.

If FinTech companies can help today's banking provide better customer services, they have long aroused concern and distrust from Luxembourg financial players. However, with over 150 FinTech companies created in Luxembourg, most of which were incorporated in the last three years (and many more to come), the Luxembourgish market has now been made aware of the dynamics and undeniable importance of these start-ups, which have already created over ten thousand jobs in the country (11% of total jobs in Luxembourg). The growing interest customers show in new technologies should accelerate the growth of the FinTech sector and give an even more important role to FinTech companies in the financial world. Luxembourg must keep pace with this technology revolution to continue to be a major player in international finance.

In the changing financial landscape, today we are witnessing the emergence of two types of FinTech: the so-called "traditional" FinTechs, which are complementary to the major players in the financial sector, and the "disruptive" FinTechs, highly innovative and more at odds with the traditional functioning of the financial sector.

Luxembourg aspires to become one of the world's major hubs for FinTech and it does have its arguments: according to the latest Global Information Technology Report published by the World Economic Forum, Luxembourg is ranked ninth worldwide when it comes to leveraging information and communication technologies. FinTech companies can also benefit from one of the most modern data centre parks in Europe.

The Luxembourg financial centre is a global market, making it very attractive for FinTech start-up companies wishing to expand internationally by providing market intelligence, access to business networks, and close connections with other major FinTech hubs in the world.

If Luxembourg is presented as a serious contender to become a major hub for FinTechs due to its flexible regulations, highly attractive tax regime, favourable IT environment, and an effective data storage system, efforts have yet to be made in order to better connect the "Fin" and the "Tech" and compete with other major European FinTech hubs such as London, Paris, or Berlin. The focus of these efforts must be on two points: innovation and flexibility.

The ability to innovate remains a major challenge to Luxembourg's ambition. The FinTech companies should not be considered as competitors threatening the major players in the sector, but rather as potential new partners. In a market in which increasing sources of funding can be made readily available to consumers, the difference now lies in the quality of banking and customer service.

Banks can benefit from FinTech companies' expertise not only for their self-service tools, but also to enhance their relationship with clients. The FinTech revolution is prompting many of the "traditional" players to review their organization as well as services offered to customers and become more client-centric.

Many Luxembourg banks still lack the necessary infrastructure to face the global technological revolution, and thus maintain a cautious approach to this type of innovation. Be that as it may, a widening approach to innovation is gaining significant popularity amongst Luxembourg financial players. Collaboration is becoming increasingly important in the financial services and technology industries.

As such, a plethora of collaborations have been created between banks and FinTech companies: some banks have decided to buy out FinTech companies, acquiring their technologies in order to develop them "in-house", while others prefer to fund them by offering loans.

If Luxembourg wishes to fulfil its aspirations of becoming a world-class FinTech hub, a major effort must still be made to access funding. Better access to funding implies not only private funding, but also public funding. By means of national agencies such as Luxinnovation, the National Agency for Innovation (founded in 1984 by several public entities), the government helps start-ups in gaining access to public funding. In 2014, the government supported nearly 300 projects and has been involved in the establishment of 45 new start-ups, of which many are FinTech companies.

Investment in FinTech companies grew by 201% globally year-over-year, bouncing from US$4.05 billion in 2013 to reach US$12.21 billion in 2014. Such growth clearly demonstrates that this sector shows promise and potential. Although the United States made up the lion's share with approximately 80% of the total amount, Europe had the highest level of growth with an increase of 215% last year. If today's banks are to benefit from the growth driven by the FinTech sector, innovation through cooperation and investment will be key.

Another major challenge for Luxembourg will be adopting flexible legislation to allow FinTechs to proliferate on a larger scale, particularly by facilitating the arrival of talent such as IT engineers. With more than 70% of its workforce being foreigners, Luxembourg is an international melting-pot. Luxembourg must promote its business-friendly environment to attract new talent and become a hub for the recruitment of high-profile IT and financial specialists.

Although the present regulatory framework eases the integration of financial technologies into the financial sector, the country must further loosen its regulatory environment, in order to allow new actors to enter financial services markets. We expect the CSSF (Commission de Surveillance du Secteur Financier), the Luxembourg national supervisory authority, to enhance the current regulatory framework in order to provide an even more suitable regulatory environment to FinTech companies.

On 20 October 2014, the Prime Minister and Minister of Communications and Media, Xavier Bettel, presented the "Digital Lëtzebuerg" initiative to the Parliament. During a press conference held after the presentation, the Prime Minister highlighted the boost in Luxembourg's economy with the arrival of FinTech companies in the country, whether in the e-commerce, cloud computing, Big Data, or e-payments technologies sectors.

With this initiative, the government wishes to consolidate the country's position in the ICT sector on a long-term basis in order to diversify its economy, while allowing citizens to benefit from better and cheaper services that innovative FinTech companies can offer. This initiative will focus on developing innovation and access to funding for FinTech start-ups and the promotion of Luxembourg's attractiveness abroad.

The "Digital Lëtzebuerg" initiative is a clear demonstration of the government's will to give a fresh face to Luxembourg as a modern, open, and connected country, ready to embrace the technological era of financial services. This initiative should bring together major Luxembourg financial players from the public, private, and academic sectors.

Luxembourg is without doubt becoming increasingly conscious of the challenge it faces, and the growing number of progressive initiatives taken – not only with "Digital Lëtzebuerg", but also with various think tanks, programmes, incubators, and accelerators – are a testament to the Luxembourg financial sector's readiness to diversify the country's economy by assisting, promoting, and developing FinTech start-ups both nationally and internationally.

We are already witnessing FinTech success stories in Luxembourg, and many major players, from both the private and public sectors, are helping FinTech companies achieve global growth. The development of the FinTech sector in Luxembourg should be increasingly successful as we observe the growing interest and support this sector is getting from the more conservative players of the financial industry.

The country is poised to swiftly adapt its already highly attractive regulatory framework to this new revolution, from which the entire national economy can benefit.

Vienna as the No. 1 FinTech Hub in Mobile Payments?

By Sebastian Haas
Co-Founder & Managing Partner, MEP Mobile Equity Partner

and Reinhold Bierbaumer
Co-Founder & Managing Partner, MEP Mobile Equity Partner

London acquired its position as Europe's FinTech centre at a very early stage. Besides the size of its well-developed banking industry, this is one of the primary reasons why London today is undoubtedly the FinTech Capital of Europe. While London maintains its dominant position, several regions and cities are investing heavily to establish their own FinTech hotspots. One of these up-and-coming players is Vienna, the capital of Austria. Vienna's FinTech hub options are different from Berlin, Frankfurt, or Zurich. Due to different historical factors, Vienna has the opportunity to be a prominent FinTech hub in a vertical sector, namely payment and ticketing.

One of the most significant arguments for Vienna's competitive advantage is its strategic location, historical banking connections, and certain unique factors. Austrian banks have approximately 50 million customers in Central and Eastern Europe (CEE) and, through their subsidiaries in the payments area formed in the 1980s, collectively hold an extraordinary strategic advantage in the mobile payment race. This factor, in combination with up-and-coming start-ups in the payments area, provides fertile soil for technological innovation which can follow on from some previous Austrian innovations, such as the Austrian health care e-card in 2005, Austrian road toll technology, or the Austrian "Bankomatkarte". It is also worth noting that Austria was the birthplace of NFC technology, the current industry standard for contactless payment.

The payment industry in general, and especially mobile payments, is essentially built on "cooperation technology". As Confucius said, "even the strongest man cannot lift himself up." The environment presents a truly unique opportunity for clever start-ups to develop world-class mobile payment solutions using this cooperation technology, due to the less complex stakeholder constellations, with just a few big banks, mobile network operators (MNOs), and payment service providers (PSPs) operating in Austria.

This chapter deals with the starting position, the players involved, competitive advantages, and what this could mean for Europe and the mobile payment industry (see the Table below).

Table: Starting basis – payment facts and figures

Austrian population	8.5m
Number of current accounts	> 8.0m
AT banks customer base in CEE	> 50m
Debit cards in AT (Bankomatkarte)	9.1m
Credit cards	2.9m
Smartphone penetration	> 70%

Practically all Austrians own at least one payment card (1.4 cards per person on average), but compared to Scandinavians or people in the UK, for example, Austrians are still quite reluctant to use their cards. Cash is still king in Austria. A total of 12 million payment cards are used for less than 500 million payment transactions per year – approximately 420 million debit card transactions (with the Bankomatkarte) and approximately 80 million credit card transactions.

Austria at present, like Germany, is still a cash country, but all the signs point towards a strong increase in cashless payments in the coming years, for a variety of reasons and factors, coming from different directions and out of different motives.

On the one hand – and this is a significant change – policy-makers have realized that a more cashless society correlates with less tax evasion, especially as far as VAT is concerned. The Austrian government recently adopted a law that forces businesses to install electronic point of sale (POS) terminals which are linked to the Federal Computing Centre (*Bundesrechenzentrum*), the IT service provider of the Austrian federal administration.

The second, and even more important factor is the specific Austrian payment infrastructure with just a few players and its relatively uncomplicated and straightforward upgrade path towards a mobile payment infrastructure from the retailer's and POS side. The interesting thing is that banks and payment service providers are in a weak position to establish user-centric and user-friendly integrated all-in-one wallets, because of their lack of neutrality. This space is reserved for either the big digital players from the US and Asia or neutral European start-ups.

Specific Starting Basis for Mobile Payments

Though at present still a "cash country", with more than 80% of transactions in cash, Austria's position in the upcoming transition to mobile payment is quite unique. It looks as though, over the last three years, Austrian banks and the payment industry were able to create the foundation for a mobile payment revolution, which could even serve as a model for Europe.

The fact that Austrian banks have more than 50 million customers with current accounts in the CEE region is also one of the reasons why Europe's payment industry should watch the mobile payment innovations that are happening in Austria.

But even more important is the fact that Austrian banks, through their affiliated payment service provider PSA Payment Services Austria GmbH, owned by all the Austrian banks, managed to get the biggest three mobile network operators, Telekom Austria A1, T-Mobile and Three, to the table for what is probably a groundbreaking joint venture: the mobile debit card on smartphones (mobile Bankomatkarte), which in 2016 will also include credit schemes. A short keyword description of this project is:

- SIM-based secure element.
- All banks and all MNOs on board.
- Android phones only (due to Apple NFC policy).
- Debit cards only (in 2015).
- Credit cards in 2016.

The decision of Austrian banks and their affiliate PSA from 2013, to replace all plastic cards by contactless NFC cards until the end of 2015, puts retailers and acquirers under pressure to upgrade POS terminals to NFC technology. This

move by banks, establishing the POS-side infrastructure for mobile payments, is happening quite fast, indeed a lot faster than in other EU countries. This means that, after 2016, the stage for mobile payments in Austria will be set.

So from Q4 2015 onwards, Austrians have the option to use their debit card Bankomatkarte as an app on their phones, via different apps from banks and mobile network operators.

What Does this Mean for FinTech Start-ups?

Austrian banks will give their customers the option to transfer their debit card Bankomatkarte to the smartphone. Though innovative and ambitious, all in all this looks a lot like fragmentation and complexity from the point of view of the customer and smartphone user. The key question remains: will the average smartphone user, as opposed to the pilot project-friendly user, adopt this? This question remains unanswered.

Austria has two options going forward. On the one hand, it may welcome IT giants Apple, Samsung, Google, with their neutral wallets, as soon as they are ready to enter the continent. On the other hand, neutral start-ups, cleverly positioned between the stakeholders and stakeholder groups, will have a tremendous opportunity here. The complexity of the EU payment space, with different regulations and different payment ecosystems, country by country, will make things difficult for the big guys from the US and the Far East. Chances are that five to ten years from now the dominant players in the mobile payment segment will be companies that nobody has heard of today, or ones that have not even been founded yet.

Local FinTech-related Venture Capital Environment

There's a small but growing pool of venture capital (VC) in Austria. But who are the relevant investors for FinTech start-ups and what types of positioning and specialization are they fostering?

A stable and crucial player in the local ecosystem is the Austria Wirtschaftsservice Gesellschaft mbH (aws), the Austrian federal promotional bank. Since 2013 the aws Founder Fund participates in Austrian ventures with high-end European scalable growth potential. The fund takes equity investments up to €3 million and has a wide set of target segments. The emphasis of the current portfolio is on digital hubs and marketplaces. Furthermore, Erste Bank plays a significant role within the aws Founder Fund, by taking part in the initial fundraising with €3.5 million, and is also represented on the fund's investment committee.

One of the VC veterans in Vienna is Speedinvest, which manages an already attractive FinTech portfolio (highlights are Wikifolio and Holvi). An impressive newcomer is Venionaire, a young, skilled team with a strong network within the relevant US venture capital centres New York (East Coast) and Silicon Valley (West Coast) which is entering the market. SevenVentures (ProSiebenSat.1 Media AG) is part of the Media Alliance Europe and therefore has the potential to scale successful start-ups, their brands and products. As a launchpad, SevenVentures offers access to over 200 million European households. Austria is serving within the group as a test market.

Even family offices offer good development potential for ventures in Austria. Leading figures and renowned personalities act as business angels in their former fields of competence and offer structured approaches, similar to EUVECA-compliant models, but endowed with more flexibility and strategic reach.

Some general trends – alongside the ongoing boom cycle in the asset class venture capital – are larger fundraising rounds and rising ticket sizes. Austria-based Speedinvest and Venionaire scheduled closings of over €50 million in 2015.

As a specialized incubator and business development hub, MEP Mobile Equity Partners is focusing on the vertical FinTech disciplines of mobile payment and mobile ticketing. MEP is acting as a cross-fertilizer between banks and MNOs, between incumbents and start-ups. MEP places seed and early-stage investments which offer a complementary and supplementary fit for the relevant mobile payment cluster. Along with others, MEP is supporting the establishment of a knowledge-driven business development hub to create a new platform for cooperation and to enhance European capabilities.

Conclusion: Unlocking the Potential

A successful mobile payment hub in Vienna will leverage an existing infrastructure and involve organizational and business development capacities, including banks, MNOs, and further specialized corporate start-ups, creating stakes in the payment industry's value chain. Austria's strategic location between Western Europe and CEE, its unique set-up of financial institutions, and relatively small market size (which wards off significant competition, yet allows for the establishment of a scalable and successful solution) make a compelling FinTech case for the country.

India's FinTech Ecosystem

By Sukhi Jutla
FinTech Thought Leader

and Narendiran Sundararajan
Manager – Research (ICT) at Centre for Innovation Incubation
and Entrepreneurship, IIM Ahmedabad

Big banks, big stock exchanges, big enterprises, big emphasis on technology, big e-commerce companies, big investments, and ambitious entrepreneurs making it big in the world's second most-populated country: all these contributing factors make FinTech breathtakingly big in India. In 2015 alone, investments in FinTech-related start-ups in India have crossed the billion-mark[1] across the spectrum. The socio-economically diverse billion-plus population of India also opens up wide avenues for FinTech activity, in terms of talent, innovation opportunities, and a massive market to serve. The numbers are telling in this regard – close to 90% of transactions in India are cash-based.[2] Online transactions are also on the rise; internet and mobile penetration are close to 20% and 70% respectively[3] and mobile internet users are forecast to pass the 200 million mark.[4] Both the public and the private sectors are reaching into these avenues, leveraging technology and innovation to create lasting solutions, from bridging the gap in access to financial services in underserved markets, to capturing the increasingly smart and networked mobile population with cutting edge mobility.

Innovation Areas

Against this backdrop of innovation and investment, one can see continued growth and opportunities in the private sector. One of India's first online marketplaces focused on personal financial products, BankBazaar has secured INR 375 crores (US$60 million) in its latest funding round.[5] Established in 2008, BankBazaar continues to position itself to keep growing its customer base and to invest in its

mobile app as customers increasingly turn to their mobiles to access such services. With more people turning to their mobiles as the first point of interaction with the site, it will become increasingly important to ensure that the company, as well as future start-ups, incorporates mobile apps as an integral feature.

Jocata is another prominent FinTech company that offers Know-Your-Client (KYC) and Anti-Money Laundering (AML) products. The technology is supporting a reduction in the cost of compliance by helping to meet regulatory expectations as well as providing standardized and reusable data from its customers. Selected for FinTech Innovation Lab run by Accenture,[6] it is clear that the world is willing to invest in Indian start-ups due to their obvious potential.

Traditional banks are perhaps feeling the heat from FinTech start-ups as they see their fee incomes from online payments decline. HDFC Bank, India's second largest bank, saw its payment fees decline by 30%.[7] In response, it has partnered with e-tailers such as Snapdeal and Flipkart to launch a shopping site on its website to encourage customers to use their platforms in an attempt to reclaim fees from e-commerce activity. The growing e-commerce sector will continue to revolutionize the payments market as more people turn to the web to buy and sell products in this diverse country.

FinTech is also disrupting the social sector, with Milaap being one of the biggest online fundraising platforms. It allows people from around the world to fund and help communities in India in need of basic facilities such as sanitation and access to clean drinking water. By pledging small amounts of money similar to the micro lending business model, Milaap uses a network of volunteers to work with field partners to review loan applications and ensure the money is delivered to the end borrower. This has proven to be a powerful way to raise funds for those who need them, by bypassing traditional banks whose processes can be bogged down in bureaucracy and unnecessary delays.

It is no surprise that the FinTech scene is now disrupting the food industry in India, known as the "Land of Spice". Foodtech start-ups in India are becoming even more popular than the booming e-commerce space. With the Indian food industry said to represent a $50 billion market,[8] there has been a rise in the number of start-ups in this space. For

[1] Trak.IN Funding Tracker: http://trak.in/india-startup-funding-investment-2015/.

[2] Knowledge@Wharton: http://knowledge.wharton.upenn.edu/article/tapping-an-appetite-for-technology-in-indias-underserved-markets/.

[3] *Time*: http://time.com/3611863/india-smartphones/.

[4] *The Hindu*: http://www.thehindu.com/sci-tech/technology/gadgets/mobile-internet-users-to-reach-213-million-by-june-2015/article6785327.ece.

[5] See http://yourstory.com/2015/07/bankbazaar-com-funding-seriesc/.

[6] See http://www.jocata.com/news.html.

[7] E27: http://e27.co/banks-gear-up-to-piggyback-on-the-e-commerce-wave-20150526/.

[8] YourStory: http://yourstory.com/2015/05/foodtech-startups-india-crowdpitch/.

example, Feazt is a platform that connects food lovers across the city by allowing them to host a dinner party or be a guest. Guests will pay a set amount per meal and hosts are charged a minimum subscription fee and a sign-up fee to use the platform.

A Collective Hub

With more and more innovations arising in almost every industry, it is no surprise that angel and venture capital (VC) funding is hitting an all-time high. Indian start-ups have now collectively raised $3.5 billion[9] in funding in the first half of 2015, which has surpassed the total value of deals in the whole of 2014. Helion Venture Partners, Sequoia Capital, Blume Ventures, Kalaari Capital, Accel Partners, Matrix Partners, Tiger Global, IDG Ventures, and Softbank represent India's mix of active local and international investors, Bangalore leading investments with $2.43 billion, New Delhi at $1.43 billion, and Mumbai at $610 million,[10] cementing the success stories of innovations with investment merit. Running in parallel, the easing of regulations encouraged by the Reserve Bank of India (RBI) has facilitated economic growth. Owing to their existing infrastructure, Indian metropolitans such as Mumbai, Pune, Hyderabad, Bangalore, and Chennai are fast becoming a collective hub for FinTech activity in the country. These aspirational cultural and business centres have the complete backbone that FinTech hubs thrive on worldwide: banking and financial institutions in public and private domains, non-banking financial companies (NBFCs), multinational companies from both production and services industries, back-end offices, start-ups and entrepreneurs, incubators, investors, and a pool of talent to drive the above.

The number of financial hubs in the country is also on the rise. In research conducted by MasterCard, seven Indian cities are ranked among the top 65 financial centres in emerging economies.[11] Mumbai, New Delhi, Bangalore, Chennai, Hyderabad, Kolkata, Pune, and Coimbatore were all listed in terms of their conduciveness to financial innovation and infrastructure, economic and commercial environment, growth and development, commercial connectivity, education, IT connectivity, quality of urban life, and security. Mumbai, the de facto financial capital of India, ranked highest among its compatriots. As an established financial services hub, it houses India's vital stock exchanges and serves as the headquarters of many national and international financial institutions. It is also an investment capital that serves as the home of many VC firms and angel investors. Bangalore is often hailed as India's start-up capital, with close competition from Delhi, Mumbai, and the upcoming ecosystem in Pune. The pioneering IT giants of India – Wipro, Infosys, and TCS – all began their operations from Bangalore, and have been key players in IT and back-end support for financial institutions. This set the precedent for the city's wealth of entrepreneurs and investment capital. These cities, along with growing innovation hubs such as Chennai and Hyderabad, have become a testing ground for various FinTech start-ups working in capital markets, payments, microfinance, trading, and institutional tools.

The future of FinTech in India is set on a playing field of high aspirations, higher expectations, and a renewed sense of optimism. The government-backed Gujarat International Finance Tech-City (GIFT city) is a big step in this direction towards the future. GIFT City is an ambitious project serving as a massive International Finance Service Centre (IFSC) built with the sole intention of providing infrastructure for global and local financial centres to establish a base for their operations. Targeting enterprises driven by Indian talent in space-constrained IFSCs such as Dubai and Singapore, GIFT City aims to be a booming FinTech employment hub. Jobs in FinTech are also generally on the rise in India. The Banking, Financial Services and Insurance sector alone generated close to 22,000 jobs. Among the centres, Pune topped the list in job creation, with all the cities mentioned above showing growth in new jobs.[12] This comes as no surprise given that companies such as SunGard, Fundtech, MasterCard, Fiserv, and First Data already have centres in Pune, with MasterCard developing their largest technology hub outside the US in the city.[13]

To sum up the outlook of India as a FinTech hub, we need to view the entire country as constituting a collective hub of FinTech activity. With its various metropolitan areas focusing on different interests and tackling diverse challenges with regards to financial services, the common backbone that drives these cities is the spirit of innovation, the support of regulators, and the promise of investment. Unlike FinTech hubs worldwide, its legacy will not be one that banks on its established status, but rather on the development it can establish across the country.

---

[9] YourStory: http://yourstory.com/2015/07/half-year-2015-funding-report/.

[10] TheNextWeb: http://thenextweb.com/in/2015/07/05/india-the-worlds-fastest-growing-startup-ecosystem/.

[11] MasterCard: http://www.mastercard.com/us/company/en/newsroom/pr_new_mastercard_research_ranks_65_Cities_in_emerging_markets.html.

[12] ASSOCHAM: http://assocham.org/newsdetail.php?id=4210.

[13] *Economic Times*: http://economictimes.indiatimes.com/articleshow/46127416.cms?utm_source=contentofinterest&utm_medium=text&utm_campaign=cppst.

Singapore, the FinTech Hub for Southeast Asia

By Markus Gnirck
Co-Founder, Startupbootcamp FinTech

and Gerben Visser
Managing Partner, Incubasia Ventures

From many perspectives, Singapore is seen as a global example for tremendous development and unparalleled growth over the past 50 years. Strategically located at the crossroads of a regional development that will consolidate a region larger than Europe (in terms of growth, population, and promising demographics), Singapore has incredible potential to bring the world to Asia, and Asia to the world.

Singapore's international presence is built on the basis of a stable country, stringent regulatory framework, and efficient administrative procedures, while its strategic positioning makes it an ideal launch-pad for regional development into larger and more highly populated countries like Indonesia, Malaysia, Thailand, Vietnam, and the Philippines.

Drivers of FinTech in Singapore

Based on the Global Financial Centres Index, Singapore is ranked the 4th largest financial centre in the world, and is also ranked in 1st place on the World Economic Forum Global Information Technology Report 2015. This confluence of financial maturity and technological readiness is critical for the acceleration of the FinTech industry, and naturally points to Singapore as a FinTech hub.

While FinTech is a global movement that has gained a lot of traction and momentum, it is important to recognize that the various geographies have different drivers in their respective ecosystems. Comparing the highly developed economies within Europe and the US against the developing economies within Asia, it is clear the drivers vary. FinTech in developed economies comes from a basis of innovation and adding value, while FinTech in developing economies is propelled by a critical need to address pain points, which are acutely felt in their respective economies.

Generalizing the drivers for FinTech in Asia is thorny as there is a healthy mix of developed and developing economies in the region. Taking a regional perspective, financial inclusion is still a key issue that, if left unaddressed, inhibits the development of financial maturity within many of these economies. Therefore, be it for altruistic reasons or merely good business sense, consciously or unconsciously, many FinTech companies in Asia are addressing issues in relation to an aspect of financial inclusion.

Another key driver of FinTech in Singapore is the conducive business environment. Entrepreneurship and innovation are heavily supported by government-related entities such as SPRING Singapore, International Enterprise Singapore ("IE Singapore"), Singapore Economic Development Board ("EDB"), and Infocomm Development Authority of Singapore ("iDA"). These organizations have been purposefully pushing initiatives aimed at encouraging and fostering innovation and enterprise in the local scene. Singapore's strong legal framework also provides a high degree of comfort and stability for FinTech companies to establish themselves here.

The heavy involvement of the Monetary Authority of Singapore ("MAS") in FinTech activities is yet another positive development for Singapore. Recently, MAS announced a Chief FinTech Officer who will serve as an entry point for FinTech companies into MAS, and an Innovation Hub similar to the FCA in the UK will be formed. They have also affirmed their strong commitment to FinTech by committing $225 million to the Financial Sector Technology & Innovation ("FSTI") scheme.

Finally, there is a tangible surge in information sourcing and content generation in relation to FinTech. Renowned educational institutes like Singapore Management University ("SMU") have established several centres such as the Financial IT Academy ("FITA") or the Sim Kee Boon Institute for Financial Economics ("SKBI"), while several local banks have been exploring executive development programmes with an emphasis on FinTech. Moving forward, the circulation and iterative refinement of shared FinTech knowledge will contribute to greater public awareness, interest, and education, which indirectly drives a higher level of FinTech activity as well.

Singapore's FinTech Ecosystem

Successful and thriving FinTech ecosystems are generally characterized by the presence of three key elements: (1) FinTech start-ups and entrepreneurs, (2) investment capital to fund the growth of start-ups, and (3) an educated community of mentors and experts.

Firstly, although it might not be immediately apparent, there are more than a hundred FinTech start-ups based in Singapore that are either looking into the Singapore B2C/B2B market or using the nation as a hub to operate across the region. Looking into the verticals within FinTech, start-ups represent common trends that are seen worldwide, from payments to trading to blockchain technology and back office solutions. Many financial professionals, inspired by the success of others and attracted by the supportive environment, are leaving their cubicle lives to start their own companies.

Secondly, in recent years many local and global venture capitalists (VCs) have been closely observing the development of the FinTech industry in South East Asia. Even though it is a fairly new industry, especially for VCs, first investments have been made and these freshly raised funds will be an important stream of capital investment for the FinTech industry. As most start-ups across various tech industries in this region are looking into B2C products, VCs are getting very excited about scaling B2C FinTech solutions for South East Asia. Additionally, many banking/hedge fund/private equity professionals are starting to invest private capital in early-stage start-ups to fund growth, while sharing insights and bridging important connections with key players in the industry.

Thirdly, it is also notable the FinTech community of mentors, experts, and angels is growing rapidly. Events like Echelon, Tech in Asia, FinTech Social, Next Bank Meetup, Hackathons, and Pitch Days draw large crowds of entrepreneurs and financial professionals that are keen to be part of the community and join the growing FinTech movement. Compared to other financial centres in Asia, the strength of Singapore's FinTech community makes a difference and provides a great foundation for entrepreneurs, financial institutions, and investors to work together. FinTech start-ups all over Asia are recognizing this fact and moving to Singapore to grow their business. Even start-ups that have a large home B2C market, such as India and Indonesia, come to Singapore, knowing that acquiring FinTech knowledge is crucial to their success, and the openness of mentors to help is unique in this region.

Taking a broader view on the FinTech ecosystem in Singapore, the key market participants include the government and regulatory bodies, investors, FinTech companies, financial institutions, technology and telecommunications companies, business associations/societies, and other stakeholders.

These market participants in Singapore have a privileged glimpse into the future by looking at some of the more mature economies in Europe and the US. Already, we are seeing the established financial institutions in Singapore mirroring some of the strategies adopted overseas, such as establishing innovation centres, partnering with accelerators and incubators, establishing venture capital arms to acquire FinTech companies, and forming partnerships and deals with FinTech companies. Though the incumbent technology and telecommunications firms have been carefully staying out of the spotlight, a closer look would reveal that they too have clearly not been idle in this critical period of the FinTech revolution.

Another exciting opportunity for FinTech in Singapore is using synergies across other tech sectors. As FinTech plays an important role in everyone's daily life, there is good reason to integrate solutions with other sectors, such as Health Tech, Education Tech and Smart Cities. The Singapore government is also investing efforts in bringing tech industries together and providing an even better environment for deeper integration. This is a welcome move, as FinTech should not just be limited to its own silo, but have the opportunity to create an impact on many different layers of a consumer's life.

For Singapore to truly emerge as a FinTech hub, there is a need for a representative organization to bring these key participants together, to create a bridge between the large corporations in the central business district, the start-ups in the grassroots, and many other organizations in the value chain in-between and also across different lifecycles.

Success Stories

The success of a FinTech ecosystem can be measured by the number of businesses that have successfully raised funds and are generating revenue. While Singapore has not had a big FinTech exit yet, a large number of companies are proving that South East Asia is the place for FinTech at the moment. The world's first Blockchain Hackathon, in 2015, produced more than 16 blockchain teams that will change the perspective on how banks and other financial institutions can work with this new technology.

Looking at some of the success stories of FinTech hubs around the globe, many of them share a common factor in having a representative/unitary organization lifting up and supporting the entire FinTech ecosystem in their respective economies.

To name but a few, "Innovate Finance" in the UK, "Stone & Chalk" in Australia, and "Holland FinTech" in the Netherlands are some well-established examples of such organizations while "FinTech HK" in Hong Kong and "The Singapore FinTech Consortium" in Singapore are quickly establishing their presence and building the FinTech community in their respective economies too.

Finally, a leading accelerator on financial innovation, Startupbootcamp FinTech, was launched during the London FinTech delegation to Singapore, led by London Mayor Boris Johnson. It has been successful through the involvement of regulators in its innovation programme, and paves the way for a more inclusive discussion on the evolution and growth of FinTech in Singapore.

Collectively, these factors have led to a rising number of FinTech start-ups in these communities, which correlates to the greater intensity of investment activities as well. Clearly, establishing such an environment would be crucial for regions/cities looking towards building their FinTech capabilities.

Conclusion

Looking ahead to the future, there is no doubt that Singapore will continue to play a leading role as a hub for the development of FinTech in the region. Singapore will be a springboard into the ASEAN countries and the broader Asian region, which represent an incommensurable pool of growth. FinTech companies in Singapore are poised to soar, as they tackle a minefield of unmapped challenges in the landscape, while exploiting lurking opportunities in the course of continuously seeking and applying innovative FinTech solutions to make financial systems more efficient.

Emerging Markets and Social Impact

4

According to the G20, 2.5 billion adults are excluded from the formal financial system. This part considers the influence of FinTech on emerging markets and the social impact that can be generated through financial technology in terms of ensuring access to financial services and products for the unbanked, i.e. democratizing finance. The cash economy is being supplemented by mobile access to digital funds. This change is not led by traditional banks but by telecoms companies who power mobile transactions. FinTech start-ups can become the engine that enables access to those in need. FinTech can help the unbanked to overcome discrimination in the provision of financial services, while decreasing friction and transaction costs for savings and payments.

FinTech: The Not So Little Engine That Can

By Susan Joseph
Founder, Leverige LLC

EMERGING MARKETS AND SOCIAL IMPACT

Back in 1930 when the financial world was in a precarious state, Platt and Munk wrote these famous words of encouragement, "I think I can, I think I can", in *The Little Engine That Could*. The world had taken a nose dive and the financial markets imploded. Since then, we have legislated, transformed, and chugged along at a modest pace. For a time, that strategy served us well in avoiding another full-scale financial meltdown, but it has also led to the emergence of a closed-off and closed-minded, but interdependent global financial ecosystem, in which regulation has kept innovative challengers at bay.

As some of the post-1930 regulations became more relaxed, we were drawn into a global financial crisis in 2008, resulting in new and sweeping regulations. Simultaneously, technology is rapidly evolving and powering the world's financial ecosystems. New regulations plus new technology lead us to one place: a full-scale revolution powered by FinTech. We are in the midst of the golden age of FinTech and it is an uncertain, exciting time that will leave us much better equipped to grow the world's economy in the future. There is a lot to do, but even tackling the tip of the iceberg to improve society by using financial technology is a great start. This is at the heart of the issues facing emerging markets.

Most emerging market economies have limited financial system infrastructure. Capital markets, to the extent they exist, and banks alike rely on legacy technology and are not accessible to poor rural populations which comprise a majority in developing countries. On the upside, there are far fewer structural and regulatory barriers in the financial system to overcome in order to serve the unbanked. It is precisely this dynamic that has enabled new technologies to develop in service of the poor, and FinTech innovators have jumped in, in some cases leapfrogging the traditional industry with new services that provide access to the previously unserved.

To understand how this is happening, we need to first understand that in emerging markets "Cash is King". The poor are invisible to the banking system. They use cash for most of their transactions and cannot access credit, insurance, or savings products we take for granted in the developed world. Most of the population is scattered across the countryside and often lives in isolated small villages. Mainstream indigenous banks have not been motivated to develop the branch infrastructure required to support this population. In emerging economies, entrepreneurship is both a necessity and a passion, as education and jobs are scarce. Unfortunately, without financial infrastructure, it is difficult for the poor and unbanked to start businesses and to pull themselves up by their proverbial bootstraps. Technology is literally the glue that bridges the infrastructure gaps.

It would be foolish to think the unbanked are not engaging in financial transactions. Surprisingly, the primary enabler in financial inclusion is not FinTech innovation per se. It is the mobile phone. Over the past 15 years, mobile phone penetration in Africa has gone from zero to over 900 million subscribers, with similar growth in other low-income regions. More impressive is the fact that around 500 million of those subscribers have no regular access to electricity.

Specifically, in Kenya, in 2007, Safaricom, a subsidiary of Vodafone, the largest mobile network operator in the country, introduced the world's first mobile money solution: MPesa. Safaricom users were able to easily adopt the service, because it was already installed on their SIM card, and, relying on a growing network of prepaid mobile networks, Safaricom was able to become a virtual monopoly in Kenya, launching a global mobile financial services industry. According to the recent GSMA (association of mobile operators and related companies) report, in December 2014 alone, mobile money users transacted a total of US$16.3 billion through 717.2 million transactions globally.

Kenya has enviable mobile FinTech solutions that developed countries can only dream of having. Systemically, this technology was able to develop freely in Kenya to serve the unbanked because banks were not willing or perhaps not able to serve the poor. The mobile technology serving the unbanked became so popular that the banked started using it. In fact, they demanded banks implement it.

So, how much of the population in Kenya uses mobile technology for financial services? An estimated 85% of all adults use mobile money services to flow monies through mobile telecommunications carriers. These transactions are not flowing through banks. Practically, this means people are using mobile wallets with accounts based on phone numbers rather than bank accounts. Secure cashless payments are flowing across different emerging market borders, bypassing banks.

The sheer volume and total amount of money transfers and big data generated by these mobile networks makes it possible for carriers to expand their services beyond payments to deposit taking and even micro-lending. Safaricom has recently launched two such services in collaboration with local banks – mShwari in collaboration with Commercial Bank of Africa (CBA) and KCB-Mpesa, with Kenyan powerhouse Kenya Commercial Bank Group (KCB).

The biggest, most earth-shattering fact to understand, and one that is worth repeating, is that the unbanked are being reached. The cash economy is being supplemented by mobile access to digital funds. Traditional banking is not leading the change. Telecommunication companies have stepped in and mobile powered transactions are the force to be reckoned with. Disruptive? Yes. Transformative? You bet!

Will digital money fully replace cash? Probably not. But the widespread reach of digital money transactions to the unbanked is fuelling emerging market economy growth, creating more wealth, and improving the standard of living.

We are about to enter the second stage of this revolution as feature phones are replaced by smartphones, with their adoption expected to reach over 70% of emerging markets by 2020. The opportunities for FinTech innovation are endless, and start-ups can become the engine that enables access and directs resources to those most in need. Now let us take a stroll through two of the most imaginative ideas around that can transform people's lives for the better.

The first creative idea is a credit insurance product that will be introduced in Rwanda via a big data platform. Only 20 years ago the Rwandan population suffered unimaginable genocide and horror, and the country is still in the process of rebuilding itself. Today, Rwanda's economy is growing at an average of 8% per year. Can the economy be driven even faster? Yes, with FinTech-powered credit insurance, which enables banks to minimize the risk of default and feel secure enough to lend to previously unreachable borrowers. Using existing and alternative data and advanced modelling, the insurer is knocking down the Berlin Wall of lack of access to credit byte by byte rather than brick by brick.

Once the secret sauce of data points and algorithms behind the product is online, the platform will be able to automate underwriting, loan origination, and the issuance of credit insurance. The loans and insurance products will be deployed

quickly and have the ability to scale. The same platform and technology can be leveraged to provide key performance indicators and indices, shedding light on the previously hidden sector, and enabling global investment in the market. As these products go live, financial education and literacy programmes will still be necessary, but the information gathered will help improve the focus and effectiveness of such programmes and the technology will help deliver them.

Imagine the economic landscape of a poor country with solidly growing small businesses – farms, produce stands, handicrafts, light industry, exports, etc. – the kinds of businesses that can create wealth and generate jobs. Also imagine you have data showing how those businesses perform and grow. Solid transparent data, easily transmitted via API.[1] Data that can be shown to investors trying to improve the country's economy and infrastructure. Data that can trigger further investment because that data proves that the investment in small businesses is working.

This is an example of how FinTech can create a voice that can be measured for the unbanked. That which can be measured can provide the basis for new policies, encouraging positive economic and social change. Change grounded in real time, empowered by the data from Rwanda's steadily growing economy. Lasting sustainable development will grow from this; strong communities will naturally evolve. Credit insurance in Rwanda will serve as a forerunner of credit insurance arrangements across other emerging market economies. Little by little, we can reach the unbanked and improve local standards of living. FinTech empowering social change? Yes, we can!

The second example takes place in Kenya. Kenya is enjoying around 6% GDP growth per year and is a financial hub for East Africa. As previously mentioned, 85% of all adult Kenyans use mobile phones, with business being transacted and liquidity being provided through those mobile accounts. The phones are not always smart phones with the capacity to host sophisticated financial apps, but they certainly are mobile phones which can at the very least move monies from place to place.

What exactly can this mobile technology do? Everything that would traditionally be done within the banking system, including supply chain finance, loans, both short-term microfinance and more standard commercial loans, savings, revolving credit,

---

[1] See the chapter entitled "Embracing the Connected API Economy" for further details.

etc. All of these financial instruments can be accessed with the swipe of your finger or the click of a button. And they are occurring outside the banking infrastructure atop elegant, secure, and neat mobile technology.

One of the more interesting lessons to be learned from emerging economies is that strong and powerful mobile tools and technologies have developed free of the stranglehold of legacy financial systems and siloed technology and regulation. It is much easier to innovate when you can start from scratch.

What has occurred to date is only the beginning. Marketplace lending is coming and can be enabled through mobile. A new FinTech start-up is developing an international lending platform that acts as an online portal for capital investment. It provides foreign investors access to local businesses that need loans for working capital, fixed assets, and other investments for growth. In particular, this platform works with local small and medium-sized financial institutions to access and originate small business loans. The platform then uploads these loans for resale to investors as graded investment

notes. That's right. Graded investment notes. Accessed via mobile. Securitization is coming through transparent instruments in Kenya and will be available in the palm of your hand. Capital markets are developing right before your eyes. Congratulations to those entrepreneurs bringing this change.

FinTech has thrown down the gauntlet. The challenge is on to move emerging markets forward. There are so many financial technology start-ups popping up each day, it is hard to know which ones will survive. What we do know is that emerging market economies using FinTech innovation are the true winners, as need gives rise to financial innovation. The very fabric of financial transactions is being rewoven and the underserved are being served through FinTech. We are in the midst of a FinTech revolution and those words written by Platt and Munk were never more relevant than today. What we dream rapidly becomes reality as we speak the ideas out loud and act to implement solutions.

It is "I think I can" at its best.

Why Am I Not Gonna Be Able to Enter a Bank?

By Francisco Meré Palafox

CEO & Co-Founder, Bankaool, S.A. Institución de Banca Múltiple

"It is so far away and I waste so much time and money to cash my paycheck. Once I arrive at a bank branch, a disgruntled guard asks me what I need. He is a bit hesitant to let me in because of my looks. I wait in line for 80 minutes to cash my check. I want to be invisible. I am never comfortable in a bank. As I leave, I tuck the money in my clothes to hide it away from robbers in the bus. Because of the rain, it takes me forever to get back home. When I arrive, I light up a small fire to get warm and spread the bills to dry. I finally breathe, this time, I was able to make it safely home."

Juan, 38-year-old Mexican

This story illustrates what millions of people who live in rural, suburban and even urban poor areas in developing countries go through on a daily basis. Financial exclusion takes a heavy toll on this segment of the population by increasing their transaction costs of managing money, not being able to participate in the digital economy, being exposed to theft and, sadly, being discriminated against by mainstream financial institutions. FinTech development is creating an opportunity to bridge many of these obstacles for millions of people and have a real impact on improving their lives.

According to the G20, close to 2.5 billion adults (about half of the working age population) are excluded from the formal financial system.[1] The story of M-Pesa in Kenya and mobile payments using a feature phone has been widely documented as a success case. And while internet and mobile phone penetration has increased substantially worldwide, reaching 40% of the population in the case of the internet[2] and, more importantly, 50% penetration for mobile phones,[3] two questions remain:

Why have mobile payments not reached a larger majority?

Why have service providers not evolved to provide a more complete financial offering such as savings and lending, nor leveraged mobile phone use to advance financial inclusion more rapidly, given the increased use of smartphones?

The answer to these questions may lie in supply-side factors, including absence of an enabling regulatory environment and a lack of digital DNA in mainstream banks, as well as in demand-side aspects, such as competition versus cash and idiosyncratic factors, including being discriminated against.

To cover and illustrate these questions, I will use the case of Mexico, since it represents an interesting case study of an emerging market facing relevant financial inclusion challenges, while having substantial mobile phone penetration and a strong and modern financial system. The banking system is solid and sound and has been assessed as Basel III compliant.[4] Mexico has also been considered as one of the most profitable markets for the global banks that have a franchise in the country. Notwithstanding, credit to the private sector as a percentage of GDP remains very low, at 18%. Also, it is estimated that close to 60% of adults in Mexico lack an account with a formal financial institution.[5] In contrast, mobile penetration is 87%,[6] with smartphone usage close to 50%.[7] Mexico is an increasingly connected society, ranking 14th worldwide in terms of population size. However, Mexico ranks globally 5th in Facebook users, 7th in Twitter users, and 5th in Spotify users.

Supply-side Factors

Seven large players that hold 90% of the market by most measures dominate the banking system in Mexico. All these banks have launched digital and mobile

---

[1] 2014 Financial Inclusion Action Plan. Global Partnership for Financial Inclusion, https://g20.org/wp-content/uploads/2014/12/2014_g20_financial_inclusion_action_plan.pdf.

[2] International Telecommunications Union.

[3] The Mobile Economy 2015 Report, GSMA. http://www.gsmamobileeconomy.com/GSMA_Global_Mobile_Economy_Report_2015.pdf.

[4] Bank for International Settlements, "Basel III implementation assessments of Hong Kong SAR and Mexico as well as follow-up reports published by the Basel Committee", 16 March 2015.http://www.bis.org/press/p150316.htm.

[5] World Bank, http://datatopics.worldbank.org/financialinclusion/country/mexico.

[6] Neomobile, "Mobile Market in Mexico", http://www.neomobile.com/mobile-market-mexico/.

[7] E-marketer, "One-Quarter of Mexico's Population to Use Smartphones in 2014", 22 December 2014, http://www.emarketer.com/Article/One-Quarter-of-Mexicos-Population-Use-Smartphones-2014/1011753.

platforms to better serve their customers.[8] However, these platforms are only available to clients that have opened an account at a bank branch. That is, such platforms do not offer digital or mobile enrolment. Therefore, the problem persists, as new potential customers have to go to a physical branch and go through a cumbersome process to open a bank account. Not only does this process inhibit clients, but also the number of branches per 100,000 inhabitants is only 15.3, which is the lowest in the Americas for major markets.[9]

Anti-money laundering regulation in Mexico was amended a few years ago, aiming to reconcile the goal of financial inclusion with the need to prevent illegal money flowing through the banking system. The most important change was the introduction of a simplified Know-Your-Customer (KYC) procedure for bank accounts that have a cap on monthly deposits of US$1,000.00.[10] The regulations allow for a "not-present" account opening process with reduced information requirements and no paper documents.[11] The potential for offering access to financial services to millions of Mexicans with this new legislation and thus fostering FinTech development is tremendous. Banks in general have not reacted rapidly to capture this opportunity, probably because of the comfortable position they enjoy in an oligopolistic market, coupled with their heavily entrenched legacy and their deep-rooted branch DNA.

In that environment there is only one branchless bank in Mexico. Bankaool is the only bank that has so far launched a digital platform that enables potential customers to open an account with just a few clicks, remotely and with no documents needed.[12] Their platform has been designed with a digital enrolment user experience, and not with just "digitalizing" an analogue process in a branch. The account has all the features of a bank account (except for the limit).

Digital and mobile enrolment for a bank account can not only improve the user experience and reduce substantial friction and transactions costs, but also, most importantly, can make a difference in financial inclusion and empower people in emerging markets to gain access to the payment system and the benefits of e-commerce. While FinTech can be a catalyst for this change, regulators must create an enabling environment to make this a reality, as in the case of Mexico.

Demand Factors

"Going to a bank branch is like going to a hospital. The minute you set foot in there, you wanna get out immediately…"[13]

Pablo, 21-year-old Mexican

"My ideal bank would be one where there are no preferred clients."[14]

Laura, 33-year-old Mexican

According to a report on financial inclusion by the Mexican banking supervisory authority,[15] 97% of adults in Mexico live in a municipality that has at least one access point to the formal financial system (bank branch, ATM, POS, or bank correspondent). However, from the sentiments expressed above, not only is there a problem with the offering, but even when financial services are available, the population is not likely to adopt them. As mentioned, close to 40% of adults have a bank account. However, only 14.5% hold their savings in a financial institution, even though 58.4% of adults save money.[16] How can FinTech help in improving the adoption of financial services, and particularly in enhancing savings rates?

---

[8] In Mexico, Telcos are barred from participating in payments or savings. Only regulated financial institutions have access to the payment system. All savings accounts or stored value accounts that are open-loop must be backed by an account at a regulated financial institution.

[9] Forty-seven in Brazil, 34 in the US, 24 in Canada, and 17 in Chile. Mexican Banking Association.

[10] At the current exchange rate of 15.5 MXN per US$.

[11] While the US$1,000 limit may seem restrictive, according to official statistics from INEGI, 80% of households in Mexico have a monthly income equal to or less than this.

[12] See further https://www.bankaool.com/web/que-ofrecemos/abre-tu-cuenta/.

[13] Focus group conducted by Bankaool, 2012.

[14] Ibid.

[15] Reporte de Inclusion Financiera, 2014, http://www.cnbv.gob.mx/Inclusi%C3%B3n/Documents/Reportes%20de%20IF/Reporte%20de%20Inclusion%20Financiera%206.pdf.

[16] The World Bank. "Financial Inclusion Data/Global Findex", http://datatopics.worldbank.org/financialinclusion/country/mexico.

Well-documented research exists on the topic of behavioural economics, savings, and financial inclusion.[17] Such research shows that we can be "nudged" into saving more and better, while using financial products. Behavioural economics also shows that people generally save for a specific purpose or goal, and not necessarily for a rainy day. And while different instruments have been used to "nudge" humans into saving, such as pension plans and Christmas clubs, the use of digital, mobile, and FinTech can represent a powerful tool in helping people better manage their money. Companies like Moven and Mint have launched platforms for personal financial management to much success.

One area where FinTech and mobile banking will marry behavioural economics is in using commitment savings accounts. Commitment savings accounts are bank accounts in which the holder sets a goal for the amount of money to be saved for a specific purpose, as well as the savings time horizon, with periodic deposits to the account to be made as a commitment. Rewards for the fulfilment of the committed savings typically are paid in the form of additional interest. Gamification may also play a role in these accounts, as well as frequent reminders of the commitment to the user when they spend money.

FinTech can thus play an important role in the adoption of these instruments as *The Economist* recently pointed out:

> … mobile technology can also help people to save … With mobile technology, providers can offer CSAs where the saver can customise the level of commitment that suits them. Bankaool, a Mexican bank, is one example. This year it will launch a mobile and online CSA for customers who wish to save a specific amount of money. The customer defines the target amount to be reached and the period over which saving will take place. The iWish account, offered by ICICI bank in India, is another example.[18]

Mexico is a country where poverty and income inequality prevail. The country ranks 1st in poverty levels and 2nd in income inequality among OECD countries.[19]

According to a survey on discrimination in Mexico, 60% of people believe that wealth creates a divide among people, discrimination being the main response.[20] Seventy-two per cent of people believe that banks are only interested in rich clients and 67% believe they take advantage of the needs of people.[21] Not surprisingly, the further removed from cities people are and the lower income they have, the fewer bank accounts they have.[22]

There have been debates on whether technology "de-humanizes" the economy. Financial services in emerging markets might well be one of those areas where less human biases would be actually desirable. FinTech and mobile banking can help overcome discrimination in the provision of financial services, by changing the terms of the dialogue. FinTech can allow for a more direct communication and conversation between financial providers and their clients, without discrimination. A person's ability to open an account digitally and perform financial transactions and save on their device will help to democratize finance and avoid discrimination. This will empower people to take control of their financial future and, no doubt, improve their (financial) lives.

The relationship between financial inclusion and economic development has now been widely documented. The challenge of including 2.5 billion people in the financial system is no doubt enormous. FinTech offers a unique opportunity to make exponential advances in such a task, taking advantage of the growing penetration of mobile technology. FinTech can help overcome discrimination in the provision of financial services, while decreasing friction and transaction costs for savings and payments. However, in order to make this a reality, a friendly and enabling regulatory environment needs to be put in place. Nevertheless, this alone is not enough. A change in the mind-set of the players in the financial system as a whole is necessary in order to bridge these gaps. Disruptive FinTech companies and banks with a FinTech DNA will be able to develop real viral solutions. Thankfully, Mexico is an example of such an environment that fosters the entry of new banking players with a FinTech DNA.

[17] Dean Karlan at Yale University has conducted extensive research on the topic. See further http://karlan.yale.edu.

[18] *The Economist*, "What technology will bring", 18 September 2014, http://www.economist.com/blogs/freeexchange/2014/09/commitment-savings-accounts.

[19] OECD, "Society at a Glance 2011: OECD Social Indicators" 2011, http://www.oecd.org/berlin/47570121.pdf.

[20] Consejo Nacional para Prevenir la Discriminación, Mexico, http://www.conapred.org.mx/userfiles/files/Enadis-2010-RG-Accss-002.pdf.

[21] Parametria, "Los retos de la banca en México", http://www.parametria.com.mx/carta_para-metrica.php?cp=4555.

[22] Consejo Nacional para Prevenir la Discriminación, Mexico, http://www.conapred.org.mx/userfiles/files/Reporte%20D-CREDITO-Web_INACCSS.pdf.

The Rise of the Rest in FinTech

By Stefano L. Tresca

Managing Partner, iSeed; Author, Mentor and Investor

Would you like to have 2.5 billion customers?

This is the number of "unbanked" – adults who do not use banks or microfinance institutions to save or borrow money. The largest proportion of these potential customers is based in Asia and Africa, with an outstanding 800 million adults living on less than $5 a day. This huge mass of humanity is not served by traditional banking because they were too expensive to reach. This is where FinTech can make a difference. Smartphones are cheaper and more popular than ever, with 1.9 billion users estimated in 2015. In this scenario, Android is the game changer. Xiaomi, a Chinese brand, came out with its first Android phone only in 2011, are on track to sell 100 million smartphones this year, and are already the second biggest start-up in the world, in terms of valuation (US$46).[1]

The consequences of this shift to being ever more mobile are massive: 2.5 billion unbanked with a smartphone are no longer unreachable! Two examples, the Malaysian start-up Soft Space and Singapore's SmartPesa, both provide mobile point of sale services and apps. They empower 600 million potential customers to send and receive non-cash payments. This evening an old lady in Kuala Lumpur can run a street food stall without cash in hand, reducing the risk of being mugged. From her point of view it is just a tap on her phone, a tool that she already uses every day. From a financial perspective, she is pumping money into the banking system. Whilst the sum is small for each merchant, when multiplied by hundreds of millions of merchants every day, this cash flow could energize entire economies. Moreover, the profit generated by the companies behind these payment systems is going to inspire more investors and more start-ups, thus generating more research and development, creating more profit opportunities, and so on in an unstoppable virtuous circle.

Being based in London – the world capital of FinTech – or even in Silicon Valley, it is easy to forget what is happening in other countries. It is the "The Rise of the Rest", and it is here to stay.

[1] http://graphics.wsj.com/billion-dollar-club/.

The Magic Cake

Alice H. Amsden borrowed the same phrase for the title of her book, *The Rise of the Rest: Challenges to the West*. In emerging economies, Amsden sees a direct challenge to the supremacy of the West. China, Taiwan, Korea, Turkey, Mexico, and all the other new members of the international financial playground want a piece of a limited global cake. In this vision, more guests at the party means less cake for everybody. Her book is brilliant, but I do not share this view about a limited amount of resources. The global cake has magic powers and its size can grow in tandem with the number of players. The West could share the cake with more guests and have a bigger piece for itself at the same time.

Think about M-Changa, a start-up from Kenya. Their app allows lending and micro-crowdfunding for school fees, emergencies, and even wedding and funeral expenses. The concept is nothing new. This practice of mutual support – *Kuchanga* – has been around for centuries, but this start-up has made it accessible to hundreds of millions of people in real time. Their escrow account also reduces the risk of travelling with cash. M-Changa was a member of Startupbootcamp FinTech, an acceleration programme based in London.

At the end of the programme, M-Changa has raised part of their funds from European angel investors. This is not a charity operation, where the West gives and Africa takes – or sometimes is forced to take against their interest. This is a business investment, where everybody wins. M-Changa gets funds, the investors get profits. M-Changa is living proof that the Rise of the Rest does not necessarily mean downsizing of the West. Micro-crowdfunding in Africa is a new market and it could serve hundreds of millions of customers. We – Western investors – may enjoy a piece of this new and freshly baked cake exactly because of the Rise of the Rest.

What Goes Around Comes Around

There is another benefit that is too often forgotten: thanks to the Rise of the Rest new cakes are baked in our own countries too.

Try to Google "prepaid meter" – the prepaid system for electricity. If you are based in the UK, you will see a list of the most advanced companies in the country, with almost half a million results. However, the first massive use and development of prepaid meters did not happen in the USA nor in Europe, but in South Africa. Back in the 1980s, a large number of South Africans without a proven address or a credit history found homes in the newly-built districts around the country. These customers tend to be served on a prepaid basis, because a subscription contract is too risky.

The most popular prepaid system at the time was inserting coins in your electricity meter. You can still see some of these old meters in London. Apparently a meter full of coins in your basement in the middle of a new South African development was considered too risky too. That is when they developed the new modern prepaid meter. Today, South Africa is seen as a world leader in prepayment technology and many other countries have adopted their standards.

There *is* Something New Under the Sun

Developing countries have large masses of new customers and few resources to manage them. This combination has produced negative results, until now. The masses with a smartphone are no longer unreachable. The combination of new customers and limited resources inspires companies and start-ups to develop low-cost but effective solutions, ready to be tested on the local market. These technologies may then be exported and adapted to the needs of the richer West.

Besides, this is not a dual market any more, with rich Westerners on one hand and poor customers everywhere else. After recurring economic crises and job losses, many in the Western population are struggling to make ends meet until the end of the month. Western customers are becoming ever more similar to their less developed counterparts than at any time in the recent past. Young unemployed and retired individuals – the first victims of this series of crises – benefit greatly from low-cost technologies. Technologies that have developed in Africa or Asia could be more beneficial to these groups of people than the new fancy apps developed by a start-up in Silicon Valley, London, or New York for wealthy millennials.

What is Really Happening?

I started taking an interest in Asia in the 1990s. It was Japan first, then teaching Italian to Koreans. Then backpacking in China and studying Chinese history. Step by step I have gone deep into the entire continent. During my years as a consultant I had a chance to work with India, Pakistan, China, Thailand, Indonesia, and Malaysia. I still follow what is happening over there and in the last few years the growth of the local start-up community is staggering.

Here are a few successful examples:

- Ezetap (India)
  Ezetap is the Indian Square. They hold almost 80% of the mPOS market – mobile Point of Sales – in India. They have a strong presence "just" in one country, India, but this market has over 1 billion customers, more than the US, Canada, and Europe combined. Most of their customers are young and avid mobile phone users. Ezetap is also unique because they do not buy third-party readers like Square, but have their own production and certification system. Their charismatic leader – Abhijit Bose – is alleged to be an Indian Steve Jobs, minus the bad temper.

- Wedlite (Indonesia)
  Want to marry in Indonesia but don't have the money? A wedding is definitely not a "business" that banks want to finance. This was a gap in the market filled by another start-up, Wedlite. They allow Indonesian couples to finance their weddings with monthly payment plans. If you think that finance is a boring and unsexy subject, reading customers' testimonials from Wedlite may just change your mind. Thanks to FinTech.

- SoftSpace (Malaysia)
  Malaysia has one of the fastest growing mobile user bases in the world, if not the fastest, when combined with their neighbour Indonesia. Not by coincidence, the most aggressive company in the Asian B2B payment solution – SoftSpace – was born in this country. They have already expanded to seven countries, including Australia and New Zealand. Indonesia alone has 250 million customers, attesting to this region's untapped potential.

- Ola (India)
  FinTech is not just a geek game in Asia. Ola Cabs provides taxis as their name suggests. They first developed an app to call a cab. Then, because in India not everybody has a credit card, they have been "forced" to develop a wallet system to pay the cabs. Once transport and e-wallets were in place, they had everything they needed to provide food deliveries. So they launched Ola Cafe.

Just one city – Mumbai – has 12 million citizens. Many of these customers are poor, but precisely because of this condition they are unbanked, without a credit card and often without a bank account. This so far neglected part of humanity could jump onto the wagon of innovation and use mobile wallets with more enthusiasm than their Western counterparts. Not by coincidence, many see Ola as the real competitor for Apple Pay and Google Pay in the near future.

- Blossom (Indonesia)
  If cabs and food are on the most traditional side of the spectrum, Blossom is on the opposite side, providing Islamic micro-financing in Indonesia through bitcoin. The ancient tradition of Islamic finance meets the latest innovation of cryptocurrency through Blossom.

- WeLend (Hong Kong)
  WeLend, a Hong Kong P2P lending start-up, has raised a series B round, raising US$160 million at the start of 2016.[2] This was solely to finance the opening of a presence in China, a market with over 1 billion potential customers.

  China is a market that I have followed since 1996, and it may be full of surprises that come to light when reading the South China Morning Post or Tech in Asia.

Conclusion

The so-called "developing countries" are not just a market that provides customers and resources to Western companies; they form the base of innovation and investments. They can create disruptive technologies that we can later see transposed in Europe and the US.

You may believe that the Rise of the Rest is going to compete for our piece of the cake, or you may believe that they will actually increase the size of the cake. Probably these opinions could both turn out to be true. In any case, these countries are already part of the game and there is no going back. The only possible choice is to embrace the new order and make the best of it. The old Chinese saying is true now more than ever:

"When the winds of change blow, some people build walls and others build windmills."

---

[2] http://www.prnewswire.com/news-releases/welab-raises-us160m-in-series-b-financing-from-khazanah-and-ing-bank-300207716.html.

Smartphones, FinTech, and Education – Helping the Unbanked Reach Financial Inclusion

By Cesar Jimenez Richardson

VP, Sales and Operations, Strands Americas

Converging trends hold great promise for the next generation of digital money management solutions aimed at helping the unbanked. According to a GSMA report, mobile money services (MMS) are spreading quickly across much of Africa, Asia, Latin America, and the Middle East, reaching over 60% of the world's developing countries.[1] However, the number of registered mobile money accounts has grown to just under 300 million around the world in 2014 and, as this represents only 8% of mobile connections in markets where MMS are available, there is significant possibility for future growth.[2]

Many current MMS solutions are now tied to legacy mobile phone handsets but, as devices get cheaper, global partnerships fight for low-priced data access, mobile operators invest to develop the necessary network capacity, and pricing models change to fit to local markets, the progress from feature phones to smartphones will soon be a reality in emerging markets. The "next billion" consumers in these regions will progressively become the focus of some of the latest innovations allowing the unbanked to be the first to leapfrog a branch-based bank and become true "digital first" banking customers.

International efforts to build data delivery infrastructure, such as Facebook's Internet.org, are looking to significantly cut the cost of delivering basic internet services on mobile phones, especially in developing countries. Internet.org is helping to promote the idea of "zero rating" mobile content, entering into partnerships with multiple operators in emerging markets to offer free mobile Facebook services such as their recent Messenger Payments Platform.

Another version of the zero-rating model – sponsored internet – has the content provider, instead of the end-user, pay for connectivity. Banco Bradesco is a leading example in the financial community, having negotiated an agreement with mobile operators in Brazil, allowing the bank's digital banking customers access to its internet banking service from their phones without incurring carrier data charges or having to use part of their monthly data package.

At the same time, network operators are also invested to develop capacity on 3G and 4G networks by introducing new and interesting pricing models better suited to the money-based realities of an economically disadvantaged consumer base. For example, delivering a "pay as you go" data plan for prepaid users has become popular in Latin America and the resulting competitive intensity has reduced service charges by over half in the last three years, also increasing service affordability.

What will this shift from feature phones to smartphones mean for the unbanked? At a very basic level, people will discover an improved user experience, gain access to more innovative products, and benefit from a more competitive environment designed to encourage affordability at a rapid pace.

Enhancing User Experience

Feature-rich interfaces and the greater ability to interact with smartphone applications will offer more intuitive experiences, facilitating user adoption in different market segments. For example, graphical and voice command interfaces (think Siri) in many local languages and dialects can help banks target people that are not comfortable with basic data services as well as consumers that are unable to read or write.

Since smartphone operating systems offer a common platform for developers – spanning specific devices and equipment manufacturers – mobile money apps can take advantage of a host of other functionalities, including integration with other features like contacts, calendars, maps, and social media apps.

App-based mobile money services will also allow providers not only to tap into new pools of data, but also to generate insights that can help improve the efficiency of their services. Some of the current frustrations in MMS revolve around their agent

[1] GSMA, "State of the Industry. Mobile Financial Services for the Unbanked" 2014, http://www.gsma.com/mobilefordevelopment/wp-content/uploads/2015/03/SOTIR_2014.pdf.

[2] Ibid.

network,[3] such as proximity or those that have cash available (liquidity). An agent locator feature (such as Find an ATM on mobile banking apps) can be especially useful to new users. At a more advanced level, customers will be empowered to rate the customer service or liquidity of a network agent. This valuable data can be used later with advanced analytics and predictive models to forecast and prevent cash flow shortages, thereby improving the overall customer experience.

On the whole, feature-rich interfaces and greater functionality on smartphones can offer a more intuitive customer experience, easing adoption and usage.

New Product Development

Greater smartphone penetration will accelerate the pace of new product development and will change how consumers engage financially, especially with merchants, businesses, and government.

To make sure this occurs on current MMS platforms, the general developer community will require easier access to the existing money rails network through the use of open Application Programming Interfaces (APIs).[4] While in-house product development teams will develop some solutions, financial institutions must embrace opening the value chain that third parties offer when they layer new products on their existing platforms. This is core to ensuring current MMS organizations modernize the money management industry in developing markets.

Personal Financial Management (PFM) applications provide an instructive example of a product that can help the newly banked learn about, understand, and control their finances. Simple features such as a calendar application allow users to easily recognize their income and expenses in a chronological format that most people can relate to, but more importantly, alerts them to future expenses and cash flow shortages. The result is a tool that, using Artificial Intelligence (AI), delivers

consumers with useful insights that help them make better decisions and take control of their finances.

Many unbanked people in developing countries face limited access to micro-savings services at formal financial institutions, forcing low-income individuals to find other ways to save. The average customer balance is over $10 for 40% of mobile money accounts.[5] This makes alternative savings propositions attractive to the unbanked, since their existing savings options tend to be risky (for example, investing in animals, commodities, or other goods as a means of saving). Moreover, people with low incomes can find it difficult to save cash, in part because the money is always readily accessible, meaning they have to continually exercise self-control.

Once again, money management technology has the potential to deliver a range of online savings solutions for consumers and businesses alike. Strands, a global financial services technology company, provides financial institutions of all sizes with a white-labelled[6] PFM application that can be customized and integrated with banks' existing core processing platforms. It allows banks to offer their customers the ability to create multiple savings goals within a single savings account, and manage progress toward those goals through data visualizations that trigger alerts and notifications if users risk falling short of their goals. Linked to a mobile money account as a source of funds, and optimized for low-income segments, such customizable savings products can serve as simple yet powerful financial tools for customers new to formal financial services.

Education: Power to the People through Financial Literacy

To maximize socio-economic impact in emerging markets, MMS needs not only to reach the urbanites but also to focus on people at the bottom of the economic pyramid.

---

[3] Agent Network: to access and utilize mobile money services, customers rely on two distinct channels. The first is the network of physical access points where customers can typically deposit cash into, or take cash out of, their mobile money account – these access points are primarily agent outlets. The second is the digital access channel – the interface that customers use to initiate transfers and payments directly on their mobile handsets.

[4] See the chapter entitled "Embracing the Connected API Economy" for further details.

[5] GSMA, note 1, http://www.gsma.com/mobilefordevelopment/wp-content/uploads/2015/03/SOTIR_2014.pdf.

[6] "White-label" refers to FinTech firms which offer their solutions to banks so that banks can brand the solution with their own brand name (i.e. banks' clients would not realize that the service has not been developed by the bank itself but by one of its FinTech suppliers).

In many emerging markets, a large segment of the population resides outside urban centres, without easy access to infrastructure like banking, transport, electricity, and roads. Rural populations represent a huge potential customer base in communities where mobile money is the only real competitor to cash.

Strategies to gain mass-market adoption require industry stakeholders to identify and track usage by women and rural customers who tend to be later adopters in the traditional technology lifecycle (usually led by male urbanites). To raise awareness and attract these users, it is important to invest heavily in Below-the-Line (BTL) marketing campaigns that deliver the required human touch points that help educate people at the bottom of the pyramid. This could include visiting villages, plantations, and districts to educate women through workshops on financial services and the use of mobile money. Following their training in financial literacy, attendees could have the opportunity to open a mobile money account and increase the rate of adoption.

Another tactic could be to use real customers who are also active MMS users to act as sponsors to educate their peers about the use and benefits of mobile money. Operators can mobilize women from urban centres who are more active in MMS, to the villages where mobile money is not yet being used.

Providing education and training for merchants is also important to gain trust and guarantee the interoperability of digital money for both P2P and the purchasing of goods and services. Clarity around settlements and how to access funds is important in helping merchants feel comfortable with the service and effectively manage their cash flows. In turn, they will be more likely to encourage customers to use the service.

The Road Ahead

The combination of digital money management, next-generation smartphone technology, and a clear strategy to help educate the population at large will be revolutionary in the delivery of financial products that help unbanked or underbanked consumers to save in ways that fit their daily realities. I personally believe democratizing access to financial inclusion in developing regions of the world has the potential not only to unleash amazing business opportunities, but, more importantly, to help millions of humans improve their quality of life in some of the toughest regions of the world. Through the frictionless delivery of digital financial products such as micro-credit or micro-insurance, more and more people will have the opportunity to become financially autonomous, help build their local economies, and provide their families with the peace of mind attained through health and life insurance solutions.

The Social Impact of FinTech in Nigeria

By Daniel Steeves

Consultant, Advisor, Architect and CEO at Beyond Solutions

The global village that FinTech enables brings markets and consumers closer, supports new businesses, and reduces reliance on the government in the process – and Nigeria, as the largest economy in Africa, is a growing and significant part of that global village.

There is no doubt that society has changed, adjusted, and progressed thanks to the technology advances of the past thirty years – and exponentially more since the turn of the century. The growing use of social media at all ages of the population is just one significant example of this change. Throughout all of this Nigerians – and the rest of the world – are really still just adjusting to a state of mind where online transactions do not pose a security risk.

From the Nigerian perspective this also provides a critical juncture to change perceptions across the global community by demonstrating not only the value and opportunities to connect with West African markets but also that doing so can be secure and fraud-free.

Members of the younger generations are being brought up in a society where mobile phones and computers are part of daily life and where they are accustomed to using technology in all parts of daily life, but the impacts of cashless transactions are clearly seen as a benefit by all. FinTech can also provide safe banking access to the underbanked, in whom the large institutions have traditionally demonstrated little to no interest due to almost fixed on-boarding costs and perceived low lifetime value in comparison with corporate customers and medium-to-high net worth individuals.

While FinTech delivers a positive impact across a broad array of topics, space limits the discussion here to the following three primary areas: consumer safety and security, contribution to state monetary policies, and support for small business and entrepreneurs.

Consumer Safety and Security

In emerging African economies where consumer and business banking are not commonplace, FinTech contributes greatly to improving personal safety: 95% of internal Nigerian consumer payments today are cash transactions creating a broad set of risks which can easily be mitigated and minimized through the use of technology.

To exacerbate things, much of the Western world perceive fraud and corruption as great risks to working with and within countries like Nigeria and have been missing great opportunities to trade and transact with these strong and emerging economies.

Start-ups such as VoguePay, based in the European financial centre of London and operating out of Lagos, can deliver secure mobile and online payment capabilities as a core part of their processes. From low-cost on-boarding and enrolment that ensures a complete match, validation and verification of user and business details through to rigorous tracking and auditing of each unique and non-forgeable online transaction, these businesses leverage volumes to deliver cost-effective value.

Secure and fraud-checked online transactions are only part of the value delivered: the simple elimination of the risks of robbery tops the list but the use of the data being accumulated can support the creation of honest credit checking facilities, using analysis of social networking patterns to help lenders assess creditworthiness.

Contributions to State Monetary Policies

The perception of banks being slow-moving, conservative, and ultimately averse to change is being disproven, primarily as the traditional banking sector is learning that it needs to react and respond to the disruption instigated by the FinTech sector. The agile start-up sector is still far ahead, leveraging market opportunities with a focused and commoditized approach. Providing user-friendly web interfaces – and accepting lower margins – on high-volume transaction areas like cross-border money transfers, delivering automation and simplicity to asset allocation, tax minimization, and investment advice.

FinTech is contributing to the national economy of Nigeria and supporting Central Bank policies to reduce the amount of cash in circulation (and cash handling costs). Reductions of this nature also help to limit corruption, leakage, and money laundering while increasing the effectiveness of other monetary policies intended to manage inflation and encourage economic growth.

Not only can Nigeria not afford to be left behind, there is a real opportunity for the country to leverage the financial and economic strength being delivered by FinTech to enable a growing maturity of fiscal policies and to seize a true leadership role.

While Nigeria does continue to spend most of what is earned from the oil sector, it has so far resisted the temptation to borrow or to overstimulate the economy, maintaining external debt below 3.5% and overall public sector debt stock at about 20% of GDP. It cannot be forgotten, of course, that banks remain at the centre of payment ecosystems – payment providers ranging from VoguePay to Apple Payments remain dependent on them for their infrastructure and as a safe (and regulated) repository for funds, although the providers of crypto-currencies are working hard to change that reality.

But this doesn't mean that there is incompatibility between regulation and rapid innovation: it is more of a disconnect, since both sides are there to serve customers' needs and it is those customers, both corporate and consumer, who will make the choice. These choices are being made daily and are different from the decisions of the past. Flexibility and convenience are offered along with these choices and it is no longer a world in which the choice of where to bank needs to be a long-term or permanent one. And, if banks and other financial service providers cannot forecast recurring revenues and customer numbers then they, by definition, are required to continue to raise the bar in terms of services and service … or watch their customer base continue to drift.

And when it comes to setting interest rates and implementing monetary policies, it is a becoming a completely different story.

Support for Small Business and Entrepreneurs

By providing training, hands-on support, pre-built shopping carts and website integrations – as well as the ability to collect and send money directly from mobile phones without the need for a website – and by leveraging local presence and cultural knowledge and implementing strict anti-fraud mechanisms, FinTech start-ups like VoguePay are enabling these changes and helping to remove the traditional barriers to technology for thousands of businesses.

Reducing both fraud and bad debts in turn keeps the cost of lending lower which directly impacts the cost of borrowing, not to mention creating more opportunities for safe lending delivering a positive result for both consumers and small business via both direct lending and crowdfunding.

It is a common thread throughout emerging economies that there is a limited use of banking infrastructure, and an even more limited trust. However, results, social-media-driven word-of-mouth success stories, and recommendations about payments, transfers, and the value of crowdsourcing are convincing an ever-increasing element of society to take advantage of modern approaches to finance for their own benefit. These innovations are global, are advertised by the users themselves, and provide compelling value to those users.

FinTech start-ups support businesses – and other start-ups – ranging from market traders and shops through to importers, exporters, and Forex traders in improving their bottom line with affordable capabilities that enable them to reach new markets and new customers – in the case of payment platforms by enabling secure, multi-currency, and crypto-currency payments across international markets.

By enabling business to start and to grow, sharing profits with developers and digital agencies, and allowing non-technology start-ups to secure their transactions, their latest acquisition goes a step further with an ecosystem that makes it possible for entrepreneurs to start new businesses with very low entry costs: another example of FinTech providing a positive impact to local and national economies.

Business as Usual is a Thing of the Past

In short, banking – and financial transactions for consumers and for businesses – is far from "business as usual". New competitors from FinTech start-ups and from other adjacent industries are flooding the market with convenient, safe, and easy-to-use products and services that were previously the exclusive domain of Nigerian banks, who are being left to watch their multi-billion Naira monopolies slip away. It takes commitment, effort, and investment of time, money, and resources but it is happening on an increasing basis due to the simple tenets of quality customer service.

To fight back, the big banks are looking to collaborate, to innovate, and to enhance social banking but are their attitudes to service, delivery, low charges, and flexibility changing in time? Will they support the "unbanked"? Will their stakeholders allow them to take more risks on smaller customers – and the smaller profits that they generate? And, finally, can they capture the tech-savvy youth and their expectations of a new paradigm of customer service?

India and the Pyramid of Opportunity

By Maneesh Bhandari
Director, CIIE

CK Prahalad's oft-cited notion states that there is a fortune to be made at the bottom of the pyramid, a fortune built on providing solutions to the impoverished and underserved millions. The population of India is extremely diverse in terms of socio-economic demographics. On such a pyramid, it shares a major chunk of these millions at the bottom and a considerable share of the wealthiest at the top, with a majority of its population in between (see following Figure). The population of 1.2 billion can be grouped by income into the vulnerable group (35%, 420 million), lower middle class (43%, 516 million), middle class (19%, 228 million), upper middle class (1%, 1.2 million), and the rich (1%, 1.2 million).[1]

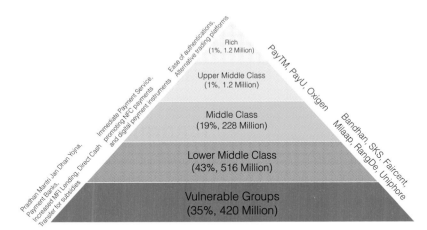

Figure: The pyramid of opportunity

Seen in terms of development, progress is a complicated issue whose scope differs across the pyramid. However, the most significant element in this complexity is the wide spectrum of opportunities available for FinTech services in India, both in terms of adoption and innovation. Both the public sector and the private sectors

(enterprises and entrepreneurs) are tapping into these opportunities with FinTech advancements being the key component in bridging the gap in access to financial services in underserved markets, and in capturing the increasingly smart and networked mobile population with cutting-edge mobility. The numbers are telling in this regard – close to 90% of transactions in India are cash based.[2] In 2015 the World Bank reported that India's unbanked adults accounted for 21% of the world's unbanked population. However, the growth in account ownership has increased from 35% in 2011 to 53% in 2014.[3] Online transactions are also on the rise, and internet and mobile penetration is close to 20% and 70% of the population respectively,[4] with mobile internet users touted to cross the 200 million mark.[5] These significantly large and aspirational numbers show not only the increasing internet connectivity component but also the large spectrum of financial products and services that can be addressed to bring in financial mobility, forming a pyramid of opportunity for FinTech in India.

On that note, the crucial areas in India's pyramid of opportunity for FinTech range from financial inclusion at the bottom right up through improving financial services and delivering cutting-edge exclusive financial payments, to the top, i.e. right from social entrepreneurship to social network-based banking and payment systems to capital markets. These are happening in the form of payment banks, lending, microfinance, insurance, foreign exchange and remittances, digital wallets, peer-to-peer, innovative payment models, investments, and trading. Enterprises and entrepreneurs have focused on simplifying technology and distribution models that create a greater impact, as well as disruptive technological advancements that have created varied use cases. Entrepreneurial success stories are abundant in this regard. Considering that India is among the world's biggest peer-to-peer (P2P) offline lending markets, P2P lending, crowdfunding, and Micro Finance Institutions (MFIs) online such as Bandhan, SKS, Milaap, RangDe, and Faircent have had tremendous success and impact by bridging the upper class market with the lower middle class and vulnerable population. Uniphore is another successful venture

---

[1] Approximate figures from McKinsey Forecasts for 2015: https://genesis.iitm.ac.in/downloads/resources/startup/tracking%20the%20growth%20of%20indian%20middle%20class.pdf.

[2] Knowledge@Wharton: http://knowledge.wharton.upenn.edu/article/tapping-an-appetite-for-technology-in-indias-underserved-markets/.

[3] World Bank: https://openknowledge.worldbank.org/bitstream/handle/10986/21865/WPS7255.pdf?sequence=2.

[4] *Time*: http://time.com/3611863/india-smartphones/.

[5] *The Hindu*: http://www.thehindu.com/sci-tech/technology/gadgets/mobile-internet-users-to-reach-213-million-by-june-2015/article6785327.ece.

that provides speech analytics and voice biometrics to financial enterprises in order to facilitate easy verification and critical information transfer to rural communities in 11 regional languages. These are examples of where challenges in lending and interaction with underserved communities are seen as opportunities that could be bridged by FinTech ideas and technology.

Up through the pyramid, consumer-facing apps and ideas have seen a strong resurgence of newer payment models in the form of gateways and wallets. Aggregators and e-commerce apps across verticals – right from FlipKart and Snapdeal to cab aggregators (Ola and Uber) and hyperlocal delivery services have all reinvigorated the payments space in India. Taking advantage of the technological penetration in the market and existing regulations with respect to payment instruments, many Non-Banking Financial Companies (NBFCs) have adopted digital wallets and helped facilitate cashless and easier payment systems. PayTM is an e-commerce and payment platform with a significant focus on mobile/digital wallets and merchant tie-ups (most successful being the association with Uber) who are redefining the perception of payments. Another early mover in this opportunity space is Oxigen, a non-Bank mobile wallet which is an RBI-approved (Reserve Bank of India) and National Payments Corporation of India (NPCI) integrated service. Using the NPCI's Immediate Payment Service (IMPS), it enables simpler and quicker money transfer and remittances to 60+ banks across communities in India. In the gateway space, both the merchant and customer side of payments were riddled with redundancy and security issues. PayUmoney is a highly secure and equally successful payment gateway integration solution across payment methods,which has simplified the process on both sides. Capitalizing on the opportunity of India's deep mobile (internet) penetration and high telecom growth, JunoTele is a start-up providing real-time and on-demand billing and payment for services directly through mobile carriers with WiFi and offline.

Investment interests in the country are also growing. Venture capital from foreign investors has seen a steady influx into India, especially for early stage ventures. These early stage venture deals accounted for more than 82% of all deals in the technology sectors over the past year in India.[6] This interest from foreign investments is due to a variety of factors offered by the pyramid of opportunity in India. Growth in the size of the consumer segment as well as mobile and internet penetration are

key factors. Tiger Global has invested heavily ($269 million over 11 deals) in the consumer space, followed by Sequoia Capital ($208 million over 14 deals) and Steadview Capital ($107 million over two deals).[7] However, only half of the venture capital flowing into early stage technology start-ups is from within India, emphasizing both the foreign investments and the smaller, yet growing, segment of local investments.[8]

On the other hand, policy-makers and the public sector have focused on easing these innovations and in creating avenues for easier adoption and diffusion. The regulatory framework from the Reserve Bank of India (RBI) has been working around financial services to create a robust infrastructure for development. The International Organisation of Securities Commissions (IOSCO) and the Bank for International Settlements (BIS) recently rated the RBI and Securities and Exchange Board of India (SEBI) highly in terms of financial market responsibility and capability.[9] The RBI in particular has undertaken various steps to ensure the flow of technology, such as removing the requirement of Additional Factor of Authentication for card-present transactions of small value, promoting NFC (Near Field Communication) technology,[10] and increasing lending caps for MFIs.[11] SEBI announced in 2015 its relaxation of norms and its move to establish an alternative trading platform for start-ups dealing in online trading.[12] This move is touted to open up trading and investment activity at the top of the opportunity pyramid. NPCI has also rolled out multiple projects such as: (1) ATM Switching; (2) mobile payments; (3) Cheque Truncation System; (4) PoS Switching; (5) Immediate Payment Service (IMPS, a 24/7 money transfer service); (6) RuPay; and (7) Unified Payment Interface.[13] The government-led Pradhan Mantri Jan

[7] The Next Web: http://thenextweb.com/in/2015/07/05/india-the-worlds-fastest-growing-startup-ecosystem/.

[8] CB Insights: https://www.cbinsights.com/blog/india-active-venture-capital-firms-2014/.

[9] Economic Times: http://economictimes.indiatimes.com/news/economy/policy/india-secures-top-most-rating-for-financial-market-regulations/articleshow/47632065.cms.

[10] Trak.in: http://trak.in/tags/business/2014/12/09/rbi-cancel-2fa-smaller-ecommerce-transactions/.

[11] LiveMint: http://www.livemint.com/Industry/LM4OfETppTduXTLQD6BovL/RBI-eases-lending-norms-for-microfinance-companies.html.

[12] Reuters: http://in.reuters.com/article/2015/06/23/india-sebi-board-idINKBN0P319K20150623.

[13] MediaNama: http://www.medianama.com/2015/02/223-npci-initiates-ecosystem-for-unified-payments-interface/.

[6] CB Insights: https://www.cbinsights.com/blog/india-venture-capital-tech-funding/.

Dhan Yojana (PMJDY) is another mission of financial inclusion in both urban and rural areas, promoting the diffusion of bank accounts, financial services, and mobile banking at affordable costs. As of 24 June 2015, 164.3 million accounts were created, with around 19,015.42 INR crores (US$2.8 billion) deposited in them under the scheme.[14] Aadhar (universal identity) and know-your-customer advancements have enabled direct cash transfer schemes, which deposit subsidies directly into bank accounts.[15] The government has also set up differentiated banking systems in the form of payment banks to provide low cost and easier banking to the underserved communities.

The public and private sectors playing off each other's actions have directly enabled the ease and adoption of various financial technologies and services. However, there are still many opportunities that remain to be addressed nationally, such as linguistic access to these services and the flow of money across accounts (51.86% of the PMJDY accounts currently have zero balances), which can happen only through enterprise development. The utilization and impact of the government-allotted 10,000 INR crores fund for development and incubation of MSMEs (Micro, Small and Medium Enterprises) is yet to be assessed. The upcoming project of setting up a Micro Units Development and Refinance Agency (MUDRA Bank) would work towards the same goal and create similar opportunity spaces for enterprise development.[16] Telecommunication developments such as Reliance Jio Infocomm Limited's highly spectrum-invested low-cost 4G services, and the government's national optical fibre network to connect rural areas and gram panchayats (rural local governments) into the grid, might enable the backbone of infrastructure to facilitate positive action on this pyramid of opportunity.

All things considered, this pyramid of opportunity is continuously evolving, bringing with it fresh challenges to be addressed and thereby creating new opportunities that could enable us to see the pyramid as an aid to the development of the economy of the country.

[14] PMJDY: http://pmjdy.gov.in/.

[15] Aadhar UID: http://aadhaarcarduid.org/category/direct-cash-transfer-scheme/.

[16] Business-Standard: http://www.business-standard.com/article/pti-stories/mudra-bank-bill-likely-in-fwinter-session-115070300655_1.html.

FinTech Solutions

Applications for Automated Text Analysis

5

This fifth part of the book summarizes the latest FinTech solutions for both established corporate players and consumers. Business-to-business (B2B) solutions have been divided into those that strategically help banks to maintain their leading roles in financial services and solutions focused on either helping incumbents to be more efficient and compliant or more secure and better equipped to make holistic trading decisions.

Business-to-consumer (B2C) solutions include disruptive business models such as crowdfunding, global remittance payments, solutions for small businesses and other sectors. We will also focus on Apple's entry into payments via Apple Pay, and the boom in wearables as the latest devices to provide financial services to consumers.

Rewiring the Deal – The Path Forward for B2B Supply Chains

By David Desharnais

Former CMO, Traxpay; SVP and GM of Digital and Commercial Platforms, American Express

Thomas Edison did not invent the light bulb. Like so many visionaries before and since, the man who once claimed that "Genius is 1% inspiration and 99% perspiration" was simply first past the post in the race to solve problems with pre-existing iterations. But even if Edison's light bulb was not the first, it was the best. While previous models had proved unfit for purpose due to cost, longevity, and reliability, his was a shining testament to the power of innovation, and a reminder that behind every broken system lies a definitive solution.

Today, the realm of e-commerce seems to be more characterized by innovative solutions than problems – at least as far as the average consumer is concerned. From the comfort of their couch, an online shopper can source and secure virtually anything at the touch of a button. Convenience is king, and our need for speed has been matched by the blurring pace of advancements in mobility, communications, and networking. With Business-to-Consumer (B2C) e-commerce sales in the already mature US market expected to increase by 18% in 2015,[1] as well as the introduction of new transaction solutions such as Apple Pay, the B2C e-commerce domain continues to grow at a breathtaking rate thanks to the ultra-convenient technology that empowers the four billion (and counting) customers who currently shop on the internet. Little wonder that China's biggest B2C player, Alibaba, raised a record-breaking $25 billion at its Initial Public Offering on the New York Stock Exchange in 2014.

As deep as the goldmine of B2C e-commerce runs, however, there is an even more lucrative territory to explore. One forecast predicted that B2B e-commerce in the US would be worth four times as much as its B2C counterpart in 2014,[2] while another anticipated a gross merchandise value of $6.7 trillion for the B2B e-commerce space globally by 2020, compared to $3.2 trillion for B2C.[3]

On the surface, such statistics paint a healthy picture of the B2B e-commerce landscape, but in reality they may be more representative of the market's potential than confirmation that everything is rosy in the garden.

Complex Commerce

While already-established B2C vendors such as Amazon and Alibaba are in a position to capitalize on the creation of consumer-like experiences for B2B buyers and suppliers, supply chains would be better served by establishing their own integrated procurement workflows and sales platforms for maximum flexibility, visibility, and profitability. The appetite for fluidity that has driven consumer e-commerce forward is equally coveted by businesses, who have billions of reasons to collaborate as quickly as possible with one another.

To some extent, existing innovations have helped to make that desire a reality. An increasing number of businesses are turning to B2B commerce networks that offer solutions to common problems for indirect spend management. The promise of these networks is automation, efficiency, and transparency to the Purchase-to-Pay (P2P) and Order-to-Cash (O2C) flows, helping to strip away some of the manual labour otherwise required. Recent years have also seen these services begin to transition to the cloud and offer mobile applications as another way of ensuring their businesses are as scalable as possible and better equipped to monitor data in real time.[4] Overall then, it should come as little surprise that 73% of enterprises[5] believe B2B commerce networks enhance collaboration between buyers and suppliers.

This integration of available B2B commerce networks is certainly a step in the right direction for businesses eager to make the most of today's technology, but there are still major obstacles in the quest to ensure the B2B customer journey reflects

---

[1] http://www.thepaypers.com/ecommerce/world-ecommerce-registers-23-6-increase-in-2013/757853-25.

[2] http://www.prnewswire.com/news-releases/us-b2b-e-commerce-companies-will-generate-1-trillion-in-sales-in-2014-eclipsing-b2c-e-retailing-market-four-times-over-280776882.html.

[3] http://www.practicalecommerce.com/articles/85970-B2B-Ecommerce-Growing-Becoming-More-Like-B2C.

[4] http://v1.aberdeen.com/launch/report/benchmark/8671-RA-accounts-payable-automation.asp.

[5] Ardent Partners Annual State of Procurement Report.

the convenience of the B2C experience. Because at their cores, B2B and B2C commerce have fundamental differences.

For starters, for the B2B set, many more people are involved in purchase decisions on the buyer side, increasing the challenge for suppliers, as they engage in long sales and approval cycles. Then there is the diversity of possible purchase channels, which makes automation and reconciliation tricky as suppliers keep track of whether their latest sale was via an online portal, an email, telesales, or a firm handshake. Another obvious but key factor is the volume purchase of goods and significantly larger size of invoices in B2B commerce. These transactions are highly relationship-dependent, and involve a degree of collaboration and coordination. In a B2C transaction, a customer is unlikely to make a distinction between buying directly from Amazon or a third-party vendor with a storefront on the site. In B2B transactions, partnerships are precious and repeat business is vital for survival.

While B2B commerce networks cater for some of these complexities, the final link in the B2B chain – payments – remains hampered by a plethora of costly variables.

The Payment Problem

If a consumer wants to buy a single item online, they will find relatively fixed prices across multiple websites, place their order, and wait for their purchase to arrive. Concluding a B2B transaction is not so straightforward. Taxation regulations come into play, prices of goods may alter dramatically from one day to the next, or be subject to volume discounts, special offers, and more. Shipping adds further complexity too, due to the high numbers of varying products involved. There is also geography to consider, with the dispersion of supply chains introducing further issues around time zones, shipping distances, customs documentation, and cultural inconsistency in how businesses expect to do business.

And what about the potential for change *after* a payment has been made? More than 60%[6] of B2B transactions require manual intervention as new business conditions or events necessitate payments to be split, combined, rerouted, rescheduled, or altered for all manner of additional reasons. These changes create a nightmare for the remittance and reconciliation of a transaction. As a consequence, over 30% of invoices are paid late, by 30 days or more.[7]

One major issue here is data. When a buyer issues a batch payment for goods to multiple suppliers, it is almost impossible for a buyer to tell a supplier exactly what they are paying for or add any additional details within current systems. If their payment covers multiple invoices, for example, there is very limited space to say so. As one expert put it, the NACHA 94-character format used by 97% of all electronic payments in the US allows for "about half of the information that a tweet gives".[8] The Single European Payments Area (SEPA) format has the same challenge. Hardly adequate for the complex data required for describing a basic B2B transaction – let alone if some variable changes somewhere in the transaction lifecycle. This issue is exacerbated by cross-border transactions where financial systems do not speak the same language and lose even more data in translation.

Such challenges make cash flow frustratingly unpredictable, and leave businesses playing a guessing game. Buyers want to optimize their working capital and better manage liquidity by introducing more visibility and control to their procurement process, but do not have accurate or up-to-date information to guide them – often missing out on supplier discounts in the process. Likewise, suppliers want to get paid predictably: on time, at the correct amount, and with the right data. Otherwise, they cannot predict cash flow and are often left in a difficult position as they attempt to raise capital to cover expenses. These issues are all too real for the vast majority of businesses – 78% of which say that they cannot forecast cash flow with accuracy.[9] As long as enterprises are unable to collaborate and transact with partners across the world in real time, visibility and control of what is happening to their money is obscured, and supply chains remain woefully inefficient (see the following Figure).

Figure: **Ironically, in today's 24/7/365, uber-connected era of business, most businesses still have little control or visibility of the status of their payment processes – and the consequences are staggering**

[6] Global Payments Report 2013, BCG.

[7] Ibid.

[8] http://www.pymnts.com/in-depth/2014/b2b-payments-are-antiquated-and-starving-for-data/#.VZWHJkY__R4.

[9] Global Payments Report 2013, BCG.

The finer details are painful to observe. Today, companies still manage 70% of all invoices via paper, and spend nearly $1 trillion[10] in fees to intermediaries just to make payments – half of which must be handled manually.[11] With the average cost of a single invoice estimated to be $14.21 in 2014, and many companies processing over 400,000 invoices each year,[12] the time and money involved in settling up is a massive waste of resources and capital. And while forward-thinking Accounts Payable departments are gradually moving off this paper trail, they remain hampered by the dearth of solutions that have existed to make the transition to full payment automation as quick and seamless as they need it to be.

A Broken System

At the root of the payment problem lie the antiquated systems that most banks offer for B2B remittance. With few competitors, and therefore little to gain by changing, banks have continued to provide "solutions" that have not undergone much alteration since Edison first cracked the light bulb conundrum. Non-standardized banking models across the globe, fragmented organizational structures that impair customer visibility, and poor collaboration between banks and financial institutions are just some of the drawbacks that render current banking services obsolete in our ever-increasingly connected economy. Unquestionably, these vestigial banking platforms are a key factor in leaving AP departments drowning beneath an ocean of paper as they manage the huge numbers of B2B exception transactions, and a reason why business cannot replicate the convenience levels now normalized in B2C e-commerce. Even existing B2B networks that claim to offer a payment component are in fact just sending a static payment "instruction file" to a bank or a link to a payment gateway. The result is exactly the same lack of transparency and loss of important data that occurs with the inflexible systems provided by banks.

This array of variables in B2B transactions underscores the fact that business conditions are too dynamic to be adequately served by such static payment methods. These methods include credit cards, wire transfers, and ACH transactions to name but a few, and any changes to the finer details of payments made in this way instantly cause B2B collaboration to become messy, time-consuming, and costly.

[10] Source: The Hackett Group (as reported in the Purchase to Pay Manifesto from Basware).

[11] http://downloads.tradeshift.com/Ardent%20Partners%20-%20ePayables%202014%20-%20 The%20Quest.pdf.

[12] Top priorities for AP in 2014 – Ardent Partners.

Thankfully, as with every persistent problem, a definitive solution can be found by taking a fresh approach.

Dynamic Payments

Today, FinTech innovators are out to create payment platforms that are every bit as dynamic as global business. Start-ups are already partnering with leading enterprises to make the all-important payment process a seamless part of their B2B commerce experience. Underpinning their work is the belief that B2B collaboration fit for the modern digital marketplace will be impossible until the final hurdle of static payments is removed.

The first step for those seeking to bring about a state of B2B nirvana has been to define exactly what constitutes a "dynamic" as opposed to a "static" payment. If payments within existing systems are sluggish, disconnected, and inefficient, it follows that any dynamic payments platform must allow for dramatically faster, safer, and smarter transactions.

In order to achieve that aim, these new players have created systems that allow businesses to execute, clear, and settle payments in real time, all the time. Key to these endeavours is a desire to marry the best of secure digital banking, rich electronic data interchange, and modern cloud-based technologies that can handle structured and unstructured data of any size or format (see the following Figure). This merging and modification of existing services and technologies has long been the Holy Grail of B2B e-commerce requirements, and the formula for event-driven payments that are truly dynamic.

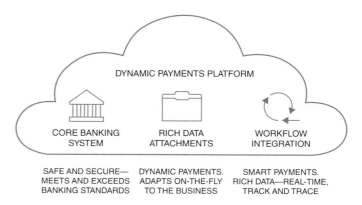

Figure: **Elements of a dynamic payments platform**

Such software solutions are empowering businesses to adapt to all the potential exceptions occurring in the aftermath of payments. B2B commerce networks offering dynamic payments capabilities are now able to get beyond the basic connection of purchase orders and electronic invoices, and truly offer an end-to-end closed-loop system for their buyers and suppliers that incorporates a 360° view of the entire transaction – enabling a whole new level of connection, collaboration, and strategic transaction. Supply chain financing, factoring, dynamic discounting, cash auctioning, and more can now be part of the equation with the press of a button.

By utilizing event-driven workflow engines that connect to existing B2B commerce systems across the supply chain, enterprises can finally trust in tech to monitor and dynamically react to any changes in the transaction, while keeping all of the details synchronized. Thanks to FinTech innovation, the payment process no longer needs to be an isolated, unpredictable step that undermines any prior efficiencies gained in the run-up to settlement.

The net result for the first businesses to turn to these platforms has been greater ownership of their capital, liquidity, and cash flow, and the removal of one of the key barriers to them working in a way they have always instinctively felt should be possible. As more companies begin to realize that the most flawed component of B2B commerce is being addressed right now, they would be doing their bottom line a disservice by not adopting the solutions available.

Of course, this light bulb moment is just part of the larger story of collaborative innovation in B2C and B2B e-commerce, and as FinTech's modern-day inventors continue to redefine and rewire the way things work in the world, there are no doubt many more sparks of inspiration still to come.

Payments and Point of Sales (POS) Innovation

By Rube Huljev

Former Sales Director, CardMobili

"Merchants have no country. The mere spot they stand on does not constitute so strong an attachment as that from which they draw their gains."

Thomas Jefferson

It was 13 February 1601 when James Lancaster slowly raised the anchor of the Red Dragon, drifting out of Woolwich to begin a journey that he never thought would change the world forever. The first step in the globalization of trade had begun with only four modest ships. At the time, valiant men had understood what connects the world – it was the ocean. The ocean allowed for the flow of goods, trade, and information. The ocean was the first internet. Unevenly distributed goods were the opportunity that these original global entrepreneurs had sensed and had the courage to act upon. Their unfair advantage was their hard-to-find knowledge of the world, long-range navigation, and willingness to face the overwhelming odds where the ultimate price was one's life. A group of London-based merchants that acted as their angel seed investors never dreamed of the outcome that would result from this initial experiment.

Today, over 400 years later, we are experiencing an almost identical moment, where the opportunities and the promise of riches abound and are even greater. The flow of spices and goods is not the big opportunity of today – the flow of data is. The internet, and more specifically the mobile internet, is the new ocean connecting different shores. The information, once a prized possession in the hands of a select few, is now at the fingertips of anyone who wants to use it and act upon it. The trouble today is that there is too much information coming from many different sources. Thus making sense of it all, correlating and putting it to a good use has become an art – not the information gathering process itself.

The merchant's situation has changed too. Once those with the biggest warehouse commanded the markets, today it is those with no warehouse or stock at all. Physical store locations are threatened and are becoming a burden and a liability.

Pure play digital merchants of goods and services are slowly creating a perception that it is the only way to go, and bricks-and-mortar enterprises could soon become extinct (or could they?). Many things have changed due to technology: from consumers getting used to ever more evolving convenience, to shorter delivery times, and lower margins and prices.

But one thing is constant and it is hard-wired from the trade of ancient times until today – human psychology. What consumers and customers really want is the experience. Whether it is exclusivity, craving something first and then bragging about it to their network, or the dopamine rush caused by the unpacking of a box whose arrival was expected. The surprise effect of receiving something unexpected. The overwhelming feeling of warmth when sending a gift to a friend. The experience of how something feels at the moment you buy (and pay for!) it. The experience of a trade, goods and money exchanging hands, changing owners. There is something incredibly personal in any trade, which is becoming lost in these digital times. People do not buy goods, but instead they buy an experience, a ritual.

Emotion. That is what people give away their hard earned money for, the feel-good effect that follows or is part of the ritual of exchange. Do you go to restaurants to end your feeling of hunger? Yes, also. But what you're really looking for is to feel good, to be served with a smile, to be recognized and pampered. To feel good and experience a great service, which also includes food.

Humans are wired for social interaction, which does not end in a digital world. The technology of today has allowed for a relationship of any type (merchant-to-person, brand-to-person, person-to-person) to start in the digital world, but the real, complete effect of that relationship is unleashed in the physical world, between two human beings. If one of them is a customer and the other is a merchant, so much the better.

And here we come to the main reason why pure play digital merchants are not a match for merchants that have both a physical and a digital presence. When the consumer walks into a bricks-and-mortar store, the opportunities to enhance and personalize the customer's experience are exponential. When a sales assistant knows the correct information about the preferences of a customer, maybe even their name and the actual context of their visit, the customer feels personally served and treated. The customer feels like a king. No pure digital play can extract that smile and that kind of bonding between a brand and a consumer.

And this small unrecognized fact is a saviour of the smart banks. Real-time personalization of customer experience, based on the best, ubiquitous, and most frictionless touch-point available anywhere – a point-of-sale terminal. Can you imagine a better point for customer acquisition and evolution of the relationship? While the whole industry is reinventing new ways to pay and creating technologies and competing standards for payments, customers do not have a problem with payment. They insert their card and can walk away in under 10 seconds with the goods under their arm. But give them something more, incentivize the customer, surprise them, offer a better personalized experience, become more human – you as a merchant will reap the results, unexpected ones. Try it on a small scale and you will be preaching this yourself in no time.

As a bank, you hold the ownership of the single most important touch-point in a consumer–merchant relationship, with emphasis on the relationship – not a transaction. Evolve your business models to sell services which bring additional value to merchants (and in turn the "kings", customers) on top of your transactions processing. Sell relationships, walk-ins, connect customers and businesses in a meaningful way. Help merchants construct a long-term value exchange with their customers, help brands construct an ad network out of their current convinced customers. Make the customers their digital word-of-mouth, a marketing channel every type of merchant has sworn by since the dawn of time. Help businesses get more smiles and referrals.

We live in very interesting times, where technology is changing everything it touches. This has been the case for quite some time, but since the mobile has taken centre stage, the "software eating the world" process has accelerated exponentially. Never before in the history of humankind has the effect of technology on everyday life been so profound or has its impact been visible so fast.

Why is that so? Because mobile is in the hands of every consumer, it is the most intimate and immediate device to reach and influence people, including the magic moment of purchase. And the consumer is, and will remain, the king (or queen, as the case may be). The more technology advances, the more it will become apparent that the real-time feedback of consumers to each other, even if they are strangers, has given them amazing power – a power feared by any type of merchant. Consumers decide the fate of merchants, who in turn decide the fate of banks.

The Three Pillars of a Financial Transaction

Let us look at these three pillars of a financial transaction: the customer, the bank, and the merchants.

Customer

"Swiper, stop swiping." A favourite quote from lovable Dora the Explorer, is also a looming curse for banks and merchants. Consumers decide where and when to swipe, touch, buy … and sometimes not to swipe at all. No swipe, no transaction fee, no merchant, no bank.

So we do agree that the customer is right at the top of the food chain.

Bank

Acquiring banks on the other hand have always been charging their merchants, which many have perceived as "tax" without any perceived value add. Therefore, given a chance, merchants will move to the nearest lower bidder. No added value, no loyalty, no country.

And there are many challengers, pretenders to the banking throne. Established banks face an onslaught of disruptors through blockchain technologies, less complicated processing, lower fees through cheaper technologies, cheaper distribution, lighter or no regulation – and finally no expensive physical and personnel overheads.

Luckily for banks, the challengers (still) compete on lower fees, prices, and no long-term commitments. There will be no winner in the race to the bottom with fees per transaction – learn your lessons from the telecom world.

The real winners will differentiate themselves with services on top of transactions that are perceived to be valuable to both merchants and end consumers. Simple, effective B2B2C services that are activated easily and sold on top of the existing merchant processing and acquiring solutions. No sale needed. Fast and effective upselling.

Merchants

And finally, the third part of the puzzle. Merchants. All of us involved in financial and tech services need to consider their simple needs and always present burning issues. Now, what is it that all merchants want?

Merchants want more profit. Merchants want new customers. Merchants want to spend less and lower their costs, especially on marketing that cannot be measured. But most importantly – merchants seek and want whatever their customers want and crave, whatever makes their customers happy and turns them into willing, sincere advocates. That something is the elusive smile. Once you have made them smile, you as a merchant, or provider of any kind of service, have done 50% of your work with your customer. You have established an emotional bond. Your customer has become more involved and tolerant. If merchants keep building on that smile, the benefits that come from that particular convinced customer (which are by the way fully measurable if the whole experience is designed well) will astound anyone. That customer experience, perceived through any touch-point, counts and differentiates more than ever before.

Building Blocks of the New Bank

With what we understand of the customer experience and touch-points, what can we say about the New Bank?

POS as the Preferred Touch-point

Banks and processors own the single most important touch-point in a relationship between a consumer and a business, which is also one of the most often forgotten. Make sure you sprinkle a bit of magic fairy dust on top of those devices in the form of services that simply acquire customer identity and can act and react to a customer's current context, paired with the back-end services that power it. There is a whole range of emerging smart new-generation POS devices (like Poynt) that will be able to make use of these services and present them to the customer in a modern way at that magic moment of contact.

Data

There are many companies that know a whole lot about customer behaviour in the digital world. There are very few that can construct a customer context in the physical environment. Banks are one of those few.

B2B2C Automated Personalization SaaS[1] for Merchants and Consumers

These services, preferably based on a performance business model, should become a core of the bank offering – a missing link that translates the obsolete into the indispensable.

Remember that centuries-old wisdom which still stands and always will in the world of commerce – the mere spot a merchant stands on (his bank and his taxman) does not constitute as strong an attachment as that from which they draw their gains (their customer's wallet).

And finally we come to an underlying conclusion – he who holds the loyalty and allegiance of consumers will have the attention of merchants too. Banks – wake up, watch your backs, offer transaction-related services to bring in more customers to your merchants. This can become your real, fully measured added value.

Will banks need to transform into technology marketing agencies? Will business models move more towards performance? Most probably. Fast. For if the banks do not do it, Facebook, Google, Apple, Samsung, Paypal, Amazon, and other contenders are surely laying the rails, since they have sensed the opportunity. They are lean, fast, and can get around regulation more easily.

The new Golden Age of Sail has begun. Are you building lean and fast ships?

---

[1] Software as a Service.

Predictive Algorithms – Building Innovative Online Banking Solutions

By Jan Michael Auer
Co-Founder, predictR and 25th-floor

Jakob Etzel
Co-Founder, predictR and 25th-floor

Georg Heiler
Co-Founder, predictR

Martin Prebio
Co-Founder, predictR and 25th-floor

Two observations motivate this chapter. Firstly, the financial crisis has shown a significant increase in the non-performing loan ratio in retail banking. One of the roots of this development is the widespread weak financial literacy of retail customers. Secondly, digitalization of retail banking is thriving and has become a key success factor. Nevertheless, quick market research in German-speaking countries shows that the evolution of online banking in the past five years has only taken place in the areas of design and user experience/interface. Thus, there is a rising need for new solutions that add improved functionality.

The idea is to bring these two observations together. Historical transaction data of retail customers can be converted into cash flow forecasts. This is tackling a real-world pain: many customers find it difficult to make a long-term forecast of their cash flows and to analyse scenarios in this context. Such scenarios can be life moments (e.g. getting promoted or losing a job) or the desire to reach a financial goal (e.g. how to fund a new car or flat). Retail customer data includes enough information to expand predictions to a sufficiently long-term period. Thus, customers can explore their financial future in interactive graphs, and bank products can be presented in the context of life decisions.

Background

In 2015, many management conference panellists claim that successful companies need to install chief innovation officers either on their board, or directly subordinated, with the power to break through company silos and turn around stuck processes. More than ever before, innovation is the key driver for economic success and the pressure on executives to generate or acquire innovation is at a high level.

A sector that has long been looked at as performing very badly in the field of innovation is banking and insurance. FinTech companies that want to disrupt the current stalemate have very high stakes and tough regulations to follow. The macro-economic environment allowed traditional products to provide enough profits, and competition happened basically on the basis of pricing and reputation, but was rarely based on innovation.

Banks and insurance companies have in the past offered both consulting services and products. Usually only the products were priced, whereas the consulting was traditionally seen as a free service. Today's near-zero interest rates and the increasing capitalization requirements of banks make these practices more challenging and it is immensely difficult to get the consumer on a pay-for-service track.

The aforementioned broader background forces banks to increasingly transform their business models and find or acquire new forms of revenue streams. Now we will take a closer look at the two main observations behind this chapter.

Financial literacy was long seen as a guarantor that retail customers would use the services and products of a bank, and would not rely on other funding opportunities (e.g. peer-to-peer lending). There has always been the basic assumption that bank relationship managers' education, training, knowledge, and experience enable them to know and understand their clients' needs and environment, find the right products, and subsequently be available at important moments in life. This could be interpreted as the retail customers being very short on alternatives other than to trust their bank advisor.

Today, however, customers can help themselves with various online forums and comparison websites. Often, clients enter bank branches with prepared print-outs detailing how much they can get with the competition. Still financial illiteracy is one of the causes of non-performing loans (NPL). A large number of bankruptcies of small and medium-sized enterprises (SME) are caused by poor financial literacy. As we see in the annual reports of all major banks, the unstable currency exchange rates and challenging economy make NPL ratios increase in virtually all markets.

Example | Online Banking in Austria

Austria is relatively well-developed when it comes to banking, and online banking statistics are similar to most Central and Western European markets. As an example, Austria's largest bank, the Raiffeisen Banking Group, has 1.6 million online banking customers. Out of 700,000–800,000 daily contacts, the bank is already handling 25 percent of them originating from mobile devices.[1]

In the European Union, out of 507 million citizens, 85% are bank customers,[2] of whom 44% use online banking.[3] According to author interviews with bank representatives, approximately 10% of online banking users are "power users" who regularly use advanced features and act as early adopters. Taking these early adopters as a target group of online banking innovation, there is a 20 million target group in the 28 EU Member States.

The Austrian market leader in online banking innovation at the moment is ERSTE Group who recently launched their new online banking service "George", and combine the largest bandwidth of functionality. Additionally, banks are experimenting with multi-channel strategies, such as account opening via email and phone or financial advice via video-conferencing (see Table below).

Table: Online banking features

Bank	Online account opening	Target saving	Rounding saving	Automatic categorization	Manual categorization	Personal finance manager	Communication channels with bank advisor additional to mail & phone	Additional features
Raiffeisen		X			X	1	Branches	Cash flow forecast for the next month
Bank Austria (UniCredit)	X					2	Branches, online (video call)	Cashback
Rest Bank	X	X	X	X	X	3	Branches	BlueCode transactions, plugin shop
Overbank							Branches	
Volksbank	(x)						Branches	
EasyBank							Mail/phone only	
Santander	(x)						Mail/phone only	
ING DiBa		X				4	Mail/phone only	
Deniz Bank	(x)						Mail/phone only	
Holvi	X				X	4	Mail/phone only	Online shop, invoicing, expense claims
Number 26	X			X	X	4	Mail/phone only	

(1) Aggregation, allocation overview and historic cash flows; external products can be added manually

(2) Aggregation only

(3) Visualization of the past and monthly statistics ("Snapshot")

(4) Only visualization of historic cash flows

---

[1] "Anpassen statt Aussterben", article in the newspaper *DiePresse*, supplement "Magazin 4.0", 27 June 2015, p. 28, Vienna.

[2] Source: World Bank, 2007.

[3] Source: usage-statista.com, 2014.

Private Customer Cash Flow Forecasts

Against this background, the idea is now to generate cash flow forecasts for private customers' current accounts. The forecasts will be made by predictive algorithms and will be based on the historical transaction data available at the bank. The prediction is done without any user interaction and is part of the customers' online banking profile. The forecasts are planned to be delivered as "software as a service" and to be implemented as a white-label solution (a product or service produced by one company (the producer) and rebranded by other companies (the marketers)).

Transaction clustering is at the core of such forecasting. Each cluster can be modelled differently and all cluster models together can thereafter be combined to aggregate estimates. Clusters can be chosen based on various parameters, for example:

- Counterpart

- Sign (income or expense)

- Category (salary, rental, food, education, leisure, etc.)

- Type (POS, credit card, standing order, etc.)

- Geolocation.

Time series clustering (shown in the following Figure) can also be based on dissimilarity measures,[4] but transaction data usually have enough inherent structure to fit the above-mentioned parameters.

The standard model generates median and 0.05/0.25/0.75/0.95 quantiles. Generally, the clusters acting as samples will be too small to give good quantiles and therefore a continuous sample is assumed and quantile interpolation is used. Other models are based on means instead of medians and/or calculate weighted estimates where stronger emphasis is put on more recent data.

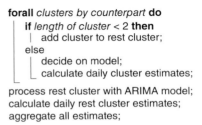

```
forall clusters by counterpart do
    if length of cluster < 2 then
        add cluster to rest cluster;
    else
        decide on model;
        calculate daily cluster estimates;
process rest cluster with ARIMA model;
calculate daily rest cluster estimates;
aggregate all estimates;
```

Figure: Time series clustering

There is a multitude of different techniques that can be applied to time series, among them:

- ATM withdrawal simulation by Hidden Markov models

- Hierarchical time series (e.g. with nested transaction categories forming the hierarchy)

- Copulae to simulate the influence of an event on multiple clusters and the clusters' interdependencies.

In 2010 SAP presented their product HANA, which is a high-performance in-memory relational database management system. The HANA platform is shipped with predictive processing tools with numerous algorithms and R integration. It might be an interesting alternative to building up a system from scratch.[5] Oracle offers similar platforms and solutions, for example column-based forecasts and automated data mining concepts.[6]

Research and Testing

Tests are currently performed on two different real-life data sets. The first includes 3,741 transactions encompassing seven years of a single current account and the second 434, derived from a three-year current account history. Within the data sets it is possible to take a subsequence spanning two years as input and compare results with existing data (see the following Figure).

---

[4] Georg Heiler. *Clustering von Zeitreihen. Ein Uberblick über Anwendungen von Zeitreihen-Clustering.* Bachelor's thesis, Vienna University of Technology, 2015.

[5] http://www.sap.com/predictive.

[6] http://www.oracle.com/technetwork/database/options/advanced-analytics/odm/index.html.

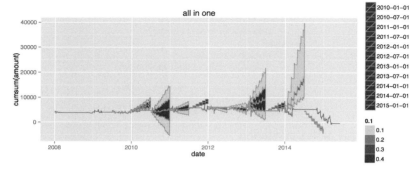

Figure: Backtesting
Source: predictR, Vienna

Figure: Integration examples
Source: predictR, Vienna

The predictive algorithms were tested on seven years of historical transaction data. Stepwise two years of input were processed and the resulting 6-month forecasts compared with the real data. The results shown above come from standard model calculations (order statistics). Results show that forecasts overestimate a negative or positive trend. This could be further corrected by using weighted estimates. When weighted estimates are used, the difference between back-testing results and real data can be used to run an optimization algorithm on the weights used. Thus, the weights can set an optimal for every specific user, but bear the risk of recent data being considered as much more dominant than older data.

Thoughts on Business and Integration

The integration into online banking can be manifold, as the pricing structure in the following Figure shows. Cash flow forecasting can, for example, be a source for an intelligent semantic search engine. It can also be part of the back-end of product calculators and so-called private finance managers (PFM).

Table: Pricing structures

Strategy	User pays for	Vendor delivers	Target
Free for all	Free	API + graphics	Get new customers
3rd party plug-in	Yearly subscription	API + graphics	Get customers to pay for service
Freemium	Premium feature	API + graphics	Get customers to pay for service
Integration into PFM	Yearly subscription	API	Enhancing PFM with prediction

The pricing structure shown in the Table above[7] can follow usual software-as-a-service models:

* An up-front fee is paid for the installation of the system. Due to data protection requirements there will be the need to deploy in a high-security data centre or directly at bank premises. There is also a need for high customization.

---

[7] See the chapter entitled "Embracing the Connected API Economy" for further details.

- A monthly or quarterly provisioning fee can be set quite low and ensures basic service level agreements and infrastructure costs. If the contract allows for automatic feature upgrades, this fee might have to be set higher.

- Finally, transaction pricing counts all requests targeted to the prediction server and bills constantly, e.g. every thousand requests.

Applying Predictive Analytics to SMEs

According to many interviews with SME executives, tax accountants, and bank managers/customer relationship managers, there is a need to provide SMEs with adequate predictive analytics. On the one hand, this helps to make better decisions per se. Secondly, this can also help in the battle against financial illiteracy and give owners and managers a better visualization and understanding of dependencies and complexity, and also allow intuitive scenario planning.

The following figures could be interesting to predict:

- Cash flows

- The impact of volatile currency exchange rates

- Demand of special products, e.g. the number of revolving credit lines, derivative instruments/hedges for specific products or currencies.

Providing powerful interfaces can enable the prediction platform to interact with a range of external data sources:

- *Macroeconomic data.* System users can be asked to give additional data such as geolocation, size (revenue, employees), sector, typical location, and sector of vendors and customers. This master data can form the basis for feeding appropriate external macroeconomic data into the forecasts.

- *CRM/ERP/accounting/data warehouse systems.* Depending on the size and sector of a company, there might be one of these systems in place. Their data can be used directly as raw input for the predictive algorithms or – being aggregated or the result of a prediction – form a factor in scenario planning.

- *Additional banks.* Once a company reaches a certain size, the likelihood is high that there are also connections to other banks. For instance, there could be a leasing contract or mortgage loan at another financial institution. There might even be syndicated loans or larger facilities. Industry standards and FinTechs like FIGO offer to connect these banks and retrieve their (transaction) data – possibly even in real time.

The disruptiveness of such methods can be quite wide-ranging. It directly impacts consultants, tax accountants, and in-house employees. For banks, having such data available could change the pricing of funding instruments and eventually even risk pricing.

Conclusions

Predictive algorithms are a highly promising and interesting field of research. Additionally, there are already the first low-hanging fruits to be harvested: solid business models can be built around them, as shown by the example of private customer cash flows.

The buzzword "treasury as a service" summarizes a couple of interesting leads towards further implementation. In particular, the use of predictive algorithms in combination with online banking and the banks' data – maybe even in combination with external sources – is promising. Ultimately, this can bring new functionalities in the customer segment of micro-corporates.

However, there are still some obstacles to overcome. Powerful statistical methods may deploy untested results and methodologically incorrect models. Also, bank back-ends might not yet be able to provide the necessary data in the requested time or data quality might simply be too poor. And in the end, there is still the risk of the users not being interested in the algorithms' output or being unable to deal with it.

A successful roll-out of private customer cash flow forecasts will be the first milestone on the journey to make predictive algorithms available to every bank customer.

Big Data is the Cornerstone of Regulatory Compliance Systems

By Thierry Duchamp
Founder & COO, Scaled Risk

Many financial institutions have been adapting their existing information systems in order to comply with post-crisis regulations. Unfortunately, the limits of their legacy technologies have been shown to be dramatic, and they have failed to meet regulators' expectations that the massive volume of data held by the banks, spanning several years, is now to be available quickly, if not in real time.

This chapter shows how big data technologies can make risk and compliance information systems easier to implement. It also describes how the technology turns constraints into business opportunities. If banks are viewed in this context as gigantic data factories, then big data technology offers the opportunity to link up previously separate functions and operating models. A single big data system can now provide an all-in-one transactional, business intelligence, and compliance solution.

As big data technology has progressively evolved from its beginnings in the web sector, it has been adapted to support the unique requirements and challenges of the financial industry. This chapter describes the architecture and the features of Scaled Risk, a financial software company, as a software solution, and explains why these components are prerequisites for the implementation of big data technologies in a financial context. We also present a small set of real-world examples of how big data can be used for compliance and risk management purposes.

In Banks, Big Data Implementation Has Been too Slow

Since the early 2010s, the term "big data" has been commonly used to describe a new generation of technologies and new approaches for data management. This technology has been created by major players of the web industry because traditional technologies were not able to adapt to an unpredictable number of users, fast-growing data volumes, and the increasing needs for processing

capabilities. The web industry was also expecting a greater level of flexibility and agility, so application look and feel could evolve rapidly without system interruption. "Big data" innovation pushed the web industry's information system capabilities to their greatest flexibility, ease of use, and power.

Surprisingly, enterprises, banks included, have mostly missed this train, with obvious implications. Enterprise innovation has evolved at a very slow pace, compared to the internet. In the end, everyday tools show high flexibility and user-friendliness, while business tools suffer from rigidity and slow learning processes.

Could "Internet Big Data" Have Been Directly Applied to Banks?

Unfortunately, direct application is not straightforward; nevertheless a huge part of the software industry is participating in the enterprisation of big data technologies. This enterprisation is progressively providing business software applications with the same level of flexibility and ergonomics that already exists on the internet. This began in the early 2010s with the noticeable success of Salesforce.com, but progress is slow and is taking more time than anyone predicted due to the following factors:

- Big data architecture is a drastic change of paradigm—implementation requires new knowledge, if not new people.

- The internet use cases mostly differ from enterprise use cases.

- The level of confidence in technology used by the internet world is (often wrongly) lower than for the other industries, especially the banking industry.

Most banks have implemented big data technologies with variable results, mainly depending on the use case for which the technology is required. The closest to the internet world, and the easiest to implement, are:

- Marketing

- Know Your Customer (KYC)

- Fraud detection.

Compliance systems need both data consistency and real-time accuracy to cope with the latest regulation requirements. Legacy technologies have been able to manage data consistently and in real time for the last 30 years – unfortunately with drastic limits. Big data technologies do not provide off-the-shelf, real-time data consistency, which is an issue.

How Can Real-time and Consistent Data be Obtained from Big Data Technology?

Combining real-time and data consistency for big data is an engineering challenge that is solved with Scaled Risk technologies. Big data technologies, as a proposition for a new architecture, rely on distributed computing, with a full lockless approach (i.e. no distributed consensus allowed). A lockless paradigm is the price to pay for getting almost unlimited system scalability, which means:

* Unlimited storage

* Unlimited processing capabilities

* Unlimited caching capabilities.

Time synchronization across the cluster is the secret to providing full lockless data consistency in time. This approach, largely inspired by Google's Spanner (http://research.google.com/archive/spanner.html), provides consistency as of any date, starting at 1 second in the past from now. This delay can even be reduced by using specific time synchronization hardware.

Standard real-time big data also needs to be enhanced, as it has different meanings in the internet world and in the banking industry. Where "interactive" is a good synonym for the former, "event-driven" and "notification-capable" are what the latter expects. Scaled Risk technologies embed both latest innovations from big data and the old recipes that have been used since the early 90s for real-time financial data feed.

Big Data Technology is the Best Technology to Implement Compliance Systems

By definition, compliance systems need data collection, from both internal and external systems:

* Trading systems

* Market data

* Referential and CRM

* External financial data

* Real-time and historical news

* Government data (OFAC, FACTA, EMIR, Dodd-Frank)

* And many others.

Data needed by compliance systems is not only getting bigger and bigger, but also becoming more and more complex. In a nutshell, big data technologies solve two major drawbacks of legacy technologies: the lack of both flexibility and of elasticity and scalability.

Lack of Flexibility

Thanks to elasticity and scalability, infrastructure can be adapted on the fly.

Flexibility

Information systems must be able to cope with rapid changes due to regulation and business pressures. The agility required is very difficult to implement with relational database management systems (RDBMs), even for a single silo in the bank. Compliance systems, by nature, centralize multiple information streams from various standards and formats. Handling the necessary, but numerous, changes in the source systems is an impossible mission with RDBMs and Extract, Transform and Load (ETL)-based solutions.

Big data technologies propose a disruptive approach regarding data schema management, because data and related data structures are stored and managed separately. The primary approach used by big data technologies relies on data schemas on read, which means data is stored in a format managed by the application. This approach gives greater flexibility, as data schemas can be changed with more ease. But there is a drawback with this approach as it offers poor visibility on data: everything is hidden by the code.

As early as 2012, Scaled Risk introduced a hybrid approach using the "Schema on read" approach, enhanced by:

- A data schema implemented on top of a meta-model;

- "Schema on read" able to smartly rely on several versions of this data schema;

- "Schema on read" also able to automatically trigger types conversions.

This hybrid approach drastically reduced the usual costs for implementing a centralized data warehouse, at the initialization stage, but also for later upgrades.

Elasticity and Scalability

Elasticity and scalability are the main disruptions brought about by big data technologies. Enabling a real lockless distributed architecture allows a big data application to offer limitless:

- Data storage

- Processing capabilities

- Caching (in-memory).

Implementing a regulatory system brings a lot of uncertainty, very similar to what happened to the web industry:

- To what degree of complexity will data evolve?

- How fast will data grow?

- Will it need more processing power (e.g. valuation)?

- Will it need to be quicker (e.g. Dodd-Frank and Clearing House)?

Combining Internal and External Data

An efficient compliance system must be able to combine data that the bank already stores in its internal systems, data provided by third parties, and public data (i.e. social networks, web). To illustrate, these are the data sources needed for detecting money laundering through company acquisitions:

- Data from banks' transactions systems

- Data from external company directories to verify the shareholders

- OFAC and similar lists

- Web search results about stakeholders.

Big data not only enables easy data collection and storage, but also provides various ways to reconcile data from different formats in a flexible (i.e. fuzzy) way. In the case of money laundering detection, this implementation will:

- Detect that shareholders are the same people as those mentioned in web search results or OFAC lists, even if names are transliterated differently from various languages;

- Compute a reputation score by text-mining the web;

- Use machine learning for weak signal detection or fraud pattern detection on account transactions.

By combining this information, a big data approach (as shown in the following Figure) will give an instant result on money laundering probability. Similar manual verification requires several hours of work and is not as exhaustive or as efficient.

Enhance Traditional Approaches

Big data is able to reduce data complexity and to detect weak signals in huge sets of information. Statistics, text-mining, and machine learning leverage the distributed capabilities of big data systems, as they can:

- Store huge amounts of data and unlimited history depth;

- Execute complex algorithms in real time;

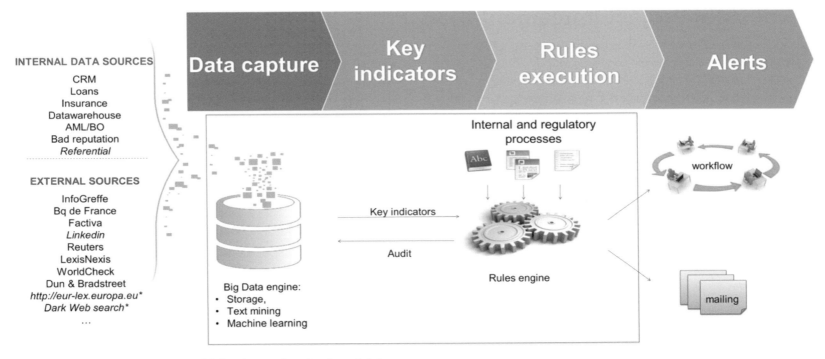

Within the figure:

INTERNAL DATA SOURCES
CRM
Loans
Insurance
Datawarehouse
AML/BO
Bad reputation
Referential

EXTERNAL SOURCES
InfoGreffe
Bq de France
Factiva
Linkedin
Reuters
LexisNexis
WorldCheck
Dun & Bradstreet
http://eur-lex.europa.eu*
Dark Web search*
...

Data capture | **Key indicators** | **Rules execution** | **Alerts**

Internal and regulatory processes

Key indicators →
← Audit

Big Data engine:
• Storage,
• Text mining
• Machine learning

Rules engine

workflow

mailing

Figure: Big data approach to combining internal and external data

Source: Scaled Risk

- Keep most used data in a fast-distributed cache (i.e. in-memory);

- Keep costs very reasonable (mid-range servers are used).

These approaches give excellent results for extracting hidden information in masses of data, with the drawback of producing false positive results.

On the other hand, traditional approaches are too rigid and restrictive and often miss real positive results. Another drawback of legacy approaches, with business rules engines based on structured data, is the difficulty of adapting to regulation changes.

The hybrid approach of feeding a rules engine with indicators provided by a big data system provides better results. Big data indicators with false positives are filtered out very efficiently by the rules engines, while more cases are detected. Regulation pressure has definitely gone beyond "time and material". Being unable to implement efficient compliance control has already resulted in multibillion-dollar fines.

Audit Everything

Controlling and implementing regulatory control is unfortunately not sufficient. Regulation requires being able to produce evidence of having actually triggered all controls. Big data is again extremely helpful in exhaustively storing results, timestamps, and related information into a single audit trail.

The audit trail is always available, which means that several years can be kept online. Archiving becomes easier as storage capability is unlimited: fine-grained with unlimited history depth.

Successful Project Implementation

Based on our experience, the successful implementation of a big data compliance system needs a set of prerequisites and best practices.

Intermediate Components are Needed

Hadoop, an open-source software framework, as a raw technology, is not self-sufficient to implement the usual financial use cases. An internal project based on Hadoop will need several man-months if not man-years just to build and integrate a set of intermediate technical components. This is certainly the most surprising fact one encounters when starting a big data project from scratch.

Another lesson learned: components that are publicly available do not necessarily cope with banking system requirements, especially in relation to data consistency and real time. This means that some components also have to be built.

Building an internal project requires a huge amount of time that can be saved by the use of an existing third-party platform, as can be seen in the following Figure.

Scaled Risk offers off-the-shelf financial big data capabilities, which means two years of time to market with our integrated platform:

- A flexible multi-version data schema for fast data collection.
- Real-time event-driven technology at the heart of the architecture.
- Instant, easy, and consistent data access thanks to search engine functionality.
- Consistent reporting capabilities thanks to distributed and real-time online analytical processing (OLAP).
- Full audit view with as of data view capabilities.
- Data visualization components.

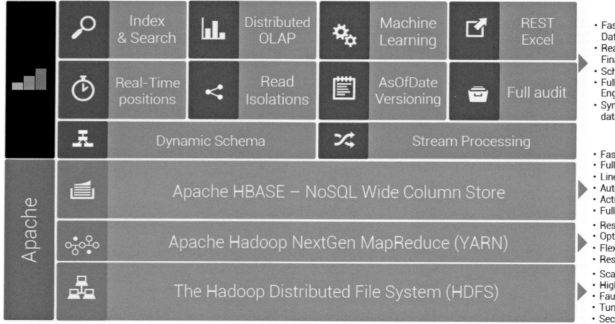

Figure: Hadoop framework

Source: Scaled Risk

Using such a solution is likely to allow you to spend extra time and money on actually implementing compliance rules and controls.

Use an Open System

This is completely compatible with off-the-shelf commercial solutions. Scaled Risk does not capture your data into a black box. Hadoop and the Open Source ecosystem provide big companies with a powerful piece of software (R, Spark, Hive, etc.) that remains entirely compatible with this system.

An open system is also about being able to extend or modify rules and data source. The technologies used to do this must be standard and open so you can easily find expert resources on the job market.

End-to-end Project Implementation

Big data technologies are still new to enterprises and banks, with the result that the focus is too often on the technology itself. In our opinion, this is a mistake that absolutely must be avoided. The financial software industry is changing rapidly with several newcomers that are able to deliver financial and big data services at the same time. They are the best providers to deliver the compliance system of a new generation.

FinTech Solutions in Complex Contracts Optimization

By Akber Datoo

Partner, D2 Legal Technology LLP

Decades of neglect are coming home to roost. In an increasingly regulated and competitive world, it is incumbent on financial institutions to fully understand the complex contracts in place with their clients. Failure to do so risks catastrophe as witnessed by the fates of Lehman Brothers and AIG. If the financial crisis taught us anything, it was that there was an extremely poor understanding of the swathes of contracts entered into. Firms were caught in a whirlwind of panic, unable to find documents, let alone identify what crucial information they contained.

Regulators globally were shocked by this state of affairs. They imposed multiple requirements on financial firms to have better management of their legal contract data. For example, on 6 March 2015, the European Banking Authority (EBA) published a consultation paper containing a draft regulatory standard on the minimum set of information on financial contracts that should be contained in detailed records maintained by financial firms, tying this in to requirements under the Bank Recovery and Resolution Directive (colloquially known as the "living wills" requirement for systemically important financial institutions).

Certainly, these regulatory demands are not unreasonable – the legal contracts are an embodiment of how financial instruments manifest themselves, through the various terms, conditions, and contractual obligations undertaken by each of the parties to the financial contracts. The stability and smooth running of the financial system relies on the satisfactory management of these contractual terms. However, the reality over the last three decades has been that many legal and documentation teams have failed to keep up with the rapidly growing business lines that they support. Ironically, this is in stark contrast to these business lines that have wholeheartedly embraced technological innovation to scale, while the legal and documentation teams have not taken the opportunity to empower themselves in a similar manner with tools, systems, and utilities available to help them manage growth.

It is a sad reflection of the current state of the financial industry, that the stick of regulation is very much trumping the significant carrot of business optimization. The stick, however, is particularly large and forceful at the moment, manifesting itself in very heavy fines and sanctions imposed on institutions, many of which stem from a failure to track and manage contractual obligations, and as a result of an arrogant "too big to fail" mind-set. Nonetheless, the stick has proved effective in forcing the use of FinTech to assist the rectification of this state of affairs by the creation of systems and processes to store and manage legal documentation and data. This is a task that would have been far less complex and time-consuming had the correct processes been in place from the start, i.e. if the documentation teams had filed and stored the contracts, and kept track of key terms negotiated in their contracts. Fixing it after a number of decades of neglect has, however, entailed a different approach due to the sheer volume of legacy contracts of relevance. This is exactly where today's technology comes into its own.

The big data excitement is all about seeing and understanding the relations within unstructured and structured data that until recently, we have struggled to grasp. Big data operates through comprehensive datasets and messiness, rather than small data and accuracy. One could argue that the challenge is not even big enough to really be a big data one, but it certainly is big enough to force legal teams to become more comfortable with disorder and uncertainty, taking on the role of a data scientist to find associations in the data, and acting on that, rather than a precise trawl through each and every word of every contract.

The initial challenge lies in simply ensuring that technology can be used to assist. Hard copy documents bound and kept safe in a vault are always going to require manual effort to obtain and read through. The legal contracts are therefore now being digitized and stored in electronic form by financial firms, using optical character recognition (OCR) and other related technologies, such as ICR (intelligent character recognition) and IWR (intelligent word recognition), to deal with some of the issues with handwritten rather than typed text. This is even being applied to areas such as the oral contracts between traders, with the use of speech recognition software to identify key terms of the verbally agreed contract and ensuring these match the trade confirmations generated by financial firms thereafter in order to avoid trade disputes.

The digitization phase is not without its challenges, such as the use of poorly defined tables in the documents. It is, however, greatly simplified through the legal documentation being drafted with reliance on precedent documents and tightly defined contract vocabulary.

Even the application of some basic classification algorithms to the electronic documents helps tremendously. The documents are now, post-digitization, searchable, and the legal department is already empowered through the ability to find the documents required, a task that was difficult for no reason other than the poor classification and filing of the documents at the time of their execution. Furthermore, through some basic management of identifiers and mapping to other data sources such as risk and client static data systems, the size of the problem can be sensibly reduced to a far more manageable one, by linking the documents to the underlying trade exposures applicable to them, and focusing on where the risks truly lie.

Finding the contracts is only the beginning of the battle. Whilst the lawyer may still be sceptical of the idea of a Google-style search delivering value on par with years of training and expertise, there is perhaps a parallel to be drawn with moments such as the success of Deep Blue, the chess-playing computer developed by IBM – the first piece of artificial intelligence to win both a chess game and a chess match against a reigning world champion under regular time controls, and more recently, IBM Watson, when it competed with and beat at Jeopardy! former winners Brad Rutter and Ken Jennings.

The automation of tasks and processes in a very procedural "if A, then B" statement is the old model of computing, in which each and every step and scenario is determined in advance by the programmer, offering little help in automating the task of reading the legal contract, understanding its nuances, and deriving key data and intelligence from it.

The FinTech approach is the application of the new model of computing, applying interpretative capabilities that learn from the data and human guidance, adapting over time as new knowledge is gained.

A number of techniques are used to excellent effect:

Correlation: at its core, this quantifies statistical relationships between data values. This allows a key legal contract data requirement to be met, not by understanding the intricate workings of it, but simply by identifying a useful proxy for it, including ones that are both multi-dimensional and nonlinear. There is no need to identify the exact nuances of the client asset and money provisions, as they are applied in the contract, through the client terms and conditions, a complicated documentation

stack, and general application of a plethora of overriding rules and regulation. Of course, even strong correlations are never perfect, and one may simply be fooled by randomness. However, that is the increasingly important guiding role of the lawyer – to avoid such issues. What the correlations do is drive the user to the high priority, high-risk areas within the legacy documentation portfolio.

Validation: data values cannot be viewed in isolation. A legal contract and underlying law and regulation impose natural constraints on the data. By mapping these out and applying them, not only is it possible to refine the search and data extraction process, but this can also highlight some of the areas of very high concern. These are ones that a human review is far less likely to detect due to the laborious and repetitive nature of the check, such as ensuring that each party has an appropriate threshold defined in the document (rather than, as seen in a number of documents, the threshold being repeated twice to the same party in error through a simple copy and paste of the language by the drafter, forgetting to then amend the important contractual party reference).

Positive feedback: increasingly, through the use of text analytics and data extraction techniques, more granular and detailed structured legal contract data can be made available to downstream consumers. There is therefore greater visibility of the nuances of the contractual obligations contained within the legal contracts. Through use of this data, in areas such as collateral optimization and credit/funding valuation adjustments (CVA/FVA), any inaccuracies in the data are immediately noticed and can be corrected through the use of workflow.

The positive feedback to cleanse the accuracy of the legal data also forces the legal team to consider the legaleze through the lens of data. Ultimately, barring a dispute with a counterparty, this is the impact of the legal documents the financial firms have entered into. Of itself, this is transforming the real understanding of the financial instruments.

The infrastructure also allows not only better understanding of the current position and risk exposure of an institution through understanding the specific contractual terms applicable across one's document portfolio, but it also allows continual optimization and improvement.

The application of FinTech need not end with the analysis and control over the legacy document portfolio. Rather, institutions are now looking at the current process of putting the documentation in place, using document generation and assembly tools to drive standardization in cases where bespoke and varied language does nothing other than to complicate the regulatory and compliance requirements applicable. It also allows, through workflow and what-if analysis of terms at the point of negotiations with clients, to really understand the risk and financial impact, enabling true optimization along the way.

The FinTech journey is set to transform the role of the lawyer, empowering and placing them in a position of truly advising and being part of the business, removing the more administrative parts of the role, and replacing them with genuine advisory decision-making.

Behavioural Biometrics – A New Era of Security

By Neil Costigan
CEO, BehavioSec

The world around us is changing – in our business and personal lives alike, we are mobile, connected, and regularly interacting with people from all around the globe. We have a range of electronic devices in our pockets, on our desks, and in our homes that mean we think nothing of grabbing whichever is closest to hand to send funds from one country to another, purchase items online from people we have never met, and manage our personal finances. It has to be fast, it has to be now, and it has to be convenient.

A lock and key is no good for protecting digital assets, and we are regularly asked to put our trust in people and systems without being able to see them face to face to verify their identity. This plethora of online information and interaction has introduced enormous opportunity for malicious hackers, seeking to highjack identities and misappropriate credentials. A recent report from fraud prevention agency Cifas shows this trend in action, reporting that the number of victims of identity theft rose by 31% to 32,058 in the first three months of 2015, compared to the same period in 2014.[1]

The highly regulated financial services sector – home to vast flows of sensitive financial and cardholder information every second of the day – is under particularly close scrutiny against this new threat landscape. Not only that, but banks are battling an extraordinary pace of change and innovation driven by technological advances, regulatory requirements, and customer expectations. The explosion in mobile device ownership and the subsequent introduction of mobile payments is just one example of where retail banks are being forced to adopt a never-before-seen level of agility to react to – and secure – new channels and business models.

A Complex Balancing Act

As banks seek to balance the all-important triangle of privacy, convenience, and security, they are having to change the way they think about security. Since virtually every authentication technique can be compromised, they can no longer rely solely on any single control for authorizing high-risk activity.

You do not have to look too far back in the news headlines to see evidence of a move towards a layered approach to security – combining the various available authentication technologies to improve both accuracy of fraud detection and user experience. Supplementary technology devices, such as card readers for verification, have been widely implemented as a means to strengthen the verification process with two-factor authentication. However, these provide a pain point for customers – another piece of hardware to carry around, and an additional barrier to entry to access the service.

Biometrics has stepped in as a potential solution to this problem. From a technology perspective, the process of verifying people by their physical characteristics has been in development ever since the emergence of computer systems in the latter half of the 20th century. Of course, the concept of "biometrics" extends much further back – people have identified each other this way since the beginning of time. Nonetheless, biometrics as a technology concept has only recently been brought into the consumer conscience, thanks in part to giants such as Apple embracing fingerprint scans to log into devices.

Behavioural Biometrics

Behavioural biometrics is a lesser-known technology, often overlooked in the headlines, that moves beyond static biometrics focused on our physical attributes (such as a fingerprint or iris scan), to rather focus on user behaviour. This takes into account details such as the way in which a person interacts with a device, the force with which they hit a key, the angle they use to swipe a touchscreen, or

---

[1] CIFAS, "Identity fraud up by 27% in first quarter of 2015", https://www.cifas.org.uk/id_fraud_first_quarter.

their typing rhythm. The technology sits in the background of an app or device, and is completely transparent to the user, aligning to the desire for a streamlined, frictionless authentication experience.

Machine learning algorithms build up a unique picture of the user – not what they are doing, but *how* they are doing it – to allow for identification of anomalies that may indicate fraud, based on previous user behaviour patterns. Importantly, this verification process is continuous, throughout the course of the session, to ensure that the user is who they say they are during the entire interaction with the device, rather than just at point of entry.

Behavioural biometrics is ideally suited to mobile, thanks to the continuous flow of rich data we are able to collect through numerous sensors on smartphones, which is not available with traditional web use. With smartphones in mind, the technology is a great fit for authenticating mobile payments.

Security and Usability

Behavioural biometrics helps to make authentication part of the end-to-end experience – that is, a natural by-product of whatever it is the user is trying to achieve, rather than calling it out as a specific step. Users will embrace stronger authentication if it is not difficult to use and – particularly on a mobile device – does not involve swapping in and out of apps on the move to locate one-time access codes.

The trend towards mobile banking means that the time taken up by security requirements at the start of each session is particularly pertinent. People log into their bank accounts increasingly frequently, for a quick balance check, or to make a payment. Service providers cannot afford for 30 seconds of a 60-second transaction to be taken up with authentication. Users will get bored, and will move on. Online retailers are battling a similar user trait, facing an increasing number of abandoned shopping carts which is damaging their revenue, and their reputation. While there are a host of reasons internet shoppers might abandon their basket, a clunky or long-winded checkout process, or user inability to remember their security password, are often cited as the top causes.

It is this "one-click buy" universe, pioneered by major internet retailers such as Amazon and Apple, which is contributing to driving greater customer expectations when it comes to banking. If we receive one type of experience in one area of our online lives, we quickly come to expect it in another. There will be an even more direct link between these experiences now that we are seeing an increasing blurring of the lines as to what constitutes a bank or payment provider, with innovators such as Apple, PayPal, and Google now competing in this space. These companies, which excel at exceptional user experience and have built their brands on this strength, are now forcing the banks to become more customer-centric and deliver the frictionless user experience that their customers demand.

Pragmatism and Perception

The conversation about usability rightly comes back to the need for pragmatic security. Users should be faced with security barriers that are appropriate to the level of risk inherent in whatever it is they are trying to do. No-one should be faced with Fort Knox level security when a bicycle lock would be more appropriate. This takes another turn when we consider that social media providers such as Facebook have their sights set on the payment space. Facebook users likely do not have a particularly strong password to log in – for uploading holiday photos and posting new status updates, they do not need to. However, with social identities increasingly being used as entry points for other services – the "login with Facebook" option – we will need to ensure that people are directed down a stronger authentication path, once there is higher risk involved.

Another interesting factor to bear in mind is the importance of user *perception* of security. Although service providers generally strive for a seamless user experience, there are some instances in which it is useful to interrupt the consumer. We might not be happy with barriers to access some services, but we are reassured psychologically that the system is secure. And so the struggle to keep up with consumer demands continues. We are complex characters and sometimes our demands conflict with one another. It is up to security experts to understand this and navigate the intricate balance between security and usability, depending on the context of the process.

Security alone is never going to be the driving factor that encourages a customer to choose one bank over another. It should therefore not be seen as a point of competition, but a basic fundamental of running a reliable service and looking after customers. The smaller market size means that banks in the Nordics have been able to take a particularly forward-looking stance on fraud, pooling their resources to take a collaborative approach to fraud. Although larger market sizes mean that this may be difficult to replicate elsewhere, there may be lessons to be learned from this refusal to compete on security.

Disruptive technology and innovation for innovation's sake may appeal to a small community of early adopters, but for banks, it is about taking on a technology that fits seamlessly into its business model, without causing any unnecessary interruption – either to business operations or user experience. PWC's Retail Banking 2020 report predicts that in four years' time "banks will organise themselves around customers instead of products or channels".[2] Strong, unobtrusive security, which balances rigorous security with minimum interruption, will be critical as they seek to deliver a seamless customer experience and service across all channels.

[2] PwC, "Retail Banking 2020 Evolution or Revolution?", https://www.pwc.com/gx/en/banking-capital-markets/banking-2020/assets/pwc-retail-banking-2020-evolution-or-revolution.pdf.

Ultra-Fast Text Analytics in Trading Strategies

By Markus Schicho
CEO, Econob

and Karin Hodnigg
Product Manager, Econob

Oh, the bitter irony. 28 April 2015 was a dark day for Twitter – one-fifth of its shareholder value was annihilated in a matter of minutes due to a tweet, published

on its own service, "#BREAKING: Twitter $TWTR Q1 Revenue misses estimates, $436M vs $456.52M expected". The tweet contained disappointing results, below what were considered to be humble earnings expectations.

Traders started to sell nearly immediately, volumes rocketed, and prices fell. This resulted in a trading halt, only to be followed by plummeting share prices. Millions of shareholder value was destroyed in minutes, as shown in the following Figure.

This example demonstrates impressively news impact on stock prices, immediately and drastically. And social media can be even more relevant when it comes to the immediacy of the impact.

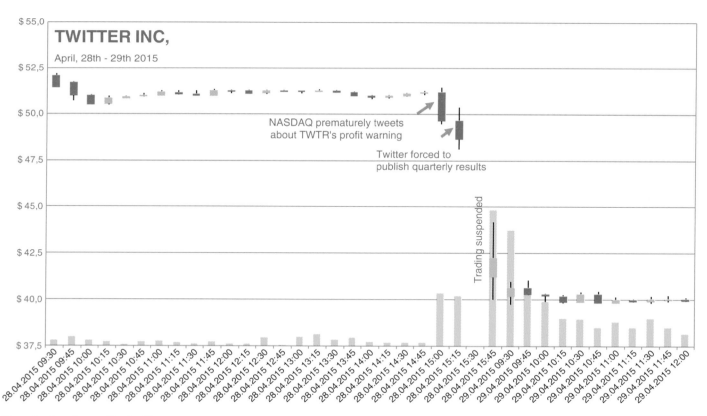

Figure: Twitter stock prices affected by news

Source: econob

Listed companies are required to publish their financial results quarterly. These numbers provide investors and customers alike with an overview of company performance. Business calendars allocate publication dates so that they are known in advance. However, companies are bound to publish any event affecting their share prices at any given time via the RIS (Regulatory Information Service) before the information is published elsewhere.

At first glance, good or bad results, expectations, and stock prices have an obvious correlation, so an impact can be easily explained. However, sometimes the expectations were not that far off, or losses were anticipated, so the price structure cannot always be determined in a straightforward manner. Markets are way more complex than one assumes at first glance, and volatility provides both risk and chances.

News beyond a mere result announcement is far more challenging. Take for example the June 2015 situation in Greece. Struggling and torn between hopes and dark fears, the market situation was very inconsistent with contradictory news and tweets. Greece had been massively talked about in 2015 – fears and hopes had been expressed in headlines, news, reports, and tweets. On Twitter, there were an amazingly high number of tweets regarding Greece, ranging from hundreds to thousands of tweets per minute, often expressing strong opinions. Optimistic and hopeful news and tweets were taking turns with very negative views – all stumbling in by the minute and massively affecting stocks.

Real-time Impact

News is far more general than an announcement that simply includes numbers. It contains analyses and reports, outlooks and what-if scenarios, rather than concrete figures. These contribute massively to a market mood, an overall attitude towards companies, countries, and branches. It is most important to state that not every news story has the potential to turn markets. But such stories do exist and have enormous stored potential. And then, it is a matter of seconds until markets react.

Profit warnings that miss or exceed targets can fiercely and immediately impact stock prices. If such news arrive during trading hours, chaos can ensue: as seen above, one tweet sufficed to annihilate one-fifth of Twitter's shareholder value. However, one should add that weak fundamentals and negative expectations amplified the effect.

Although not true for Twitter, where the negative effects persisted for months, the agitation triggered by news often calms down after only a few minutes. The ripples decrease and the effects are rather short-lived. Most importantly for traders, experience shows that *the major adjustment to the information released (and the window for trading profits) lasts about 40 seconds.*[1] This means traders have less than a minute to read the news, compare the numbers against their expectations, decide whether to buy, and trigger a trading action accordingly (and correctly). And still finish second, or third.

The News Impact Triangle

There are three major players when it comes to news trading. First, renowned news agencies such as Dow Jones, Thomson Reuters, and Bloomberg distribute thousands of news stories per day, thoroughly researched. Then there is the rather new channel of social media, reacting faster, but less well researched, more emotional and emotive, but acting upon thousands of opinions that may or may not reflect the market sentiment. And finally, there are stock exchanges and regulatory services that target market stabilization. This means that the publication of quarterly results is likely to be handled outside of stock trading hours to avoid high volatilities.

Automatic Text Analysis Fundamentals

When extracting information from any given text, many issues arise. Finding words, sentences, numbers, named entities, concepts, and ideas while keeping the context, both semantically and grammatically, are major topics in linguistics. However, these approaches are all far from being feasibly executed in real time. When analysing financial texts, the financial and economic perspective requires a focused analysis that can be executed in milliseconds. Thus, any software that hopes to support traders must enhance the analysis and diminish execution times.

Entity Identification, Wordings, and Indicators

First, the named entities and concepts such as countries, companies, and persons, such as CEOs and political leaders, need to be categorized. Secondly, number identification must be precise; and as different formats and number representations

---

are critical, any automation must be able to handle different alphanumerical formats and translate them into concrete values. In the financial context, only concepts that the trader is interested in need to be found to avoid information overflow. An application that truly supports a trader must thus offer possibilities to select interesting concepts and allow them to configure what they would want to react to. Configuration, selection, and personal interest and experience are essential.

Here, the distinction between wordings and phrases and indicators is crucial. While wordings consist of phrases such as "low demand, decreasing sales, reducing forecast", describing what economic situations or events can occur, financial results and numbers are more delicate. Indicators are always referenced with a number, and often with a time period connected to it. Readers easily distinguish between the numbers 2015 and 2016; software needs to be taught to enhance pure numbers with time or unit information.

Considering the short news text in the Figure which follows, a lot of information is presented in an unstructured manner. Red/dark-grey annotations highlight the company to be found in the text, green/medium-grey annotations show indicators, and light green/light-grey highlighting shows the numbers found in the text. Now comes the most critical step: these different indicators, wordings, time periods, persons, or companies are linked and are interrelated in their context. So we discover that in this example IBM's revenue fell to $22.4 billion in the third quarter. Traders could use this precise information to sell shares if their expectations had not been met, or otherwise buy them.

IBM posts 4 pct drop in quarterly revenue <IBM.N>

Oct 20 (Reuters) - International Business Machines Corp <IBM.N> reported a 4 percent drop in quarterly revenue, hurt by weak sales in its software and services businesses.
    Total revenue fell to $22.4 billion in the third quarter ended Sept. 30 from $23.4 billion a year earlier. [ID:nBwXt86Na]
    The world's largest technology services company's net profit from continuing operations fell to $3.46 billion, or $3.46 per share, from $4.14 billion, or $3.77 per share.

(Reporting by Anya George Tharakan in Bangalore; Editing by Don Sebastian)
((anyageorge.tharakan@thomsonreuters.com; within U.S. +1-646-223-8780; outside U.S. +91 80 6749 7118;; Reuters

Figure: Annotated text
Source: ATRAP

With ATRAP, you can have real-time news trading software that is capable of these textual analyses and has immense potential to configure trades after unstructured text has been analysed. To be precise, a trader configures that they sell their IBM shares if their expectations of $25 billion are not met, and buy shares, if they are. Whenever news arrives, ATRAP checks for the facts and if these conditions are met (either way), it automatically places an order in the market. The following Figure shows an ATRAP screenshot with a successful trade. The analysis performance allows ATRAP to place orders often ahead of others, and before any trading halts may occur.

Wordings are easier to detect – either they are present in a text or not. However, often the impact on stock prices is more difficult to estimate. But with higher risks come higher profit opportunities. On several occasions, ATRAP has demonstrated its capabilities and has been amongst the first trades worldwide after an event occurred.

Events and Investment Decisions

The identification of analyst ratings in texts such as "Credit Suisse raised Daimler from HOLD to BUY" can be performed with an automated analysis. Credit Suisse is the rating agency, Daimler the rated company, and the rating event "raised from hold to buy" indicates a positive development. Using this in the private investment sector where no structural data feeds are available could be interesting.

Since the identification of rating events is possible – how about the identification of more generic events? Political events, business events such as company mergers, resigning CEOs, or even natural disasters – people can learn about all of these. Using this information, traders can be warned immediately, or informed if an event occurred or posed a high risk to their investments.

Sentiments and Opinion Mining

Emotive news, or polarizing social media coverage can have an enormous impact on company or asset perception, both positively and negatively. This emotional perspective, the "guts" of the market mood, is often expressed in analyses, market reports and, increasingly, on social media channels. A news- and Twitter-based evaluation of market moods must reflect the newest tweets, reports, and analyses

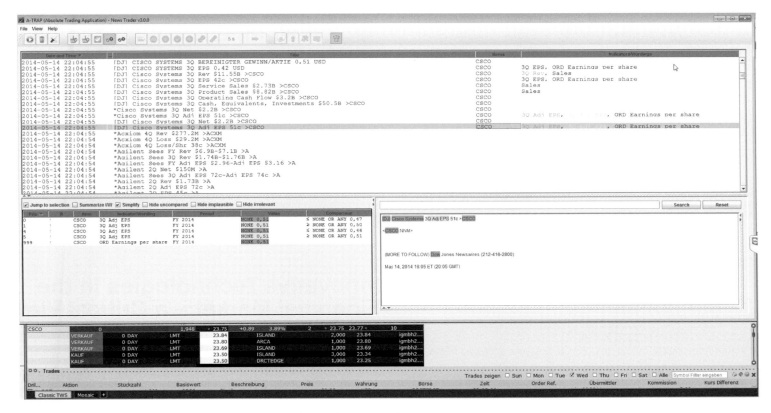

Figure: **ATRAP screenshot – a successful trade after information extraction**

Source: ATRAP

to be of use. Repeated media coverage of a topic is more likely to have an impact than a single news item and the credibility of the author or news source has its part to play too. Automatic assessment of sentiments in text (linguistically-based opinion mining and sentiment analysis) requires both expert financial knowledge and a deep understanding of how different opinions are conveyed on different media platforms – Twitter has a distinct vocabulary, each language and even each domain has diverse patterns and phrases used to express opinions.

The identification of concepts and entities such as analysts, companies, or countries in texts has been discussed before, explaining how concepts can be identified. Linguistic patterns expressing positive or negative sentiment can then be assigned to the identified company. The example in the following Figure

allows two different assessments (growing/stalling outlook) to be assigned to the corresponding stock.

The question for investors shouldn't be why Facebook is growing while Twitter seems to be stalling ; it should be where will Twitter land with the public .		The question for investors shouldn't be why Facebook is growing while Twitter seems to be stalling ; it should be where will Twitter land with the public .	
concept	Facebook	concept	Twitter
orientation	Polarity	orientation	Polarity
value	↑	value	↓

Figure: **Sentiment analysis example**

Source: lingrep.com

The Twitter item is described as "seemingly stalling", while Facebook is presented as "growing" – resulting in a negative assessment for the former and a positive assessment for the latter. The distinctive assignment of each assessment to the correct item is fundamental to econob's linguistic engine and crucial for any further analysis. A set of different opinions regarding one concept can be aggregated, resulting in one single assessment for a company in one piece of text. An analysis of even shorter texts helps gain an overview, especially if there is a lot of information present. See for example the tweets about Greece in the following Figure.

RT @UnisonDave: Greece woes show how the politics of debt failed Europe. Look at how austerity impacts on household debt https://t.co /f2VmN...

2015/06/23 09:07:07 (93ms), Nikos, Melbourne

Greece May Strike Deal Already This Thursday: A ray of hope emerged in what seemed an endless standstill over ... http://t.co/yoJCAsDxlK

2015/06/23 09:06:27 (85ms), iro | forex, http://ircforex.com

Figure: Greece tweet assessment
Source: twiction.lingrep.com

Hope and a positive outlook are rated "good" while austerity, debt, and failure are negatively connoted; they result in a "very bad" evaluation of a tweet. The automatic evaluation of thousands of tweets and news items thus allows an ultra-fast, impartial, and extensive evaluation of market sentiment, one which is up-to-the minute rather than being available one week later. The most important aspect, though, is that these results are transparent, comprehensible, and repeatable.

Applications for Automated Text Analysis

Extracting information from natural and unstructured text, the compilation of events described, and the detection of sentiment or assessment is a fascinating capability that has enormous implications for workflows (no need to read thousands of texts) and manifold applications. Applications for information deduction and identification are

first and foremost making direct use of given information as fast as possible – when trading the news. But this is by no means the only application imaginable. Derived information can be stored in a news information database. Such a huge knowledge base can then connect news items, events, results, and numbers (all enriched with temporal information).

Sentiments do not affect stock prices the way events and ad-hoc news do, since stock markets are more reliant on volumes, and a crowd-based assessment of moods on particular topics, so their application is by nature different. Sentiments can first and foremost serve two purposes in the financial market (apart from a financial application, sentiments are immensely important for journalists, marketers, and public relations officers). First, alerts can be provided if the market mood is changing. Second, sentiments can serve as a filter for emerging hot topics, companies, or branches.

Innovative Technologies in the Financial Market – a Critical View

In Europe, news-based trading is still in its infancy. Traders are rarely confronted with both the possibilities and necessities of news trading; instead trading still remains based on fundamentals or solidly established traditional models. Investors and traders who are aware of the novel possibilities presented by news trading often already use the latest technologies and incorporate them into internal processes. However, financial institutions are sometimes not able to adapt internal processes to incorporate news-based trading, with budgetary questions proven to be a critical and sensitive issue.

The potential of automated text analysis in news trading is immense. Although workflows have to be adapted and thus bear an inherent risk, this is the next challenge that needs to be taken on in financial technologies. Stamina is required on the part of the FinTech companies. Potent industry partners are important and workflows need to be adapted.

But there is no alternative to innovation when one is aiming for success.

Regulated Crowdfunding Ecosystems

By Oscar A. Jofre

Founder & CEO, KoreConX

Regulated crowdfunding is where an online portal is used to sell securities (shares or debt instruments) in a company to a crowd of investors. Securities regulators govern regulated crowdfunding, and they determine the conduct between the issuer (company), investors, and the broker/dealer that is required to operate the regulated crowdfunding portal.

It is important for all the participants in the regulated crowdfunding ecosystem to understand how it all works and their role within that ecosystem. The ecosystem requires infrastructure to be fully integrated and seamless, providing the benefits of compliance and transparency with respect to regulatory requirements. Mutual cooperation between all participants of the ecosystem will help it become effective, efficient, and successful.

The following Figure shows the participants of the ecosystem and some of their responsibilities.

The goal of the ecosystem is to help the issuer and investor come together in the most efficient manner through the regulated crowdfunding portals. Below are more details about each of the participants that need to work together on a global scale.

Securities Commissions are mandated by their respective governments to enforce and administer securities laws and govern the securities industries in their jurisdictions. In the area of regulated crowdfunding, the Commissions regulate which investors and issuers can participate, how portal operators conduct business, and report back to the Securities Commissions. The primary goal is to protect investors and ensure a straightforward, compliant marketplace.

A great example of such a regulation is the Jobs Act Title II, Title III, and Title IV in the United States. The US Securities and Exchange Commission (SEC) clearly outlines all the rules and regulations that relate to crowdfunding in the US. The Jobs

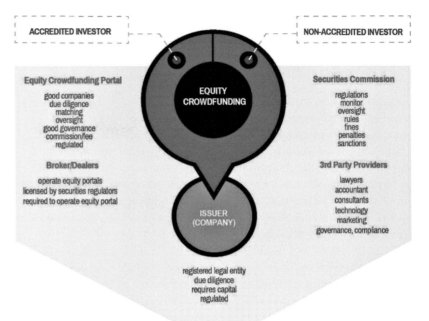

Figure: **Crowdfunding ecosystem participants and responsibilities**
Source: Koreconex

Act provides clarity for issuers (companies), investors, third-party providers, and portals on how to operate, manage, conduct, and report.

By providing this clarity, the USA has flourished with the implementation of the Jobs Act. On 23 September 2013 Title II went live and $118 billion was filed with the SEC for those intending to raise capital up to November 2014. What is even more remarkable is that over $30 billion of what was filed was raised. This clearly demonstrates that the ecosystem is working and only getting better. On 30 October 2015, the SEC voted 3–1 to allow Title III to go live. Under this Title, non-accredited investors can invest a minimum of $2,000 up to a maximum of 10% of their income or assets in companies that are raising up to $1m in funds. This means that there are now a potential 233.7 million new investors in the US, up from 8.5 million, and that companies doing this type of fundraising could have 500 new shareholders to manage.

One of the key reasons why regulated crowdfunding is a global phenomenon is the marketing that the USA, the SEC, and the promoters of the Jobs Act have done to advocate the value to investors, issuers, and governments that are being pressured to create jobs and increase the flow of capital.

Accredited investors are those investors deemed by the Securities Commissions to be high net worth individuals who would not be catastrophically impacted financially if an investment in a company seeking funds through regulated crowdfunding failed. These investors are considered to be sophisticated and able to make appropriate judgements about their investments. Typically, in any country around the world, 3–5% of the population would be considered accredited investors. What is surprising to many in the global marketplace is that only a very small percentage of even accredited investors get the opportunity to see and invest in private placement financings.

John Kaiser, a researcher in private markets in North America, conducted a research report focused on investors in private placements in Canada. Mr Kaiser points out in his report that in the past 10 years in Canada, in the private placements available to the accredited investors, only 1% of those qualified were given the opportunity to invest.

Non-accredited investors are the "rest of us", the rest of the country's population that does not meet the requirements to be registered as an accredited investor, and have been demanding access to early-stage investment opportunities. In most countries this type of investor needs to be of legal age (usually 18 years of age) and will be given restrictions on the amount they can invest in one particular issuer (company). The regulators have done this to protect unsophisticated investors. Regulators may ease these restrictions over time, in order to allow the non-accredited investors to invest more, but the ecosystem will first need to demonstrate the positive progress and impact regulated crowdfunding is making.

Examples of countries that have been very progressive in allowing non-accredited investors to invest in companies through the regulated crowdfunding portals are:

- Canada, providing investors over the age of 18 with the opportunity to invest in private or public listed companies through an exemption called the "offering memorandum". This gives a private issuer access to over 28 million Canadians.

- Other countries such as the UK, the Netherlands, New Zealand, Italy, Thailand, Spain, France, Germany, and others have also created rules over the past 12 months to allow non-accredited investors to invest in private placements.

Now that Title III has been given final approval in the USA, equity crowdfunding is about to become truly democratic. As a lead market, the USA has set the example, and the rest of the equity crowdfunding world is sure to follow.

Regulated crowdfunding portals bring issuers and investors together. It sounds simple, but in order to operate a regulated crowdfunding portal in most countries in the world you need to be a registered broker/dealer. The reason for this requirement is to ensure that issuers are being vetted properly to protect the marketplace and investors. The portal has a regulatory responsibility to perform due diligence on each issuer to make sure it meets all regulatory requirements in the jurisdiction in which the regulated portal is operating. The portal can also choose to add further due diligence steps and demand additional information to further enhance their screening process. The portals are also required (depending on the exemption being used in the private placement) to do investor accreditation, anti-money laundering, and in some cases suitability checks, to make sure the investment is right for the investor. The portals have to be registered with Securities Commissions and it is often necessary to take securities and compliance courses to meet regulatory requirements. There are portals providing investment opportunities for accredited and non-accredited investors. Portals can choose which sector or sectors they would like to operate in. In a very short period of time, the market is showing that investors are attracted to regulated portals operating in specific verticals. Today you can find regulated portals in: mining, oil and gas, real estate, technology, cannabis, restaurants, franchises, life sciences, and mobile apps, among others.

The most successful regulated crowdfunding portals globally have very similar characteristics: they operate fully transparently, and they have dedicated individuals to the growth of this newly emerging sector. The entire global marketplace owes the emergence of regulated crowdfunding to "ASSOB", the world's first regulated crowdfunding portal, operating for 12 years with *zero* fraud, and having helped companies in Australia raise over $150 million. The ASSOB success story has been an example of how regulated crowdfunding works and the benefits it can provide for investors, issuers, and the country.

The most surprising part of regulated crowdfunding has been that the real estate industry sector has been leading the way with the highest level of investments. Real estate has taken the regulated crowdfunding sector by storm with global leaders such as Prodigy Networks, RealtyMogul, and FundRise taking centre stage. This is only the beginning, and other industry sectors, such as mining, oil and gas, biotech, life sciences, and technology, are just starting to emerge. What we see around the globe today is that regulated crowdfunding portals are building trust with online investors. The key to this is the focus on transparency under which the ecosystem operates. Without this transparency, regulated crowdfunding would fail.

Issuers exchange shares or debt instruments, which are considered securities under current regulations, for investors' money. For issuers, regulated crowdfunding is the holy grail of raising capital, as it allows them to be in direct contact with their investors. Crowdfunding brings great exposure to a new crowd, and that can assist with future rounds of financing. Private companies in the United States, Israel, and the United Kingdom have used this regulated crowdfunding model with much success. However, one of the biggest responsibilities issuers have in a regulated crowdfunding ecosystem is the requirement for transparency. They must be open to providing information at each stage of a crowdfunding campaign: pre-transaction, during the transaction, and post-transaction to keep the investors, regulators, and portal operators happy.

Third-party providers are also very important in the ecosystem. Think of them as the chassis in a car. You can have the best engine, fuel, and tyres but without the chassis you go nowhere. Yes, they are that important. They are essential as your first internal crowd to get you started.

In regulated crowdfunding you need your lawyers and accountants, as you would in most financing rounds, to ensure you meet regulatory requirements. You may be required to have audited financial statements and, likely, to have some form of offering document. You need them to make sure that what you are putting out in the market meets regulatory conditions, and to maintain your ongoing legal obligations.

The participants in the background provide technology and services to the entire ecosystem to facilitate the process of pre-during-post regulated crowdfunding transactions. These participants can include pre-crowd service providers, video production companies, investor networks, social media and marketing professionals, and many others.

The regulated crowdfunding ecosystem is possible today because of these four key pillars:

1. Technology
2. Internet
3. Social media
4. Progressive governments.

The nature of these markets and the way business is done can change rapidly and governments are responsible for laying a proper foundation on which businesses and people can grow and conduct their business. The advances in technology and social media allow us to bring a message to billions of people across the globe in seconds. The way we communicate, collaborate, and invest has changed forever.

Regulated crowdfunding uses the four pillars and brings together all the participants to work together cohesively. For anyone, anywhere in the world, involved in regulated crowdfunding, these are very exciting times.

Remittances – International FX Payments at Low Cost

By Michael David Wolper
CMO, GlobeOne

A major paradigm shift is afoot in the financial world. Specifically, we are poised to see explosive growth in the mobile banking space that would not have been possible at any prior time in history. Currently, there are 2 billion underserved adults when it comes to traditional financial services. Couple that with the 1.93 billion readily connected smartphone consumers, and it becomes clear: the move toward mobile banking is all but inevitable. Real-life events show how mobile banking growth has the potential to positively impact countless lives.

Consider a remote, underserved village in Mexico, where every month a designated townsman is tasked with driving several hours to the nearest money transfer office, to retrieve funds wired by relatives in the States. After haemorrhaging money on fuel, transaction fees, and other expenses, our ambassador returns home holding a fraction of the amount originally sent. Now consider the same transaction done over a smartphone app, without having to travel, at a cost significantly less than that associated with traditional bricks-and-mortar banks. Not only is this methodology eminently possible, it is all but inevitable! Indeed, this evolved way of doing things could very well become "the new normal". You need simply view the technological landscape through a younger generational lens to appreciate it for the reality it is en route to becoming.

"Digital Natives" and "Digital Immigrants"

In the march towards the use of advanced technology, there is clearly no turning back. But for millennials and younger-aged consumers, the writing has *always* been on the wall. Simply put: the use of internet technology and electronic gadgetry is all they have ever known. In a 2001 essay, writer Marc Prensky coined the terms "digital natives" and "digital immigrants" to describe generational differences in digital usage. Essentially defined, digital immigrants' lives have straddled both the pre-digital and digital eras, whereas digital natives have only ever known the latter.

And there is no question which group will have a greater economic influence on banking – and all other sectors, for that matter – as they grow to occupy a larger percentage of the consumer base.

The "natives" versus "immigrants" distinction is mostly about perspective. An immigrant using a retail banking website to pay a bill is apt to consciously notice: "I'm paying bills online instead of visiting a branch", whilst natives do not have that consciousness. For them, branches never factored into their lives. Due to this phenomenon, retail banks must retrofit their ways of doing business, by stepping up their migration from physical platforms to electronic solutions. Failure to do so could result in their outright extinction. To be fair, banks largely know this, and are slowly but surely embracing electronic distribution formats. But they are making electronic delivery systems add-on components, when they should be making them their chief focus, *second* to their bricks-and-mortar operations. This is a case of the proverbial tail wagging the dog.

One way to remedy this is by giving customers the option to bank over mobile phone applications, which should be as fundamental to retail banking models as ATMs were in the 1970s, call centres were in the 1980s, and internet channels were in the 1990s and the early 2000s. It is up to each banking establishment to fully honour the changes to come – and likely profit by doing so.

The Power of Remittances

The potential social aspect of mobile phone app transactions can be astounding, especially when it comes to global remittances. Defined as the "transfer of money by a foreign worker to an individual in his or her home country", remittances currently amount to more than $583 billion annually. As of 2013, in the US alone, more than 41 million people could be identified as international migrants. Furthermore, according to the World Bank, in 2012, Mexico received $23 billion in remittances from the US – about 50% of the total outflow, followed by China ($13 billion), India ($11.9 billion), and the Philippines ($10.6 billion).[1] What is to be gleaned from this phenomenon? Apparently, the desire to give back is a universal impulse.

---

[1] Andy Kiersz, "Here's Where Migrant Workers In America Send Their Money", *The Business Insider*, 8 April 2014, http://www.businessinsider.com.au/world-bank-us-remittance-map-2014-4.

Economist Dilip Ratha describes the promise of remittances as "dollars wrapped with love", as the money sent offers untold potential for economic development and social change. "Remittances empower people," says Ratha. "We must do all we can to make remittances safer and cheaper. It can be done and I want to help people break free from the cycle of poverty."

But while the majority of funds sent home go towards helping family members with regular monthly bills, philanthropic motivations have recently come to occupy a larger role in the remittance space. We are witnessing a pivot, where it is no longer just the migrant labour force sending money to their families for sustenance. Expats are now sending philanthropic remittances as a way of helping their native countries in times of need. The 2015 Nepalese earthquake killed more than 9,000 people and injured more than 23,000. It flattened entire villages, leaving hundreds of thousands of people homeless. After the tragedy struck, large sums of money flowed to the country from the Nepalese diaspora. Compassionate people yearned to help their fellow countrymen with the rescue and rebuilding efforts – a collective act of good will that truly made a difference. After all, Nepal is one of Asia's poorest countries, with little ability to fund major reconstruction efforts on its own.

A bit further back in time, the 2004 Indonesian tsunami killed at least 230,000 people across 14 countries, including India, Sri Lanka, Thailand, the Maldives, and Somalia. Combined, the Nepalese quake and the Indonesian tsunami inspired some US$14 billion in remittance aid, funnelled through worldwide relief organizations. Philanthropic remittances are a very good thing. They contribute to a country's overall inflow of capital, ultimately serving to lower that country's borrowing costs in times of distress.

But sending money can be costly. Whether the recipient is an individual, a family, or a relief organization, the senders are saddled with the same hefty transaction fees, which can cost an average of 7.72% of the total amount sent.[2] And these costs can quickly add up. In 2014, fees from the $485 billion in remittances sent worldwide exceeded the total funds Mexico received in remittances overall.[3]

---

[2] Source: The World Bank, https://remittanceprices.worldbank.org/en.

[3] The World Bank, "Remittances to Developing Countries to Grow by 5 Percent This Year, While Conflict-Related Forced Migration is at All-Time High, Says WB Report", 6 October 2014, http://www.worldbank.org/en/news/press-release/2014/10/06/remittances-developing-countries-five-percent-conflict-related-migration-all-time-high-wb-report.

Putting the transfer fee burden in even sharper context, according to an Overseas Development Institute remittance report released in 2014, two of the world's largest money transfer operators – Western Union and MoneyGram – account for two-thirds of the money transfers to Africa, where an average of 12% of the amount sent back to relatives in sub-Saharan Africa is lost to transfer fees. This is enough to pay for the primary school education for 14 million children in the region!

Technology offers the promise of reduced fees, placing more funds into the hands of the remitters' intended targets. With streamlined transactions like GoMoney slashing up to 5% from the 7.9% global average transfer fees typical with traditional banking structures, mobile banking services can direct some $34 billion back into the pockets of those people who need it the most. It is a new way for banks to give back to the community, and a humanitarian outreach made possible by smartphone technology.

Millennial Outreach

Companies boasting charitable components are likely to resonate particularly loudly with millennials, who champion a robust urge to give back. Smart businesses are taking notice.

Take online glasses retailer, Warby Parker. Riffing on the old adage "Give a man a fish and you feed him for a day; teach a man to fish and you feed him for a lifetime", for every pair of glasses Warby Parker sells, the company sends cash to a non-profit partner that helps teach local entrepreneurs in low-income countries to start their own glasses business. In essence, Warby Parker earns profits, while simultaneously helping poor communities to help themselves. It is a win-win scenario.

The Future of Banking

In any discussion about banking, the question invariably arises: "Will cash use ever become obsolete?" This is an important question to ask, but a nearly impossible one to answer since there are conflicting views on this topic.

On the one hand, people have been predicting the demise of cash for years, spurred on by the buzz around Apple Pay and crypto-currencies. But as recently as

2013, cash was still used for about 85% of global consumer transactions, according to a MasterCard report.[4] In most developing countries, it remains the default mode of payment for the vast majority of consumers – even in places like Kenya, where mobile payment tools have experienced a runaway success.

It is easy to see why many analysts maintain the belief that cash is here to stay. But there are equally persuasive reasons to believe it will go, especially when governments seem to be eager to jettison cash. A case in point: the US is making federal payments like Social Security and veterans' benefits exclusively by electronic means. And India's government has issued biometric IDs to its citizens, laying the groundwork for a cashless society and opening the door to financial inclusion. Adding to that, mobile access has spread around the world, as both feature phones and smartphones are making their way into the hands of consumers everywhere.

Young people are likely to outgrow cash. The practical timetable for this to happen is a judgment call. But a mobile phone banking app that will allow people to seamlessly conduct banking business in both cash-based or a cashless environment is likely to truly capture market share, and make banking easier.

John Lennon famously asked us to "imagine all the people, sharing all the world". Could he have ever predicted just how globally connected the world would one day become, due to advances in FinTech?

---

[4] MasterCard, "MasterCard Advisors' Cashless Journey. The Global Journey From Cash to Cashless", 15 September 2013, http://www.mastercardadvisors.com/_assets/pdf/Master CardAdvisors-CashlessSociety.pdf.

FinTech Solutions for Small Businesses

By Luke Hally

CEO & Founder, DragonBill

Who would have thought that the combination of finance and technology could result in something exciting? It may have seemed unlikely, but FinTech has emerged as the hottest sector on the planet. No doubt, this is due to its heart being centred in London, the start-up and finance capital of Europe. But it is also a global phenomenon. In the US, New York City has retained its position at the top of the finance industry. It is keeping tech talent away from the west coast with a thriving FinTech community and collaboration between established players and emerging start-ups. In Africa FinTech is helping the unbanked perform transactions in a secure and convenient manner. South East Asia also has a number of emerging FinTech hubs. Hong Kong and Singapore are building on their existing trade and service economies, creating FinTech hubs such as the FinTech Innovation Lab in Hong Kong run by Accenture and partnering with banks from around the globe. Startupbootcamp FinTech was launched in Singapore. In Australia, a number of co-working spaces and incubators have appeared.

The traditional financial players get a lot of press time in FinTech-related news: Goldman Sachs in New York, Barclays in London, and Accenture in Hong Kong, while banks in China are quietly snapping up as much FinTech talent as they can. We are hearing about great improvements in efficiency and usability in existing systems. Any improvement is good, but are all these revolutionary? Are they disruptive? I see entrenched market leaders leveraging regulation to keep competition out. Performing counter-disruption manoeuvres, disrupting the disruption before it begins.

In New York, we may be seeing the emergence of a new trend of outsourcing disruption, or in modern parlance, "Disruption as a Service". Acqui-hire used to be seen as the lowest rung of the exit ladder for start-ups. Now we are seeing start-ups set this as their goal, turning would-be entrepreneurs into employees. The banks are successfully using the FinTech boom as a recruiting platform. Isn't a revolution supposed to be replacing existing systems with better ones? This brings us to the question: what is disruption? Is disruption something we should be aspiring to? Clayton M. Christensen, the creator of the *theory of disruptive innovation* said:

"Disruptive technologies typically enable new markets to emerge."[1] Disruption is not merely the unseating of the market leader – that is successful competition. It means changing the rules of the game, which enables a new player to beat the record holder.

The record holders in finance have been playing for a long time and have amassed enormous wealth and power. So much power that governments have become dependent on their continued operation – as we saw with $1 trillion bailouts in the US during the global financial crisis. This large centralization of wealth, power, and regulation makes competition difficult and leads to a lack of it. We all know who the losers are when there is a lack of competition – consumers. Consumers lose either through price or lack of access.

Power in the market means the control of supply and distribution of goods or services. If you have power, you can dictate price and access. Disruption is the decentralization of this power, and once supply is democratized, so too is demand because consumers now have a choice. In the case of FinTech it will coincide with a spread of wealth. As more players enter the market, wealth will flow from the banks to these alternative players. As consumers get a better deal due to competition and more efficient solutions (banks have large legacy systems they must support), more wealth stays in their pockets, making everyone a little better off. Disruption is the free market in action, slowly being freed from the shackles of existing legacies by technology.

Small and medium-sized enterprises (SMEs) are the key beneficiaries of disruptive start-ups. Their talent pools are shallower and their needs less complex than large enterprises, so they rely on outsourcing expertise. They are willing to try new tools that will have a tangible impact on their business. This also suits small agile start-up teams. SMEs function as the engines of many economies, globally responsible for 80% of economic activity. And they are now beginning to benefit from the FinTech revolution. In Australia, SMEs are a critical part of the economy, making up 97% of business and employing 47% of the workforce. Melbourne – in the Australian south-eastern state of Victoria – is the traditional centre of finance and a city of diverse cultures. The government is supporting entrepreneurs through a number of initiatives. The AU$60 million Start-up Victoria initiative was launched to develop high-growth innovative businesses, including FinTech, as well as the AU$200 million Future Industries Fund, which has a focus on professional and financial services.

---

[1] Clayton Christensen, The Innovator's Dilemma: When New Technologies Cause Great Firms to Fail (Harvard Business Review Press, 1997).

The government will draw on a $500 million Premier's Jobs and Investment Fund to support high-priority initiatives. With these factors and support it is no surprise Melbourne is the home of a wide range of FinTech start-ups servicing SMEs.

Good financial advice can make or break an SME. A qualified adviser can fill gaps in knowledge. Importantly, they can also identify opportunities, reducing risk and increasing efficiency. FinancialAsk, for instance, makes financial advice easy to get by offering it through apps and the web, making quality advice accessible. With the right advice, businesses are equipped to make decisions, but they need tools to track the implementation. Cash flow is a concern for many SMEs. Boomeringo is a budgeting and a cash flow management tool, originally aimed at consumers and income earners. After launching their app, they discovered that a significant portion of their users were SMEs. The app connects with banks, credit cards, and loan accounts and, using algorithms, sorts spending and cash flow into categories as well as merchants. It not only helps with budgeting, but also with bill payment reminders. The powerful analytics platform increases users' financial intelligence through experience.

In addition, even if an SME has good cash flow, they may still need loans for capital or expansion. Moula is a data-driven alternative lending platform for Australian SMEs, providing quick and simple funding based on an SME's transaction data and corporate profile. Its online application process has been designed to be fast, making it easy for a business to access funding without the process and paperwork of traditional banking. Like many start-ups, Moula was born out of personal experience, in this case, the challenges of obtaining finance for a family business.

Of course, all the tools in the world are not going to help a business unless they are getting paid. Civilizations have been using money as a transactional device since around 600 bc. Payment for goods and services in a face-to-face transaction is straightforward. You make your payment and receive your goods. Receiving payment where the customer is remote is a problem as old as business itself. Customers are hesitant to pay before receiving goods or services and businesses are hesitant to provide them before they receive payment.

After being foreseen in Edward Bellamy's 1888 book, *Looking Backward*, we saw the first multi-merchant card, the Diners Club Card, in 1950, and in 1982 electronic funds transfer at point of sale (EFTPOS) was introduced. The introduction of credit cards and EFTPOS saw a consolidation of institutional power. Banks were no longer just for business accounts and places for loans and savings. They became the central facilitator of transactions. While this may be seen as disruptive to cash, it

does not satisfy our earlier definition. If your business does not accept electronic payment, it will lose business. We have seen examples of this in Australia. Several of the "Big Four" banks had system crashes, meaning businesses could not accept card payments. The media reported customers leaving stores without purchasing because of this. This is every business's nightmare.

This throws into sharp relief the need for competition and the need for disruption of payments. After some false starts in the 1990s with NetBank and DigiCash, in 1999 the original disruptor PayPal was born, now being followed by numerous others. As business and technology have evolved, we have seen the nature of payments change to suit the context of the transaction. In some instances, we are seeing the blurring of the online and offline worlds. Think of paying for an Uber trip, no swiping, no PIN codes, just get out of the car. As these platforms have built trust, and as online shopping grows in popularity, we have witnessed the emergence of payment escrow, where payment is held until the goods are received. This obviously benefits the customer because they know they will maintain control over the payment until they receive the goods. It also benefits SMEs. If the business is not well known, they have no reputation and no reason to expect trust from the customer. The customer is taking a risk that the business will deliver on the agreement once payment is made, especially from overseas. If the business accepts escrow options from a well-known platform, they in effect leverage the trust and reputation of that platform. It is interesting and representative of online trading that escrow has become widely accepted online, before entering traditional offline business transactions, when offline business and customers both have much to gain from such a system.

User context is something that is particularly important for SME tools. The lack of a defined process across businesses means it needs to be low-friction and streamlined to fit into existing processes with low workload and a shallow learning curve. Processes have to be specialized, so the SME can do what they need to do and get back to business – they should not be navigating around features they do not need or use. SMEs are typically run by few people wearing many hats, so the hats need to be as light as possible. The user context of the SME and customer should be encapsulated in a good FinTech payment solution, providing payment options that suit the business, customer, and transaction alike. FinTech is giving SMEs the tools they need to have flexibility of payment so they can get paid and get back to work. These benefits will then flow on to consumers, through a smoother, less stressful transaction, where a better customer experience will emerge. These benefits contribute to a stronger economy and happier population. Viva la revolucion!

Payment Solutions Including Apple Pay

By Denis Thomas
Management Consultant, KPMG

"Are P2P Payments next for Apple Pay?"

"Roger Federer slams Wimbledon all-white dresscode."

"Pluto shows its spots to NASA probe."

These are some of the headlines captured from some of the well-established newspapers. Time is a key factor with regards to news. The platform that publishes the news first receives the most traction and eventually the most TRP (Television Rating Point/Target Rating Point) ratings. At this juncture, the network effects work in its favour and all this builds credibility for the news channel and eventually the news network. This chain reaction raises a few questions in my mind:

• Timing is critical to news but is it to entrepreneurs? Would timing play the same role for serial entrepreneurs?

• Is there really a first-mover advantage or does it differ on a sectoral basis?

• Does timing affect tech giants?

We have often heard budding entrepreneurs complain: "That was exactly *my* idea, and that firm just received $5 million in funding which should have ideally been mine!"

In my view, in today's dynamically evolving world of payments, timing matters and Apple has done a phenomenal job with regards to timing the Apple Pay product launch at the crux of the FinTech and Payments tsunami wave sweeping across the universe. Kudos, Apple! However, the main success of Apple Pay is dependent on its widespread adoption; a world devoid of credit cards and cash. Is that sci-fi or reality?

The Payments Ecosystem

Apple, Google, or Starbucks? Did you say Starbucks?

Apple is a limelight baby and receives all the media attention. Google closely follows Apple but the silent player in the payments space is Starbucks, which should definitely get a mention. Starbucks has combined the ease of payments for ordering a Frappuccino via their mobile app and provided additional value to customers by providing a single source for keeping track of all reward programmes in one space. This move has seen a huge adoption amongst consumers that prefer using the mobile app to order to skip the long lines typical of Starbucks outlets in New York and other university joints that witness huge traffic during certain hours of the day. This is in line with CEO Howard Schultz's ambition of making mobile payments a top priority as Starbucks is the only company that claims 90% of the $1.6 billion spent in US stores was made using a smartphone in 2013.[1]

The following Figure shows a sample ecosystem.

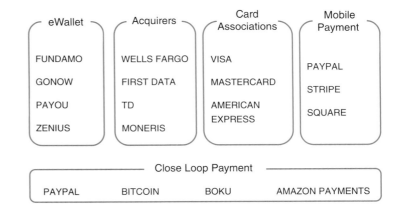

Figure: A sample payment ecosystem

Categorically speaking, there are several players in the payments space, classified across e-wallets (Google Wallet, Visa Checkout, Apple Pay, Swap), bank credit cards (Wells Fargo, HSBC, Chase), business credit cards (Best Buy,

---

[1] See http://www.starbucks.co.uk/coffeehouse/mobile-apps and https://news.starbucks.com/facts/starbucks-mobile-order-pay-national-rollout.

Target), e-wallet platforms (hyperWallet, Fundamo, GoNow, Payou, Zenius), card associations (Visa, MasterCard, American Express), acquirers (Wells Fargo, FirstData, TD, Moneris), processors (Chase, GlobalPayments, FirstData), third-party processors (Stripe, PayPal, Square), ISOs (Everlink, Pivotal Payments), point-of-sale terminal technology (Ingenico Group, Verifone, Magtek), integrated systems (Micros, Vivonet, Profitek), in-store terminal payment providers (Chase, Payfirma, GlobalPayments), e-commerce payment providers (Stripe, Payfirma, Apple Pay, PayPal), recurring billing payment providers (Stripe, PayPal, Payfirma), mobile payment providers (Square, Venmo, Intuit), and tablet POS providers (Vend, NCR, Square, Payfirma).

Another layer, denoted as the close loop payment networks (Amazon Payments, Bitcoin, PayPal, Boku, Sometrics, Dwolla) would operate across the entire payment ecosystem layer between consumers and merchants.

The examples cited above cater towards the American market but provide a good overview of the players across categories and can be easily used for comparisons across countries.

In 2015, Google Wallet announced its plans to launch the P2P network and Apple quickly followed suit. The evolution of such technologies will give rise to newer authentication norms at the device level and position Google/Apple as an evolutionary payment bank. Apple has always drifted away from the complexity of financial transaction processing but the benefits of building one in-house are not a far-fetched idea. We could ask Starbucks who recently did that and enjoy over a million transactions as part of their own payment network.

So, would Apple transform into a payment bank? Perhaps, if the benefits add up. However, as Starbucks has proved, Google and Apple need to provide something extra so that people begin adopting their technologies. For consumers, it is no longer about payments but about the extra added value.

Energizer Effects

Apple will continue to innovate on the FinTech platform but Apple Pay displays Apple's vertical integration efficiency through seamless blending of hardware, software, and user-friendly interfaces into a harmonious ecosystem. The above

attributes are specific to Apple Pay and this will definitely energize the iOS ecosystem.

Privacy

Apple does a phenomenal job on privacy concerns by not storing the following:

- What you bought
- Where you bought it
- How much you paid for it.

Apple also refrains from exchanging any credit card information with merchants during transactions, which further boosts its security mechanism.

Merchant Adoption

Apple Pay is a new but comprehensive payment solution as 83% of financial institutions across America have already adopted it. An average of 22,000 stores have already signed up to adopt Apple Pay. Some of the names include Starbucks, Whole Foods, Bloomingdales, Disney, etc. Service providers like Uber and Groupon have also climbed aboard.

The above network numbers and the potential to add several more over the next year pack plenty of adoption potential for this technology amongst bigger merchants, but would similar tactics attract smaller merchants?

Consumer Adoption

Merchants are adopting Apple Pay and Apple recently published that over 700,000 merchants are on board that have set up operations to accept Apple Pay as a form of payment. But how many of you out there walk into a store with just a phone and no card and no cash? I don't know any of my friends who do that in developed economies.

Let us change gears a bit and look at the following Figure. What do you see?

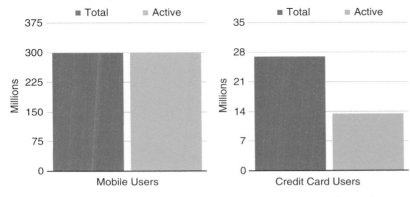

Figure: Penetration of mobile users vs. credit card users in India

Source: Secondary Technology Research Providers

The graphs show the penetration of mobile users vs. credit card users and the percentage of active users in each segment in India. The interesting part to observe is that the penetration of mobile devices and adoption is along similar lines for most emerging economies. This means that technologies that drive usage of payments via a mobile device would prove to be more successful in emerging economies. But, in order to arrive at the ultimate goal of transferring to a world with no cash or credit cards, we also need to shift focus from customer benefits to merchant benefits, as smaller merchants are not jumping on board due to the transaction fees involved. As long as smaller merchants do not adopt Apple Pay, the common people are always going to carry an alternative mode of payment. Apple needs to provide incentives for smaller merchants to enable the widespread adoption of Apple Pay. If I am using Apple Pay, I would like to use it at my grocery store, my service station, my laundromat, and also the street food stall across the corner that serves hot dogs and burgers. The list of usage scenarios is endless but you get my point.

Potential for Data Analytics

Apple is not storing transaction information and one might contend that the potential for big data usage is almost missing in this scenario. Apple alluded to the above through its Cupertino event as data being used for a bigger purpose, which could hint at advertising or other revenue streams. However, Apple could use big data

through technologies like iBeacon to provide live feeds or additional spot discounts on products within one's vicinity while shopping in a physical store. This approach to analysing big data as it flows in would avoid transactional data storage and spur the development of several applications around this domain. Apple Pay and Apple Watch users would eventually benefit from all these network externalities.

Industry Economics

Gartner (a technology research firm) states that the payment market is expected to generate a total of $721 billion in global transactions by 2017. This depicts a 35% CAGR (Compound Annual Growth Rate) from 2012. Mobile payments are expected to constitute 45% ($325 billion) of these transactions. The NFC (Near Field Communication) segment is expected to be 5% ($36 billion) by 2017 but is growing at 64% CAGR. Overall, this looks extremely lucrative.

Summary

- Apple Pay re-energizes the iOS ecosystem and provides a new stream of revenue for Apple.

- The existing user base of 800 million, plus iTunes' accounts that already contain credit card information would contribute hugely to its success.

- Apple Pay has hit privacy concerns smack on their head.

- Payment industry economics and resulting network externalities may or may not work in Apple's favour.

- Regulatory bodies will pay a huge role in the adoption of Apple Pay like similar technologies in emerging economies.

Apple Pay emerges to be by far the most innovative disruptor in the FinTech space. Its simplicity of use, current iTunes' user base, privacy policies, security features, and comprehensive financial networks that have already been constructed promise a bright future for Apple and several start-ups that would eventually evolve around this domain.

FinTech Solutions Benefiting other Sectors

By Rael Cline

Co-Founder & CEO, MediaGamma

The idea of a contract for the future delivery of an asset of a specified volume is not new, actually it finds its origins thousands of years ago in Mesopotamia, Egypt, and the Roman world. The obvious use case is risk management for both sides of the contract: guaranteed future revenue for the seller and guaranteed future supply at a known price for the buyer.

Fast-forward in time, the oft-cited Dutch Tulip Bulb Mania of 1637 allowed speculation on future prices via forward contracts, and the first "futures" contract is generally accepted to be the Yodoya rice market in Osaka, Japan around 1650. In modern times, deregulation resulting in increased price volatility, coupled with the newly available computing power from the 1970s, proved to be the catalyst for an explosion in the right to buy or sell at a future date contracts ("options") and standardized forward contracts, known as futures contracts. Today, the global derivatives market has grown to an astounding US$700 trillion in notional value, across 30 currencies, and is widely used as a risk management tool by companies, investment managers, governments, insurers, energy and commodities firms, and banks alike. Whilst most people think of interest rates, currency, equity, or credit derivatives (or even the more exotic weather and electricity derivatives), this chapter will focus on two other burgeoning opportunities for FinTech companies interested in derivatives: the cloud infrastructure market and the online advertising markets.

Within the current FinTech mind-set, both of these markets present fantastic opportunities, as they both rely heavily on technology, prices are volatile, the underlying assets are (largely) commoditized, and there has been limited skills and knowledge crossover between finance and cloud or online advertising.

Of course, fields such as payments, crypto-currencies, and crowdfunding will be enormously valuable, but the best opportunities lie at the intersection of industries. Nowhere is this more apparent than in combining derivatives with cloud infrastructure and online advertising. The cloud infrastructure market (also referred to as the "Infrastructure as a Service" or "IaaS" market) is the computing infrastructure (computing power, memory, and storage) that is used to power internet applications. Data is stored and processed off-site and made available on demand from a remote location. The market is worth roughly $16.5 billion, projected to grow at 43% annually for the next five years according to reports.[1] Amazon pioneered this market in 2006 in terms of offering cloud-based services to other companies, after solving their own infrastructure scaling problems. Large companies such as Netflix, Dow Jones, Pfizer, and Comcast all use Amazon Web Services ("AWS") today. Although behemoths such as Microsoft, Salesforce, IBM, Rackspace, and Google are investing billions into the market, Amazon is still leagues ahead, by some accounts four times larger than all its rivals combined.[2] The interesting feature of cloud services is that they are on-demand. So, for instance, if there is a sudden increase in the demand for a service, one is able to click a few buttons and fire up some additional infrastructure to meet this demand. AWS introduced this spot market in 2010; however, the volatility in spot pricing creates a large amount of uncertainty for companies that buy in the spot market.

An important step took place in 2013 when Deutsche Börse announced its Cloud Exchange AG, a joint venture with Berlin-based Zimory, which enables participants to trade spot capacity. Although none of the vendors mentioned in the above paragraph is included in the exchange, there are still five vendors to choose from. The exchange offers standardized products and procedures for admission, trading, settlement, and surveillance, and one is able to switch between vendors within the same contract. To get a sense of the contract specifications, storage capacity is traded in data units of at least 1TB, and processing capacity is denominated in at least 10 Performance Units (PU), with one PU representing 8 GBs.

Interestingly, when thinking about derivatives, the industry already has the idea of a "reserved instance" or a forward contract that one can re-sell. Currently, however, one can only re-sell back to the same vendor and so the market lacks true price discovery. However, given that there are clear use cases around why a buyer would want to hedge future costs for, say Christmas (just think of Netflix's demands to stream on Christmas Day), it is surely just a matter of time before futures and

---

[1] TechNavio Report titled: Global IaaS Market 2015–2019, http://www.gartner.com/newsroom/id/3055225.

[2] Business Insider, http://www.businessinsider.sg/aws-revenue-is-bigger-than-its-four-closest-competitors-combined-2015-4/.

options are introduced. Andy Jassy, SVP of AWS said that "AWS has the potential to be the largest business at Amazon long-term, which is significant given that our retail business is a $70 billion business". This bullishness may not seem so far-fetched, given that this infrastructure will power large parts of the Internet of Things (IoT) market, a market that is estimated to reach $7.1 trillion by 2020.[3]

Another large, exponentially growing and volatile market where derivatives could be useful is the online advertising space. Not many people know this, but large parts of display advertising slots are bought and sold in real-time auctions using computer algorithms in fractions of a second. The technology is called "programmatic advertising" and the spot market is referred to as "real-time bidding". Display advertising includes the banner ads that are ubiquitous across the web, mobile, video, and social media. Buyers such as brands or media agencies input certain targeting rules for an ad campaign (travel websites or males in New York for instance) and when a user arrives at a webpage, an auction takes place to show the user a particular ad. Data such as browsing history and customer relationship management (CRM) is overlaid and releases information as to how much a buyer is willing to pay. Once the winner of the auction is chosen, the winner shows the ad to the user. This means that two users visiting the same webpage simultaneously can view two different ads, and the buyers may have paid vastly different prices to show those ads. Remember, this all takes place in about 200 milliseconds. So the infrastructure here is not unlike the high-frequency trading infrastructure in financial markets.

Globally, this is estimated to be a $53 billion primary market by 2018[4] and although one may think that digital advertising budgets are still relatively small compared to TV budgets, the UK is the first country in the world where over half of all ad spend is on digital.[5] There is little doubt that this will be replicated throughout the world. Once IPTV gains traction in the future, this will add a further $79 billion to the market size by 2020.[6]

Our measurements, however, show that this spot market is actually 12.5 times more volatile than the S&P 500 Index. This means that a buyer of ad space (a brand or ad agency for instance), is never sure whether, firstly, they would win an auction to show an ad, and, secondly, how much they would pay for the ad. This makes planning media budgets for future campaigns extremely difficult and hurts cash flow planning too. From the point of view of a seller, such as a website or a mobile app that hosts the ads, this affects revenue.

Use cases from a website's point of view would be to combine the futures and spot markets into a better yield management system. Using both futures and spot prices, they could create algorithms that allocate ad slots between the futures and spot markets in order to maximize revenue. This could be similar to how airlines manage their ticketing yields as they both share the characteristic of non-storable inventory (ad slots shown at a particular time and seats for a particular flight).

From a hedging viewpoint, index-based exchange traded funds could prove to be useful hedging tools. A seasonal website such as a travel website could hedge against future unfavourable price movements by taking a short position in a correlated index. Similarly, a buyer could hedge against potential price increases by maintaining a long position in a relevant index. Furthermore, for buyers, having a forward curve of prices could help the media planning function and aid future costs per acquisition (i.e. how many ads do I need to show to achieve *n* number of people purchasing my product or signing up to my newsletter?).

Even option contracts would be extremely useful: often when pitching to a potential brand for new business, an agency would love to say that it has secured certain ad slots in the pitch. In an options case, all the agency would need to pay is the upfront premium and exercise it, only if they win the pitch. From a seller's point of view, option premiums would be another source of revenue.

Of course, there already exists a forward market in media buying. In fact, the forward market in media buying has existed for decades, long before the spot market came of age a few years ago. A large buyer (brand or agency) would sit down with a large print publisher or TV network and agree a deal for the forthcoming year. This "upfront" market continues to exist today in deals where personal relationships are important or where the product is customized. So

[3] IDC forecast, http://www.forbes.com/sites/gilpress/2014/08/22/internet-of-things-by-the-numbers-market-estimates-and-forecasts/.

[4] Global Media Suppliers Advertising Revenue Forecast, September 2014, MAGNA GLOBAL.

[5] eMarketer report, http://www.theguardian.com/media/2015/mar/27/half-ad-spend-digital-media.

[6] Transparency Market Research report, http://www.digitaltveurope.net/318352/global-iptv-market-to-reach-us79-billion-in-2020/.

this over-the-counter forward market will always have a place in media buying, but the majority of ad slots are conducive to being traded in an exchange environment.

The potential gross notional size of a derivative market in either the cloud IaaS or programmatic media markets is difficult to estimate, but there are clear use cases for participants in both these markets. In both the cloud IaaS and programmatic media markets, the technology foundations for an exchange-based derivative market are well underway. Moreover, both already have functioning forward markets. With the standardization of contracts beginning to take place, there can be no doubt that a very large opportunity exists for FinTech companies to make their mark in these markets.

FinTech Innovation for Wearables

By Dominika E. Bajer
Director, DEB Marcomms

The growth of the wearable industry sector has been years in the making. In 2013, a Fortune magazine headline read "Bloomberg report estimates that Apple could see revenues of up to $3.6B with a successful smart watch".[1] A year later *Forbes* was predicting that the "smartwatch industry will grow in 2014 to $2.5B globally. In the years to follow, the smartwatch industry will keep growing at a 3-digit rate."[2]

In September 2014 CB Insights noted that "over the last 5 years, the wearables space has seen more than $1.4B of investment into emerging, private wearable start-ups", concluding in their analysis summary that "it is conceivable that 2014 might be the first year to see more than $1B of investment flowing into wearables".[3] In November 2014, a group of Morgan Stanley analysts wrote in a note: "Wearable devices will far surpass market expectations, and become the fastest ramping consumer technology device to date, in our view."

And then in 2015 the NFC wearable boom exploded. Near Field Communication (NFC) is a short-range wireless connectivity standard that uses magnetic field induction to enable communication between devices when they're touched together, or brought within a few centimetres of each other. With Apple's Smartwatch rolling out into international markets, technology giants such as Google, Sony, Microsoft, and LG putting their stamp on the wearables market, and lifestyle/ fitness bands manufacturers such Jawbone, FitBit, and Misfit offering a more and more compelling product range, the wearables boom is certainly on. From week to week, wearables hold increasing media headlines for business and technology. From global companies to disruptive start-ups – everyone seems to be competing for their share of the big wearables pie.

What is All the Fuss About?

Wearable, adjective, Oxford dictionary definition: "Denoting or relating to a computer or other electronic device that is small or light enough to be worn or carried on one's body: a wearable computer could monitor your heart rate and other bodily functions."[4]

Alternatively, it can be described as: wearable technology, wearables, fashionable technology, wearable devices, or fashion electronics. They are clothing and accessories incorporating computer and advanced electronic technologies. The designs often incorporate practical functions and features, but may also have a purely critical or aesthetic purpose.

Lifestyle bands. Smartwatches. Wearable goggles. Fitness trackers. Body wear cameras. Wearable orthopaedic casts. Health monitors. Virtual reality headsets. Data storage NFC rings. Festival "dog tags". Stadium access control bands. RFID key fobs … The emerging landscape of wearable technology is as wide and unpredictable as most of the socio-economic revolutions that have been led by technology. The scope of the current product range and the speed of new wearable solutions launched across the globe this year alone promises to change the way we run our lives, monitor our health and lifestyle, exercise, learn, play, heal and, last but not least, how and what we communicate. With the latest business analysts' predictions of wide market adoption happening soon – the future of wearables is promising and possibilities are endless.

Wearables – A FinTech Solution?

Not so long ago, during London Technology Week 2015 someone asked me why wearables are a FinTech solution. A wearable is a tech product, no doubt, and venture capital interest in that market is a remarkable one, but where exactly do wearables fit into FinTech?

The answer is a simple one: by enabling NFC payments on wearable devices. Imagine being able to turn any wearable device into an alternative payment device.

---

[1] http://fortune.com/2013/03/04/how-big-might-the-market-be-for-an-apple-smart-watch/.

[2] http://www.forbes.com/sites/arieladams/2014/03/07/the-size-of-the-smartwatch-market-its-key-players/.

[3] https://www.cbinsights.com/blog/wearables-industry-venture-capital-2014/.

[4] Oxford dictionary: http://www.oxforddictionaries.com/definition/english/wearable.

Imagine that on top of all the features which a favourite wearable already has we add the convenience of "all-in-one", being able to pay. Imagine a payment device that measures heartbeat, monitors sugar levels, calculates alcohol intake, and on top of this sends out alerts as to how much you spent and what that does to your balance and savings. Imagine a world where as a consumer you do have a choice of how to pay using a globally accepted Visa, MasterCard, or American Express network with a novelty of device form – without the hassle of keeping an eye on your wallet, Wi-Fi enabled smartphone, or heavy coins in your pockets.

NFC wearable payments *are* a FinTech solution. Admittedly, currently still more an emerging one than a fully-fledged boom, but with constantly increasing consumer demand for ultimate convenience, a solution that is soon to become as big as market predictions. The revolution has already started: Apple Pay on Apple Watch, Jawbone's cooperation with American Express to launch payments, Wirecard's Payment Band proposition for the EU area, or the UK-centric Barclaycard bPay relaunch. Not to mention the constant market gossip about handsets and fitness wearables manufacturers looking into adding contactless payment features to their existing products. Every month the financial services and banking industry is commissioning wearable-centric proof of concepts, focused on enabling open loop payments into more and more flexible devices.

Everything You Always Wanted to Know About Wearables

Innovative financial services solutions are always on the verge of a hype. A decade ago when prepaid had more opponents that supporters, I advocated for it as an example of the endless possibilities of programmes and consumer convenience. It was the range of product offerings that provided a fresh approach to payments, the cards industry, and end-users. Further market adoption happened thanks to transit solutions (such Oyster in London, UK) and the expansion of e-wallets launched all across Europe. Now this is business as usual, rather than an innovative solution. In 2015, it was the Apple Pay mobile payments hype that made the industry rethink the customer approach; followed by Samsung Pay – the rest of the market will soon follow.

I spent last year monitoring the wearables tech market and became somehow hooked on witnessing another technology revolution, which has bigger financial and sociological potential that those just described. Wearable payments may actually change the way we perceive money, payment devices, and technology-enabled solutions (more and more often included in the Internet of Things). Wearables seem as emerging and innovative as prepaid cards and e-wallets were back in the day.

The "must have" global shift in the marketplace will happen on consumer demand, whether the industry wants that or not, as Generation Z's quest for ultimate convenience is in full force. According to *Forbes*, "71% of 16-to-24-year-olds want wearable tech."[5]

I have witnessed first-hand how many obstacles and limitations the current wearables market has to overcome to enable payments on radio-frequency identification (RFID) devices. A complicated ecosystem and an overcomplicated value chain, which nevertheless aims to build partnerships between handsets (e.g. Samsung) or wearable hardware manufacturers (e.g. Misfit, Fitbit, Pebble, ID&C), and semiconductor manufacturers (e.g. NXP), FinTech solutions providers such as TSM companies (Gemalto, Oberhur Technologies, DigiSEq Ltd), and financial services players (including but not limited to payments networks, issuers, programme managers, and acquirers), results in a complex formula.

I could not help but conclude that to really witness the biggest consumer trend since the invention of mobile phones, the industry must invest in the collaboration and dialogue between parties. This year alone, wearables-centric summits across the world show an increasing interest in engaging.

That is how the NFC Wearables Boom Everything You Always Wanted to Know About Wearables* (*But Were Afraid to Ask) cross-industry knowledge sharing concept emerged. NFC wearable boom is currently present as a group forum on LinkedIn[6] and provides an industry headlines overview on PaperLi.[7] In real life, during London Technology Week 2015, members of the FinTech and Financial Services (FS) industry met to share their views about the recent boom during a NFC

---

[5] By Victor Lipman. *Forbes*: "71% Of 16-To-24-Year-Olds Want 'Wearable Tech.' Why Don't I Even Want To Wear A Watch?". 22 September 2014.

[6] http://linkd.in/1LMbLm6.

[7] http://bit.ly/1UodXE1.

wearable boom event organized by DigiSEq Ltd. International attendees exchanged views with SMEs who provided a comprehensive review of the current state of the industry. A showcase of wearable tech (including Misfit, Boom Pay Band, and NFC Ring) was followed by insights from both sides of the fence – FS represented by DigiSEq, Visa Collab and Carta Worldwide and NFC wearables creators – ID&C and IVS (focused on a multimillion wearables market for RFID stadiums and festival solutions), and concluded with a panel discussion Wearables – hype or opportunity? The event illustrated the old rule that collaboration is a base for all progress.

As with any innovation, for NFC wearable boom to continue and have a long-lasting place among FinTech solutions, there is a need for ongoing cross-industry collaboration. More companies entering into the mix with innovative business models may offer seamless delivery and/or further the technology boom.

"The future of payment is wearable. Wearables are the new trend in the field of internet-based devices"[8] says Markus Braun, CEO of Wirecard AG. Wirecard prototype Pay Band is working as an NFC wearable payment device already. UK-based Barclaycard decided to relaunch their bPay brand to respond to increased consumer interest. As of July 2015, customers can choose between an NFC wristband, a key fob, or a sticker – reflecting what is happening on the NFC wearables market. Devices can be linked to any account and yes, they are a little bit more expensive than standard card fees, but they are still far cheaper than lifestyle or smartwatch products, and can be used to pay anywhere that the contactless symbol appears. Another UK-based company, DigiSEq, has the mission to make today's innovations part of tomorrow's daily use. DigiSEq can enable payments on any RFID device.

There are more and more market players looking into NFC wearables and it is only a matter of time before we recognize real industry influencers who will shape payments on remote RFID products.

Endless Possibilities, but Within a Contactless Limit

The fairy tale of NFC wearable boom should be concluded only by optimistic statements: how it is not just a hype, but an opportunity. And it is.

The technology used in wearables is becoming more and more revolutionary and accessible, wearable devices are evolving into fashionable items and device unit price goes down as more and more competitors are trying to win consumers. Recent entries of budget products such Xiaomi can soon ensure a wide adoption of the mass market. Within the first six months of 2015 some of the wearable players such as GoPro and FitBit are already capitalizing on the current wearables boom.

The FinTech world is feeling increasingly excited as wearable technology blooms. Financial services are already counting predicted profits and what was once a niche market now seems to be the next global "must-have" consumer trendy investment, business venture, and personal gadget.

However, payments on NFC wearables, even if they can be run via limitless systems and offer flexible fashionable factor possibilities, somehow will always be limited. Limited by a contactless spending limit varying from country to country and limited by a market-by-market acceptance network of contactless POS terminals infrastructure.

So whether NFC wearable boom will soon become an NFC payments wearable boom and reach $1.6 trillion global spend only the future will tell. There is, however, no doubt that in 2016 it is one of the most interesting, consumer-centric FinTech solutions.

---

[8] Wirecard: https://www.wirecard.com/newsroom/press-releases/newsdetail/wirecard-presents-first-payment-wearable-on-hce-basis/.

Capital and Investment

6

This part of the book is focused on capital raising options for FinTech businesses and investment trends for retail and professional investors. We review the finance ladder from start-up financing through to growth capital, private equity, and exits/IPOs and discuss the importance of building an investable platform. You will learn about angel investing and why it is important to attract smart money while also sharing the many benefits of being an angel investor. We will outline the growth of crowdfunding and marketplace lending as a leading FinTech sector and look into the future of wealth management, deep diving into the robo-advisory space and business models.

You will gain insight into the latest technologies which facilitate higher investment performance by collecting and leveraging the knowledge of the crowd, including how a crowdsourced hedge fund could operate. Finally, we widen the perspective and look at underlying opportunities and challenges within the investment sector and the power of governments to create frameworks supporting both fundraising and the (Fin)Tech sector globally.

Investment and Capital – Back to Basics

By Richard Goold

Head of Tech Law, EY (UK & Ireland)

In this chapter, we will look at:

1. The "finance ladder": the complete corporate finance process from start-up financing through to growth capital, private equity, and exits/IPOs; and
2. Building an investable platform – key legal, accounting, and tax issues that all founder teams should be aware of.

The Finance Ladder

I will consider the lifecycle of a FinTech company by looking at the financing options and stage-posts of a high-growth trajectory:

- What is meant by venture capital, growth capital, and expansion capital? What are the differences and the fundamental aspects of each type of financing?

- When might private equity come into play?

- What are the advantages and disadvantages of taking a FinTech company public?

Venture Capital – The Basics

Venture capital describes the more risky forms of equity investment that investors can make in companies (the "venture" gives the clue away). However, many of the mechanics used by venture capitalists (VCs) are designed to de-risk the investment from an investor's perspective. Before we dig deeper into those protections, I will describe in a little more detail the various stages of venture capital in today's FinTech ecosystem.

Often companies start their capital raising journey by either bootstrapping (eking out an existence without raising capital) or raising the bare minimum to get going – this is normally called a "friends and family round", which is descriptive of the typical sources of that initial capital.

This would then be followed by an angel round, which may lead to a seed round, although the two terms are being used almost interchangeably now. Typically a seed round is a round of investment of generally up to £1 million. Seed round investors are often high-net-worth angel investors, although we are beginning to witness an increase of the US phenomenon of institution-led seed rounds. At this stage of a company's development, this investment is the most risky money – there may be little more than a team and an idea, with the seed capital being used to develop the product. Seed rounds normally have investor protections such as warranties, restrictive covenants, and certain other covenants on the company but investors normally do not expect the heavier style of institutional protections that a VC would require. This cuts down on the legal process and therefore the cost of raising money.

An A round (generally in the £1m–£7m region currently, but they are getting larger) will often be led by an institutional VC and the terms would be more protective and extensive than an angel would push for.[1] The model documents contain a term sheet, a shareholders' agreement, and a set of articles of association. They are not for the faint-hearted (the shareholders agreement alone runs to over 60 pages) and are complex by necessity, as the protections that VCs insist upon to guard them (in down rounds and in the event that the company becomes insolvent) are multi-layered.

In essence, VCs generally want their money back in case the company becomes insolvent ("a liquidation preference") and to have comfort that if money is going to go into the company in the future at a lower valuation than that at which they are investing, they will get recompense (through an "anti-dilution protection").

Other key elements are:

- Warranties
  These are contractual promises from the company (and possibly the founders) as to the state of the legal, tax, and financial affairs of the company;

- Restrictive covenants
  These are covenants from the founders that they will not compete with the company or do other things to harm the company's business; and

---

[1] Those of us that have been involved in the investment community for some time have been part of an initiative in conjunction with the British Venture Capital Association to pull in the parameters of negotiation for such processes and a set of model documents can be found at http://www.venturecentral.co.uk/model-documents/4585713181.

- Covenants

  These are both found in the positive (e.g. management agreeing to do certain things, such as provide information to the investors) and in the negative (e.g. management agreeing *not* to do certain things, such as deviate from the agreed business plan).

B Rounds and Beyond

B rounds, C rounds, and beyond are often described as "expansion capital". By the time that a company has moved on through a successful A round, hopefully the technology is gaining some serious traction, customers are being won over week-on-week, and it is time to scale up the workforce – particularly the salesforce. That is where expansion capital comes into play. Expansion capital is a competitive space for the VCs and by the time a company is profitable and ready to expand, it is time to be picky and choose the investor with the right network and the right experience for you.

Growth Capital

Growth capital is sometimes used interchangeably with expansion capital but in the UK it is more typically put into less risky companies that are already profitable and that have not been through extensive rounds of institutional venture capital.

Private Equity

Private equity can be found in several different scenarios, but most commonly it is an alternative to a trade sale and it is capital that is used to buy out the existing owners (replace those owners who may also be directors with a new tier of management). The private equity house will then incentivize those managers to grow the company through equity.

Different forms of management buyouts using private equity are as follows:

a. *MBO* – management buyout – when the existing second-tier management utilize private equity to buy out the existing top-level management;

b. *MBI* – management buy-in – when new management of the business come on board at the same time as the incoming private equity investor to replace the old management entirely; and

c. *BIMBO* – buy-in management buyout – a hybrid of the above where some existing management may stay along with new management coming in.

When to Go Public?

In the last five years, capital markets have not been operating in Europe as well as any of us would have liked, but the public investor appetite for FinTech has increased hugely, and with the alternative investment market (AIM), the new high-growth segment on the London Stock Exchange and the main market itself loosening up, public markets are certainly a consideration for companies. Whilst many FinTech companies are not quite ready to go public just yet, I think that we will see a significant number of FinTech IPOs over the next five years.

The public markets are of particular interest to companies that have any level of consumer facing element to them – if brand awareness can be raised through an IPO and that can be linked to raising capital and creating an exit event for some of the earlier-stage investors (without the founders losing control of the company), an IPO can be a win-win for the company, management, and the investors.

Entrepreneurs beware, though: the life of a public company CEO, with all the investor roadshows and corporate governance to consider, is certainly not for everyone. Those that like the closed boardroom, the more nimble touch of a smaller board with less governance, often prefer to raise capital privately (to build towards a trade sale).

Building an Investable Platform

Having the best idea in the world does not mean that you will build the best company in the world. The rule of law, tax bear-traps to avoid, and key accounting issues all need to be slotted together to create an investable platform.

The frenetic pace of a FinTech start-up means the tax position of the company and founders can easily be overlooked. Getting the paperwork right at the outset is so important. Part of that is getting the right team of advisors involved, but all management teams need to be aware of the key accounting, legal, and tax issues that institutional investors will want to see in place before they invest.

Beware of the Taxman

On an exit which delivers the returns FinTech entrepreneurs are likely to be hoping for, having your house in order from day one can mean, at least here in the UK, the difference between a 10% tax bill and a tax bill in excess of 45%. Not only that, but the tax bill will come at the end, rather than as a nasty surprise at an earlier stage in the growth cycle. The name of the game is to ensure that all of the upside is treated as a capital gain rather than income, which is taxed more punitively.

Founder Shares

The starting point is for the founders of the business to incorporate a company and issue shares to themselves in the agreed allocations at the outset. The share issue will require a minuted board meeting, the issue of share certificates, and most importantly entering the founders' names in the company's shareholders' register. A situation to avoid is leaving these formalities until the first investment round. By then, the company will have value, which means that the taxman may say that he wants income tax on the value of the shares issued to the founders because they are employees. That is money that does not yet exist, of course. Depending on the rights which the shares have, it may be necessary for the founders to sign what is called a section 431 election to make sure all the exit proceeds are subject to capital gains tax and not income tax.

Management Share Options

If things go well, then the founder team may want to bring in and incentivize fresh talent. Issuing free shares to the management team would give rise to income tax on the value of the shares when they join and they probably will not have the money to pay for the shares. Much better to give them EMI share options which have a market value strike price. EMI stands for "enterprise management incentives", a share option arrangement specifically designed to provide a powerful tool for the recruitment and reward of employees in growth companies. They are turbo-charged from a tax viewpoint: there is no tax up front and no tax when the options are exchanged for shares, and provided that a year has passed since the employee was given the EMI options, only 10% tax when the shares are eventually sold.

Angel Investing – Access to "Smart Money" to Fund the Best FinTech Companies

By Susanne Chishti
CEO & Founder, FINTECH Circle; Chairwoman, FINTECH Circle Innovate

The "angel round" is normally the first external funding round to inject cash into a FinTech start-up by accredited, high-net worth (HNW) investors. Most great tech success stories were backed by fantastic angel investors who really believed in the team and their vision and helped to make it work. Thus each FinTech firm needs great FinTech angels backing them up all the way. This chapter helps finance and technology leaders to find out how they can personally benefit by becoming FinTech angel investors.

So how can you personally benefit from the enormous growth of the FinTech sector? The two main options are to either become an entrepreneur trying to build the next FinTech success story or to become a FinTech angel investor. As an angel investor you invest your personal funds to help the best FinTech entrepreneurs build their business in order to sell it or go public many years later to make a good return. The most valuable companies of tomorrow's finance sector are being formed today and if you only invest via the stock market into publicly listed stocks and funds, these opportunities will not be available to you. Private investors can be part of the journey from the beginning by providing much needed capital to the best start-ups and small and medium-sized enterprises (SMEs).

David S. Rose, founder of New York Angels, summarized it so well by providing the following example: "This form of investment can be extraordinarily lucrative. When Ben Silberman approached New York Angels in April 2009, seeking a small investment in his interactive mobile catalog idea, he valued his company at $2.5 million. Today, just over four years later [2013], Pinterest is valued at $3.8 billion – an increase of 152,000 percent."[1] So angel investors who backed the initial funding round have done extremely well. In 2015 Pinterest Inc. raised $367 million, giving

the online site a valuation of $11 billion and making it one of the most highly valued start-ups by venture capitalists in the world.[2]

So how can you get involved, how can you become an angel investor? Two key principles should apply – first only invest in what you know and secondly, only invest the money you can afford to lose. Similarly to crowdfunding, there is no guarantee that you will get your investment back. HNW investors often use an asset allocation strategy when building their investment portfolios which might consist of a core portfolio of passive investments (for example exchange traded funds) in combination with a range of satellite investments such as property, hedge funds, private equity, and commodities. The key thing is to never put all your eggs in one basket – a lesson we have all heard before.

So where does angel investment fit in? What differentiates successful angel investors from the rest is their passion for a certain industry because of their previous experience and skills. Often this passion and deep domain expertise drives and empowers them to pick the winners. Post investment smart angels like to play an active role in the success of the company by doing anything in their power to help the company grow. That is why all FinTech entrepreneurs need their angels!

FinTech angels often come from the financial services and/or technology sectors combining deep domain expertise in retail, corporate, investment banking, asset management, private wealth management, or transaction banking with technology understanding and the curiosity to explore new technologies such as blockchain innovation, for example.

So where do angel investors make the best returns? Very few statistics exist and many are outdated. However one recent survey of business angels was published in the UK, featuring responses from 403 angels, and drawing data from angel syndicates and networks comprising 8,000 individual investors, entitled "A Nation of Angels" which shared the details of their best- and worst-performing investments.[3]

---

[1] David S. Rose, *Angel Investing – The Gust Guide to Making Money & Having Fun Investing in Startups* (John Wiley & Sons, 2014).

[2] *Wall Street Journal*, Article written by Yoree Koh on 16 March 2015, http://www.wsj.com/articles/pinterest-raises-367-million-at-11-billion-valuation-1426538379.

[3] "A Nation of Angels, Assessing the Impact of Angel Investing across the UK", Enterprise Research Center, January 2015, http://www.enterpriseresearch.ac.uk/wp-content/uploads/2015/01/ERC-Angels-Report.pdf.

Financial technology came out on top with FinTech as the most lucrative sector for angel investment, delivering the highest growth compared to any other industry.

The report also found that these early-stage investors are getting younger in the UK, more female, and are increasingly likely to back companies outside their local area. In 2008, the median age of a UK angel investor was 53. In 2015, 44% of UK angel investors are under 45 years, and almost three-quarters are under 54. The proportion of female angels stands at 14%, up from just 7% in 2008. The rise of women-only angel networks has helped the gender gap to narrow slightly, but the UK still lags behind the US where 20% of angels are female. Thus the FinTech sector needs more angel investors and more female angels to join to ensure that the best companies get funded.

So how do you become an angel investor? What are the key areas you should be aware of when starting to invest?

- Diversification is king.
  Among private investors and VCs it is often expected that at least half of their investments will fail, thus out of 10 investments, you would assume that at least five will fail, three to four might return the original investment, and one will be the big winner, where the exit will be so extraordinary that it compensates for all losses. Thus you rely on 10% of your portfolio generating enough return, so that the overall portfolio return is attractive.

  The problem for investors is that nobody knows who the winners will be and therefore investing in early stage companies is a numbers game. David Rose summarized it in this way: "Several studies and mathematical simulations have shown that it takes investing the same amount of money consistently in at least 20 to 25 companies before your returns begin to approach the typical return of over 20% [per year] for professional, active angel investors."[4]

- Understand the investment lifecycle/finance ladder of a start-up.
  Angel investment normally comes after the friends and family round and before VC funding and is normally focused on amounts between £100,000 and £1 million.

[4] David S. Rose, *Angel Investing – The Gust Guide to Making Money & Having Fun Investing in Startups* (John Wiley & Sons, 2014).

However, these lines are blurring as we have seen with FINTECH Circle, Europe's first angel network exclusively focused on FinTech opportunities, where we co-invested with early stage VCs during 2015. You also need to be aware that every successful company will need more money to grow and your stake will be diluted unless you are able to join the follow-on rounds.

- Dealflow is key to identifying high-potential opportunities.
  The better your dealflow, the more likely it is that you will pick a winner. Therefore the best strategy is to align with like-minded investors and become well known in the marketplace so that the best FinTech companies approach you before approaching others. Most frequently angel investors join syndicates where angels combine their knowledge and expertise in evaluating companies and then co-invest together. Without great dealflow, you could be the best stock picker but it would not help because the opportunities you see are limited.

- Top angels will provide "smart money".
  When companies start to grow they not only need money, but mentors/advisors (whose interests are aligned with the founders) to help them grow their business. This help could mean introducing them to your contacts and network of potential partners and customers. It could mean helping them to validate important business assumptions, providing resources (to which they would not otherwise have access) or helping them with their value proposition and business model to achieve product/market fit. Being an angel is such an opportunity to be both an investor and mentor/supporter of the start-ups you have backed. You are on their side and they know it.

- Angel investing is personal.
  As an investor you need to back the founding team wholeheartedly, which normally means you must like them, trust them, and believe in them to execute their plans. You will want to spend time and energy with the FinTech firms you back to understand their backgrounds and if they have what it takes to succeed. Angel investing takes time to build the rapport on both sides as it is equally important for the entrepreneurs to feel comfortable with their investors. A well-known FinTech entrepreneur once told me that he does not take on investors whom he does not enjoy going to lunch with. That makes perfect sense – being invested as a private investor is like a marriage which neither you nor the entrepreneur can leave easily.

- Evaluate their pitch, presentation and technology.

Key documents investors often look at are executive summaries (that's an important document because if that does not sell the opportunity, the investor will not look further), investor decks, business plans, or financial forecasts. Thus it is key to spend time preparing the investor deck well and also to make it visually appealing. First impressions count on paper, online, and in person. In order to assess the proposed tech solution, angels will leverage their own expertise and network of relevant industry contacts.

Now let us assume you have found a great FinTech company at an Angel Network Event, met the founders in person, really liked them and their product, discussed their pitch with other FinTech angels who also want to back it in the form of a very complementary angel syndicate (in terms of combined expertise and available networks across financial services and technology), and now you want to take it further. This next phase is called "due diligence", where it is key to explore the details of the management team, the products/services and traction to date, the market size and opportunities for global expansion, route to market strategies, competitive advantage, and exit options. Due diligence can be done together or one angel can take the lead.

The difficult next step is agreeing on a valuation. Normally FinTech firms will have an idea about their valuation and about how much money they are looking for. This will normally be part of the pitch deck made available to angel investors. However valuations are never set in stone and can be negotiated taking into account:

- Competitive metrics, i.e. what are other FinTech firms worth in this vertical at this development stage?

- What are the growth and valuation expectations for the company in the future?

- How much can you afford to invest taking into account that you want to build up a diversified angel portfolio of companies and what equity stake would you like in return?

This is obviously not a complete list as books have been written on the topic of valuation, which is a difficult combination of science and art especially for start-ups.

The negotiating process is again an opportunity to go into more details on company leadership, and discuss important questions in terms of control and decision-making, including the protection for minority shareholders, all summarized in the important "shareholders' agreement". In addition there will be other documents to sign depending on which country you are based in, a process which can be very complex and tiring for the FinTech entrepreneurs who are always relieved when the fundraising process is over as it is a distraction to their business.

After the investment the key objective of smart angels is to add value to their FinTech firms. Assuming that you are an angel investor with great domain expertise in some of the verticals across financial services such as retail, corporate or investment banking, asset management, private wealth management, transaction banking/payments, or crypto-currencies/blockchain technologies, your contacts and previous experience will be extremely valuable to the founders and you should try to help them wherever you can.

Finally, a very important benefit of angel investing is non-monetary – being an active angel is fun. It can be very rewarding to meet inspiring entrepreneurs, mentor and coach them, actively participate in their journey, feel the excitement when things go well, and try to find solutions when challenges occur. Creating your FinTech portfolio of angel investments will be an amazing experience. It is entrepreneurship without the responsibility and helps you keep up with the latest disruptive technologies and trends and it is satisfying to be able to give back. Thus there is definitely a social side to angel investing. For those investors who want to invest in FinTech start-ups but have no time to be active angels or might not be permitted to pick their own investments (as there might be a conflict of interest with their day jobs), specialized funds exist which focus on investments into FinTech companies.

FINTECH Circle angels attend great start-up and educational events, are invited to mentor the best FinTech entrepreneurs, and are intellectually challenged and stimulated which helps to see the future of finance and personally benefit from the FinTech revolution. You and your angel network can fund the best FinTech start-ups, laying the foundations for their future success!

Crowdfunding and Marketplace (P2P) Lending – Online Capital Marketplaces as New Asset Classes to Access Funding

By Brian W. Tang

Managing Director, Asia Capital Markets Institute (ACMI)

Online capital marketplaces are FinTech platforms that facilitate fundraising by accessing "other people's money".

In relation to this category of internet finance, equity crowdfunding portals are disrupting the venture capital (VC) market by enabling investments directly into private company start-ups, and peer-to-peer (P2P) lending platforms are disrupting the banking market by facilitating lending to small and medium-sized enterprises (SMEs). This new mode of capital pooling and securitization is currently also being expanded into areas such as invoice trading and real estate investment. On their face, these kinds of investments can provide opportunities for individuals and asset owners and managers to make potentially uncorrelated portfolio allocations. Concurrently, this form of alternative finance allows originators to syndicate balance sheet risk exposures, and risk-taking SMEs and entrepreneurs, including other FinTech companies, to fund innovation and create jobs.

The growth potential is tremendous. Goldman Sachs' 2015 report entitled *Socialization of Finance* called crowdfunding "potentially the most disruptive of all the new models of finance". The World Bank estimates that crowdfunding investments in developing countries alone could reach US$96 billion a year by 2025. Venture capital firm Foundation Capital, whose portfolio includes a stake in Lending Club which staged 2014's largest US tech IPO, asserts that marketplace lending is a US$1 trillion market.

It is, therefore, not surprising that debates have already begun regarding whether such online capital marketplaces are creating new investment asset classes. But does the sector have the critical ingredients to create one or more sustainable asset classes?

Disclosure Paradigm as the Basis of Modern Global Capital Markets

Key to the integrity of all capital marketplaces and exchanges that seek to tap "other people's money" is the requisite trust in the quality of the fundraiser's transparency/disclosure and independent gatekeeper due diligence/credit rating analysis.

In the lead up to the creation of the US Securities Act of 1933 and Securities Exchange Act of 1934, upon which the regulation of modern capital markets globally is based, US Supreme Court Justice Louis D. Brandeis famously quipped: "Sunlight is said to be the best of disinfectants; electric light the most efficient policeman."

The principle behind the Disclosure Paradigm is fairly straightforward: limited liability corporations were historically created to seek "other people's money" for high-risk and high-growth enterprises (such as merchant expeditions to the Orient) when traditional lenders were unwilling to extend credit. In return for a proportionate share of the profits, capital raisers were obliged to periodically disclose all material information relating to their financial condition and operating performance to enable investors to make their investment decisions to buy, sell, hold, and price such securities. Such disclosure should be complete and should not be misleading nor contain material omissions.

On this basis, first moneyed families, and then institutional investors followed the advent of the pension system and insurance policies, and eventually more ordinary "moms and pops", could invest and trade, directly or indirectly, in these securities. These new asset classes included investments in shares of public companies listed on stock exchanges, in sovereign and corporate bonds, as well as in private companies through VC and private equity firms.

The Disclosure Paradigm has proven to be a relatively cost-effective investor protection policy mechanism. It implicitly relies upon the critical judgment of capital markets professionals regarding what information is material that should be disclosed to different classes of investors, depending on their assumed levels of financial sophistication. Platforms tapping retail investors thus need more disclosure and investment protection than institutional and accredited investors. Enforcement regarding any deficiencies is effected through regulatory action and/or private litigation, depending on the jurisdiction.

Accordingly, the professionalism of capital market gatekeepers both external (such as stock exchanges, investment bankers, lawyers, auditors, and credit ratings agencies) and internal (directors and officers such as CEOs, CFOs, company secretaries, general counsel, and investor relations), as well as adequate investor financial literacy, are imperative to the efficient functioning and integrity of our global capital markets.

The Global Financial Crisis' Aftermath of Regulations, Penalties, and Loss of Trust

The 2008 global financial crisis, triggered by factors including a widespread mis-selling of sub-prime mortgage-backed securities, resulted in an initial wave of prudential regulation focused on systemic risk, financial stability, and capital levels to address financial institutions that were deemed "too big to fail". A tsunami of legislation and regulation followed. For example, the US Dodd-Frank Wall Street Reform and Consumer Protection Act consisted of a record-breaking 849 pages and 396 rule-making requirements that Brown Brothers Harriman has estimated will total more than 25,000 pages when completed. In March 2014, US Attorney-General Eric Holder clarified that "[t]here is no such thing as too big to jail". Since then, several global banks have been prosecuted and pleaded guilty to criminal charges such as tax evasion, US sanction violations, and currency market manipulation. Based on CCP Research Foundation research, bank conduct risk costs (including provisions) for 2010–2014 have risen to more than £200 billion, with charges including misconduct, mis-selling, and fraud. At the same time, securities regulators are increasingly focused on ensuring effective disclosure by communicating with and enlightening investors in plain language, rather than obfuscating risks with voluminous boilerplate and repetitive language that arises from a tick-the-box "mere compliance" mentality.

Conduct Risk as a New Core Focus of Financial Regulation and Supervision

In the wake of the Libor interest rate manipulation scandal, the UK Joint Parliamentary Commission on Banking Standards published its 2013 report, *Changing Banking for Good*. Around the world, the high-level focus of central

bankers and securities regulators, ranging from the UK Financial Conduct Authority and US Federal Reserve Bank to the Hong Kong Securities and Futures Commission, has shifted to cultural and ethical aspects of financial institutions to address the perceived "ethical drift" that gave rise to the increased conduct risk. Regulators now expect greater management and individual accountability for misconduct.

Proposals for industry-wide codes of conduct are gathering steam, such as the Netherlands requiring banker oaths and the Fixed Income Currency and Commodities (FICC) Market Standards Board proposed in the Bank of England's recent Fair and Effective Markets Review. Voluntary initiatives abound, including the Australian Banking and Finance Oath initiative, the UK Banking Standards Board, and the Malaysian Financial Services Professional Board. The Harvard student-originated MBA Oath initiative demonstrates the importance placed by millennials on pursuing careers with purpose and positive contribution. Yet the greatest challenge ahead lies in "bringing to life" and operationalizing such codes and oaths to promote professionalism in the service of clients and as part of society.

Trust and Regulating Rapidly Evolving Online Capital Marketplaces

Proponents of crowdfunding, marketplace lending, and other new fundraising platform business models must similarly be willing and able to exude a level of trustworthiness in their processes and standards. This is especially true at a time when their legal status may be murky. Otherwise, crises will arise and distrust in the emerging industry could result in forms of investor protection regulation that may excessively hinder the nascent growth of the sector. And this requirement to exude trust applies to the platforms themselves as well as the emerging ecosystem actors.

In the meantime, developments are rapid as this space evolves quickly. In the UK and US, the ongoing low interest rate environment has led to institutional investors becoming the dominant marketplace lenders. At the same time, the "private IPO" market has seen explosive growth with unicorn companies of US$1 billion plus pre-IPO valuations reportedly exceeding the value of all VC-backed tech IPOs in the year to date – this demonstrates the tremendous interest in being able to invest in private companies that could be the next Google or Facebook.

Perhaps ironically, online capital marketplaces have achieved greater levels of democratization in retail investor participation in countries such as China, which according to Wangdaizhijia had at least over 1,500 P2P platforms operating at the end of last year. Some of the reasons for this include their competitive offerings compared with state-owned bank incumbents, and a high mobile broadband penetration that helped create a strong culture of online transactions via internet giants Alibaba and Tencent. The tremendous rise of the Chinese A-share stock market since the end of last year has also excited entrepreneurs and individual investors alike in relation to the fundraising and rapid wealth creation possibilities that capital marketplaces can provide.

However, the bubbles of today can lead to herd mentality, mispricing of risk, an increase in the number of speculators, a decline in asset quality of offerings, and pressures to cut corners. That, in turn, can lead to the tears of tomorrow.

Professional Education for Advancement of the Online Capital Marketplace Ecosystem

According to Edelman's 2015 TrustBarometer, financial services remain the least trusted industry globally. It is this loss of public trust that has in fact helped FinTech to emerge and quickly gain traction over the past few years. A critical lesson internet finance participants should also learn from the progression of financial services' regulatory focus is the importance of reputation and reinforcing professionalism as a self-regulatory mechanism to help gain the trust of both consumers and regulators. Academic research from the Carnegie Foundation for the Advancement of Teaching identifies three critical elements in professional formation: professional identity, analytical skills, and practical know-how. In relation to the capital markets, this means cultivating participants' core values and roles in dealing with "other people's money" and financing real economy growth. It also means honing professional skills in giving voice to such values in the face of organizational dynamics, competitive pressures, and complexity in addressing systemic information asymmetry.

Policy-makers and industry participants will and should continue to debate the extent to which retail participation in online capital marketplaces should be expanded beyond accredited and professional investors. Different approaches will emerge, as can be seen from Malaysia's annual cap on each individual's crowdfunding participation to the US JOBS Act's licensing of crowdfunding portals. The Australian Securities and Investment Commission's recent creation of an innovation hub is a great idea to allow for ongoing stakeholder dialogue and small-scale piloting of new business models. The industry can also benefit from practice guidelines that are not mere checklists for minimum disclosure. Ultimately, quality capital markets rely on quality due diligence and quality disclosure.

FinTechnologist professionalism and investor education of this new form of investment and its risks are essential to gain consumer confidence and avoid costly over-regulation and prosecutions. This has been recognized by various industry initiatives such as the European Crowdfunding Network's recently updated Code of Conduct for platforms and new Charter of Crowdfunding Rights for users.

More can and should be done. Only then may online capital marketplaces live up to their promise of facilitating new and sustainable investment asset classes that benefit investors and entrepreneurs alike, and to cost-effectively fuel innovation and real economy growth to serve our broader society.

The Digital Investment Space — Spanning from Social Trading to Digital Private Banking — A FinTech Sector Made for Disruption?

By Michael Mellinghoff

Managing Director, TechFluence

In the mid-1990s the mutual fund industry introduced distribution fees to reward their distribution partners for promoting their own mutual funds to private investors. The reduction in margin for mutual fund providers was immense. A fund which at that time charged a management fee of 1% suddenly had to pay on a recurring basis half of the management fee to the distributor, who sold the fund to the client. This decreased the margin of the product provider by at least half. This marked the starting point of a negative market development for product manufacturers, and especially investors in these products, in favour of product distributors. Clients over time paid the bill via higher management fees, as product manufacturers increased their management fees, and thus charged even higher distribution fees, since the fee level very often was expressed as a percentage of the management fee of the investment fund: a vicious circle decreasing the yield of the investor and increasing the profit of the industry.

These high profit margins are one of the reasons why digital competitors entered the field of wealth and asset management and why they have a chance to capture enough market share to survive even fierce future competition between the traditional and the digital world, which will most likely lead to an overall reduction of fees. Moreover, decades of underperformance by active mutual funds have led to a massive outflow from the category to the benefit of low-cost passive and ETF options as well as alternative asset classes and instruments. At the same time, client demand changes rapidly as the very low interest rates across the globe foster the need of savers and investors to act more proactively than in the past, i.e. take higher risks and invest more than previously or start investing in risk-bearing asset classes.

Furthermore, technology in the past few years has enabled retail clients to become more and more independent from their product advisors in banks or advisory firms. Clients simply start applying their digital behaviour from the e-commerce sector to their financial needs and thus are open to digital financial offers. These digital behaviours changed more quickly than banks could adapt their services offer, especially because post financial crisis they had to focus on saving the industry by adapting to a new regulatory regime rather than keeping up to date regarding their digital offerings. Digital challengers have jumped onto the opportunity and the early movers among the FinTech start-ups have attracted substantial attention because of this, and continue to drive the change in the FinTech sector, which is complex by definition, as the regulatory environment is more demanding than in other sectors.

Extrapolating these trends, it is fair to assume that available assets are going to increase for digital challengers and thus increase the margin pressure for traditional players that will be forced to cut costs and re-focus their business models. The first digital challengers to traditional players in the field of digital investment were social trading companies and companies offering automated investment advisory services ("robo advisors") both focusing on retail investors. The first market entrants in the robo advisory field innovated by business model and did not compete over price. As robo advisory enables all market participants to compete for the private client, many players in the financial universe will tap the market of automated investment advice: banks, online brokers, asset managers etc. will start offering robo advisory services for free. The US market unsurprisingly started to move first into this direction as Charles Schwab counters Wealthfront's successful market entry by offering robo advice for free. Similar developments are now being witnessed in other markets, for example in Germany where ebase, a subsidiary of Commerzbank, entered into the robo advisory business in July 2015. A question mark for the moment remains, whether non-financial players will enter the automated advisory space, as they did successfully in other areas, for example the supermarket banks in the UK like Tesco Bank, M&S Bank, or Harrods' Bank. These developments are likely to result in reduced margins in the retail space and traditional players will focus their activities on more complex areas of the market (for example, private banking), which will foster competition here and lead to a market concentration in this part of the market over time, too.

The more robo advisory models mushroom – white-label versions are already available for example from start-ups in Germany – the more different algorithms will be competing in future and will align over time. The independent robo advisory providers are forced to continue striving for innovation and will over time offer more connected services like a concept that can be labelled as the "talking portfolio". The Internet of Things will create completely new business models and markets in all aspects of our current lifestyle. Money matters are not excluded from this. For example, self-driving cars, plus the Internet of Things, plus insurance will in the future allow a bunch of tailored solutions in the InsuranceTech space.

The Internet of Things will also have an impact on our savings and investment culture. The investment world will see similar developments as the insurance world: why should only petrol stations and hotels be shown on Google Maps? Why not the next available (human) investment advisor? Why should a navigation system in a rental car not offer the option to choose a portfolio-optimized route? Such a service would provide information on companies that are directly or indirectly linked to the current portfolio holdings of the investor: only Royal Dutch Shell gas stations, no other fast food locations than Starbucks would be displayed, and of course respective vouchers would be given to shareholders first, etc. As self-driving cars are connected to fridges and other household appliances, the "driver" has time to consider decisions about whether today he would like to optimize his daily household spending on optimization of his short-term trading portfolio, or instead the long-term investment portfolio. Based on the global real time and projected drive thru waiting times at McDonald's, the portfolio itself will issue buy or sell recommendations on McDonald's stock. Also the connected fridge or freezer will have a button to order portfolio-optimized food only, telling you every morning that if you and all other users of this service use this service, the joint financial gain will be "x" % p.a. on invested capital. The portfolio holdings and its expected return will be automatically readjusted based on the aggregate buying activity of all connected smart fridges. Such a trend could result in the formation of special interest groups/communities based around investment styles. Analysis of investors' private and business lifestyle through smart appliances will certainly result in buy or sell recommendations for certain asset classes or securities.

While these developments seem like fiction today, we currently see only the beginning of robo advisory structures that enable start-up companies to enter a high margin business. In the US robo advisors are mushrooming already.

Techfluence assumes the number of automated advisory services to at least rise tenfold globally in the next few years. Advisory services become a commodity. More sophisticated tools, which allow investors for example to exclude certain product providers from the portfolio or single asset classes or even single stocks, will be able to offer this as a fee-generating premium service, which can be paid in fiat currency or social currency, i.e. personal data sharing models.

The traditional competition among portfolio managers on the best (risk-adjusted) performance will at least partially be replaced by competition of the best algorithms of the automated analysis providers. The technological developments thus impact all parts of the value chain of wealth management. Successful sophisticated investment algorithms will also be offered through B2B channels as robo advisory with a human touch. UBS is already using smart data verified by client advisors to optimize portfolio returns. As more social trading platforms emerge and grow more user profiles, advisory services – online and human – will be added to the platforms, helping investors to select the best user mix in their social trading portfolio.

As robo advisory services entered the market only recently, especially in the next few years, there is going to be direct competition between automated advisory and human advisory services, be they branch-based or online. Over time, this will lead to hybrid models as it is fair to assume that the growing complexity of algorithms will lead to the need for human support, thus creating new job opportunities, too. The investment advisor of the future does not pick stocks or asset classes on behalf of the client but consults on algorithms or even helps tailor them.

In summary, the FinTech industry is set to disrupt the digital investment area as a whole, starting with B2C business models, with B2B to follow soon. The whole value chain of wealth management will be under tremendous pressure to change and adapt. The new competitors have the ability and agility to offer products and services digitally and the successful players will continue to innovate. The Internet of Things and wearables will boost this development. Traditional players should use their grace period as they still earn high recurring fees from the past by investing these wisely and try to compete with the new FinTech players and actively seek collaboration with tech companies.

Leading the Way with an Investor-led Approach to Crowdfunding

By Christopher Smith

Former Content Editor, SyndicateRoom

In June 2015, the word "crowdfunding" was added to the Oxford English Dictionary along with the verb "to crowdfund" and the adjective "crowdfunded". So does its inclusion in a dictionary mean that crowdfunding has become mainstream and that it is no longer part of the alternative finance market? The answer is: not yet.

Crowdfunding is still a relatively novel funding concept. Globally, it is growing rapidly, but it is also diverse and in constant evolution. Moreover, its development and growth vary from country to country, depending on local regulatory, economic, and social factors amongst others. Awareness of crowdfunding, in comparison to the established financing market, is still low and there are some critical challenges – in particular around education, transparency, and the protection of investors. These issues need to be addressed before crowdfunding can reach its full potential.

The term "crowdfunding" can mean different things to different people, as there are a number of diverse models. Broadly speaking, they divide into those which do not provide a financial return (donation-based or reward-based models, such as Kickstarter) and those whose goal is to provide a financial return (equity-based platforms such as Companisto and SyndicateRoom, or lending-based platforms such as Funding Circle).

Of the different models, the most complex is undoubtedly equity crowdfunding which sees investors receive shares in the company in return for their investment. Much of the complexity is due to the regulatory aspects of this type of financing.

In the United States, legal barriers have slowed the development of equity crowdfunding, although this is changing since the new Regulation A+ rules came into effect in 2015. Companies can now secure funding via equity crowdfunding, provided they comply with a set of specific laws and standards.

In the case of Europe though, the rapidly increasing popularity of equity crowdfunding has caught many by surprise – especially the regulators. Equity crowdfunding is more advanced here than in other regions of the world. However, the market is highly deregulated and there is a patchwork of different national legal frameworks.

A review published in December 2014 by the European Crowdfunding Network states: "We are still far from a harmonised single market for crowdfunding, maybe even further than last year."[1] Instead, an increasing number of EU countries are implementing specific national crowdfunding regulations of their own. The top three European crowdfunding markets have each gone to different lengths to facilitate crowdfunding. In France, the government has been strongly supportive of crowdfunding, and introduced rules and regulations for both peer-to-peer lending and equity crowdfunding in October 2014. These are aimed first and foremost at protecting investors.

Across the border, in Germany, new regulations were approved in April 2015, which were not as onerous as some in the crowdfunding industry had feared, but which still imposed limits on retail investors such as an investment cap of €10,000 if they show they can bear the loss, or €1,000 if they cannot.[2]

In the leading European market for crowdfunding – the UK – the approach taken by the Financial Conduct Authority (FCA) has been to fit crowdfunding into the existing regulatory framework, rather than creating an entirely new regulatory regime.

Differing regulatory frameworks are not the only challenge to be overcome before crowdfunding platforms can operate on a pan-European basis. As the European Crowdfunding Network has said, a harmonized single market for crowdfunding is still some distance in the future. However, there are a number of other key issues to be addressed by the crowdfunding industry in the meantime.

Crowdfunding, and equity crowdfunding in particular, is still very new; its existence is measured in years rather than decades, or centuries in the case of banking.

---

[1] http://www.eurocrowd.org/files/2014/12/ECN-Review-of-Crowdfunding-Regulation-2014.pdf.

[2] http://www.eurocrowd.org/2015/04/germany-adopts-crowdfunding-rules/.

Although it is growing rapidly, it still represents only a small fraction of the financial sector and many people are unfamiliar with it. There is, therefore, a clear need for education both in the case of investors and also on the part of investment-seeking businesses.

A survey carried out by NESTA in the UK for their report "Understanding Alternative Finance"[3] revealed that "sixty per cent of surveyed consumers said they are 'unlikely' or 'very unlikely' to begin/continue using alternative finance platforms, citing concerns about perceived risks and a lack of information about those individuals and businesses that they would be funding."

Similarly, a European Commission report[4] states that in many instances investors remain insufficiently informed about the real risk of investing, what exactly they will receive in return for their investment, and other aspects, such as voting rights.

Some crowdfunding platforms' websites do provide this type of information in their FAQs, "help" pages, or in investment documentation.

It is not only a question of educating investors, but also one of transparency and protecting the interests of stakeholders. The "crowd" is composed of individuals who may or may not have experience or knowledge of financial markets. How then can the crowd do their best to ensure they are making the right decisions? It is not always easy for them, as certain elements of investing via crowdfunding are less obvious on some platforms than others.

One of the key differences between crowdfunding platforms, which can have the greatest impact on investors, is the investment model. There are two current equity crowdfunding investment models: investor-led and company-led.

With the "company-led" approach to crowdfunding, the company seeking capital sets its own terms of investment and decides its own valuation. Naturally, it will seek to set the best possible valuation for itself, giving away the minimum amount of equity to secure the funding it requires. Prospective investors are then left to decide whether they want to invest at that valuation, or not.

This approach is good for the company but may not be the best for the investor. In the UK, in recent months, several company-led crowdfunding valuations have been the subject of heated discussion, with some commentators feeling they are unrealistically high and that investors may lose out as a result. How then can an investor ensure that they are investing in a company at the best possible valuation? The answer is to have an angel by your side.

Anyone who has watched Dragons' Den or Shark Tank will occasionally have seen the dragons/sharks rip an entrepreneur's valuation of his or her own business to shreds. To some extent that is understandable, because start-up or early-stage companies often have little in the way of assets or revenue and, as a result, valuations tend to be highly subjective.

Of course this makes for compelling TV viewing, but the important point is that dragons/sharks, or business angels as they are more commonly known, generally have years of entrepreneurial experience on their side.

Away from reality TV, the investor-led crowdfunding model involves a business angel or lead investor agreeing a valuation at which they are willing to invest in the company. The goal is to arrive at a negotiated valuation that both parties are happy with. In the process, the angel will usually carry out extensive due diligence, willingly expending the necessary time and resources, as they are potentially investing a considerable sum of money. A report by NESTA – "Siding with the Angels"[5] highlights the value of this approach, revealing that angels who perform at least some due diligence, even just 20 hours, experienced fewer failed investments than those who did not.

For their part, the ordinary equity crowdfunding investor is then able to benefit from the involvement of the angel and invest under the same or similar terms as them.

AngelList – based in the US, and UK's SyndicateRoom are two of only a handful of platforms operating an investor-led model. Their investment opportunities involve one or more angels and, on occasions, VCs. This provides investors with the reassurance that an experienced professional is carrying out the necessary due diligence and negotiation to ensure that the investment is properly priced. The fact

[3] https://www.nesta.org.uk/sites/default/files/understanding-alternative-finance-2014.pdf.

[4] Crowdfunding Innovative Ventures in Europe: http://goo.gl/Ol8Clv.

[5] http://www.nesta.org.uk/sites/default/files/siding_with_the_angels.pdf.

that the angel is putting their own "skin in the game", by investing their own money, gives added reassurance to investors. This reassurance does not come entirely without cost for AngelList investors, though, as syndicate-leads get carry (a tax on investors' profits).

Properly priced investments are not the only factor in helping to protect the interests of investors. In the case of SyndicateRoom, an aspect of their investor-led approach that benefits investors is that they receive the same share class and price as the angels, whether they are investing £1,000 or £100,000. They also have the same rights in following their money in later rounds, enabling them to avoid excessive dilution.

This is often not the case on crowdfunding platforms that operate the company-led model, as companies can choose to issue more than one class of share. Often founders get A shares, whereas ordinary investors get B shares, that come without voting or pre-emption rights. This matters because ordinary investors may well see their stake heavily diluted if the company embarks on another round of funding at a higher valuation.

The investor-led model of crowdfunding has clear benefits for investors over the company-led model. As crowdfunding continues to grow, issues such as the protection of investors, transparency, and education will assume an ever greater importance, not just in the UK market but across Europe as well. Companies that put the investor first will be well-placed to take advantage of these changes. Will "investor-led" be added to the Oxford English Dictionary one day? Surely it can only be a matter of time.

My Robo Advisor was an iPod – Applying the Lessons from Other Sectors to FinTech Disruption

By Paolo Sironi

Thought Leader, Wealth Management Investment Analytics, IBM

FinTechs are hitting the headlines for their potential to disrupt banking services, unbundle financial institutions, and tear down barriers to entry by means of digital weapons.

Within the FinTech ecosystem, robo advisors have gained momentum to advise or manage private wealth at the expense of established institutions and are poised to become the new price-makers of the banking relationship. They first appeared around 2010, and leapt to the top of the chart of disruptive innovation a few years later due to a set of concurrent factors:

- A change in market regulation to favour fee-only advice, which is affecting global markets;

- A significant growth in assets under management that robo advisors could harvest in a relatively short time;

- The recognition of appealing not only to low-margin clients, but also to affluent and high-net-worth investors, which were previously thought to be an exclusive *target segment* of traditional more expensive advisory firms.

Yet, not all FinTechs addressing personal finance can be classified as robo advisors, and not all robo advisors are pure FinTechs.

"What is a robo advisor?"

The terminology "robo advisor" is quite journalistic: they are not always robotic, nor do they always provide advice.

Robo advisors (1.0) are automated investment solutions which provide automated portfolio rebalancing using trading algorithms based on passive investments and diversification strategies, which engage individuals with digital tools featuring advanced customer experience, to guide them through a self-assessment process and shape their investment behaviour towards rudimentary goal-based decision-making. It follows that robo advisors must display at least some of these four elements, if not all of them:

- Provide full digital access;

- Perform automated portfolio rebalancing;

- Adopt indexation or passive management;

- Personalize to customers' goals and behaviour.

"Is robo technology truly disruptive?"

We will answer this question by referring to the theory of innovation, which enables us to establish a parallel between the iPod's disruption of the music industry and the game-changing nature of robo advisors in banking.

First of all, we do not confine technology to a concept linked to the usage of algorithms or digital instruments (e.g. tablets), but we define technology as any process by which a firm (e.g. a bank) transforms information and data, human labour, or economic capital into products or services of greater value. This is of the utmost importance because most banking transactions are essentially "immaterial" and we can ascribe to the technology concept the three elements of digitalization, automated portfolio rebalancing, and goal-based investing (GBI) principles. We will explain why the latter plays a key role in the evolution of robo advisors.

Second, technology evolves continuously inside and outside individual firms. The introduction of new technology modifies the way firms operate and the way consumers access services and products. Therefore, we use the term innovation to indicate any change of existing technology used by a firm and recognize that such a change can take two forms: disruptive innovation or sustaining innovation:

- Sustaining innovation refers to any improvements in product performance, being of incremental nature or more radical, that allow a firm to increase the quality of its offer, to fend off competition, or to increment commercial margins, by operating either at lower costs or with higher affordable prices. Structured finance or hedge funds would be some examples.

- Disruptive innovation instead might well result in worse product performance, at least in the near term. Such revolutionary products are usually cheaper, simpler, or more convenient to use and appeal to new customers or create new needs in existing clientele.

Robo advisors classify as disruptive technology because they are cheaper than traditional advisory services, they are simpler to access, they appeal to new customers, and create a new need among existing clientele.

Goal-based investing, which robo advisors represent in a rudimentary fashion, is instead a case of sustaining innovation, which will grant the smarter robo advisors the opportunity to move outside the disruptive though unpleasant corner of low margin businesses and achieve margin-driven growth over time.

Traditional firms typically face two challenges in their lifetime: deciding how much investment needs to be dedicated to sustaining innovation and, most importantly, recognizing which disruptive innovation can be the main reason for failure or success of established brands, although such innovation might seem to be anti-economical in the near term. Banks are not excluded from the need to solve this dilemma.

"How do sustaining and disruptive innovation interact to shape the future of banking?"

According to Clayton M. Christensen,[1] there is a relationship between innovation and industry/product performance over time (i.e. the quality of banking services): there seems to be a fixed amount of innovation that a regular customer can absorb, all industries being equal, hence a capped amount of money that investors are willing to pay to receive better products or services. Clearly, not all investors

[1] http://www.claytonchristensen.com/key-concepts/.

are equally constrained, which permits banks to tier their offers across different segments: retail, affluent, high-net-worth (HNW) and ultra-high-net-worth (UHNW). This is represented in the following Figure.

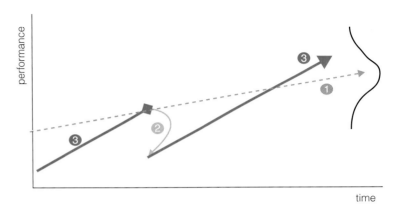

 improvement rate: innovation a client can absorb and its variability

 disruptive innovation: introduces simplified and less expensive products/services, to appeal to new or less-demanding customers

sustaining innovation: higher margins and more demanding customers once products gain foothold, improvement cycle restarts

Figure: **Innovation and industry/product performance over time**

Yet, time goes by, industries evolve, technology changes, and so does investors' behaviour. Thus, markets or segments can saturate: no further innovation can lead to higher commercial margins. This is when disruptive innovation, such as robo advisors, has the highest chance of succeeding. Initially, disruptive solutions are seen as a phenomenon confined to less appealing low margin clients (e.g. retailers) or distant markets (e.g. emerging economies). But disruptive innovation can downshift the product paradigm globally, across markets and segments, so that customers start favouring the new solutions and move en masse towards new offers. This can displace established players who have no time to adjust their traditional workflows or business models. Market leaders become laggards (e.g. Nokia) and new entrants gain momentum (e.g. Apple) and start climbing the hall of fame of successful brands. Thereafter, the cycle of sustaining innovation re-ignites and successful firms can achieve higher commercial margins by improving once very simple disruptive products.

To exemplify why robo advisors have all the potential to be disruptive technology, we can briefly discuss what happened in the music industry, when the iPod was first launched.

The first Compact Disc (CD) player was sold in Japan by Sony in 1982. The CD levelled up the music industry by setting a higher standard and inducing fierce industry competition by means of sustaining innovation. A period of tech spending involved a large number of consumers who were buying new appliances offering higher levels of sophistication. Within a decade, many households were equipped with advanced High Fidelity sets (Hi-Fi) featuring equalizers, subwoofers, powerful amplifiers, and fancy head-sets that parents were willing to buy to reduce noise late at night. Soon, individuals reached a peak point in consuming satisfaction, and in the late 90s they could not possibly justify paying higher prices for a declining marginal improvement in music quality. The music market saturated.

Steve Jobs grabbed this chance and in 2001 launched the Macintosh version of iTunes and the first Apple iPod (think of a robo advisor). The key selling point of the iPod was not better music quality compared to existing CD players. The fact is that the product was cheaper, more portable, and certainly cooler than CD players. Those who thought that it would have been a phenomenon confined to young consumers, walking up and down the streets with white cables in their ears, were proved wrong. The era of the Hi-Fi was over, the traditional way of buying and listening to music was disrupted and changed forever. Most importantly, today the dependence of Apple's revenues on iPod sales is very limited, as Apple entered a new wave of sustaining innovation to release higher margin services and devices, such as iPhones and iPads up to the Apple Watch in 2015 (think of GBI).

"What does this tell us about the fate of wealth management?"

Digital trends are a mix of technology advances and changes in consumers' behaviour which are facilitating the creation of new entrants to compete with traditional banks. Robo advisors are FinTechs which attempt to democratize advisory services that have always been an *exclusive privilege* of private banking institutions. They started to target retail investors needing financial advice, but lacking the resources to pay for the required services. With an entry level investment of around US$5,000, robo advisors were meant to appeal to low-margin customers and mostly to a very young clientele whose needs remained unheard

by traditional bankers, as they did not account for a large contribution to their balance sheet figures. Yet, robo advisors proved to be very attractive solutions not just for low-income customers, but also for affluent and high-net-worth individuals. Banks, already reconsidering their focus on wealth management operations due to increasing cost of capital in investment banking, yet challenged by tighter market regulation, were quite abashed to see that new entrants were threatening their once dominant positions, filling the headlines of newspapers, and attracting within a short time a considerable amount of venture capital funding.

We can conclude that robo advisors possess all the elements to be a disruptive technology and relegate the banking industry to simpler and low-income business models. Clearly, although new entrants use digital weapons and dump incumbent businesses, neither robo advisors nor the financial institutions willing to invest and transform have any interest in engaging in a huge transformation effort to corner themselves in low-income shops.

Goal-based investing will provide a way out for all the players that master the battle of disruptive innovation. GBI principles are already present in robo advisors' propositions, but to a level of simplicity that cannot afford them any leverage and increase commercial margins. Yet, the tendency will be for financial advisory and financial planning to converge within robo models. This will allow robo advisors to tier their offering to appeal to a more diversified client base and will enable them to price up their services by competing on more added value services. The sustaining innovation that GBI can provide is supported by high-end technology advances, such as cognitive computing and risk-based portfolio management.

"Will banks be extinct or will they transform?"

We cannot predict the future of an industry nor of an individual firm, and we cannot say if today's banking will become extinct or will transform under market and consumer pressure. The latter is the more likely outcome, given the unique characteristics of banking as a regulated and, to a point, a protected industry. However, the industry landscape is truly changing fast. What lies ahead is not a one-sided competition, FinTechs versus traditional banks and advisors, but rather a likely situation where a handful of digitally transformed firms will become new dominant players, while traditional institutions unwilling or not able to embrace change will become laggards.

Crowdsourced Alpha

By Vinesh Jha
CEO, ExtractAlpha

In August 2007 many established market-neutral institutional investors experienced sudden losses when some large investor – seeking liquidity to cover losses in another part of his portfolio – liquidated an equity book that had been dedicated to quantitative ("quant") strategies, which used computer models to select stocks. Because this investor held similar stocks to other quants, the liquidations led to adverse moves across such strategies, and a domino effect ensued as other affected investors liquidated to prevent further losses. Prices snapped back to their previous values, but by that time many investors had locked in large losses.

The following Figure, from Khandani and Lo's paper "What Happened to the Quants in August 2007?",[1] shows the returns to quant strategies at the time. These were market-neutral strategies designed to be very low-risk, and a 2% move in a single day was an extreme outlier event.

Quants had a hidden risk: they shared strategies, and therefore positions, with their peers. Shared positions led to liquidation risk, high correlation of returns, and a

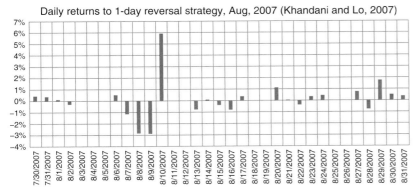

Daily returns to 1-day reversal strategy, Aug, 2007 (Khandani and Lo, 2007)

Figure: Daily returns to 1-day reversal strategy, August 2007
Source: Khandani and Lo, 2007

---

[1] *Journal of Investment Management*, 5, 29–78.

lack of differentiation from the perspective of underlying investors. The strategies were similar in universe, risk modelling, research techniques, and, most importantly, sources of alpha.

But why were the alphas so similar across established firms? Because their data sources were identical. Systematic investors rely on historical data to design strategies. A handful of data sets – financial statements, market data, and broker earnings estimates – dominate these strategies and the academic research which inspires them.

The Need for New Data

Lately, demand for differentiated alpha has increased, and has been met thanks to greater data availability and processing power. New data leads to improved outcomes for managers who are proactive in sourcing the data and implementing models based on it. The question then arises: where does this new data come from? First, an investment manager could dig deeper into traditional qualitative content. FinTech companies such as AlphaSense and RavenPack provide structured data derived from such unstructured sources as conference call transcripts and news. Secondly, data sets can be formed as "exhaust" from other processes. Transactional data such as point-of-sale data, or foot or web traffic, originally collected for other purposes, can find utility among investors. Finally, data can be crowdsourced. Crowdsourcing can be an *active* process: a data supplier could ask people to collect data, or to provide their opinions. Premise Data Corp crowdsources the collection of pricing data on foods worldwide, leading to accurate inflation expectations. *Passive* crowdsourcing is also possible: opinions can be harvested from blogs, social media, product reviews, etc.

There are, however, some caveats. Historical data may be short, or may exhibit survivorship bias if it excludes defunct companies; or it may be thin, including only names in one particular industry. These limitations make it harder to draw inferences in a backtest, or to partition historical data into in-sample (testing) and out-of-sample (validation) periods. The data can be in a nasty format, with no clean identifiers such as ticker, and one must often do the hard work of extracting sentiment or other information from unstructured data. These difficulties are not insurmountable, and the rewards to those data vendors or consumers who put effort into sourcing and cleaning this data can be significant.

What is Crowdsourced Alpha?

Crowdsourced alpha is *the use of multiple humans' forecasts to make investment decisions*. These humans need not know their forecasts are being used – as in the passive crowdsourcing examples above. They need not actually be explicit forecasts. There are many companies attempting to create alpha out of Twitter feeds, extracting company sentiment from 140-character posts.

To crowdsource alpha, we need a *measurable thing to forecast*, which we *need help in forecasting*; and we need *humans to make the forecasts*. We need some platform for the collection of forecasts. We may need to provide some incentive for the forecasts to be provided – monetary (pay me to make a forecast), pride-based (I want to be the best forecaster), marketing-based (I want to tell everyone I am the best), or community-based (I want to share my opinions). We need to clean up noise in the data. A diversity of opinions or knowledge is helpful, allowing us to benefit from the wisdom of the crowd in the generally understood way. It is also useful to have an objective way of measuring forecasting skills. The persistence of skill is valuable. If the good forecasters remain good over time, then skill is an inherent characteristic of the forecasters. We can then have confidence that the top forecasters' ideas will be worth listening to in the future.

An early example was the IBES (Institutional Brokers Estimates System (I/B/E/S, as part of Thomson Reuters)) broker forecast data set. Though commoditized now, the idea was once novel: collect brokers' earnings per share (EPS) forecasts and combine them into a consensus expectation of earnings. IBES fulfils our needs: a platform for structured forecasts of useful, relatively noise-free forecasts by incentivized humans. We can debate whether those incentives are great ones, but the data is indisputably valuable. It exhibits many of our wants: the opinions are somewhat diverse, though less so in cases of herding or management guidance, and there is persistent skill in analyst forecasting, as proven in work done at StarMine – now part of Thomson Reuters, but then independent – in the early 2000s.

We can use the crowd to forecast many things. A few examples can be seen in the Table below.

Table: Examples of forecast types which can be crowdsourced

What	Who	Where
EPS, Revenues	Sell side	IBES, FactSet, CapIQ
	Buy side, Independents, Individuals	Estimize
Returns	Sell side research	IBES, FactSet, CapIQ, TipRanks
	Sell side sales desks	TIM Group
	Financial bloggers and newsletters	Seeking Alpha, Motley Fool, TipRanks
	Individuals	PredictWallStreet, StockTwits
Social Sentiment	Twitterers, Facebookers	Gnip, and many others
Macro	Governments, Economists	Reuters, Government, Consensus Economics, Estimize
M&A	Rumor mill	Mergerize by Estimize
Strategies	Fund managers	FoF, multistate firms
	Algo developers	Quantopian, QuantConnect

Example 1: Crowdsourced Earnings Estimates

Estimize is an innovative platform in which the crowd – amateur and professional analysts or investors – supplies forecasts of a company's future EPS and revenues. Contributors may disclose their name and professional status (buy side, independent researcher, individual trader, student, etc.). The pool of 7,000 contributors is equally split among these groups.

A simple average of the crowd's forecasts is more accurate than Wall Street 61.8% of the time when there are at least three contributing forecasters. These numbers increase to 64.8% and 66.3% when requiring 10 or 20 forecasters, respectively. There are several hypotheses as to why the crowd would be more accurate than the experts. Although services such as StarMine have brought more accountability to sell-side research, EPS accuracy is only one input into an analyst's compensation and prominence. There are behavioural biases in sell-side earnings estimates, including herding. A forecaster is unlikely to make a notable estimate away from the consensus, for fear of being incorrect. Regulatory constraints on sell-side analysts constrain their ability to produce timely research updates. So changes in sell-side forecasts tend to be gradual. Institutional biases may also exist. Many analysts are employed by institutions which also include investment banking arms. If these banks want to retain the advisory business of their corporate clients, there may be pressure to provide optimistic forecasts on certain issuers.

We can gauge whether the greater accuracy helps investors by looking at the stock price reaction to firms which beat the sell-side's expectations, versus those which beat the crowd's expectations. Prices react much more strongly to surprises as benchmarked against the crowd; the expert-benchmarked market reaction is half the magnitude of the crowd-benchmarked reaction, and it reverses after a day, whereas the reaction of the crowd is more permanent. So crowdsourced data better represents the market's expectations of earnings, and an investor who uses it can profit from unexpected earnings (see following Figure).

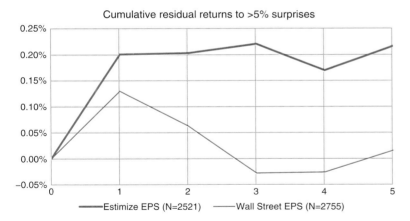

Figure: Cumulative residual returns to >5% surprises

Contributor accuracy is persistent from quarter to quarter: better-ranked contributors are 36% more likely to remain better ranked in the future, and poorly-ranked contributors 36% more likely to remain poorly ranked, than they are to switch to the opposite. So we can improve our forecasts by focusing on the best contributors.

Example 2: Alpha Capture

"Alpha Capture" refers to institutional investors' use of trade ideas from sell-side research sales and specialist sales to drive the investment process. These ideas are distinct from recommendations issued by brokers' research analysts' desks, and are privately communicated to clients, who compensate the brokerage firm for the ideas with trading commissions or cash. Ideas are shorter-term than their research desk counterparts and are more evenly distributed between Buy and Sell.

TIM Group offers the industry's leading alpha capture platform, called TIM Ideas. TIM Ideas has a unique data set of trade ideas on global securities from 2006 by 300 brokers and 3,000 unique "authors". Trade ideas are not otherwise aggregated into a single database, and only by using TIM can we understand the benefits of aggregating disparate forecasts.

We examine the returns to a trade idea – in the following Figure we have flipped the sign so that we expect the returns to both Buy and Sell ideas to look positive. We have restricted our analysis to stocks with at least US$100m market cap, $1m daily trading volume, and $4 in price, and we have adjusted returns to account for industry and common risk factors.

We see strong returns out to ten trading days in all regions. Because of the short horizon of trade ideas, acting on them in a timely manner is important.

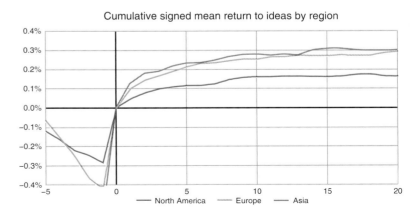

Figure: Cumulative signed mean return to ideas by region

CAPITAL AND INVESTMENT

Author performance is persistent: authors who have had profitable ideas in the past continue to provide superior trade ideas in the future. Authors are 47% more likely to stay in an extreme performance group (top or bottom quintile) than they are to fall to the opposite quintile.

The top ideas can also be combined into a stock selection signal, the TIM Indicator. The long/short returns to this signal are shown in the following Figure. The gross Sharpe ratio of a trade idea-driven strategy is, remarkably, over 5, and the numbers comfortably survive transaction costs, indicating that crowdsourced trade ideas can be used to generate significant alpha.

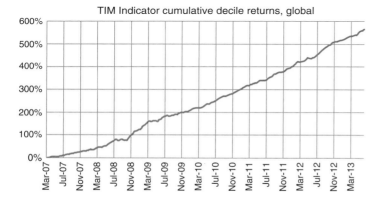

Figure: TIM Indicator cumulative decile returns, global

Example 3: Financial Bloggers

Attention to crowdsourced alpha has focused on identifying sentiment on Twitter. Microblog sentiment is well explored, so we focus on a more finance-relevant subset of social media, financial bloggers. Blogs such as Seeking Alpha and Motley Fool produce content which is designed to predict stocks, but is underexploited by institutional investors. TipRanks collects investment advice from 65 news and financial blog sources, and applies Natural Language Processing (NLP) to derive sentiment measures. 122,000 recommendations from more than 4,000 authors on over 2,000 US equities have been collected in real time, creating a robust collection of qualified sentiment. These blogs are targeted to financial readers, with articles by buy-side investors and industry experts. Contributors are often compensated, and typically disclose existing positions to mitigate the effects of potential conflicts of interest.

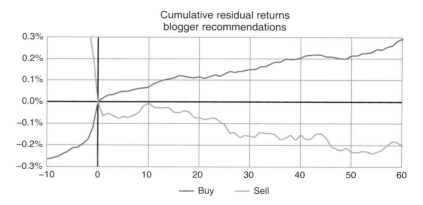

Figure: Cumulative residual returns blogger recommendations

Table: Historical returns of equity market neutral portfolios built using the TIM Indicator

Region	Decile Annual Return	Decile Sharpe Ratio	Decile Hit Rate % days	Stocks per Decile	Decile Daily Turnover
Global	29.61%	5.52	69%	336	12%
North America	20.84%	2.56	59%	164	11%
Europe (excluding UK)	42.17%	5.02	65%	56	13%
United Kingdom	44.73%	3.7	61%	25	15%
Japan	31.70%	3.19	59%	50	12%
Asia (excluding Japan)	35.60%	2.79	59%	36	12%
Australia and New Zealand	36.84%	2.02	57%	13	13%

In the following Figure, we show the residual returns to Buy and Sell recommendations from financial blog posts, with the universe as before. Due to the retail focus of these blog posts, 84% of the recommendations are Buys.

Clearly there is alpha in financial blog posts. A market-neutral investment strategy which buys the stocks with recent Buy recommendations and shorts those with recent Sell recommendations is significantly more profitable, as shown in the following Figure, which uses the TipRanks Expert Sentiment Signal (TRESS).

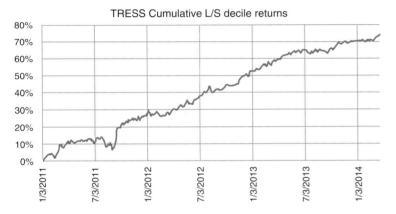

Figure: TRSS cumulative L/S decile

A financial blog-based strategy demonstrated an annualized return of 18.8% and a Sharpe ratio of 2.13 over this time period in market-neutral terms, demonstrating the relatively unexploited power of financial blog data when implemented in a systematic way.

In summary, investment managers now have access to innovative data sets which crowdsource alpha, and which allow them to differentiate their return streams from those investors who continue to use commoditized data sets. These data sets offer significant, measurable performance improvements over traditional sources. As more data becomes available to investment managers, and as the types of forecasts which can be crowdsourced proliferate, investment managers and their clients will benefit.

To Crowdsource a Hedge Fund

By Andrew Campbell

Data Analyst, Quantopian

Quantitative investing, using computer algorithms to run a portfolio, carries enormous economic incentives. Five out of the top six hedge fund managers in 2014 were quants. Quantitative investors Kenneth Griffin of Citadel, James Simmons of Renaissance Technologies, and Ray Dalio of Bridgewater each earned over $1 billion in 2015 alone. Bridgewater itself has $169 billion under management. Their algorithmically informed Pure Alpha fund has an average annualized return of 18%, having lost money in only three years of its 20-year life.

Yet, in a world of 7 billion people, there are only around 5,000 professional quants. Why should we believe that only such a small population of managers is capable of harnessing algorithms to generate top returns? Daily leaps in engineering and the widely documented finance-to-tech brain drain are proof that not all investing talent resides in the cubicles of elite hedge funds. Individuals from a wide range of backgrounds are capable of beating the market. When aggregated, this talent has the potential to compete with Wall Street's finest institutions. There is a significant opportunity for the crowd to disrupt the guarded world of quantitative investing.

Why is quantitative investing not bigger? Should the financial upside not draw more people to the profession? The answer lies in two barriers to entry: technology and track record. For individuals, algorithmic investing tools are hard to develop and data is prohibitively expensive. A lone quant will spend much more time building and maintaining a trading rig than he or she will creating actual strategies. Even if you do have a trading platform, attracting investors is nearly impossible without a viable track record. Who would trust you? As an aspiring manager, your only hope is to land a job at an accredited hedge fund.

But what if this was not the case? What if everyone had the tools they needed to create a track record and raise capital backing? Surely, given the right tools, many of the world's scientists, engineers, and hobbyists would apply their intellect to the markets. This democratization of quant finance is already well underway. Accessible data sources, free education resources, low-cost cloud-based research, back-testing, and execution platforms are levelling the playing field. But even with the right tools, individual quants need a third party to give their back-testing and live trading results a stamp of legitimacy. Without an impartial scale on which to compare managers, investors will never throw their capital behind the crowd. The time has come to give aspiring quants the chance to earn their stripes. Competitive forums in other fields have given birth to efficient hiring networks. TopCoder's competitive arena for programmers and Kaggle's data science leaderboards have become go-to resources for job-hunters to communicate their skills to prospective employers. Surely, the world of quant finance can follow this model. Nothing more than a good idea should be necessary to begin developing the track record needed to attract investment.

The structure and implementation of this quant crowdsourcing platform are not to be glossed over. It is very unlikely that any good manager would be willing to simply show their algorithm code to potential investors. What would stop the investor from stealing the idea? This market failure was explored by Kenneth Arrow in his famous "Arrow Information Paradox". The paradox states that valuable intellectual property (IP) will only change hands when the buyer feels confident that they are buying good technology at a fair price. Yet, if the invention is revealed to the buyer in the pre-sale process, it has in effect been given to him or her. As a result, valuable IP is unlikely to change hands without patent protection. To avoid these IP trade frictions, all algorithm evaluation must be based on analysis of a strategy's returns, not on the underlying code.

To verify the validity of a return's track record, the investment platform must itself run tests on the algorithm being judged while keeping its code encrypted. Allowing individuals to submit their own data would leave investors vulnerable to fraud. This mass execution and comparison of investing algorithms is only feasible when the algorithms themselves are written in a standardized format. To make this common format and evaluation process attractive to quants, a robust all-in-one algorithm creation and comparison package is necessary. When a platform for researching, writing, back-testing, deploying, and comparing trading strategies becomes an investor in its own user base, a symbiosis emerges. The quants get a free platform for researching and writing algorithms that will always remain their own intellectual property and the chance to win significant capital backing. While the rest of the world is left analysing quarterly returns on a few dozen strategies, the platform-investor gets to build their portfolio by looking minutely at returns from hundreds of thousands of strategies. With this mass of data in hand, a fund can more accurately invest in the strong and uncorrelated algorithms needed to form an elegantly diversified portfolio.

To understand the full beauty of a crowdsourced hedge fund, we must first define the portfolio theory term "diversification". Diversification is the systematic dampening of risk through the ownership of uncorrelated return streams. Think of the daily return of an asset as the sum of its true underlying growth rate and a risk term. Each day, that risk term draws a value (which can be positive or negative) from a normal distribution and adds it to the price of the asset. This random element of price movement defines the volatility of the asset. When we hold a diverse basket of assets, we expect the correlation of their risk terms to be lower. With uncorrelated risk terms, we expect those daily fluctuations in price to cancel each other out. By isolating the growth rates of our assets, diversification allows us to achieve our target return with lower volatility.

Money managers use the "Sharpe ratio" (a portfolio's annual return in excess of the risk-free government bond return divided by portfolio volatility) to quantify the balance between a strategy's past risk and reward. The Sharpe ratio is particularly useful when it comes to exposing the results' diversification. For example, some simple maths tells us that a portfolio of 15 uncorrelated return streams, each with a Sharpe ratio of only 0.2, is likely to yield an aggregate Sharpe of 1.0. Even if you are chasing high returns, a strategy with low volatility relative to returns may be preferable. Leverage, broker loaned funds that can be used to purchase more assets, can be used to raise returns while keeping volatility below an acceptable threshold.

For the last 30 years, most portfolio diversification occurred through the inclusion of uncorrelated types of assets. Each new "thing" that was securitized became an opportunity to offset the risk of another asset class. However, at a certain point, relying on traditional assets to diversify has its limits. New frontiers for diversification are unlocked when the assets in your portfolio are actually portfolios themselves. Imagine a portfolio of trading signals where each signal has a given rate of poor decision-making and good decision-making. To minimize your risk at a given level of profitability, you would want poor decisions by each of the signals to be uncorrelated events. Given a low correlation between the daily decision qualities of your signals, even a slight bias towards good decision-making is very likely to generate a steady profit. The key to lowering the correlation between signals is diversity in data sources and data interpretation.

The recent explosion in data availability has raised the potential for signal diversification immensely. According to a 2014 IBM report, 90% of the data generated by humankind has been created in the last two years. As the pool of available data grows, the potential for diversification through data interpretations expands at a significantly faster rate. With the rise of "big data" has come a reinvigoration of R&D activity in statistics, machine learning, and distributed computing. Data is being mined for new insights and optimizations in ways that were impossible even a few years ago. For each additional dataset that becomes available, there are dozens of ways in which that dataset could be used to generate a trading signal.

This is where crowdsourcing comes in. By investing in a collection of fine-tuned quantitative strategies drawn from the crowd, the inputs, parameters, and underlying theory behind each of these strategies become potential sources of diversification. Aggregating strategies into a portfolio is not a new idea. First introduced in the 1960s, the "fund of funds" model has attracted substantial mainstream attention and investment. However, no fund has ever capitalized on the potential benefits of aggregated investing talent at a massive scale. If we assume that manager skill among independent quants is normally distributed, given enough algorithms, the probability of finding a promising collection of uncorrelated strategies is very high.

For the last hundred years, hedge funds have been run as highly centralized institutions. Only a select group of highly educated and proven managers are privy to the investment process. Even at a large fund, it is not uncommon for one star player to call all the shots. This concentrated decision-making paradigm is set to be challenged by the collective wisdom of the crowd. When individuals everywhere are given the tools to build a track record and win investment, genuine meritocracy becomes a reality in quant finance.

Providing Capital and Beyond

By Kayar Raghavan
Angel Investor and Non-Executive Director

People use the words money and capital interchangeably but that is a mistake. Capital is scarce. Do not believe anyone who says otherwise. Money on the other hand is plentiful. That is why we see near zero or negative interest rates for money kept in banks. Money is not of much use if it is not productive. Capital on the other hand is money productively invested and deployed. It is, therefore, even scarcer when it comes to angel or venture capital, which is sought to be invested in enterprises run by *others*. A blog from Reid Hoffman says that a general partner looks at a few thousand (you read that right) companies before investing in two firms at best, in a given year.

Why am I saying this? Whether it is scarce public capital provided to start-up firms by governments in the form of grants, loans, equity, and tax rebates or private capital provided by angel investors, venture capital, corporate VCs, and private equity firms, it is a responsibility enjoined upon them to ensure that the funds are put to extraordinarily good use. However, there are not many young firms that reach that threshold of good use, that of a potential to yield multiple returns and other benefits such as employment creation or environmental sustainability to their stakeholders. No wonder, too, that almost four out of five start-ups do not even return the invested capital. This is also, unfortunately, for a good reason.

Investors, both private and government, put money into start-ups whose idea, product, team, and execution skills, put together, can create value, *immense* value, for them. The value may take any form. It may be pure financial returns to the private investors, while for governments and quasi-governmental bodies it may in the main be the creation of greater employment opportunities or be advantageous in areas such as public health and education. However, in order for these forces to create value, they require underlying drivers to operate in tandem and at their optimum potential. All these underlying variable/drivers are interconnected and, if they all exist, can substantially increase the likelihood of success. They do not always operate in isolation and are often part of a larger ecosystem. This is where the private and public investor communities can, should, indeed in my opinion, badly need to, play a much more effective role.

While a few private investors such as angels and early venture capital firms do take up active roles such as board director, advisor, mentor, Entrepreneur in Residence (EiR) and the like, helping the investee companies from within and without, this chapter addresses the larger issues in the public space which both private capital and government may collaborate to address. Addressing some of these issues is so transformational that it may take up to a generation for the drivers to be fully effective. This is because there are structural weaknesses, although a few of these may be country-, region-, or culture-specific. Some other deficiencies and drawbacks may be addressed in a shorter time horizon. What is not in doubt is that these areas are in need of massive regeneration and re-engineering, and unless this task is undertaken very swiftly, the future repercussions may be catastrophic, not just in terms of lost opportunities for employment creation, a first-order problem in much of the world, but also in causing further damage to what may already be a fragile social cohesion, at least in some inner cities.

The Great Digital Divide

Access to technology is a fundamental infrastructure issue, at several levels, with huge ramifications, but in particular to developing a healthy and employment-generating tech ecosystem. On the one hand, a large percentage of the population in many countries simply does not have the wherewithal in terms of literacy, much less, digital literacy, to access digital knowledge, means, and assets. As technology and innovation continue to advance at a rapid pace, the divide becomes even more acute for the digitally disadvantaged. This is a very marked divide even in advanced countries, let alone developing and underdeveloped countries. Lack of digital literacy, combined with an ageing population in much of the European continent, is a case in point. Let me amplify this with a real life example.

Thanks to technology, much of banking and financial services has moved online. However, banks, even those starved of capital, are compelled to keep open totally unviable branches to serve those who cannot go online and use internet banking and, therefore, require in-person services. Post offices are kept open to accept small savings and to dispense benefit payments to the elderly. The result of this is that the cost of distribution and delivery remains high to the detriment of the taxpayer. This also deprives those start-ups that provide these services digitally of an opportunity to scale up to serve all those in need of financial services. The result is capital loss on both counts: one, a case of higher public expenditure and the other, a case of potential revenue loss.

Lack of digital awareness and literacy also have other deleterious effects on society. The number of cases of personal data breaches, people being cheated out of their funds, and crimes of an even more serious nature such as personal security being compromised, is on the increase thanks to the literacy divide between the digitally aware and the digitally deficient. This obviously puts a huge burden on the exchequer as governments have to spend a vast amount of resources to protect the digitally innocent from the unscrupulous but digitally sophisticated.

The other major reason for the digital divide is simply lack of access. In many countries, communication infrastructure is neither uniform nor fully reliable. Vast areas are still unconnected by internet with reliable bandwidth. Then there is the need for digital education and training in these far-flung areas. How then do young firms make their products and services available to people and businesses in these places? Even if they can do so, is it at affordable price points for both buyers and sellers? How many potential customers are lost to the start-ups due solely to this issue?

Large-scale Revamping of Education and Training

One of the biggest drawbacks in the realm of formal education, seen across the world, is the fact that much of the curriculum remains unchanged for years. Add to this the fact that it is often conducted independent of the realities of life outside school and another significant gap emerges. Technology is moving at supersonic speed, while much of the school curriculum moves, if at all, like a bullock-cart. The pace of product growth in consumer electronics, financial services, big data processing, delivery services growth through cloud, mobile, and social media is not just unmatched by the pace of education and training, but the difference is huge and increasing by the day. This causes, and has already caused, a massive supply deficit in terms of technical resources to businesses in general, but more particularly to the start-ups, which can hardly afford the high costs associated with hiring the very few and rare resources available in these technology-driven fields. Speak to any start-up cluster in any city in the world today and the lack of technical resources will be flagged up as the number one issue.

Yet another facet of much of the formal education system is its dependence on rote and the premium it places on high grades. This concentrates young minds on the immediacy of getting a higher grade and into the best schools and universities. Barring some major universities, there is almost no recognition given to experimentation, innovation, risk-taking, and public leadership in the curricula of most universities, much less schools. There is also the inherited culture in most societies where failure invites harsh criticism and public disgrace. This is hardly conducive to promoting an environment where starting a private enterprise or investing in one, both of which involve an inclination to take risks without fearing potential failure, is encouraged.

Education, training, and keeping pace with innovation is only marginally better at the big corporate and regulatory levels. Regulations lag by a big margin, even in relatively older domains such as medical devices and drug testing, crowdfunding, and e-commerce not to speak of a number of recent innovations such as bitcoin, blockchain, etc. When only one in five thousand synthesizers tested are used and only one in three drugs finally passed for use breaks even in terms of numbers, what is required of regulators is an adaptive approach that is outcome-oriented. The recent case of fast-tracking experimental Ebola drugs should be very instructive. But do we always have to wait for an emergency to drive innovation faster?

In addition, big corporations need to re-engineer their supply chains to accommodate the purchase of products and services from small firms. The time and resources spent in attracting big corporations as clients, notwithstanding a good business case, are simply unaffordable to most start-ups.

Growth Financing and Exit Opportunities

The start-up ecosystem can only be as strong as the encouragement and opportunities available for young risk-takers and innovators to leverage. One of the essential pillars of this ecosystem is the availability of finance at the early and seed stages. However, this is only possible, or in any case facilitated, by recycling old seed and early-stage monies, in addition to the injection of new monies. In essence, early angels need to recoup their early investments so that they can invest and de-risk new entrepreneurships.

Raising money from other people to fund one's start-up business is never easy. It is particularly hard to do so in the early stages where there is little empirical evidence within the firm to back up any claims or projections. Angel investors understand this and there is hence a smaller burden of proof imposed on founders and start-ups at this stage. When it comes to growth capital, though, fundraising assumes new dimensions in terms of complexity. Start-ups often have to show a minimum viable product or service, a level of customer traction and, importantly, product or service stickiness. While founders are understandably disinclined to dilute much at this stage, venture capital requirements are often fairly steep: 25% to 30% ownership at series A level. Given where their businesses are, many start-ups do not attract the level of valuation to be able to give away a big chunk of their firm, on the back of a prior round of angel funding and dilution. The VCs on the other hand are not prepared to engage with a start-up where their quantum of funding is below a minimum threshold. As VCs generally invest in no more than two firms per general partner per year on average, it is in their opinion sub-optimal for them to spend much time with a start-up that cannot absorb a level of funding that they are comfortable with.

Then there is the point about intellectual property (IP), or rather the lack of it, trotted out by some venture funds as the reason for not funding start-ups. These are days of open sourcing that developers can tap into and where the crowdsourcing of ideas and design are almost the norm. When Elon Musk is throwing open Tesla design principles to be copied by other car manufacturers, IP should not be of great value to anyone – barring a rare case of drug discovery – other than keeping some patent attorneys busy. Facebook, Apple, and Google have umpteen patents but they don't make their monies from their patents, nor is any of their functionality totally irreplaceable. It is ultimately all about execution; that is, how nimble the company and the product are in receiving user feedback, adding new functionality, and iteratively making available to users feature-rich products, all of which can be done without making a great effort to protect patents.

VC funding is not available to start-ups that have not been substantially de-risked, as we have seen above. The level of de-risking expected of start-ups by venture funds is high, particularly in areas where precedent is lacking. The exceptions are start-ups founded or angel-backed by investors who have already had successful exits or the start-up is in a domain that is the latest fad and backed by several VCs at the same time. All others have to kiss several frogs before they find a VC prince. Even when they find one, the terms are prohibitive in terms of anti-dilution provisions such as full ratchets and the like, not to speak of unreasonable cash

costs on account of due diligence and stock options allocation for mentorship imposed on the start-up. Much of this is simply unaffordable for many young companies. No surprise then that the delta between angel funding and VC funding is often referred to as the "death valley".

The demand–supply mismatch for growth funding is thus too pronounced, resulting in the effort becoming monumental, causing distraction and consequent disruption in the start-up's life with the result that many firms struggle to get growth funding. What then is the remedy?

A small country like Israel, which is second only to the United States in the number of technology companies listed on Nasdaq, has a lot to teach us here. In 1993 the Israeli government created Yozma, a $100 million fund of funds that in three years spawned 10 venture capital funds. In each one, Yozma, an Israeli private partner, and a foreign private partner with proven fund management expertise, all invested approximately equal amounts. From the start, the Israeli government gave the private sector partners an option to buy out its interest in the funds at attractive terms – a fact often overlooked by other governments that copy the Yozma model. That option was exercised by eight of the 10 funds, profitably for the government, by the way. Five years after the founding of Yozma, its remaining assets were liquidated by auction. The government's exit served as market proof that real value had been generated and is one of the reasons that the Israeli venture capital industry not only became self-sustaining, but simultaneously achieved a quantum leap in growth.[1]

In countries such as the United Kingdom, there exist at series A stage several opportunities to access grants and government or quasi-government co-funds. By their very mandate, these grants and co-funds are tasked to encourage start-ups through funding and investment, or to fill in the void where angel or VC funding falls short. This happens not only in areas of long gestation such as drug discovery and medical devices manufacturing and sales, but also in technological innovations that are disruptive, that promote public health, clean energy, a better environment and, often, simply create productive employment. These have indeed spanned firms from drug discovery to e-commerce, to analytics, to mobile health. Other countries and governments may emulate this model too.

---

[1] Source: HBR.

Many countries can also follow the example of the UK and a few other European countries as well as places like Singapore in Asia, where there are liberal tax concessions provided to angel investments. This will have the effect of attracting, once again, large-ticket angel investments, thus obviating the need for start-ups to look for series A funding early on, before attaining product/project maturity and market penetration. Indeed, the UK government's EIS/SEIS programmes are likely to have a phenomenal cascading effect in terms of additional angel investments once early angels start exiting profitably.

Also, if the VCs and later-stage funders, including government funds, can offer secondary exits at series A/B as a matter of course, even if only partially, to angel and seed investors, the latter would be prepared to fund start-ups more liberally, thus postponing the stage at which the start-ups look for growth funding. This will enable series A/B to come in at a slightly later stage when the start-ups will have had enough traction and are in a position to provide the requisite comfort to VCs.

Yet another avenue to provide exit opportunities for angels and early-stage investors is to create exchanges for purchase and sale of private securities, which can provide much-needed liquidity to these investments. These can be appropriately regulated, as India has sought to do, so that there is full transparency in the system.

Participation by private and public funds in these exchanges would provide phenomenal opportunities for liquidity and consequent recycling of capital, resulting in constant regeneration of the entire start-up ecosystem.

What I have outlined above are just some important areas to which private–public partnerships and governments should pay immediate attention. Large funds, businesses, and governments must continually prioritize a number of other aspects of business so that we can all cope with several competing demands – a youth bulge seeking employment leading to a large-scale labour migration, technological progress and innovation driving consumption patterns and climate change, demographic stagnation in Europe and China versus demographic dividends in Africa and South/Central Asia, are just some of the most pressing issues that will shape the FinTech sector of tomorrow.

These other areas encompass capacity building in the form of constant creation and maintenance of a healthy private and public investment climate, improved market access to small businesses, reduced friction and cost of doing business, help in scaling up businesses and, finally, creatively constructing financing and exit opportunities for risk-takers. We can see that human capital matters at least as much as traditional investment capital.

Enterprise Innovation

7

Innovation has not been the focus of financial institutions since the financial crisis as established players had to keep up with constantly changing regulatory requirements globally. This part provides the reader with an overview on how established financial companies innovate by leveraging both internal and external partnerships and innovation methodologies. The authors recommend an effective internal governance and stakeholder engagement model and share detailed insights on innovation labs, a very popular enterprise innovation strategy. The authors also focus on the collaboration options between established financial institutions and FinTech firms, including Corporate Venture Investing, explaining how to manage a successful internal investment arm. Finally, the insurance sector and the potential opportunities for innovation that exist within insurance are discussed.

Can Banks Innovate?

By Alessandro Hatami

Founder, The Pacemakers

2015 is the year when it became clear that the digital revolution has finally hit the banking industry. A couple of headlines illustrate that: global investment in Financial Technology (FinTech) has tripled in 2013–14[1] and the British Bankers Association announced that mobile banking has become the preferred way for customers to engage with their banks.[2] Most banks (although still not all) have finally come to realize that they need to start engaging with their customers with levels of speed, transparency, precision, and fairness that are simply not possible with the traditional branches and telephone banking approach. Banks are spending substantial amounts in IT, but their total investment globally is only expected to grow at 4.6% in 2014–15, and most of this will be spent on the maintenance of existing legacy systems.

With these changes underway, the leadership of most banks is increasingly keen to explore ways to become more innovative, and a growing amount of investment is being allocated to innovation. Some banks have established innovation teams – often headed by non-banking "disruptors" from other more innovative industries – and have allocated reasonable budgets to invest in delivering new ideas. Some banks have engaged in partnering with business accelerators and incubators – these are organizations that select promising FinTech start-ups for the banks to mentor, fund, and even partner with.[3] Last but not least, some banks have established investment funds to be able to invest directly in early-stage companies in the sector.[4]

All these initiatives have had the desired effect of creating a certain level of excitement within the banks, with a good number of PR opportunities to underscore their commitment to renewal and innovation. They have also generated long lists of possible innovative propositions. Some of these have even progressed to pilot stage – but very few have actually been delivered at scale to the banks' customer bases. This is because banks are fundamentally not designed to be innovative.

The business culture of most banks values consistency, reliability, predictability, and short-term profitability. These values have served the banks very well in the past, but they are very ill-suited to a marketplace that is being disrupted and requires the ability to respond quickly, often with an action plan that is not yet well-defined. This cultural disconnect has left banks unable to embrace the continuous innovation approach of businesses like Google and Amazon, built to constantly innovate. Most of the innovation that we see in banks is based on expensive, and hard to replicate isolated efforts.[5]

Does this mean the banks will not be able to innovate and meet the digital challenge? Not necessarily.

Banks build things all the time. They have well-established procedures and guidelines to do this that are extensively used and well-tested. To build new propositions, the innovation team within a bank needs to learn to apply the same approach to innovation propositions. Most new things banks build have certain requirements in common. They all have:

- A sponsor with sway,
- Engaged stakeholders,
- Confidence of customer buy-in, and
- A business case with a strong investment justification.

To start delivering at scale, a bank's innovation team needs to use a similar approach for all propositions they believe their bank should launch. These propositions should have business cases comparable to the banks' other investments.

---

[1] "The Future of Fintech and Banking", Accenture Study, March 2015 http://www.fintechin-novationlablondon.net/media/730274/Accenture-The-Future-of-Fintech-and-Banking-digitallydisrupted-or-reima-.pdf.

[2] "The Way We Bank Now: World of Change", report by the BBA and EY – June 2015 https://www.bba.org.uk/news/press-releases/mobile-phone-apps-become-the-uks-number-one-way-to-bank/#.ViEDdH6rSM8.

[3] See Startupbootcamp FinTech, Barclays Techstars, and Startup Accelerator with Wells Fargo.

[4] Corporate Venture Funds have been established by Santander, BBVA, Sberbank, American Express, Citibank, and Visa to name a few.

[5] A few examples of these are Pingit at Barclays, MoneyManager at Lloyds Bank, and BankAmerideals at Bank of America.

In order to put together these business cases, the innovation team need to create a delivery process that will enable them to run and afford several experiments every year, with an allowance for many of these not to succeed and to ensure that all those that do succeed meet the requirements of being eventually launched at scale. The key components of this process are a strong engagement with the bank, a deep understanding of how it does things, and the ability to experiment and test new ideas with customers quickly and cheaply. True innovation is based on experimentation, and it should be acceptable that the outcome of some experiments may be not to go ahead. Without failure, it could mean that the innovation efforts are being too conservative and not enough risks are being taken. Addressing costs and duration are also fundamental needs – most things banks do take too long and cost too much. This makes failure unaffordable. If the traditional delivery procedures are applied to innovation, failure cannot become an option.

Let us take a closer look at what needs to be in place to deliver innovation:

Sponsors with Sway

One of the key principles of delivering change in a big organization is that things are built on behalf of someone. This someone can be the regulator, the Compliance/Legal Division, or more often a P&L (profit and loss) owner. Even the greatest ideas, without the support and sponsorship of a business owner will not get built. Should this support not be there, it is often better for the Innovation team to focus on propositions that do have it and to pass on those that do not – even if these seem great ideas. A decent innovation that is actually delivered at scale is better than a great one that is not. The most important point to ensure is that the sponsor is committed to support a full-scale launch of the proposition if it is proven with customers and meets return targets.

This approach does have a downside, however. What should the innovation team do about strong ideas without adequate sponsor support? This can be common, especially in situations of channel conflict. There are no easy solutions in this case. An option is to shop the idea around to other potential sponsors – if the product teams are not supportive, then maybe the compliance teams, worried about customer treatment, could be. Another option is to escalate within the bank's hierarchy – but this option often leads to political complications and should be used sparingly. The third option is to wait and to move on to the next idea – good ideas

do have a tendency to resurrect themselves. All in all, though, it is helpful to realize that sometimes good ideas will not get built.

Engaged Stakeholders

It is best that the innovation team identify and engage with the various stakeholders – or gatekeepers – as soon as possible in the lifecycle of the experiment, right after having secured the sponsor buy-in. Stakeholders include employee representatives from Compliance, Fraud, Risk, Finance, HR, Operations, IT, Procurement, and more. These are the people that can stop the launch of a project. It is key that representatives of all these areas be at least informed of the experiment. It is important to involve all interested internal parties of an innovation experiment early on, because if the stakeholders will stop a new idea it is better for this to happen before too much time and effort is spent on it. In my experience, early engagement softens the stakeholders' stance when it comes to final approval.

Stakeholder engagement is not only a necessary precaution. Stakeholders can in fact often be strong contributors to the quality of the experiment. I have been involved in a project where the representative from the legal team came up with a nuance that fundamentally changed the propositions for the better. But it is important to be cautious of not losing control of the experiment because, when left to their own devices, stakeholders can also easily damage an experiment – so the engagement with them has to be treated with the utmost care. Stakeholders are necessary, but need to be managed well.

Confidence of Customer Buy-in

The best way to understand if customers want something is to let them use it. So the next important step is to create a prototype that, as far as possible, looks and feels like the end product to the customer. The non-customer-facing back-end, though, can sometimes be done less rigorously. Imagine an app that looks great to the customer, but the back-end integration is done by a colleague typing very quickly to enter the data into the system. The real objective of prototyping is to get first-hand customer feedback from a large enough sample of customers to either stop the idea or put together a realistic business case. It is important that a prototype is both inexpensive and quick so as to make potential failure affordable and to enable the bank to run several experiments a year, not just a handful. Small scale, speed, and cheapness are not attributes generally associated with the normal delivery capabilities of a bank, and therefore the innovator should explore building an alternative delivery process, possibly outside the bank, to build their prototypes.

Business Case

A strong business case is the key prerequisite for building anything in a bank. This is a document that has structure and content that is a reflection of a bank's culture and beliefs. As such, it is fundamental the innovation teams understand how to build one. Luckily, if they have got this far, they are likely to have all the necessary components aligned.

A business case needs an owner – in this case the sponsor fulfils that role. He or she will act as the advocate for the investment in the proposition at the appropriate decision-making fora. The business case will need an analysis of the return on investment. All the components are to hand. The results of the prototype will provide the base data to forecast a revenue number. Several of the stakeholders will provide the other needed inputs: IT and Operations will contribute to the costs analysis and Finance will validate the financial analysis. Other stakeholders will ensure the business case meets the regulatory, fraud, and compliance requirements.

Done right, the business case of the innovation proposition will look like any other project to be financed by the bank. With this approach, innovation will be disguised as business-as-usual, substantially increasing the likelihood of it being actually delivered at scale.

This approach is very helpful with innovation that has a clear path to profitability. As we know, this is not the case for many innovations. What should the approach be with non-profitable innovations? In some instances not having a path to profitability means that the idea should not be delivered at scale in the first place – in fact, the key objective of the prototyping is to identify these ideas before too much time and money has been spent on them. In some cases, however, the innovation proposition should be built even without a clear path to profitability. This can be because of competition, public opinion, regulation, and more. In those cases also the sponsor, stakeholders, prototype, and business case approach will still deliver the right framework to get the proposition built.

Innovation and digital change are changing the banking industry. It is the role of the effective Innovation team to help the bank understand, accept, and deliver innovation to customers – even without having to fundamentally change their culture.

And as more and more innovative ideas are delivered, it is possible – even likely – that the culture of the bank will change.

So, You Think the Innovation Lab is the Answer?

By Andra Sonea

FinTech Thought Leader

In the public perception, the banking world has remained almost unchanged while other industries have remodelled themselves in response to the global crisis and, recently, increasing pressure from digital customers. Bankers, consultants, and regulators on the other hand would state that the banking world has changed dramatically and they can even point to the thousands of millions spent in transformation programmes across the financial services industry. I would argue that clients do not see or feel this "transformation" – they largely get the same products and services as they used to get 20 years ago. While all banks now offer a mobile and web platform, the type of information offered is still the same and there is no sign of product personalization or contextual financial information allowing the customers to make the best financial decisions.

Life has undoubtedly accelerated as compared to 20 years ago. I can now buy online items ranging from books to electronics, even on my commute, within a timeframe which previously required days of browsing on the high street in order to make the final purchase. Now, mere seconds of impulsivity can unbalance people's finances and lives because they do not have, at their fingertips, the information needed to take financial decisions with confidence. While everybody thought real change in banking would come from regulatory change and large transformation programmes, it seems the combined pressure from customers and start-ups is a stronger disruptive force. The quick reaction of many banks was to set up an innovation lab in order to understand and meet the demands of this "new" customer and to react to them with the speed of a start-up. If the intention to change is not just a display of "innovation" for PR purposes, then I believe there are two key areas which should be taken into consideration if one wants to establish and run an effective innovation function:

1. Creativity and innovation need fertile ground to manifest themselves and the environment needs to be purposefully created.
2. Consistent methods for absorbing the outputs of creativity and innovation in the larger organization need to be enabled.

Foundations

Early decisions in setting up an innovation function lead to different work dynamics and, as a consequence, to fundamentally different innovation outputs.

Key questions for management are:

- Do you have a vision about the level you want to play at? Globally? Nationally?
- Are you focused on certain customer segments or products?
- How do you want your bank to operate in five years?
- Do you want your innovation function to explore and experiment in order to discover the path to that "future state"?

To illustrate the point, let me outline just two possible scenarios and how they impact the innovation function. Let us assume one bank's view is that the world moves towards financial services being consumed as utilities, and they will provide the forever-elusive pipes which will enable open innovation on top of its infrastructure. Another bank could hold the view that they should be your platform of choice for viewing your complete financial status through facilitating aggregation of all your financial data. These are two very different visions of the future, which both require important changes in the existing modus operandi of a retail bank. Their infrastructure does not yet have the fluidity or connectedness of the "pipes", nor can they provide their clients with a centre of control, analytics, or contextual advice. However, the innovation function in those banks will have something in common: they *focus* on a future scenario, and the innovation is aligned to it strategically – see the following Figure.

An innovation lab set up on such a path of discovery would be very different from one with a free agenda for "experimentation". Such innovation initiatives could be like "Google's 20% projects" where Google employees can spend one day a week focusing on side-projects which have the potential to bring new products to the table. These projects, while not clearly aligned to the company strategy, often end up in the company's product portfolio.

The most common form of experimentation in financial services within innovation labs is with a "business-led pipeline" or an "independent pipeline". The first type

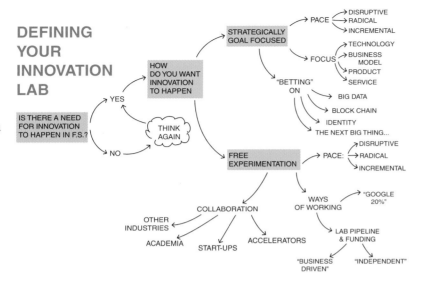

DEFINING YOUR INNOVATION LAB

Figure: **Defining your innovation lab – decision tree**

works with a pipeline constantly adjusted, depending on priorities and funding from "the business", while in the other model the lab has decision-making power over the priorities for experimentation, but probably less financial resources under its own control. Both types of innovation functions – let us call them "goal-focused" and "free experimentation" – need to explicitly answer some more questions in order for them to be effective:

- What is the bank's appetite for disruptive innovation?

- Do we want the lab to focus on discovering disruptive business models and formulate the accompanying requirements for technology delivery?

- Or would we like the lab to focus on incremental innovation[1] supporting other functions like strategy and planning or architecture, which together define the path to the "future state"?

---

[1] I would leave aside the discussion of whether there is such a thing as "incremental innovation". I would argue in this case that the organization is looking for "creative problem solving", not true innovation. See Tina Seelig, "Insight Out: Get Ideas out of Your Head and into the World" (*HarperOne*, 26 May 2015) for more.

The choices you make – disruptive or incremental; technology, product, service, or business model focused; betting on identity, big data, infrastructure, or blockchain – will lead to fundamentally different ways of delivering innovation – see the following Figure. One lab could be focused on disruptive product innovation using big data, while another could be focused on incremental innovation for customer experience. Both could exist within the same organization and also in parallel with free experimentation.

INNOVATION LABS FOCUS AND APPROACH

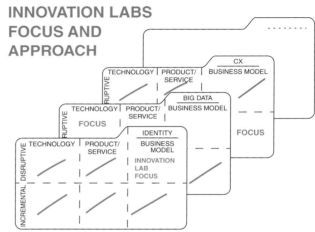

Figure: **Innovation labs – focus and approach**

For each model, there are obviously pros and cons. For an effective innovation lab, it is very important that the bank makes its intentions transparent to those working in the innovation function and to those using the outputs of this function, so the efforts and expectations are aligned and no resources are wasted in the decision process.

People

People are definitely the most important resource for the success of an innovation function. If you need people to deliver incremental changes along the bank's established functions or if creators are required who can envision "new worlds", the personalities and skills of your lab must be constructed to align with that vision. Most innovation labs I know end up, unfortunately, with a collection of the same type of people and skills and very often with too many project managers. There should also be UX designers, the CX specialists, and people versed in strategy and formulating propositions. There should also be developers not borrowed from an agency. I would always involve architects – people who know the bank by heart and can tell you how or if a shiny new technology could be applied in the real context of that bank. Diversity is key to enabling creativity. Bring people with different professional and cultural backgrounds together; take people from other industries, younger and older generations, and veterans from within the organization.

Just because "innovation" is young and hip, your lab should not be exclusively a collection of young hipsters. Managing diversity and people with deep expertise is never a simple task. Whoever will manage the labs will need to nurture, not stifle the diversity, enable, not suppress critical thinking, and manage deep expertise for a common collective purpose.

Methodology

An innovation lab is a Noah's ark of professions and specialisms. Each profession has its own methodology and language and each individual can in principal create an end-to-end solution to a problem within the confines of their specialism. However, the premise of an innovation lab hinges on the collaboration process of a cross-section of expertise. Therefore, a common "language" must be developed to allow a service designer, who has never been exposed to Financial Services, to communicate with the banking decision-makers or architects. To be clear, it is very difficult to coalesce skills and people with very different professional backgrounds – but this is precisely the combination needed for "real" innovation to happen. It is imperative, that the different voices and ideas are not silenced or suffocated. Thus, active and paramount effort must be placed and maintained in creating a communal "language" and, in turn, methodology.

Another key dimension of diversity is melding the ways of working in the start-ups and enterprise environments. The lab exists within the remand of the enterprise but has to deliver like a start-up. Therefore, it is acutely important that the lab methodology enables both "ways of working".

If you choose Design Thinking, Lean or Agile Methods, or if you develop your own method – train the whole team. Do not let them play by the ear. Simply put, through the common methodology, you initiate interactions between specialisms that are

unlikely to happen within the larger organization, and allow them to feed off each other's energy and ideas.

Resources

Is the innovation function a physical space, or can innovation happen through virtual collaboration?

I have seen both work. People can simply use the resources of the organization available for normal business (rooms, technology, and processes). There is no definite need for that shiny space, with coloured modern furniture. However, most financial services labs now have dedicated physical spaces,[2] some of them located with the rest of the business, and some in global tech centres. There is no "best" choice here, however there are implications. A remote location might allow the lab to develop new ways of thinking, away from the restrictions of the organization. This positive aspect can, however, be negated afterwards when the lab wants to feed back their findings. They can be perceived as out of touch with the organization, or they simply might not have the means to forge the necessary relationships with the key internal stakeholders who would be affected by their findings and need to take a decision about their innovation proposals.

What makes the actual difference to the output of a lab is what type of resources they have access to. Ideally, a lab would have its own infrastructure and tools. They would need collaboration tools, which enable them to communicate safely with external organizations that are very often involved in the idea development. The lab would need access to platforms where they can securely store and analyse data. Some labs developed a mini-bank stack, to which projects connect when needed and thus the experiments are not lost, but rather they build on each other.

Access to data is essential, as the collaboration with technologists from within the bank in understanding how various legacy systems work is crucial. Ignoring the needs for a technical infrastructure for innovation limits considerably the scope of work and success of a lab. The results of lacking an IT lab infrastructure can be unambitious proposals which undermine the desired innovation role of the lab.

---

[2] "Peek Inside 7 of The Banking World's Coolest Innovation Labs", *The Financial Brand*, 8 June 2015, http://thefinancialbrand.com/52177/7-of-the-coolest-innovation-labs-in-banking/.

Governance

"Innovation governance" is much misunderstood, by people from both inside and outside the banking world. Outsiders often look puzzled. "What is it to govern here?" (see the following Figure). This shows, however, a lack of understanding of how a bank works. As a heavily regulated industry, needing to operate 24/7 without fault, while dealing with highly sensitive data, banks function according to strictly governed processes and rules. Insiders and especially the guardians of governance would say on the other hand that everybody, including the innovation function, would need to respect the same rules as the rest of the bank. This is not true for many reasons. Innovation projects have a very different purpose and lifecycle than the business-as-usual projects: they might not use live client data; most often they do not connect to the productive infrastructure or do not have a chance of "going live" in their respective set-up.

Most of the bank's governing rules have evolved over the years from the era of a paper-based business and nine-to-five opening hours, before the cloud or cyber-security threats existed. Financial institutions are now a mixture of old and new, trying to cover all aspects of risks. They were, however, not defined for the case where somebody in the bank wants to experiment a bit, connect and combine technologies, or use client data for live testing.

Figure: Author's Twitter feed

Source: Twitter Feed from Private Twitter account from the Author and a contact, 23 June 2015

If you want to repetitively but rapidly set up proofs of concept which use a new technology, real data, and are tested by bank clients, the rules of such engagements need to be formally defined. It is not "blank sheet" governance as some imagine, which allows experimentation within the bank, but precisely the opposite. The governance should contain a clear definition of what the innovation function needs to do in order to have access to resources and what experts and governing bodies it needs to consult in order to make sure the data is not compromised and large risks are not created through experimentation.

Innovation "Consumption"

While in the pharmaceutical, technology, and energy industries R&D and innovation functions are by definition at the heart of their competitive edge, financial services have neither the culture nor the experience of setting up innovation functions and absorbing their products. There are countless stories of missed opportunities, too painful to hear: Xerox not knowing what to do with Alto, IBM letting go of the SAP founders … the list goes on. This is why I think right now it is more important than ever for the financial sector to genuinely learn how to incorporate innovation, otherwise the future will slip straight through their fingers.

What outputs does one expect to see from the bank's innovation function?

If a bank sets up a lab with a mandate for disruptive innovation focused on the use of data with big data technology, one would expect in a certain timeframe to clarify some real opportunities and choices of technologies which the bank will follow up on, given its expressed view that the bank will create business value out of data. If, however, the innovation function does not have a clear mandate, but delivers experiments in response to a varied set of business questions, the output would be just that: a set of answers to those questions only. It is thus very important to align the way the innovation lab functions with the type of output the bank expects to get.

Most of the outputs from a typical bank innovation lab could be included in one of the categories below:

- New feature(s) of an existing product and/or platform (e.g. web, mobile)

- New product

- Identification of new technology or combination of technologies for a specific use case

- Improved Customer Experience (CX) journey for a particular product or channel

- Industry trends

- Strategy reports

- FinTech scouting and news

- New business models.

There are many ways, of course, to measure the success of an innovation lab. In my view, that success is by no means represented by the delivery of many experiments, but rather by the delivery of the relevant information to the relevant people in the organization in such a way that enables them to take decisions, adopt the solution proposed, or learn from the tests performed in the lab. Without enabling the handshake between the innovation lab and the larger organization, the organization as a whole will waste resources and, more importantly, lose valuable opportunities.

Can the handshakes between the lab and the larger organization be predefined?

I strongly believe they should. In some cases the lab could search a while for the relevant stakeholders for their particular findings. However, in most cases, depending on the type of output, the clients, the audience, and the mechanisms to promote and distribute the innovation can be predetermined. The following Figure gives some examples of how typical lab outputs need to be handed-off in order to be converted into genuine action.

FROM OUTPUT TO ACTION

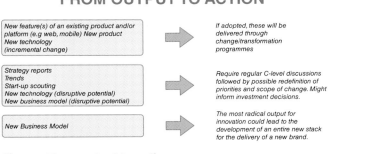

Figure: From output to action

So, you still think an innovation lab is the answer?

My advice:

- It is not one lab but many labs – set up focused labs, but also allow free experimentation in the organization.

- Innovation governance is not a "blank sheet" as many believe, but a clear and simple framework which allows the lab to function creatively and have rapid access to resources (people, infrastructure, data, etc.) in a highly regulated world, which functions at a different tempo. Make sure you have a framework in place from the beginning and keep it updated and relevant.

- Find, retain, and nurture people knowledgeable and passionate about their field of expertise, who are not put off by repeated trial and error and problem reframing, but who, on the other hand, thrive on challenges. Nurture them. Find that leader who loves the "nerds" and knows how to create the environment which allows them to work at their best.

- Diversity creates fertile ground for creativity – do not go for a lab staffed only with young, white, male hipsters who all know "agile" and "Ruby on Rails". Do not ignore the hard technical skills, or you end up with too much PowerPoint material. Do not forget innovation needs must be fed back into the organization and somebody needs to speak the language of the organization in order to be able to advocate for the required changes.

- Do not focus only on the tip of the iceberg. Innovation in banking focuses very much at the moment on the visible part of banking – a new feature in the app, on the web, or a brightly coloured branch with modern furniture. If you assess the content of most of the FinTech conferences around the world, the ideas presented attack the visible business model or the presentation layer of the banking world. For those who understand how a bank works, this is just the tip of the iceberg. Where is innovation in Assets & Liability Management, or Treasury, or even Regulatory Reporting? All these functions continue to be delivered in silos and in the "old ways".

- Changes in the deep layers of the bank would have a massive impact in the way a bank functions and would surface immediately in better CX, better products and services. What sort of lab allows experimentation in the core of the bank? How can we allow for experimentation of the incredibly powerful combination of hardware and software, which transform and disrupt all industries? This is the type of change I strongly believe in and I hope to see and contribute to in the years to come.

The ultimate "innovation lab" in my view would deliver an in-house full-scale "challenger bank". With the budget of yet another massive transformation programme, instead of trying to add a layer of polish to systems on life support, the banks have the option to build their own challenger banks. The customer in search of a better proposition would, as before, migrate. But at least now, they will be able to migrate inside your bank.

FinTechs and Banks – Collaboration is Key

By Bjoern Erik Juengerkes
Head of Business Development, biw AG

Banco Bilbao Vizcaya Argentaria (BBVA) with Dwolla, Royal Bank of Scotland with Funding Circle, National Australian Bank with Bugwolf, Wirecard Bank with Holvi and Number26, biw AG with auxmoney, fashioncheque, and others. These are just a few examples of collaborations between banks and FinTechs that have emerged over the last two years.

In earlier times, also retrospectively referred to as FinTech 1.0, FinTechs took a very radical and disruptive approach aiming to replace banks and established financial systems. Young and entrepreneurial start-ups have since tried to close the gap between the "dusty" service offerings of incumbent banks and customer needs. Using innovative digital technologies, they intend to improve customer experience, to streamline processes, and to more efficiently offer a wide variety of financial products and services such as investments, lending, payments, and remittances.

Things have changed and, meanwhile, an increasing number of FinTechs collaborate with banks. Experience from partnerships with several European FinTechs has shown that for FinTechs to succeed, it might be worthwhile thinking twice whether to disrupt or to collaborate.

Partnerships between start-ups and traditional companies are not new. Since barriers to entry in financial services, set among others by regulatory standards, have traditionally been very high, start-ups so far largely avoided this segment

Experience with several European FinTechs has shown that FinTechs and banks can collaborate at different stages of development. There are many reasons for both parties to do so, with the right partner, good preparation and the necessary openness towards the other party's requirements.

Collaborating Makes Sense for Both FinTechs and Banks

Collaborations between FinTech companies and banks can take different forms. Some FinTechs are bound to services that can only be offered by those holding a banking licence. Hence, they either need to apply for the licence themselves, or enter into a strategic partnership with a regulated partner, a bank. Funding Circle went its own way. In the UK, it is regulated by the FCA.[1] Others, such as Dwolla (Veridian Credit Union, USA),[2] Number26 or Holvi (Wirecard Bank, Germany)[3] and Savedo or Zinspilot (biw AG, Germany)[4] have partnered with banks.

Some FinTechs focus on bank partnerships in order to enlarge their customer base and at the same time enrich the product and service offering of the respective bank (e.g. Lending Club and Union Bank, USA).[5]

Unrelated to the stage in which FinTechs and banks engage in a partnership, both bring valuable assets to the table. FinTechs are tech-driven, test new technologies, and explore what is technically possible, not being bound to legacy systems. Applying innovative concepts, they create an enormous number of ideas in a very agile way. On top of this, FinTech entrepreneurs innately use social media technologies to support their work, from idea finding to consumer contact after launch.

Banks are usually risk-averse and act much more slowly due to their regulatory boundaries and their liabilities. Their banking capabilities allow them to open accounts, hold money, give out credit, and offer other regulated products

---

[1] See Funding Circle 2015, available at https://www.fundingcircle.com/uk.

[2] See Dwolla 2015, available from https://www.dwolla.com.

[3] See Number26 2015, About Number26, available at https://number26.de/en/support/number26-partner-bank-2 and Holvi 2015, *Customer Support*, available at https://support.holvi.com/hc/en-us/articles/201434362-Making-payments-to-Holvi.

[4] See Savedo 2015, *AGB*, available at https://www.savedo.de/agb and Zinspilot 2015, *Ueber uns*, available at https://www.zinspilot.de/de/ueberuns.

[5] Lending Club 2015, *About us*, available at https://www.lendingclub.com/public/lending-club-press-2014-05-05.action.

and services. Further, they can add their industry expertise, regulatory, legal, compliance, and risk management know-how and can give FinTechs access to global payment systems as well as their own customer base. Overall, they can lower the barriers of entry for FinTech firms into the financial services space and provide customers in a partnership with an increased level of trust.

Together, FinTechs and banks create an ecosystem that allows them to better fulfil client needs and close the gap between the services offered by traditional banks and actual customer demands.

Needs for a Collaboration

FinTechs have to choose the right partners and prepare wisely for their partnerships. Depending on a FinTech's needs and its status, partnership choices are different.

Setting up a business requires in-depth preparation and, at a certain point, a decision whether to look out for a partner or go it alone. Experience shows that the point of approaching potential partners needs to be well chosen and prepared. Selling into banks – no matter whether it is a partnership required to run the business, or to accelerate and grow the business – is very often a long-lasting process. And it is not a straightforward process either. Due to generally high investment costs, great business risk, and the need for strategic fit, banks choose their FinTech partners wisely, applying similar criteria to those on which venture capitalists base their investment decisions.

FinTechs that are already operative need to make the choice whether a partnership will accelerate growth or whether it is wiser to continue to approach the market alone. There are no hard decision criteria and, in the end, as in every partnership, it is a choice about whether to stay independent and take a longer and harder way to grow your business, or to partner and potentially compromise. Many FinTechs that have reached a critical mass to operate their business models are meanwhile approached by banks in a search for innovative solutions to enhance the banks' product and service portfolios. In consumer-oriented business models, one can find partnerships based on referral agreements such as that of Santander with UK-based Funding Circle

and Crowdfunder.co.uk.[6] Other business models show full integration of services, such as the integration of document analysis and semantic technology services of the German FinTech GINI into the online banking front end of Deutsche Bank.[7]

FinTechs still in their set-up phase need to respect both regulatory requirements and the nature of their business model in a decision to go for, or without, a partner.

As fully regulated entities, banks can support FinTechs to manage regulatory requirements. FinTechs have to be aware that, depending on the partnership, they can still offer their services under their brand; however, the bank as a regulated entity is (also) in almost all cases a contracting partner to the customer.[8] This set-up is completely independent of which entity maintains the client contact, does the marketing and sales, or provides the service with its IT system. A good example of a FinTech that has partnered with banks for regulatory reasons is auxmoney, a German online marketplace for P2P lending that acts as an agent and has partnered with two banks, for regulatory purposes.[9]

Different Banks, Different Benefits

In searching for a partner, it is important to differentiate between retail and transaction or specialized banks, as both types have different needs and wants, and both can be attractive for a FinTech company, depending on a FinTech's development stage and focus.

Retail Banks

Partnerships with retail banks usually take place once the FinTech has set up its business and wants to rapidly enlarge its customer base, increase customer trust, and/or the retail banks intend to enrich their product and service portfolio. There is currently a huge appetite from retail banks to cooperate with FinTechs. However, there are also numerous retail banks that believe they can innovate by themselves, or others that simply ignore the trend or still resist hooking up as second movers.

---

[6] Santander 2015, *Alternative funding*, available at http://www.santander.co.uk/uk/business/alternative-sources-of-finance.

[7] Available at https://www.gini.net/en/b2c/.

[8] Concept called "Co-" or "white" labelling.

[9] Auxmoney 2015, *FAQ*, available at https://www.auxmoney.com/faq/anleger.

An existing customer base is attractive if FinTechs can use it in the way they would like to run their business. Once they have reached a certain market position, access to larger banks is much easier, and so is their negotiation position when it comes to using the customer base and making the bank's customers also the FinTech's customers (with all the rights attached to this from the corporation's point of view). As long as a start-up is small, it is very often faced with resistance on questions such as "Who owns the customer?"

Partnerships with retail banks are not always easy, as most retail banks lack open infrastructures, use legacy systems, and are still, despite an official willingness to open up to digitalization and innovation, slow movers. Very often, there is also political resistance, which makes FinTechs selling into retail banks difficult and time-consuming. The higher IT integration is, the more new products and services compete with existing ones, and the more difficult it is to successfully initiate a partnership.

Transaction or Specialized Banks (Including Challenger Banks)

Partnerships with transaction or specialized banks are of importance in setting up a business model, in case regulation requires licences to operate the business. Usually these banks do not focus, or only to a lesser extent, on end clients and are instead focused on corporate clients such as distribution partners or sales agents that maintain client relationships. Many of the transaction banks, which have opened up to FinTechs, have agreed on cooperative partnerships, offer their partners co- or white-label services, act in a way which is more similar to start-ups than regular retail banks, and have created open infrastructures that allow easy interfacing. In Germany, we see three banks front-running in FinTech start-ups. Two of them, biw AG and Wirecard Bank AG, are pure transaction banks that white-label their services to their partners.[10]

Selling into bank partnerships is often very time-consuming. With increasing size, decision processes in banks become immensely lengthy. To avoid being stalled, FinTechs need to be well prepared and, ideally, analyse organization and decision processes on the partner side up front:

---

[10] See http://paymentandbanking.com/2015/05/17/cooperations-between-banks-and-fintechs-in-ger-17-05-2015.

- How is my desired partner organized, i.e. who benefits from the partnership, who does not, and what needs to be done to foster decision-making?
- How are decisions made, i.e. am I talking to the right people, who is making decisions – a single person or a committee?

Sometimes it might not be wise to talk to the CEO first. However, it is useful to approach a person such as the Treasurer first, as they might benefit most from the desired partnership. For decision-making, it is thereafter sensible to build up a relationship with the decision-making bodies.

Into the Collaboration – Avoid Frictions

Partnerships between FinTechs and traditional banks are special, as partners with completely different backgrounds, risk appetites, and liabilities intend to work and function together. In particular, for collaborations that are necessary to run the business, it is of the utmost importance to get a good understanding of the other party's mind-set, its goals, and restrictions up front. Expectations and common guidelines should be set very early in the partnership. FinTechs need to understand why traditional banks do not develop at the speed of the start-up, demand certain security levels when it comes to IT systems, have publishing restrictions, to mention only a few of the topics that very often lead to frictions. All of this may seem trivial, but experience shows that FinTech/bank partnerships that are not well prepared can lead to great dissatisfaction and at worst to a termination of the partnership.

Why Collaborate at All?

If a FinTech can replicate the bank's IT, if it has enough money to set aside for the bank's equity capital and can convince the regulator to get the approval for a banking licence, if it believes customer trust is not an issue since its (new) brand is trustworthy enough and is convinced it can attract enough customers on its own, it should start its business without entering into a partnership. If this is too time-consuming and complex, it should look for the right banking partner.

Outlook

Partnerships between start-ups and traditional organizations such as those between FinTechs and banks are not new. Other industries have seen them much earlier and have demonstrated how relationships develop. While banks have been very reluctant to move into the FinTech space in the first place, the number of collaborations between FinTechs and banks has meanwhile increased enormously worldwide. There is no doubt that the financial services industry will be disrupted in the same way as other industries beforehand. Partnerships and collaborations between existing and new players are key to ending up on the winning side.[11]

---

[11] For example BBVA acquired online bank Simple in early 2014. Simple 2014, *Company News*, available at https://www.simple.com/blog/the-next-chapter.

Partnerships Are the Key to Addressing Financial and Digital Exclusion

By Marc Lien
Director of Innovation & Digital Development,
Lloyds Banking Group

and Nick Williams
Consumer Digital Director, Lloyds Banking Group

It is an exciting time to be involved in FinTech, and at Lloyds Banking Group we are determined to play a big role in the FinTech ecosystem, by engaging in debate, contributing to continual innovation, and investing in its future. The face of the banking industry has changed, with customers now choosing to bank in new ways at a time and place that suits them. Finance has had to adapt to keep up with rapidly accelerating customer and technology-driven trends to enable customers and communities to benefit. The power of digital can bring increased prosperity to individuals and organizations that harness its potential. Conversely, it can work against those who are left behind, either due to a lack of basic digital skills, or a poor understanding of online opportunities (the "digitally excluded"), or those who are unable to make use of core banking services (the "financially excluded").

There is a growing risk that digital exclusion is leading to financial exclusion. We know some low-income families are without a bank account and they risk paying a "poverty premium" because they don't make their regular payments using direct debit or standing orders, for example. Perhaps more surprising are the findings of a recent Halifax survey that shows customers who are able to manage their money more regularly and more easily online have more than double the amount of savings and are less likely to go into unplanned overdrafts.

By opening up the power of digital to everyone in the UK, we can tackle digital and financial exclusion head-on. At our organization, we are extending an open invitation to the FinTech community to join forces with us so that the FinTech revolution does not just result in private gain, but in the shared legacy of a fully inclusive and digitally and financially savvy society that contributes to everyone's wellbeing.

The Financial and Digital Inclusion Imperative

Many of our personal, business, and not-for-profit customers are already taking advantage of the power of digital. However, over ten million adults and more than one million small businesses and charities in the UK are not only missing out on the benefits of digital, but are at risk of being left behind and excluded from a society that will in the future have digital at its heart. Our own research, conducted as part of the 2015 Lloyds Bank UK Business Digital Index,[1] shows that, on average, organizations that adopt the power of digital have a more confident outlook, gain access to wider markets, and are one-third more likely to have reported an increase in their turnovers in the last two years, than the least digitally mature organizations.

Banks and FinTech communities can and must work together to reduce exclusion. Some progress has been made, as we will see below, but there is much more for us to do.

About Us

Our day-to-day relationships with our customers are evolving, not because their financial needs are fundamentally changing, but because they want to interact with us in different ways. Their expectations of how we should serve them are being set by how the best businesses in the world harness digital. For this reason, digital sits at the heart of our strategy and underpins our overall mission to help Britain prosper.

You can now order a taxi, jump into it, and get out the other end without even reaching into your pocket for a wallet. That sets the bar for all organizations, not least our industry. Customers choose to bank digitally because it's simpler and easier; it allows them to transact when and where they want.

For this reason, we have established a transformation programme to improve our own digital products and services and help ensure we are being digitally inclusive for all our customers.

---

[1] Started in 2014, the Lloyds Bank UK Business Digital Index uses detailed analysis of small and medium enterprises (SMEs) and charities to understand how they use and feel about digital technology.

Our Digital Transformation

As a Digital 100 Leader, our guiding principle is simple: it is to be where our customers want us to be. Only four years ago, none of our customers was using a mobile banking app. Today we have six million active mobile users and for many of these customers mobile is their main way to get online. In the past 12 months alone, our 11 million digital customers have logged on to our secure site 1.3 billion times, while transactions totalling £2.2 trillion were made through our commercial online channels in 2014 – that is not far off the UK's entire GDP.

In 2014, more than 40% of our customers' new product needs, such as current accounts, personal loans, or credit cards, were fulfilled via digital. To keep up with this shift in customer preference, we deliver enhanced propositions and experiences to our customers every month. To truly be effective in a more digital world, we realize that we cannot stop there. We are reinventing the core services that we provide for our customers by starting afresh with the sole objective of designing brilliant experiences that meet our customers' needs. Digital is no longer the domain of a few people within our Group – it is everyone's job. The same is true of innovation. Our journey has taken us from talking about digital, to digitizing the channel, to digitizing the bank, to digital being in our very DNA.

One key part of our digital progress in this era of rapid and pervasive change has been creating a digital platform that allows us to quickly innovate both internally and with the FinTech community. We have invested £750m over the past three years in a single digital architecture that provides consistency and resilience across all desktop, mobile, branch, and telephony touchpoints.

This investment is important, but to create a culture of experimentation and to drive innovation across the Group we have also set up LBG Innovation Labs to constantly test new ideas and concepts. More than 50 innovation ideas have been built and tested with customers this year alone and many of these are, or soon will be, with our 11 million digital users. We have created a safe controlled environment where it is "okay to fail" and we can test quickly. As a result, we have sped up the customer feedback cycle and we are helping the business de-risk future investments.

We are the first major bank to have a Digital Division reporting directly into the Group CEO, centred around a specialist digital hub housing 1,200 colleagues in London. This division has a mandate not just to focus on digital performance and delivery for the Group, but to be a catalyst for change for the entire organization, facilitating our ambition to be the best bank for customers in the digital age.

Our Digital Future

We believe opening up the power of digital to everyone is a key element of achieving our mission of "helping Britain prosper". In the next three years we are investing a further £1bn in digital, on top of our investment in IT resiliency, to transform ten customer journeys across physical and digital touchpoints. We are starting with a clean sheet and a simple question: what will "brilliant" look like for our customers?

We can and will make digital more accessible for all our customers and one way we are directly doing this is by committing 20,000 Digital Champions, recruited from Lloyds Banking Group colleagues, by 2017. These Digital Champions pledge to actively help customers, friends, and family to get more out of being online by helping them to understand the benefits of the internet and inspiring them to increase their basic digital skills.

Our Digital Champions initiative was launched as part of our commitment to the digital skills charity Go ON UK, whose vision is to empower all people, small businesses, and charities across the UK to reach their digital potential. Go ON UK works in partnership to achieve digital inclusion and Lloyds Banking Group is proud to be a founding partner and board member. One of the many exciting projects on which we are collaborating is the creation of the new Lloyds Bank Digital Index, which will provide a measure of basic digital skills and map the links between digital and financial exclusion.

While we are determined to seize opportunities such as these to make digital accessible to all, it is the *collective* power of banks, with their regular and frequent interactions with millions of people and organizations across the UK, and the entrepreneurial drive and technological expertise of the FinTech community, that will ultimately help maximize the potential of digital. For this to be truly achieved, we must collaborate – and do so in a way that is inclusive to everyone.

Collaborative Partnerships are the Key to Digital and Financial Inclusion

FinTech points the way to our digital future and we need to nurture and harness the creative and visionary power of FinTech through strategic partnerships, collaborations, sponsorship, and championing of the ecosystem. Lloyds Banking Group is mobilizing around FinTech and we are already reaching out through partnerships such as the one with Startupbootcamp FinTech Accelerator, where we were involved in launching the first Global FinTech Insurance Accelerator programme.

We are also delighted to be a founding member of Innovate Finance, a new trade body for technological innovators working to support the FinTech ecosystem in the UK. We supported Innovate Finance's London Tech Week, which brought together key players and influencers. London is the best place for FinTech start-ups and the city is the top location for FinTech job creation,[2] at a time when financial services is alight with innovation. With FinTech generating over £20bn for the UK economy and a half of all investments in Europe being taken by the UK, it is a great time to be part of such an important movement.

We joined forces with Innovate UK, the Government's Technology Strategy Board, and four other partners to launch the first FinTech Open Innovation challenge to the start-up community. The challenge was: "How can digital innovation be used to improve financial literacy and help people better manage their finances for themselves and their families?" What we were looking for was a start-up that would improve financial literacy and skills among consumers in an engaging and intuitive way, making a real difference to people's lives.

Small businesses and start-ups are well placed to explore financial innovations and tackle the types of issues we pose through the Innovate UK challenges. Lloyds Banking Group can provide these FinTech companies with access to 11 million online customers who can benefit from this kind of innovation. The synergies and mutual benefits from such sustainable partnerships are plain to see – we are not only using our digital platform to innovate for our customers, we are collectively raising the level of our ambition to make a more profound and lasting impact.

The Opportunity to Work Together

Technology is driving changes in how we work, how we bank, and how we live our lives. Many individuals and organizations are already harnessing the power of digital. Others are either unable to, due to lack of knowledge or expertise, or they are simply unaware of the opportunities passing them by. We cannot tolerate digital exclusion and allow anyone to fall behind. For the sake of our citizens and businesses, our economy, and the future prosperity of our country, we must develop high digital capability throughout our society.

Lloyds Banking Group can and will play an important role in helping provide the necessary access to digital, but to harness its full power and make a lasting impact, organizations such as ours and the FinTech community must combine their strengths and work in close partnerships. Only by working hand in glove can we tackle digital exclusion and create a lasting societal legacy for everyone in the UK. We want to be part of the movement and we invite you to join us because we know the best ideas come from collaboration.

Let's work together.

---

[2] Source: startupbootcamp FinTech Trend Report 2014. London has surpassed New York and Silicon Valley for FinTech job creation, with 44,000 specialist roles in the City of London alone.

Corporate Venture Capital – The New Power Broker in the FinTech Innovation Ecosystem

By Nicole Anderson

CEO, FINTECH Circle Innovate

> "In an economy where innovation spells the difference between success and failure, corporate venturing can spur tomorrow's innovations while it helps build an organization in which innovation is business as usual."
>
> *Boston Consulting Group, October 2012* [1]

Corporate Venture Capital (CVC) is not synonymous with, but rather a specific subset of, Venture Capital. How capital is mobilized and managed for return varies considerably across company investor profiles. The coming of age of the "corporate investor" in FinTech is some way off, but if deployed strategically in support of innovation, CVC becomes a real contender in the investor landscape. Lessons learned from other industries can be applied. FinTech is high-octane and an emerging segment in its own right. It calls for speed and agile sourcing in a global marketplace. The challenge is simple – the CVC function often needs to undertake its own attempt at re-invention. How the Corporate Venture Division is structured, its evolving culture and skills all play a role in its future success.

There is an increased amount of funds focusing on FinTech globally. In exchange for the high return that venture capitalists assume by investing in smaller and less mature companies, they usually get significant control over company decisions and a significant portion of the company's ownership (and consequent value).

Corporate venture is much more varied in its approach to investing, given the differences in drivers and measures of success. The typical drivers behind corporate investment mandate are:

- Strategy – to advance the future vision of the enterprise;
- Expansion – to extend the company's portfolio of products and services;
- Innovation – to improve the competitive position and enhance customer experience or take strategic bets;
- Finance – to improve the financial return of the company

In 2014, 40 CVCs invested in a combination of venture capital funds and accelerators, equating to over $29 billion. In the same year, at least 10 CVCs had fund sizes exceeding $250 million. [2]

Whilst 2014 was a big year for corporate-backed exits, with the US enjoying two-thirds of the market value, one of the major revelations was that corporate funding was fast becoming the most active "seed-to-series A cliff" player with a whopping 212 first-round (series A) deals in a single year. [3]

The momentum is set to continue. VC firms and CVCs continue to align in co-investing and, while committed capital in VC firms is contracting, corporate venture is growing. More large corporates understand the potential for sustainable business returns and competitiveness by blending corporate venture strategy to innovation acceleration priorities. Considering the benefits venture investing offers, the real question is whether corporations can afford not to join the game.

CVC and the Opportunity for the FinTech Ecosystem

Dozens of banks and financial services companies are already committing to "seed investing" and many more are sponsoring large FinTech accelerators around the world. The "David and Goliath" connection is proving itself out in the search for strategic gains and predictable returns. It is very early days.

[1] Boston Consulting Group, "Corporate Venture Capital: Avoid the Risk, Miss the Rewards", https://www.bcgperspectives.com/content/articles/innovation_growth_mergers_acquisitions_corporate_venture_capital/?chapter=5.

[2] Nicole Anderson: https://medium.com/the-fintech-book/corporate-venture-the-new-power-broker-in-the-fintech-innovation-ecosystem-21bdfbad4ccb; Global Corporate Venturing Annual Report – June 2015 .

[3] *The Economist* (2015).

In an attempt to get "closer to the innovation ecosystem", some tier 1 players have launched high profile labs – BBVA, Capital One, Wells Fargo, Deutsche Bank, UBS, etc. – whilst others have opted to sponsor accelerators such as Lloyds and Barclays.

The budgets for these activities are impressive, with the average lab costing an average of $2 million to launch.[4] The focus on attracting start-ups to showcase, cohort, and collaborate has meant that millions have been spent on the infrastructure, hiring key talent, and leveraging the "benefit" of the positive PR.

Switching to the high-profile CVC investments such as Goldman Sachs (OnDeck, Kensho), JP Morgan (Prosper, Motif Investing, Square), Citi (Square, Betterment, Platfora), HSBC (Kyriba), BBVA (Simple), Mastercard (iZettle), and AmEx (SumUp, LearnVest), there is little evidence to suggest corporate strategy has caught up or is supported by innovation and investment mandates. They are almost, for now, separate worlds.

Accelerating Open Innovation in FinTech

The need to innovate is impacting dozens of product and service areas across the financial services supply chain. Jamie Dimon, CEO of JP Morgan Chase, was famously quoted as saying: "Silicon Valley is coming. There are hundreds of start-ups with a lot of brains and money working on various alternatives to traditional banking."[5]

Lloyd Blankfein, CEO of Goldman Sachs, has publicly confirmed that he fully expects that "partnerships, acquisitions and competition will be the key to the way the vertical develops".[6] If you marry the pace of innovation to the potential of business disruption, the enterprise has to act quickly. The rules of the game have changed and the once privileged position of building internally and staying competitive are flawed models to a successful future.

The partnership needed between heads of innovation, corporate venture, the CTO office, and risk and compliance are all essential in searching for and shaping deals, working with business units, defining measures of success, and ultimately supporting the change in cultural appetite for risk and willingness to test, trial, and collaborate with the outside world.

Investment sustainability takes planning and an appetite for risk. It also requires patience and embedded margin for "error".

For those FinTech-focused CVCs who understand the power of portfolio management – targeting early-stage, higher-risk deal flow, but balancing that out with later-stage, lower-risk in-sourcing of technology – stand a greater chance of repeatable future returns.

Setting up for Success

Ask any Head of Innovation at a bank how they are measured and how this aligns with other business units/functions, and the answers are likely to be just as varied as the individuals being asked the question.

If you turn to the CVC arm, many are under-resourced and desperately need augmentation from experienced venture and innovation professionals working with them, and in the key global locations. Past processes and measures are unlikely to meet the needs for now and the future.

The internal collaboration and fusion of planning between innovation and investment functions is vital. Structure, relationship to parent/enterprise, talent/skills, approach to portfolio management, and venture philosophy are all vital areas to assess. Challenging each element is necessary – and some of the key questions need to be asked – these are sampled in the following Table.

---

[4] *Forbes,* "FinTech Startup Labs on Growth Path from London to Hong Kong", September 2014; Accenture, "The Rise of FinTech, New York's Opportunity for Tech Leadership 2014".

[5] Jamie Dimon, A Letter to Shareholders, http://files.shareholder.com/downloads/ONE/15660259 x0x820077/8af78e45-1d81-4363-931c-439d04312ebc/JPMC-AR2014-LetterToShareholders.pdf.

[6] John Seward, "Is There Technological Turmoil in the Financial Services Industry?", Benzinga, 14 March 2015, http://www.benzinga.com/analyst-ratings/analyst-color/15/03/5326198/is-there-technological-turmoil-in-the-financial-services#ixzz3hG7UJcfV.

Table: Key questions for success

Structure	Relationship with Parent	Talent/Skills	Portfolio Management	Ventures
• How has the Corporate Ventures Function (CVF) been set up?	• How do you set expectations for results?	• Partner/Managing Director profiles?	• How do you get access to the best deal opportunities?	• How do you build your reputation in the ecosystem?
• Strategic Goals – financial/ strategic – what is the proper balance?	• How do you ensure fast decision-making?	• Size of team and profiles, outside hires vs. internal knowledge?	• Deal flow funnel?	• What stages do you invest – seed, A, B, C?
• Measures of success (KPIs)?	• How do you get involvement of business groups (BGs) in the process?	• Compensation and implications on acceptance CVF by organization?	• Board/observer seats in ventures?	• How do you generate a high quality deal pipeline?
• Governance structure?	• How to keep the parent company and BGs involved in CVF's activities?	• VC reward policy or Corporate reward policy?	• What does CVC offer the companies and co-investors?	• Majority/minority stake?
• Composition of investment committee and advisory board?	• How do you bring portfolio companies into the parent and BGs?			• Do you co-invest in syndicates?

Moreover, the role of the CVC function needs to act and move more like a VC to support the innovation strategy. Many argue that CVFs can be more successful, if placed outside the organization under the governance of an investment committee.

A balance has to be struck in such a model. The considerations are many, but building on the above, some guidelines for setting up an external CVF (sponsored by a corporate parent) would be found in the Table below.

Table: Guidelines for setting up an external CVF

Structure	Ventures
• A clear investment focus essential	• Minority stakes are most common
• Tenure – needs to be long-term – investments need time to mature	• Co-investment options should be the norm
• Efficient investment process to keep up with market speed	• Board/observer seat in venture and involvement in major decisions
• Success metrics covering financial and strategic elements	• Active support of portfolio companies
• Location close to corporate office or major business groups for internal networking	• Stable and consistent network in venture ecosystem
	• Reputation and track record is key for ensuring quality deal flow

Relationship to Parent	Talent/Skills
• CVF should have broad and resilient network within parent and business groups (BGs)	• Team size for fund: 5–8
• Dialogue between CVF with BGs and Corporate Centre needs to be systematic	• Employees representing a mix of VC and internal background (50/50)
• Early BG involvement during investment process	• Match CVC comp packages to those of VCs
• Portfolio companies need regular exposure to BGs	

FinTech CVC – Lessons to Live By

CVC should be a true business partner both to its internal stakeholders and to its investment portfolio companies. It should blend internal investment skills with the best industry standards in corporate venture funding. It needs to strike the balance between strategic and financial returns, working always to balance portfolio risk in either discreet investments or co-investments, but never alienated from the innovation agenda or group strategy.

The cost of venturing is considerable. However, the rate of change of innovation makes it an obvious choice given that inactivity can be more costly. The time is now for FinTech to create a perfect storm for corporate venture to be the new power broker in the innovation ecosystem.

The Insurance Opportunity

By Péter Orlovácz

Former Head of Digital, AXA Bank Europe

Insurance is a massive 4.64 trillion-dollar industry, yet most of the focus within FinTech has been on banking (investments and lending) and payments. The issues faced by customers from the insurance sector are very similar to those of banks, i.e. sub-par customer service, opaque pricing, and complicated products. The trends of digitization, new distribution models, and transparency that gave birth to many FinTech start-ups also apply to the insurance world.

Distribution

People are less inclined to buy insurance themselves, instead engaging with agents who will typically approach the customer and "push their products". This has largely shaped distribution into an agent-broker type model where the agent's role is more about sales.

As digital alternatives shape customer needs and behaviour, it is distribution which tends to change first. Advances in technology and insurers' desire to get closer to customers (to better capture data and provide a more consistent customer experience) have started to change the distribution model, but the emergence of digital distribution will change it even more. In addition, distribution poses some of the largest costs for modern insurers. Some insurance carriers started direct distribution, especially for simpler, one-off products like travel and motor insurance. Very few, however, went all-in on direct insurance, fearing competition with their own agent networks. As a solution to this classic innovator's dilemma, some of them have branded their direct offer differently as "modified pricing and products" to ensure agents will not be too negatively affected. This relationship is quite similar to how banks feel about their branches. Agent networks too will also need to find their added value in addition to sales.

One of the most significant technology-driven disruptions in distribution has been the rise of aggregators, which are websites that compare quotes from multiple insurance providers. These are most developed in the United Kingdom and other advanced European markets, but some companies have started to do the same thing in the United States – Google is one of them. Aggregator sites started with simpler products like motor and travel insurance. Looking towards expansion, their big challenge is to find new products where customers can be self-directed. For this, they will need either simpler products, requiring fewer data points for the underwriting algorithm, or to find a way to provide better user experience – either by using public data or proprietary information the insurer already has to help customers obtain their insurance. Another way of expansion for comparison sites is vertical; to turn into highly personal advisors, with more added value.

The future of digital distribution will not arrive at the same time, everywhere. Direct distribution has achieved only a small share: only 2% and 5% respectively for P&C (Property and Casualty) in France and Italy, and even smaller percentages in Japan, where agent networks still rule. In other countries, like Canada, the Netherlands, and emerging markets like China and the Czech Republic, there are remote distribution shares of 15–25%.

The distribution model may also be changed by companies providing services where insurance is just one component. This may take many forms:

- An infamous example is payment protection insurance (PPI) bundled with loans and mortgages in the UK. This insurance policy was said to be protecting its holders in case they were not able to repay a loan or mortgage.

- Trov, a mobile app, provides a service that lets its users catalogue and keep track of all their belongings with their current value. This service lends itself to insurance, be it motor, home contents, or any other specialty P&C product.

- Monsanto has acquired a big data company, The Climate Corporation, which had built an insurance product to protect farmers against weather risk, based on individual data and real-time weather feeds. Monsanto will offer this product as part of its Integrated Farming System that provides farmers with recommendations for their farm.

While digital distribution is gaining market share quickly, it is still relatively small. Agent networks will likely adopt digital too, augmenting their own service. Distribution is not just influenced by market maturity as customer preferences and the regulatory environment will affect this. Blending insurance with other services is a great model and risk is still underwritten by insurance carriers. Is this not a threat then? In the long term, this might weaken insurers' ties with their customers, relegating insurance policies to commodities.

Big Data

Insurance is the world's first big data business as companies have been using data to model and price risk way before the term became fashionable. Insurers' past loss and underwriting data is one of their most valuable assets.

However, the insurance industry's lead in collecting and making sense of large amounts of data is fading quickly. Companies like Google, Facebook, and Amazon are collecting much more data and have arguably better tools and human capital to make sense of it. The growth of sensors (call them telematics, wearables, or Internet of Things (IoT)) around us will very soon produce vast amounts of data insurers do not have access to. A very good example is MetroMile. This company offers pay-per-mile auto insurance where you connect their small device to your car. The MetroMile device, besides measuring how many miles you drive, collects data on your driving habits too. No company has tracked such data before (at least for regular customers), so insurers have a much smaller data advantage. If MetroMile is able to collect data on driving behaviour and use it for actuarial purposes, it will have a strong advantage.

While it is too early to say that the insurance industry has nailed big data and is using it fully, it is definitely an area where traditional players still have a head-start. Most insurers have started initiatives like AXA's Data Innovation Lab or German Allianz's net joint venture with Fraunhofer Labs. Using big data to customize insurance products in theory is a step in the right direction, but it will surely give rise to privacy concerns. While customers will enjoy better prices and tailor-made products, it is still uncertain how intrusive they could find the very techniques that make it possible. Consumers and insurers will need to find a balance between discounts and the extent to which the company owns customers' data and profile. Another risk of using IoT for insurance is cyber-security, or rather the lack of it. These smart data collection devices are not always designed with security in mind. According to studies, 70% of the most commonly used IoT devices contain vulnerabilities that a hacker can exploit.[1] This is not the kind of risk insurers can or would like to price into their models.

New Entrants

Insurance is a tightly regulated market and starting a new carrier is very expensive. Oscar, a New York-based health insurance firm had a minimal capital

---

[1] Eduard Kovacs, "70 Percent of IoT Devices Vulnerable to Cyberattacks: HP", *Security Week*, 29 July 2014, http://www.securityweek.com/70-iot-devices-vulnerable-cyberattacks-hp.

requirement of US$45 million. Quick growth is also difficult as regulatory capital increases with new customers. Yet, new entrants to this market could arrive from two directions.

First, from some of the companies who collect vast amounts of data in their daily operations (the Googles, Amazons, and Facebooks). Besides data, they have a very large customer base with whom they have much better relationships than insurers do. These companies could in theory offer insurance by leveraging their proprietary data. What is not yet clear is where in the insurance value chain these companies would want to be. The first logical place is distribution. Google is already there with Google Compare for auto insurance.

Second, start-ups could and will enter profitable niche markets with focused, simple products. Just as TransferWise can do international money transfers better than the banks, there will be insurance products where new entrants perform better than current players. In the US there are start-ups like Oscar, Gravie, and Navera that are working on providing better health insurance, a major pain-point of customers.

Another interesting model is peer-to-peer insurance, and Friendsurance is an example of this in Germany. This model is as old as the insurance industry itself. The early models of insurance were based on the sharing of risks and rewards by a community of people (in the mutual insurance model, the community actually owns the insurance company – Benjamin Franklin introduced this model in the US in 1752). Online communities have reached a large enough scale for the mutual insurance model to work efficiently, this time not bound by geographical barriers. Coupled with low-cost distribution, forming small communities that insure themselves may atomize previously homogeneous insurance markets.

A Note on the Digital Insurer

While looking at new market trends and how existing insurers could adapt is useful, digital transformation has more mundane opportunities for established players too. The simple digitization of existing insurance processes (straight through processing of quotes, rapid product configuration, etc.) could yield improvement to profit margins. Combined with existing companies' scale, if done well and in a timely fashion, this too could make existing carriers rather formidable competitors in the digital age. In itself, this may not be enough, though.

More Success Stories

Throughout the book we have heard from successful FinTech companies about their cutting-edge products and solutions and from FinTech thought leaders working across large organizations implementing ambitious FinTech innovation programmes. Here we share success stories from both entrepreneurs who founded FinTech firms that followed their vision and "intrapreneurs" who implement innovation in large global organizations. We look at businesses servicing consumers as well as other enterprises. What all these stories have in common is that we asked our authors to look below the surface of public relations and tell us more about the founder, their vision, and the companies' growth over time.

You will be inspired by the founder of eToro, the world's largest social investment network, discover Avoka's story as a leading customer experience management platform, and be motivated by Bankable's founder who is building "banking as a service" for all.

In addition, we examine how Citibank has rolled out a global FinTech challenge based on the vision of an intrapreneur and how SWIFT was able to spot and successfully respond to the FinTech opportunities for entrepreneurs and its global membership base of financial institutions. Both stories clearly demonstrate that even established financial institutions have the capacity to innovate and embrace change.

eToro – Building the World's Largest Social Investment Network

By Yoni Assia
CEO & Founder, eToro

It is a cold Monday winter morning in the Netherlands and Noa Strijbos has gone out to the stables to tend to her horses. She is one of the world's most popular horse trainers, but her 27,000 followers are not interested in her love of horses.[1] On the social investment network, eToro, Noa has transformed herself from an amateur observer of the financial markets to a professional trader in just three years. Her global following is waiting to see what her next investment moves are on the world's financial markets. After all, in 2015 her investment portfolio has already risen by 25%.

I am Yoni Assia, the founder and CEO of the world's largest social investment network. As a child growing up in the 80s, I was constantly surrounded by innovation. My father, David, established the technology company, Magic Software, which in 1991 became the first Israeli software company to list on NASDAQ. Surrounded by this technological revolution, I was inspired to start coding aged 14, hoping one day to play a significant role in the next stage of innovation. Like many teenagers, I began to work at weekends, collecting small amounts of change to put in my piggy bank. As a result, I wanted to put this money to good use. Feeling uninspired by seeing my hard-earned cash just sit there on the shelf and equally uninspired by the local banks, I decided that I would take control of managing my own money.

It was the 90s, tech was booming and the bulls were on the charge – both in the NBA and in financial markets. Men in suits, in their fast cars, working in big enclosed office buildings were trading on the world's markets with a great deal of success. With my tech experience, as well as my aptitude for numbers, I decided to give trading a go from the comfort of my own bedroom. Why could I not join those on Wall Street and be connected myself to the world's financial markets? Unfortunately trading was not as simple as I initially envisaged. From a practical point of view, it was all rather inconvenient and laborious. In order to get started I needed to purchase a few extra screens for my desktop computer. Once I was set up with my screens, I was able to analyse financial charts, but the whole experience seemed lonesome and helpless. In fact, my older brother, Ronen, found my fascination and struggles with finance all rather comical.

In the end, though, we both agreed that this really was no laughing matter. We understood quickly that global markets and economies were connected to one another, yet somehow 99% of the world was disconnected and disengaged from this ecosystem. With the emergence of technology and social connectivity globally, we realized the power was shifting to the disconnected 99%. Once equipped with the right tools and infrastructure, the masses could not only influence financial markets, but could take control of their own investment decisions. This vision and realization led to the establishment of eToro in 2006.

Building the Network

In 2006 our founders, Ronen Assia, David Ring, and myself, decided to try and solve the problems that I had encountered whilst trying to trade online. We attempted to tackle the complicated, lonesome experience of online trading and create an online trading platform that was simple and enjoyable. Why should finance be boring?

Initially our platform was designed as a financial challenge, with traders competing against one another in the global markets. However, we soon realized this contradicted our initial vision. Rather than competing against one another, it would be better for our users to learn from one another and we decided to revolutionize trading by allowing traders to see each other's performance and portfolios. With the world in recession after 2008, we understood there was a demand for financial transparency and the masses had lost faith in traditional financial institutions. Against the background of increasing global debt levels, the credit crunch, and Bernie Madoff, by seeing what other traders were doing, we were adding a layer of transparency within the financial ecosystem that had never previously existed. We decided to make finance social.

Scaling the Network

In 2010 we established the world's first social investment network, the eToro OpenBook, where members of our online community were able to follow one another. This built not only a network of traders, but a smart crowd curating

---

financial news and investments within personal news feeds. Traders were now able to consume financial news on their personalized feed, and in response trade according to this information, promoting their investment decisions to millions of people on other social networks. Financial products were now in reach of the mass market, not just the chosen few. The secrets of successful traders were no longer concealed from public view, but rather out in the open, being scrutinized or being copied, depending upon your own interpretation.

The ability to copy the traders on the eToro OpenBook not only allows members of our community to mimic other trading strategies, it enables investors to build people-based portfolios, creating a financial asset class of their own.[2] As well as bringing forth greater levels of responsibility and accountability, social trading generally outperforms independent trading, according to data analysed by MIT Media Lab. The movement of money in and out of these people-based portfolios is being done at the discretion of the investors on the network, creating a frictionless form of asset management. Almost anyone can open an account on the network, of any net worth, creating their own diversified portfolio. We have dramatically lowered the barriers to entry for anyone wishing to invest and manage their own funds, creating a network scalable in reach to millions, giving traders access to the financial markets that they had never had before. Since we launched our social investment network, we have not turned back.

The success in establishing and scaling our community was born out of a deep understanding of global technological trends. We examined the social revolution and, rather than believing that this was a fad, as many did, we quickly understood that this was the future of all forms of finance. By transitioning our platform to how the world was evolving, we became an early adopter and first mover in this space. This also enabled us to further embrace our vision of opening up the global markets for everyone to invest in a simple and transparent manner.

Breaking the Banks

Being copied and followed can be a lucrative business for our most popular traders. Our Popular Investor Program allows traders to receive 2% of the assets they are passively managing. This is the future of money management, a sector well known for its exclusivity, expense, smoke-screens, and mirrors. Many of the traders on the platform are now building their own profitable fund-of-funds. Today (June 2015), eToro's network includes 4.5 million registered users in 170 countries. Hundreds of financial instruments can be traded on eToro and our investors can copy, follow, and interact with one another in virtually any language, all over the world. As of today, we have raised a total of $62 million of investment. Our most recent investment round "D" included significant funding from three major global financial institutions, PingAn from China, Sberbank from Russia, and Commerzbank from Germany – eToro being the latter's first ever FinTech investment. The convergence of a FinTech company such as eToro and leading financial institutions demonstrates the force behind our disruption of the old world of finance.

For years, only the privileged few had access to the kind of information and the investment that gave them the power to move markets. The financial system is being significantly disrupted. What was once the exclusive domain of those men in suits down in Wall Street and the City is now more accessible to anyone, anytime, anywhere.

---

[2] *Decoding Social Influence and the Wisdom of the Crowd in Financial Trading Network,* by Wei Pan MIT, Media Lab Yaniv Altshuler MIT, and Alex (Sandy) Pentland MIT, http://web.media.mit.edu/~panwei/pub/socialcom12.pdf.

Avoka – An Overnight Success, 13 Years in the Making

By Derek Corcoran

Chief Experience Officer, Avoka Technologies

"OMG!" (meaning "Oh My God!"). I was familiar with the phrase, but it was the first time I had ever heard an executive, never mind a C-level at a global bank, use it in a meeting. She had realized what Avoka could do for her company and I realized that we really had built something special at Avoka.

It felt like the culmination of an intense 5-month period of positive press – we had won back-to-back Finovate "Best Of Show" awards in London and California, we were awarded "Most Innovative Customer Engagement Solution" in the Citi Mobile Challenge, and we were called out in Inc. Magazine's "22 Financial Technology Startups You Need to Know". It felt like 13 years of hard work and four significant pivots (perhaps more "refinements" than "pivots") in our business had led to Avoka becoming an "overnight" success. And the journey started . . .

In 2002, Philip Copeland and Howard Treisman, already successful businessmen and IT veterans, established Avoka as their next venture (Philip's third start-up). Avoka was focused on delivering on the promise of Business Process Management (BPM), namely "Business Agility". After completing a number of successful projects in financial services, government, and aviation, Philip and Howard realized that many of the clients they were selling to already had one, if not four, BPM or workflow systems already. They did not need another one. What they really needed was a way of connecting those systems to customers that were outside the organization. They needed to allow customers to apply online, and it needed to be a great customer experience.

PIVOT 1 – Customer Experience, not Business Process Management

Avoka shifted the focus from managing an organization's internal processes to allowing customers to kick off a process such as applying for a loan or opening an account. The reality was that Avoka's primary customers in financial services and government had hundreds and in some cases thousands of these types of transactions. The highest volume transactions were available online (e.g. Open a Current Account, Apply for a Credit Card) and the rest were still paper-based. The issue was that the traditional way of delivering an online experience to replace a paper or PDF form was to get the IT Department to custom-develop code using programmers. This was not cheap or fast, hence only the highest volume transactions were online. Avoka saw a need for a faster way to build these online experiences without programming – something that put the "business" in control, with IT in a support role. And that created a second need – a solution to manage these online experiences. After all, if you have got hundreds of online transactions, then you will need somewhere to maintain them. This led to the development of the first iteration of Avoka's product, Transact.

We learned a lot during this period about consumer behaviour and what makes a good customer experience. We took these learnings and we baked them in to our product, so each subsequent client benefited from the lessons of those that went before them. As a result, Avoka was now a customer experience company.

PIVOT 2 – Mobile, the Game-changer

On 9 January 2007 at the Moscone Center in San Francisco, Steve Jobs introduced the world to the iPhone. It changed everything – from how we check the weather to how we communicate, from how we find information to how we shop. Initially our clients told us "people do not want to apply for a loan or open a bank account on an iPhone, the screen is too small", but we were not so sure.

In the following years, it became apparent that customers wanted to do *everything* on their mobile phone, including applying for a bank account, a loan, or lodging an insurance claim. One insurance company explained to us how they wanted to make it easy for customers displaced by a storm to be able to lodge an insurance claim on their smartphone, tablet or PC ... whatever they had access to after a natural disaster. It needed to be convenient, not an app the customer had to download.

Building the capability to support mobile and desktop devices from a single design was probably the most significant single product development we invested in. But later we would realize that it was absolutely the right thing to do. Avoka was now a customer experience company focused on the new frontier of the "digital channel" encompassing PCs, smartphones, and the new wave of tablets.

PIVOT 3 – Cloud Computing Comes of Age

At the same time that Steve Jobs and mobile were changing the customer experience, Jeff Bezos and the Cloud were changing how organizations built and hosted their software applications. And this provided an enormous opportunity for Avoka.

At this point, Avoka's product was one that was installed in an organization's data centre and our typical clients were banks, insurers, wealth managers, and government agencies. Getting a new server in to the data centre of an organization like this was hard, really hard. The data centres were typically managed by large IT outsourcing companies who provided additional services such as installation, security, back-up, redundancy etc. on top of the bare-metal server. A $10,000 server could easily cost $100,000 per year in total costs and 2–6-month lead times to order, receive, and install a server were not unusual.

For a business like Avoka that was already experiencing 3–12-month sales cycles, adding additional months before customers went live was crippling. "Agility is the new black" and traditional data centres were far from agile. Using the Cloud, we could set up a brand new instance of our product for a customer in a single day. Hallelujah!

At this point, we also made a decision to move to transaction-based pricing. If a customer completed an application, for example, for a new bank account, a charge was incurred. This allowed Avoka to better align the cost of our product to the value it was delivering. There was some resistance to this new approach at the time – organizations were used to thinking in terms of "buying" software and paying for maintenance and support. But as products like Salesforce continued to grow in popularity, so did the idea of Software as a Service (SaaS). We stood our ground on the new SaaS model and in about 18 months the objections pretty much disappeared. Avoka was now a SaaS company focused on digital customer experience.

PIVOT 4 – Focus. Focus. Focus.

At this time, Avoka was growing nicely and had customers in banking, insurance, wealth management, government, pharmaceuticals, engineering, construction, transportation … and so on. We felt the time was right to look for a way to drive explosive growth. Everything we knew and read said that we needed to "focus".

It was obvious that we should focus on financial services and particularly banking and wealth management – but what exactly should our value proposition be? Why should a bank engage Avoka as a new vendor? We helped with operational efficiency, IT productivity, time to market, customer acquisition, but it was still too broad. What would Avoka's unique value proposition be for our target clients? What would our elevator pitch be? That was probably the hardest question we ever had to answer. The thing was, we already knew the answer – we just hadn't joined the dots yet.

Eight years earlier, an executive at a large bank had told us that "abandonment rates for online personal loan applications are running at around 92%". "Imagine," he exclaimed, "if 92% of customers that walked in to a branch left before completing a transaction or if 92% of calls to our call center went unanswered – we would be out of business pretty quickly." Abandonment of online sales transactions (account opening, loan applications etc.) in financial services is a huge problem and it seemed banking was the only industry willing to accept such poor conversion rates. And as the digital channel was growing in importance, the problem was getting worse. In an environment with low interest rates (post-financial crisis) and new offerings like peer-to-peer lending, traditional financial institutions had become very focused on acquiring new customers. They were investing heavily in digital marketing to ensure that if a customer was in the market for a product, their bank "got found". The problem was, when the customer hit "Apply Now" the experience was pretty similar to how it was in the early 2000s, and so abandonment rates remained high.

Then we got lucky. We were introduced to a financial institution that was absolutely focused on writing more personal loans and was willing to work with us to achieve that. We delivered a new personal loan application in just 10 days and then our team jointly started watching the abandonment statistics we were generating. We asked ourselves "where are customers abandoning and why?" We would form a hypothesis ("maybe if we changed X"), talk to the customer about it, and their reaction was "get on with it … make the change!" So we did and immediately monitored the abandonment. Lo and behold, it reduced, meaning more completed loan applications. So we made more and more changes – always just changing one thing at a time so we knew if it was positive or negative.

It worked! In just six weeks, we had worked together to reduce their loan application abandonment rate from 64% to 49% – a significant increase in loans written every week. This experience helped increase our knowledge of the problem, but also gave us proof that abandonment could be effectively combatted, or at least reduced. By looking at the friction or effort associated with completing an online loan or account application and identifying ways to minimize that friction (i.e. make it easy for the consumer), everybody wins. I cannot overstate the importance of having a customer and real data to prove our value proposition is real, not theoretical. Prospects connect with stories, not PowerPoint slides.

We took the concept of frictionless digital sales to Finovate, the leading conference for cutting-edge banking and financial technology (with a unique demo-only format) and won three back-to-back "Best of Show" awards. This provided confirmation that what we were talking about and delivering was valued by the finance sector. Avoka was now a SaaS company focused on frictionless customer experiences in financial services.

We had found our home.

Lessons Learned

In FinTech, there are two types of company:

Disruptors – those that offer an alternative to traditional banking such as peer-to-peer lending.

Collaborators – those that offer banks an alternative way to do business.

Avoka is a collaborator.

Now, to say we pivoted four times is not entirely accurate. It was more a refinement of our solution and business model. But they were significant changes. And along the way, we have learned some valuable lessons.

Sell something that makes your clients successful – if your product/service can be directly connected to helping make your clients successful, in particular acquiring new customers (as opposed to reducing operating costs etc.), focus on that. And when working with clients, listen and learn, and embed those learnings into your offering.

Tell your "story" with results – as soon as you can, build a case study (even a blind/anonymous one) with hard cold data showing the value you have delivered. And deliver this as a story, like you would tell at a BBQ. People connect with stories.

Adapt to change – if you are in FinTech, the only constant is change. You cannot respond to every suggested "game-changing technology", but you should keep your finger on the pulse of the industry and be prepared to move. If a technology looks like it has the potential to help consumers and make their lives easier, there is a good chance they will adopt it (iPhone, peer-to-peer lending, etc.) so give these technologies your special attention to establish how they could help or hinder your business.

Bankable – Banking as a Service

By Eric Mouilleron
Founder & CEO, Bankable

I founded Bankable in 2007 when the word "FinTech" had not even been coined.

It all started at a dinner party in London in November 2006 where I met a lady who had invested in the prepaid payments space in the United States. Prepaid was already a high-growth industry in the US and I thought this growth would spread to Europe. I had a closer look at the payments industry and discovered an opaque world with abusive fees, huge inefficiencies, and lack of real-time processing. I realized this industry was ripe for disruption by adding a real-time component, flexibility, efficiency, and transparency to the new payment equation. I wanted to launch a new software venture from scratch, which would be innovative and disruptive, yet not capital- or resource-intensive. Payments were exactly the right space.

I come from a technology background. At Valtech, an IT project-based consultancy that I previously co-founded in 1993, our growth was by definition limited by our headcount. The more billable team members we had to deliver software projects, the more our capacity to invoice grew. I wanted to break that fatality and build a scalable business not strictly dependent upon recruiting new staff. In six years, Valtech grew from two founders in one office to 1,200 employees with 12 offices in eight countries. The company was financed with money from friends and family, which quickly translated into revenues from clients. In April 1999, Valtech went public on the Paris stock exchange and at its peak in 2000, reached a market capitalization of US$1.5 billion.

Recognizing the gaps in the payments industry, I was determined to displace payment inefficiencies with efficient, real-time, affordable, and secure solutions. Realizing the scalability achievable in a business that is driven by technology, I envisioned powering payments with globally scalable technological innovation. I attended the first MasterCard Prepaid Conference in Prague in May 2007. The energy brought about by such a large concentration of people at the conference confirmed my belief that prepaid payments was a booming sector with tremendous growth potential. I wanted to be part of it.

I restarted discussions with the company I had visited in the US with the aim of importing their prepaid payments technology to Europe. However, this proved impossible as their software issuing platform lacked the flexibility to become global. Based on my previous experience of delivering scalable software solutions to clients, I then decided to develop an in-house flexible transactional platform which would suit the needs of large financial and non-financial institutions targeting the payment pain-points of both corporates and consumers.

However, regulation prevented non-bank financial institutions from launching a payments service in Europe straight away. With the industry moving swiftly in the US, where a growing number of start-ups were redefining financial services, I waited in anticipation of a wave of change that would hit Europe as well. Meanwhile, I continued working on the business and legal architecture for Bankable. Two years later, I was finally rewarded for my patience. In November 2009, the Payment Services Directive was implemented by most EU Member States in order to stimulate competition in the marketplace to provide consumers with transparent and efficient financial services. This was the necessary regulatory change that would allow us to operate in Europe as a new payment technology enabler. Also, in December 2009, this change of regulation helped me close a first round of funding of EUR1.5 million from a single private investor. Bankable started operations in January 2010 as a payment programme manager headquartered in London.

I chose London, as the Financial Conduct Authority (UK) has always encouraged competition in the finance industry and the UK government in general actively promoted business. A majority of e-money institutions are headquartered in the UK. London's position as a global trading hub with a large concentration of financial technology businesses and headquarters of large corporates and financial institutions is unmatched in Europe. Thus, London also attracts a highly skilled and diverse talent pool.

As a co-founder of Valtech for 12 years, I had always encouraged a multicultural and diverse environment. I applied the same values to Bankable and employed people who brought specialized skillsets and were experts in their respective fields – from consultancy and law, to defence and the telecommunications industry. I wanted to build a team of brilliant people who brought in fresh ideas and did not hesitate to speak their mind. My experience has taught me that putting such people in a room together generates ingenious ideas and solutions. I met my first employee through the former Head of Prepaid at MasterCard Europe. He brought in extensive experience in the prepaid industry, which was vital in laying the foundations of Bankable. I was then introduced to my partner and Bankable's current Chief Operating Officer through a friend at a party in May 2010. Given his consultancy background, I shared my business proposal with him to get feedback. He saw opportunity in the business and eventually decided to join Bankable in September 2010. I gradually built the rest of my team mostly through connections made during the two years that I waited for regulation to change.

With a team in place, I reached out to some Deutsche Bank representatives who I had also met at a conference for non-bank financial institutions. They were keen on learning more about challenger banks and FinTech and were willing to provide their feedback during every step of the development of the transactional platform I had in mind. We worked on building the first version of the Bankable platform and simultaneously scheduled meetings and put contracts in place with payment processors, the card bureau, and banks for BIN[1] sponsorship. With these partnerships in place, the first successful transaction on the Bankable platform was processed in March 2011.

Subsequently, Bankable's platform underwent an 18-month audit by Deutsche Bank Global Transaction Banking, making us the sole "Global Approved Vendor" by Deutsche Bank in our space. We then created a corporate disbursement prepaid card programme for Deutsche Bank which went live in October 2013. Having such a brand attached to Bankable was very beneficial as it created instant trust and built credibility with potential clients and partners. Today, Bankable has over 80 clients across Europe.

Over five years, Bankable has evolved and broadened its scope to offer innovative payment solutions by shifting focus from prepaid cards as a means of payment to the company's vision of providing "Banking as a Service". To meet the business needs of large financial institutions and disruptive FinTech players alike, we have evolved our platform into a highly flexible transactional platform which works as a core to provide bespoke payment solutions. Our platform enables any regulated or non-regulated organization to launch targeted payment solutions quickly.

For instance, a French serial entrepreneur, who also happens to be my neighbour, identified an opportunity to launch a financial tool targeted towards the younger generation. I introduced him to Bankable's platform while having coffee with him one morning when he realized that the platform's bespoke functionality could power his idea. Bankable then provided a set of APIs[2] allowing him to quickly build *Anyti. me*, a solution which replaces cash as a child's pocket money with a prepaid card, while providing parents with monitoring tools. The solution has been very well received in France and resonates with the idea of providing essential payments services and transaction monitoring in real-time.

Today, Bankable's team is based in offices in London and Paris, represents five nationalities, and speaks eight languages. As FinTech spreads globally, Bankable wants to play a part in the ongoing revolution by continuously providing efficient and cost-effective payment solutions for everyone. We are looking to expand our services to emerging markets where the robust and innovative Bankable platform will help to displace cash. My priority now is to make Bankable a success and for it to become the "Intel Inside" of payments.

---

[1] A Bank Identification Number (BIN) is the first 6 digits on a payment card and identifies the bank that issues/sponsors it.

[2] See the chapter entitled "Embracing the Connected API Economy" for further details.

The Next Chapter in Citi's Story of Innovation

By Jorge Ruiz
Global Head, Digital Acceleration, Citi

Looking at the financial industry today, competition is fierce and companies have a clear opportunity to innovate – to step up to the demands and expectations of their clients, create new products and experiences, and fuel progress in the industry. At the same time, there is a huge population of developers and designers around the globe who are poised to help make those changes but they need to be invited to join the conversation. As a result, we see these innovative individuals creating financial start-ups instead of joining major corporations. We read about these start-up companies all the time; either they are taking market share from established banks or being acquired by them. They are often viewed as competition but it is not that simple. At Citi, we are disrupting the norm by encouraging and empowering individuals to work with us to help innovate and change the financial industry.

The Onset of FinTech

Financial Technology (FinTech) is transforming the way individuals and institutions engage with money. Almost every major bank is doing something in the FinTech space – from hiring consultants to creating competitions, hackathons, accelerators, venture funds, and developer programmes. It has only been within the past few years that these major players have begun paying attention to the start-ups and small businesses that are making amazing contributions to the banking ecosystem. It used to be that an industry dominated by global players with banking licences would pose a barrier to entry for young brands and innovators. But now, long-standing brands should be looking to these smaller players to shake up the status quo and collaborate to enact change within the once stagnant financial industry.

Banks have the opportunity to rethink how they approach innovation and to transform themselves using some of the creative applications being conceived and brought to market by non-traditional financial players. At Citi, we are looking at developed ecosystems as well as other unexpected places around the globe, to find the next big thing in banking. Building relationships and spending significant time in markets that were once considered far-flung is critical for us to really understand the location-specific challenges that our clients face. The ideas and solutions we are unearthing as we explore could help us keep a step ahead of a disruptive market.

The pace of FinTech innovation today is a challenge for traditional banks. Large banks have ingrained planning processes and face regulations that can result in a long go-to-market cycle and complicated approval processes. They are not regarded as nimble or particularly responsive. Start-ups, while lacking the resources of global corporations, are boundless when it comes to leveraging new technology and have thus been able to work nimbly to innovate and respond to customer feedback at a fraction of the cost.

One specific area in which Citi is fast-tracking FinTech innovation and development is through the Digital Acceleration team. This global team was created to fuel progress by working with FinTech organizations and leveraging outside-in innovation to unleash the power of the tech community, develop new solutions, and disrupt the way banks innovate.

The Path to Acceleration

In looking at the financial industry as a whole, there are clearly two paths major institutions can take. The first is a defensive position – the idea that there is little that the start-up community can contribute and that they do not need to be viewed as serious competition. Countless companies across numerous industries have taken this path and have not only lost relevance but also market share to the very start-ups they should be collaborating with. The second path, and the one that we at Citi have chosen, is finding avenues to work with as many innovative companies as possible in helping them design and innovate our sector, which ultimately benefits us and our millions of customers. While we have incredibly talented developers working internally on everything from our dot-com presence to first-of-its-kind mobile technology, there's a limit to what we can accomplish on our own. We know that global markets each have their own specific needs and desires shaped by infrastructure, culture, mobile adoption, Wi-Fi access, and countless other factors. We realized we needed to create a platform to give talent a voice while also helping drive the type of innovations needed locally by our customers.

Once we decided we wanted to collaborate with developers, we needed to find a way for them to get their foot in the door. It is not always easy to get a meeting or sign a deal with an executive at a global financial institution. How could we make that a possibility? After looking at all the players we wanted to include – developers, designers, technology thought leaders, and governments – we created the Citi Mobile Challenge (CMC). The programme is a next-generation accelerator that does not limit itself to a physical location but conducts a three-month programme virtually around the world, leveraging Citi's unparalleled global reach to discover and incubate solutions across more than 100 markets.

Creating the Citi Mobile Challenge

Citi's approach to banking innovation is more than a competition. It is an opportunity for us to transform the financial industry by working with top developers and designers who can take us to the next level and truly change the way the world banks. CMC is connecting developers and resources in a way that is not happening frequently or quickly enough elsewhere in financial services.

The CMC takes place wherever the developers are – the choice of when and how to work is entirely in their hands. Developers from around the globe are given access to APIs[1] from Citi and from leading technology companies to build solutions that can change the world. Finalists are selected and prepare for Demo Days, where they have the opportunity to present their prototype solution in person. Leaders from Citi and dozens of other companies judge these events and meet directly with the developers. Top innovations are selected and incubated by Citi to help turn their prototypes into viable pilots.

Citi Mobile Challenge Launches in Latin America

Citi Mobile Challenge launched its inaugural programme in Latin America in spring 2014. One hundred and fifty ideas were submitted by over 500 developers from 19 different countries. The speed and early results of the programme were remarkable – and we knew that we were on to something that would truly transform digital banking. Eleven top innovations were announced and project managers were assigned to each team to help these developers navigate Citi's businesses and processes. Citi has launched pilots with two of those teams. The first is PAQ, a full-cycle mobile commerce platform that connects a microfinance institution, a tech provider, a small retailer, a corporate distributor, and Citi to promote financial

inclusion. The second is PideloRapido, an integrated personalized e-commerce solution. These pilots are excellent examples of how we can connect with external developers and even other financial institutions and enable progress for more of our clients all over the world. For those of us at Citi, it's also a wonderful illustration of how we can connect across business lines and geographies to fuel progress for a variety of our clients.

Citi Mobile Challenge Travels the World

After a successful initial programme in Latin America, Citi Mobile Challenge travelled to the United States in autumn 2014 and to Europe, the Middle East, and Africa in spring 2015. With each Challenge, the programme added new elements, deepened relationships with sponsors, and grew its community of FinTech thought leaders.

In the United States, our call for submissions attracted more than 700 registrations from 62 countries. We reviewed 61 working prototypes from finalists at Demo Days in Silicon Valley, New York, and Miami, and named 12 top innovations in mobile solutions and the Internet of Things. We grew from three sponsors in Latin America to 18 in the US and added value to developers through increased mentorship. The conversation around the competition expanded beyond the walls of the Demo Days through press coverage and social media engagement. We decided this was the right moment for Citi to launch another way of engaging with the developer community, through Citi FinTech Meetups.

In December 2014, we announced the inaugural Citi FinTech Meetup in Miami, which focused on the city's significance as a financial technology hub connecting the Americas. The programme's goal is to further empower and engage thriving local developer ecosystems, deepen connections with the best thinkers, and stimulate digital progress in the industry. We continue to hold regular Meetups in Miami and are looking forward to expanding to new markets.

The next stage of the Citi Mobile Challenge world tour was Europe, the Middle East, and Africa (EMEA) in the spring of 2015. We expanded the scope of the programme to include more countries than ever before and added new elements to benefit developers. Major sponsorships were formed with companies including IBM, MasterCard, and Uber, which resulted in more APIs for developers to use and a series of webinars to help participants enhance their solutions before the Demo Day events in Nairobi, Jerusalem, Warsaw, and London. Local government officials joined us as guest speakers and our judges included executives from collaborating firms and

[1] See the chapter entitled "Embracing the Connected API Economy" for further details.

even some alumni from past Challenges. Developers in EMEA completely reimagined what FinTech is and how far it could go, helping to make banking even more personal and connected. Our experience in the region has broadened our thinking on what this programme can achieve and the huge potential of outside-in innovation.

What's Next?

As we turn our attention to other regions of the world, the Citi Mobile Challenge team is excited to continue our journey, build our community, and discover new applications for FinTech. The top innovations and resulting pilots from Citi Mobile Challenge are only the tip of the iceberg. We have been very lucky to work with thought leaders throughout the FinTech community and deepen relationships with many of our clients, collaborating companies, and colleagues. Meeting and working with these developers has been truly inspiring and the response from our colleagues at Citi is energizing. As we look at our product portfolio today, it is clear Citi Mobile Challenge has accelerated outside-in innovation. We are committed to growing the programme, as well as adding new elements to make the experience even more valuable for developers, Citi, and the entire banking industry. As we see it, the programme is Citi's next step in FinTech innovation and will connect players at all levels of the financial ecosystem as they strive to reimagine digital banking and improve the financial experience.

FinTech Trends from the Frontline – Building Collaborative Opportunities for Start-ups, Market Infrastructures, and Wholesale Banks

By Fabian Vandenreydt

Global Head of Securities Markets, Innotribe & The SWIFT Institute at SWIFT

As an integral part of SWIFT, Innotribe has a unique position within FinTech innovation – identifying key trends and opportunities, leveraging talent, and ensuring that the financial services ecosystem benefits from fresh thinking from start-ups. Innotribe was one of the initial facilitators that helped to accelerate and spread the first wave of FinTech innovation, and it continues to play an important role in this process. Leveraging SWIFT's expansive global network, Innotribe collaborates with investors, venture capitalists, strategists, banks, and financial institutions. Innotribe also supports the growth of FinTech innovation globally with its Start-up Challenge programme, strategic partnerships, thought leadership, and its forum at Sibos, the world's premier financial services event for the financial industry.

The FinTech landscape has changed substantially since Innotribe was launched back in 2009, and the number of major players has rapidly increased. Five years ago "FinTech" was far from a household term. The pace of change is swift and has a profound impact on how the financial services industry operates. We see this first-hand in the exponential growth of our Start-up Challenge, for which applications have more than doubled in just two years – from 175 companies in 2013 to 370 in 2015. In addition to the overall expansion of FinTech, the topics that these players focus on are becoming more mature, and reach deeper into the core of wholesale banking and market infrastructures. There is clearly a developing understanding about what needs to evolve in banking systems, both retail and wholesale. Moreover, the professionalism of start-ups is increasing, thanks to improved coaching and mentoring programmes. Start-ups are becoming much savvier in terms of how procurement processes work in banks and they better understand how to come up with the facts and figures required to successfully present an idea.

These hungry young companies are changing the competitive landscape. They are adopting new technologies and business models to meet the needs of financial institutions in everything from lending to securities and payments. In parallel, the industry as a whole is becoming ever more curious to understand and potentially capitalize on new ideas. This is evident in the number of entities, such as incubators and accelerators, who exist to help nurture start-up talent and bridge the gap between the financial community and the start-up ecosystem. We have also seen a major change in the relationship between start-ups/early growth companies and banks. It used to be an "us against them" dynamic, but the sentiments have evolved significantly. The banks now see FinTech as an integral part of their innovation strategy, and there is a need to recognize it as such. There is an emerging sense of collaboration between banks and new FinTech companies.

Geographical trends are also interesting. FinTech innovation tends to emerge in specific cities, or financial centres, rather than at the level of countries as a whole. Nevertheless, the overall number of hubs is rising and we predict that the expansion of FinTech will continue. Long-established financial centres are broadening their horizons and increasingly embracing FinTech. Frankfurt, Luxembourg, Dublin, and London are just a few examples of a growing network of FinTech havens popping up all over Europe. Part of their recipe for success is being very open to all professions and nationalities. A combination of financial backing, real estate backing, and academia is equally important. This valuable mix makes such environments attractive destinations for start-ups. In addition to the larger financial centres, the Nordic region has – from a technology and an enterprise standpoint – typically been at the forefront of things, and is now increasing its presence in FinTech as well. Spanish banks have also been active in prioritizing subsets and pockets of FinTech innovation. Beyond Europe, from the Asia Pacific to Latin America, we are witnessing the development of new start-up hubs in markets which are fertile for innovation and disruption. For SWIFT and Innotribe, Africa is a region of emerging importance across the business, but also in terms of innovation. It was for this reason that we brought the Start-up Challenge to Cape Town this year for the first time, which was a great way of drawing attention to innovation happening on the ground in African communities and outside the "traditional" Start-up Challenge geographies of London, New York, and Singapore.

Ultimately, if you are in a financial centre, you will attract investors as, more often than not, it is a safe place to invest. But it helps if there is also a unique selling point – such as talent. Most aspiring FinTech communities realize that they need to import talent to some extent, but some ecosystems are more advanced than others. You want to start small, but the sooner you open up, the better. Singapore is a prominent example. The start-up scene has opened up to importing talent with very specific skills, such as cyber skills or venture funds skills, in order to boost their ecosystem and to scale it faster. We have also noticed a growing demand from governments or banking associations to create a positive environment for FinTech innovation. In the US, for example, there has been the conscious development of a culture of controlled risk-taking and an environment has been created that allows people to fail gracefully. This mind-set shift ensures that start-ups are not considered "unsuccessful" if they fail the first time round, and it becomes much easier to pick up and start again.

It may sound simplistic to highlight the importance of such a positive, "can do" environment, but it remains integral to the success of innovation in Silicon Valley and it is an ethos that is also reflected in New York. Moreover, if an entrepreneur asks a potential investor for $100k in the US, the response is likely to be: "What can you do with $1 million?" Whereas in Europe, if a start-up asks for $100k, the investors might ask: "What can you do with $50k?" It is a very different approach to risk and ambition.

Another important theme is fostering diversity of talent. This year, we have tracked the gender of the founders of firms applying to participate in our Start-up Challenge. At 23% female and 77% male, the figure is unbalanced and we hope to stimulate improvement. Considering that there was only one female CEO among the current list of top 50 European FinTech companies (by venture funding), our numbers are not bad – but clearly it is not 50/50. This is an issue that has been raised a lot in debate among industry players recently, and we hope to address it further from an educational perspective.

Looking to the future, we now have an alumni network of more than 650 start-ups. We are very proud of this, and we hope to empower this vibrant ecosystem to work together on specific areas of innovation that truly add value for the wider financial community. And as a company, SWIFT plans to work closely with start-ups and growth-stage companies to develop proofs of concept which will empower our strategy going forward.

We feel that it is essential for companies to identify opportunities to collaborate, share experiences and learning, and debate common challenges. If we want to move forward as an industry, collaboration across the various FinTech communities is more important than ever. As a global cooperative, SWIFT is eager to support innovation and to find ways of bringing scalable, real-world change to address the many change drivers prevalent in the financial community. As technological innovation continues to evolve, Innotribe will play a vital role in continuing to bring the start-up ecosystem and financial services expertise together.

Crypto-currencies and Blockchains

This part focuses on digital currency and the various applications of the blockchain.[1] Until now, the most important manifestation of blockchain technologies has been Bitcoin. What comes next? What are alternative applications of the underlying blockchain technology to financial services?

Most Bitcoin 2.0 applications are still at the emerging stage, but they promise to improve the architecture of transaction-based industries. The authors in this part envision several categories of blockchain technologies that will impact the financial industry: digital currencies, asset registries, application stacks, and asset-centric technologies.

---

[1] A blockchain is a permissionless distributed database based on the bitcoin protocol that maintains a continuously growing list of data records hardened against tampering and revision, even by operators of the data store's nodes. The initial and most widely known application of blockchain technology is the public ledger of transactions for bitcoin.

FinTech + Digital Currency – Convergence or Collision?

By Manie Eagar

President/CEO, DigitalFutures; Director, Bitcoin Alliance
of Canada

Crypto-currency Meets Digital Finance and Mobile Value Exchange

In just two short years crypto-currency has grown from a hobby project to a multi-billion dollar global digital finance industry. With new competing alternatives and technologies advancing beyond simple currency-based payments, to all manner of value exchange, financial instruments, smart contracts, and blockchain-based distributed ledgers, everyone is waking up to the fact that bitcoin was just the beginning.

Arriving just in time for the great convergence of mobile payments, digital branchless banking, and digital-value exchange, bitcoin, alternative currencies, and digital finance innovations promise a major disruption of global finance.

Originally an *outlier technology*, the business of bitcoin, and its broader digital money applications, has now grabbed the attention of all major financial institutions, consumer technologies, and regulators all over the world. We will explore the tension between decentralization versus the "new channels to market" play of the various incumbents.

The bitcoin proposition: In his seminal paper "A peer-to-peer electronic cash system" dated November 2008, Satoshi Nakamoto envisaged that "A purely peer-to-peer version of electronic cash would allow online payments to be sent directly from one party to another without going through a financial institution."

From this simple premise the bitcoin phenomenon has grown in scope (2 million plus current users projected to grow to 5m according to Juniper research[1]) and

---

[1] http://www.juniperresearch.com/researchstore/commerce-money/cryptocurrency/
bitcoin-altcoin-impact-opportunities.

size ($3.7bn market capitalization as of early July 2015) to grab the attention of media headlines worldwide thanks to the infamous MtGox and Silk Road debacles. Bankers and regulators still quote these two factors as the specific reasons that they don't "trust" bitcoin, confusing business malpractice with the legitimate applications of a highly disruptive financial innovation.

But what is unstoppable is the convergence of two major FinTech sectors with that of bitcoin and newer digital currency and blockchain-based technologies – the crossroads where Digital Banking and Mobile Transactions meet the Crypto-currency Protocol(s). Will this be a natural convergence or a collision? What are the implications, opportunities, and challenges for FinTech start-ups, entrepreneurs, investors, and established legacy players alike?

The Internet of Money: A Radical New Business Model

The key drivers for the emerging FinTech and digital currency innovation are to provide services that are secure, frictionless and almost free, in real time, anywhere. The efficiencies that these technologies alone offer are incentive enough for every traditional financial services provider to sit up and take notice, whilst entrepreneurs in the crypto-currency space have attracted more than $1.5bn in investments, with the broader FinTech sector projecting $22bn in 2015.[2]

What will drive the adoption of the overlapping technologies and the efficiencies and disruptive business opportunities? The 2015 World Economic Forum report on "The Future of Financial Services"[3] highlights that incumbent players are most likely to be attacked where the greatest sources of customer friction meet the largest profit pools.

Customers, consumers, and users are becoming the new co-creators of value. This requires a value transfer system that rewards each respective contribution incrementally and directly, regardless of the kind of services or goods being offered anywhere in the world in real time.

---

[2] http://www.fintechinnovationlablondon.co.uk/media/730274/Accenture-The-Future-of-Fintech-and-Banking-digitallydisrupted-or-reima-.pdf.

[3] http://www3.weforum.org/docs/WEF_The_future__of_financial_services.pdf.

Digital Asset Management and Value Exchange

Digital asset management and value exchange are fast becoming the virtual market spaces where globally distributed organizations and communities connect to barter, exchange, transact, settle, and interact around different modes of digital value exchange. Key sectors of the digital economy will participate in closed or open digital economy market spaces facilitated by secure distributed ledger applications.

As the digital economy becomes global and pervasive, key focus areas will be digital asset management and value exchange; distribution and logistics; Internet of Things (IOT); Machine-to-Machine data (M2M); distributed, online and mobile payments; and global remittances and settlements via smart contracts.

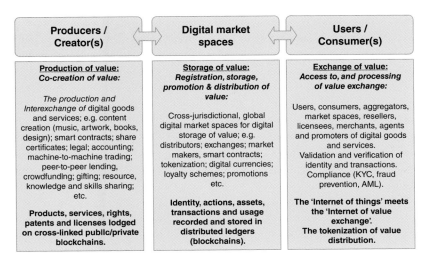

Figure: Digital asset management and value exchange

Key sectors that the distributed ledger (blockchain) and related tokenization (read digital currencies) plus smart contracts applications will address are:

- Government-to-government (G2G) verification and validation of assets and data related to finance, development aid, asset registers, taxation, duties to discover money laundering and to monitor sanctions and trade agreements.

- Government-to-business and business-to-government (G2B2G) information tracking, auditing, taxation, foreign exchange, remittances, and foreign trade monitoring have historically been challenging. Banks have notably been coming under scrutiny and have received heavy fines for not complying or for not properly monitoring the activities of foreign agents, customers, and branch offices.

- Government-to-citizen (G2C2G) services cover every aspect of services to citizens such as registration, taxation, issuing of passports, voting, and the engagement of citizens with government agencies at every level. Vast disparate systems cannot cope with the demand and the multiplicity of duplicate public records, creating silos and multiple points of failure open to hacking, personal identity risk, and fraud.

- Business-to-business (B2B) covers aspects of inter-business trade and settlements, manufacturing and distribution, logistics, supply chain management, to digital rights and online services.

- Interactive business-to-consumer (B2C2B) in physical and online retail and services, linked to social media will increasingly become a driver for national

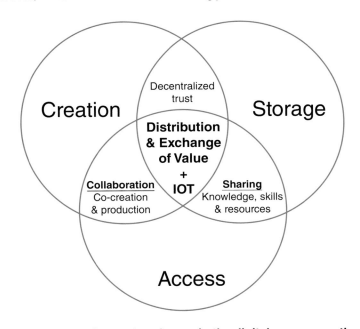

Figure: Value creation and exchange in the digital economy + the Internet of Things

and global economies. Business will in turn leverage consumer databases and performance tracking to streamline their services and deliver value at scale.

- Citizen-to-citizen (C2C) economic engagement will increasingly manifest in the shared and digital economy with crowdfunding, peer-to-peer lending, informal trade, barter, and exchange as drivers.

Hybrid Digital Finance Platform Convergence

Digital finance will be distinguished from the old ways of banking and traditional financial legacy systems through the convergence of digital banking, mobile value exchange, and crypto-currency applications in a variety of forms suited to different jurisdictions, market evolutions, and the differentiated needs of the banked versus the so-called underbanked (estimated at 2bn) worldwide.[4]

There is increasingly talk of the "Internet of Money", converging with the "Internet of Value" (exchange) and the "Internet of Things" and greater understanding of the opportunity in digital finance services and distributed infrastructure development.

The digital finance landscape is evolving to address these opportunities, creating huge system-wide convergence and integration, and niche players alike. At the end of the day, the users/consumers of all these offerings will decide which variations suit them best based on ease of use, access, stability, store of value, security, reduced friction, exchangeability, transferability etc. – ultimately the best user experience (UX) for the money.

Delivery platforms from every sector of the industry will vie for a stake in this lucrative and necessary business – from the so-called over- to underbanked parts of the world. There is no question that the world financial system needs an overhaul, or at the very least sound and viable alternatives to the current legacy system-driven offerings and the latest innovations emerging through branchless banking and mobile transactions/payments. There is a great chance that bitcoin itself could become dis-intermediated, as crypto-currency technologies, business processes, and alternative currencies and protocols emerge or become adopted by existing and new players in the FinTech, digital currency, and mobile payment sectors.

What this implies is a "hybridization" of digital finance technologies and a combination of decentralized and centralized platforms and delivery channels. There are a number of reasons why this dual economy is likely to emerge, including the ease with which digital currencies can unite global consumers and merchants: the low cost of digital currency payments, the openness of consumers to new innovations, and the growing influence of technology companies according to Gareth Murphy, director of markets for the Central Bank of Ireland speaking at the BitFin 2014, Digital Money and the Future of Finance Conference in Dublin.[5]

He envisions a hybrid Bitcoin-Fiat future where "The existence of a 'euro-denominated economy' and a 'virtual currency economy' raises the prospect of an internal balance of payments between two sub-economies where suppliers may prefer one currency over another as a means of payment (for different goods and services)."

He continues: "Multi-currency economies are not unusual. For example, the US dollar is accepted in many economies alongside the local legal tender. Also, there are a number of regional currencies in existence in many parts of the world that aim to encourage transactions in local goods and services."

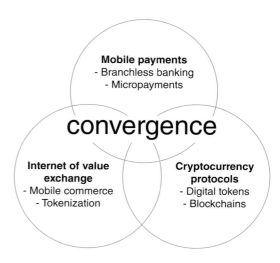

Figure: Convergence of FinTech

---

[4] http://www.worldbank.org/en/news/press-release/2015/04/15/massive-drop-in-number-of-unbanked-says-new-report.

[5] https://www.centralbank.ie/press-area/speeches/Pages/GarethMurphyBitFin2014.aspx.

One area of convergence highlighted by long-running venture capital firm Kleiner Perkins Caufield & Byers (KPCB), after announcing their blockchain investment fund,[6] is the rapid developer adoption of the technology with fundamentally new capabilities and agile applications enabled by blockchain. Permissioned or permission-less (e.g. bitcoin) blockchain scripting interfaces give developers the ability to program distributed contracts on top of the bitcoin and competing blockchain networks. They highlight the ability to create programmable contracts, which allow developers to programmatically manage value exchange with an unprecedented level of control, which will simplify and minimize the trust required in many common transactions done today. They highlight use cases that have emerged around standardized contract types, such as micropayment channels, which are indicative of a broad range of applications that are now possible, such as mobile wallets, gifting, and social media value exchange.

Figure: The value chain

Digital Currencies and Mobile Transactions

Branchless banking is the key distribution channel strategy used for delivering financial services without relying on bank branches and is also being used as a separate channel strategy that entirely forgoes bank branches. Overriding even

this will be the fact that the majority of customers now prefer online or mobile banking.

Internet access (all devices, but especially mobile) with customer centricity, affordability, ease of use and affordable secure access anywhere, especially at point of sale, are becoming the key drivers.

- Mobile is a lead driver for change in payments technology – specifically the remittances and money transfer markets. Nearly half of all online sales are now made over mobile devices (IMRG Capgemini)[7].

- "Business models, technology, and consumer behaviors are changing. Electronic payments, digital commerce, predictive analytics, and mobility are converging, along with contextual marketing, digital advertising, couponing, loyalty, and social media. The opportunities to enable magical new commerce experiences for consumers and more meaningful interactions between brands, merchants, and their customers are endless" (Paul Galant, VeriFone).

- Dramatic uptake of smartphone devices and mobile phone penetration in emerging markets (not just the "unbanked"). 67% of the people on the planet now have a mobile phone conducting an estimated 300bn transactions valued at $860bn. There are already 1bn mobile banking users (Mobile Commerce revolution).[8]

M-Pesa – Lessons for Integrated FinTech + Digital Currency Merchant and Consumer Adoption?

A leading example, and great case study for alternative digital transaction adoption, is the emerging market success story in Kenya, namely M-Pesa.

It was originally designed by Safricom (Vodafone) as a system to allow microfinance-loan repayments to be made by phone, reducing the costs associated with handling cash and thus making possible lower interest rates. Once you have signed up, you pay money into the system by handing cash to one of 40,000 agents (typically a street vendor or a corner shop selling airtime). It has since broadened to become a general money-transfer scheme – loans and savings products, bills and salary payments, etc. Having established a base of initial users, M-Pesa then benefited from network effects: the more people who used it, the more it made sense for others to sign up for it.

6 https://www.kpcbedge.com.

7 http://internetretailing.net/2015/12/45-of-ecommerce-sales-now-made-via-mobile-devices/.

8 http://ptgmedia.pearsoncmg.com/images/9780789751546/samplepages/9780789751546.pdf.

Interoperability – The Integration Challenge (and Opportunity)

The challenge is that emerging financial technologies do not trust or have access to established financial institutions and services, whilst the latter in turn do not trust or have access to the emerging technologies. Nevertheless, both worlds are already exploring strategic partnerships and relationships and soon we will see a large-scale convergence and meshing of legacy and emergent digital finance offerings and delivery platforms. Blockchain-based "proof of concepts" are sprouting up everywhere. Imagine centralized meets cloud, meets distributed solutions. Here lies the true competitive advantage and innovation for digital finance players.

The digital currency of the future might take on many forms. It will break down barriers and increase access to increasingly large audiences across geographies, with different levels of income. Crypto-currency innovations initiated by the bitcoin protocol and its later derivations have opened up a range of applications and potential solutions for an increasingly globalized economy, inviting further exploration. Emerging digital finance models and technologies for financial inclusion can positively impact those who are "unbanked" or excluded, creating greater access, equality and efficiencies in established markets, and delivering a digital finance future that is "flexible, frictionless, and almost free" for all.

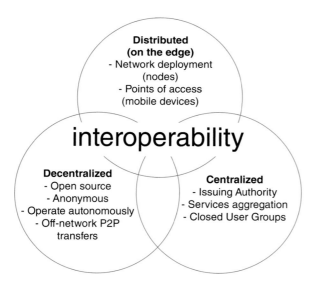

Figure: Distributed deployment challenges

Blockchain and Crypto-currencies

By Adam Hayes
Co-Founder & CEO, ChainLink

and Paolo Tasca
Economist, Deutsche Bundesbank

The notion of an entirely digital form of money has captured the curiosity of economists, computer scientists, and philosophers alike from the time the computer was still young. There was, however, always the nagging problem that a currency consisting entirely of ones and zeroes could be exactly copied over and over again, the same way that ones and zeroes allowed for the infinite duplication of audio in the form of compact discs. What good is money that could be counterfeited at will? The solution, which spawned bitcoin and its various daughter digital currencies, was the marriage of cryptography and decentralized networks. Both technologies had existed independently: cryptography, useful in encoding email messages, sensitive information and digital files; decentralized, distributed networks with ARPANET giving birth to the internet.

How Does Digital Currency Work?[1]

In 2009, Satoshi Nakamoto satisfied the long-held curiosity of economists, computer scientists, and philosophers with the creation of Bitcoin. The system relies on a disparate network of participants, each trying to essentially break an encrypted message. Rather than the nodes of the network working together in cooperation, Nakamoto put them in competition with each other to solve this puzzle with the first to do so winning a prize: a block of newly minted bitcoins. This became known as "mining" for bitcoin. Furthermore, the system was hard-wired with a certain rule at the outset: a new block would be found on average once every ten minutes; if more participants enter the competition and the time to solve the puzzle shrinks to say eight or nine minutes, the difficulty of the puzzle will be increased to re-establish that target time.

---

[1] For more on how digital currency works, see https://bitcoin.org/en/faq. To avoid confusion, we use *Bitcoin* (singular with an upper case letter B) to label the protocol, software, and community, and *bitcoins* (with a lower case b) to label units of the currency.

Let us take a roulette wheel at a casino as an analogy for bitcoin mining, where the prize for landing on double-zero is a block of bitcoins. There are 36 numbers on the wheel, plus a zero slot and a double-zero. The chance of the ball landing on double-zero is one out of 38. The casino owner knows that 38 games of roulette can be played over a 10-minute interval, and wants to ensure that there is only one winner per given interval. As one final rule, in our hypothetical example, only one player can sit at a single roulette table at a time.

A second player enters the casino and sits down at a second roulette table. The owner of the casino is upset to see that twice as many games can be played in any given period, and that in fact he is now paying out to two winners every 10 minutes. The casino owner restores his target payout interval by increasing the number of slots on each roulette table. As a third, fourth, tenth, hundredth etc. person walks in the casino to play at their own private roulette table, the casino owner must keep increasing the size of the wheels.

It is important to remember that each spin of a roulette wheel is an independent trial: the chances of the ball landing on a black number do not increase merely because a string of red numbers has occurred. Bitcoin mining, and our increasing roulette wheel size analogy, is also a series of independent trials performed in tandem by competing players. Good luck may produce two winners in a row, even though the odds have increased to one out of 38,000 instead of 38. But just as in a fair coin tossed over and over again, the long-run average will revert to the expected mean, and our casino owner – and bitcoin miners – can always expect a payout once every 10 minutes.

Bitcoin mining serves a dual purpose; it is not merely the method of introducing newly created bitcoins. Of more importance, it serves to validate and confirm each transaction on the network, creating a tamper-proof data structure underlying the system known as the *blockchain*. The blockchain is essentially a public ledger which everybody mining for bitcoins has a copy of. Every time there is a winner, each copy of the blockchain is updated and all the transactions that have taken place in between this winner and the last are recorded indelibly into it.

Again, consider the roulette wheel. Not only are there people playing simultaneous games of roulette, but there are also non-players who are simply taking side bets on the action. Only when there is a double-zero will those side bet transactions be confirmed.

Bitcoin works in much the same way: miners compete with each other to solve a puzzle just like the roulette players hope to score double-zero. As more miners enter the game, the problem gets more difficult to solve, maintaining a 10-minute interval between creating new bitcoins. All the while, people are transacting with bitcoin to buy and sell goods and services, to speculate on its price, and to pay wages. Each time a miner solves the puzzle, all of those accumulated transactions are validated and confirmed in the blockchain. The important difference between bitcoin and our casino is that bitcoin has no owner, and no central authority to oversee it. Rather, those rules were hard-wired into the initial code and agreed upon by its participants.

While that is all very clever, it is fairly self-serving: bitcoin mining finds new bitcoins and at the same time validates and confirms internal bitcoin-bitcoin transactions. But what if this same powerful time-stamped validation engine could be harnessed to confirm and verify *external* non-bitcoin specific transactions?

Bitcoin 2.0 and Future Trends

Until now, the most important manifestation of blockchain technologies has been Bitcoin. However, anything that requires trust or proof is a good candidate for the blockchain, as bitcoin miners will naively validate and confirm those transactions too – because those miners are always trying to solve the next block and earn bitcoins as a reward. Title of ownership, deeds, contracts of all shapes and sizes, and notary, are examples of information that can be permanently recorded into the blockchain – and which can unambiguously be transferred to subsequent owners without the need for a central authority. This has huge ramifications for how business is transacted and may prove disruptive to everything from the legal to the financial sector.

Indeed, after the first wave of early enthusiasts and overly ideological bitcoiners "blinded" by their belief in a rapid displacement of the US dollar and other hard currencies, the Bitcoin community started focusing on alternative applications of the underlying blockchain technology.[2]

Most of these Bitcoin 2.0 applications are still at their dawn, but they promise to improve the architecture of transaction-based industries. We envision four categories of blockchain technologies that will impact the financial industry: digital currencies, asset registries, application stacks, and asset-centric technologies.[3]

Digital Currencies

At the time of writing, there are over 500 alternative *altcoins*.[4] These are digital currencies much like bitcoin, with specific monetary supply mechanisms and transaction networks. We glimpse a future characterized by the creation and diffusion of community-based digital currencies that will be used in closed-form environments as tools for internal rewarding, customer loyalty programmes, or incentive and governance schemes. The communities will either be organized via state institutions or by private corporations who will issue their own specifically branded "coins". There are already platforms which allow anyone with a rudimentary knowledge of software programming to create their own digital currency according to their own unique rules and usage limits within the community and the organization. Moreover, there are already payment networks such as Ripple, enabling various digital currencies to be sent easily between members.[5] In the near future, it will be possible for every single smartphone user on the planet to possess a digital wallet for each branded coin, instantly exchangeable in the form for example of loyalty points, for other altcoins, or for hard currencies. This all functions under the auspices of a unique global market with a distributed, decentralized clearing mechanism. This will massively upgrade transaction efficiency and increase the currency-utility of reward.

Asset Registries

These applications refer to the possibility of linking real assets (stocks, bonds, certificates, etc.) to a digital token which can then be exchanged among network users by simultaneously transferring ownership of the underlying asset. The changes of ownership are automatically registered and recorded in a multi-asset public ledger without the need for a central authority or for any institution to provide clearing and settlement services. For the time being, the technology still needs refinement. Critical issues include the potential for overloading the blockchains

---

[2] On this matter, an interesting comment was given by the Reddit CEO (Mr Yishan Wong), who praised the technology but called out the bitcoin community for being overly ideological. See http://www.coindesk.com/reddit-ceo-thinks-world-dogecoin-slams-crazy-bitcoiners/.

[3] See Paolo Tasca (2015), Digital Currencies: Principles, Trends and Opportunities, ECUREX Research Working Paper.

[4] See https://cryptocointalk.com /forum/178-scrypt-cryptocoins/.

[5] See https://ripple.com.

with additional external data (a phenomenon referred to as "blockchain bloat") that will require additional mining power and create scalability problems.[6] Thus, although asset registry applications have already been brought to the market (examples include Mastercoin (now OmniLayer),[7] ColoredCoin,[8] Namecoin,[9] and Counterparty[10]) at the moment, the banking industry at large cannot fully exploit the potentialities of this technology. The good news is that solutions such as *sidechains* are being implemented to solve the bloat problem, and in the near future asset registry applications will indeed be a common tool used by the whole of the finance industry.[11]

Application Stacks

These are "non-currency" blockchain-based platforms that will be used for the development and execution of complete applications on top of decentralized networks.

By complete applications we mean Distributed Autonomous Organizations (DAOs). Any business organization can be defined as a combination of a set of properties and also a set of rules which govern the roles of, and interaction among, the individuals composing the organization. The idea of DAOs takes the traditional concept of business organization, decentralizes it, and encodes a division of labour between Artificial Intelligence agents and humans under the control of a verifiable and incorruptible set of enterprise rules. Thus, DAOs are established by employing a decentralized network of autonomous agents, each of which perform output maximizing production functions according to pre-established rules which are auditable, open-source, and distributed across the processing power of their stakeholders (who are humans or even other DAOs). DAOs are the most complex form of decentralized automation to date. Simpler forms of this concept consist of

smart contracts, autonomous agents, decentralized applications, and decentralized organizations.[12] Current application stacks that allow for implementation of decentralized automation are NXT, Ethereum, and Eris, which distinguish themselves based on their core focus.[13]

Asset-Centric Technologies

Asset-centric technologies are based on a new concept of distributed consensus which gets rid of the expensive and resource-wasting *proof-of-work* system which is the default consensus mechanism utilized by Bitcoin.[14] Stellar, Ripple, Hyperledger, and Namecoin are the most famous examples of asset-centric technologies.[15] These decentralized ledger infrastructures allow for the exchange of real assets like currencies, metals, stock, or bonds and in some cases even without the need to use a native digital token as in the case of Hyperledger.[16] The element that distinguishes these asset-centric technologies with respect to the other blockchain-based technologies described above is the fact that these represent distributed *exchangers* where network users can exchange among themselves various heterogeneous real assets.

Conclusions

An entirely digital, decentralized, peer-to-peer currency is now a reality. Bitcoin has ushered in the crypto-currency age, for better or for worse. The potential for crypto-currencies to revolutionize money and disrupt finance is enormous, but it is only the beginning. Perhaps even more important is the blockchain, the distributed ledger data structure which crypto-currencies rely on. Capital investment in blockchain-related start-ups is a recent trend that started only in 2012; however, since then, the annual growth rate of investment, 150% year over year, is faster than even the dot-com boom. Blockchain applications spanning a number of sectors promise to

---

[6] In June 2015, it was announced that the maximum block size for the Bitcoin blockchain would be increased to 8 MB.

[7] See http://www.omnilayer.org/.

[8] See https://www.coloredcoins.org and https://www.coinprism.com.

[9] See https://namecoin.info/.

[10] See https://www.counterparty.com.

[11] Sidechains are separate and distinct from the main bitcoin blockchain, but which would be interoperable with a two-way peg. This could allow for the transfer of assets between the side-chain and the main blockchain, without eating much storage space. See the paper "Enabling Blockchain Innovations with Pegged Sidechains" at http://www.blockstream.com/sidechains.pdf.

---

[12] More information of decentralized automations can be found here: https://blog.ethereum.org/2014/05/06/daos-dacs-das-and-more-an-incomplete-terminology-guide/.

[13] See http://nxt.org/, https://ethereum.org/, and https://erisindustries.com/.

[14] By one estimate from 2014, Bitcoin consumed as much electric power as the entire country of Ireland. See http://karlodwyer.github.io/publications/pdf/bitcoin_KJOD_2014.pdf.

[15] See https://www.stellar.org, https://ethereum.org, http://hyperledger.com/, and https://name-coin.info/.

[16] Unlike Bitcoin, Stellar, Namecoin, or Ripple, Hyperledger does not have an in-built digital currency but at the same time it guarantees a distributed ledger base which gives each partici-pant freedom in choosing which combinations of other participants to trust.

change the way companies and people transact, send payments, sign contracts, transfer ownership of things, and much, much more.

The hope is that this new technology will instead turn the digital divide, among and within our countries, into digital opportunities. The reduction of transaction costs and the elimination of costly – and sometimes obscure – layers of intermediation have the potential to favour financial inclusion for the benefit of society.

However, blockchain technologies will also introduce new risks to users and market participants as well as new risks to financial integrity: e.g., fraud, money laundering, and cyber-crimes. Therefore new forms of "tech regulation" should be designed and implemented in order to boost innovation and guarantee market stability in those new areas that will be affected by the adoption of blockchain technologies.

The Future of FinTech

10

This concluding part of the book aims to chart the future course of FinTech over the next decade. What will happen to the global insurance and banking industry? Will they survive and maybe even thrive by learning from successful transformation programmes by tech giants and the innovation culture of FinTech start-ups today? What will happen to FinTech firms who disrupt the finance industry? Will they be the winners, having responded to new client demands faster and better than anybody else? Will existing banking and insurance services become "utilities"? If big data is the competitive advantage will the data which is controlled by incumbents within their organization be more valuable or will it be the data outside their IT firewalls which can be analysed by FinTech entrepreneurs using cutting-edge artificial intelligence, machine learning, and analytical data mining solutions?

Everybody agrees that collaboration is key. Are Application Programming Interfaces (APIs) the secret tool to implement partnerships in practice? Could APIs even help banks to escape their legacy systems and compete at start-up speed? Will we see global FinTech banks emerge which – thanks to their own banking licence – will no longer rely on established players or be at the mercy of long procurement processes? Will "FinTech Marketplace Banking" reverse the existing value chain completely where established players become actual suppliers to FinTech banks?

To serve customers well in the long term, should we forget what customers ask for today and figure out what they would be asking for if they knew it was possible? Disruptive technologies such as mobile, blockchain, the Internet of Things, and wearables enable so many new financial services that we are really only constrained by our imagination. In order to look into the future we have asked a diverse group of authors ranging from FinTech entrepreneurs, Challenger Banks, established banks, consulting companies, tech giants, and global FinTech thought leaders what to expect and how stakeholders in the FinTech ecosystem could respond to guarantee their successful future.

How Emerging Technologies Will Change Financial Services

By Manoj K. Kashyap

Assurance Partner, Banking and Capital Markets, Global FinTech Leader, PwC

and Grégory Weber

Director and FinTech Leader, PwC Luxembourg

The financial services sector is in the nascent stage of digital disruption. Its main functions are the same today as they were yesterday – people use financial services to exchange money, to save or invest, to finance, or to insure against risk. All financial services are a response to these four basic needs, and this will not change. What is changing, though, is the way these needs are being addressed. New technologies are delivering convenience, speed, and volume in quantities we have never seen before, making financial transactions easier, cheaper, and more convenient. As Jeff Stewart, CEO of Lenddo, an online platform which uses data from social media and other sites to form a profile of the borrower, declared: "Financial Services is about to have its Napster moment". FinTech is, indeed, reshaping the financial services industry, which will undoubtedly look very different tomorrow than it does today. And the penetration of technology-driven companies in the financial sector is set to go deeper, since finance offers them an ocean of opportunities.

Many Opportunities for FinTech Are Yet to be Explored

By the year 2020, over 1 million payment transactions will take place every minute in the world.[1] While cash still remains the primary method of payment for low value transactions, we have observed a declining trend in its use during recent decades in conjunction with increased adoption of new alternative payment methods. On a large scale, governments are taking notice of the cost differential between cash and non-cash solutions: cash can cost up to 1.5% of a country's GDP,[2] which is around five times more than the cost of non-cash alternatives.[3] The volume of non-cash payment transactions will be driven by global GDP growth, especially in SAAAME (South America, Africa, Asia, and Middle East) countries, the ongoing improvement of payment systems infrastructure, as well as the continuing growth of e-commerce at the global level.

As a matter of fact, according to eMarketer, B2C e-commerce sales are set to reach US$2.36tn by 2018 soaring from US$1.23tn in 2013. In this regard, mobile represents a powerful vehicle for digital sales and we expect the global value of mobile payments to increase to US$1,271.8bn by 2020[4] (from US$235.4bn in 2013). On the other hand, the digitalization of currencies and their acceptance by customers and merchants is on the rise. Crypto-currencies such as bitcoin, Ripple, and hundreds of other crypto-technologies will surely foster the digitalization of the payment systems and the globally-connected economy.[5]

Boosted by increasing infrastructure requirements and growing numbers of middle classes, global financing needs will exceed three times the world GDP by 2020. While alternative ways of financing such as PE/VC, crowdfunding, and P2P lending are still small markets, accounting for a mere 0.5% of European GDP, they have been growing at a fast pace in recent years. In this respect, global crowdfunding gathered a strong momentum in 2014, expanding by 167% to reach US$16.2bn raised, up from US$6.1bn in 2013.[6] Concerning P2P lending, Lending Club, the largest of the marketplace lenders, reached over around US$13.4bn in loan issuance at the end of September 2015, compared to US$7.6bn at the end of 2014.[7]

Investable assets will reach US$200tn by 2020.[8] The highest increase will come from mass affluent and high net worth individuals (HNWI). More specifically, mass affluent assets in SAAAME regions will more than double from 2012 to 2020.[9] The importance of institutional investors is also on the rise and we anticipate that the assets of pension funds, insurance companies and sovereign wealth fund (SWF) will reach US$100.5tn (a 5.8% CAGR[10] from 2013 to 2020).[11]

---

[1] PwC Market Research Centre based on Goldman Sachs data.

[2] MasterCard Advisors' Cashless Journey, September 2013.

[3] PwC analysis based on ECB data.

---

[4] PwC Market Research Centre based on Goldman Sachs data.

[5] See also PwC, *Virtual Currencies: Out of the deep web into the light*, 2014.

[6] Massolution, Crowdfunding Industry report, 2015.

[7] https://www.lendingclub.com/info/statistics.action.

[8] PwC Market Research Centre based on Credit Suisse data.

[9] Ibid.

[10] Compound Annual Growth Rate.

[11] PwC Market Research Centre. Past data based on Credit Suisse, SWF Institute, The City UK, OECD, and Insurance Europe.

A rise in investible assets translates into increased demand for asset management, which should support the growth of automated financial advisory solutions. On a global basis, robo advisors directly managed about US$19bn as of December 2014, according to a study by Corporate Insight,[12] and this figure is set to grow since virtual advisors are providing personalized portfolio allocation, tax aware portfolio design, smart rebalancing to maintain a target risk, and 24/7 access with lower fees than other types of advisors.[13] Market players will also increasingly take advantage of every new piece of information for investment decision-making, distribution, compliance, and reporting purposes.

Global Insurance Premiums Will Amount to US$800 per capita in 2020[14]

The global value of insurance premiums will reach US$6.2tn by 2020 growing at a 4.2% CAGR from 2013 to 2020. The highest growth will come from developing markets such as Asia-Pacific, Latin America, the Middle East, and Africa. However, Europe and the US will remain the two most important regions accounting for 63% of global insurance premiums by 2020. The long-term opportunities for insurers in a world where people are living longer and have more wealth to protect are evident. But they are also bringing fresh competition, both from within the insurance industry, and a raft of new entrants coming in from outside. The entrants include companies from other financial services sectors, technology giants, health care companies, venture capital firms, and nimble new start-ups.[15]

Telematics (a term that refers to any device which merges telecommunications and informatics), for instance, offers new applications to manage risk and enhance customer relationships. On a global basis, the value of telematics insurance soared from EUR 3.4bn in 2009 to EUR 13.5bn in 2014, a 31.8% CAGR over the period.[16]

---

[12] Corporate Insight, *Transcending the Human Touch*, 2014.

[13] PwC/CACEIS, *Reshaping the retail fund distribution – Winning strategies and tactics in a disrupted environment*, 2015.

[14] PwC Market Research Centre based on Credit Suisse data.

[15] PwC, *Insurance 2020 & beyond: Necessity is the mother of reinvention*, 2015.

[16] PwC Market Research Centre based on GSMA data.

Property & Casualty insurers are particularly keen to embrace this technology, which allows them to match premiums more closely with actual risk. On the other side, drivers benefit from the opportunity to lower their insurance rates by driving more safely. In addition, governments in various countries have announced plans to launch telematics-related mandates on services such as emergency call and stolen vehicle tracking (e.g. the eCall initiative in the EU and the mandatory "Black Box" law for all new cars in Italy).

The Future of FinTech Largely Depends on Five Game-changers

In this highly dynamic environment we have identified five main game-changers (customers' experience, Fin & Tech connection, data monetization, crypto-technologies, and regulation) which are set to influence the future development of the financial industry, but the definitive impact of those factors remains unknown.

Customer Experience (CX)

Internet, mobility, social networking, and the rise of price comparison websites have changed the game over the past decade and have created a new generation of customers who demand simplicity, speed, and convenience in their interactions with financial providers and even with their peers (e.g. P2P models). FinTech is placing clients at the centre of its business model. It is moving towards strengthening front-end tools and adopting a multi-channel approach in order to provide clients with multiple touch points and enriching customers' experience. "We understand our customers are changing the way they consume financial products, and we focus on enriching our value proposition to them, looking for opportunities in the areas of Personal Financial Management Services (PFMs), Blockchain, API-based banking,[17] insurance and more."[18]

The increasing flexibility of IT architectures, open networks, and API[19] is facilitating a dynamic and diverse financial services environment. This raises a critical question for incumbents: to what extent will they be able to adapt their business models and IT infrastructures to cope with this new competitive landscape.

---

[17] See the chapter entitled "Embracing the Connected API Economy" for further details.

[18] Santander Innoventures website.

[19] API = application program interface, is a set of routines, protocols, and tools for building software applications. The API specifies how software components should interact.

Fin & Tech Connection

The connection of Finance and Technology is producing a collaborative spirit in both sectors that is blurring the traditional business lines. Experts in the financial sector bring to the table a specific knowledge such as risk management, financial analysis, and regulatory compliance, while IT players contribute with technological expertise and an understanding of the customer's experience in a digital age. "Silicon Valley is coming [...] we are going to work hard to make our services as seamless and competitive as theirs. And we also are completely comfortable with partnering where it makes sense."[20] Going forward, what will be the dominant approach for combining expertise in both finance and technology? Will players enhance in-house capabilities by themselves, by outsourcing, by partnering, or by acquiring strategic stakes?

Data Monetization

Financial services providers are sitting on a veritable goldmine of untapped data which will play an important role in FinTech development. As a matter of fact, the emergence of powerful, low-cost analytical tools and computer technology enables companies to mine big data, identify emerging trends, and develop unique insights. These insights can translate into better, faster, smarter business decisions – and can drive the development of breakthrough products, reveal hidden markets, and spark other innovations that give companies a competitive edge.[21]

The question is: will data analytics no longer be a competitive advantage, but rather a competitive disadvantage for those who do not embrace it? And most importantly, how can financial institutions secure clients' data privacy and strengthen trust in the industry?

Crypto-technologies ("Blockchain")

The truly disruptive innovation will certainly come from crypto-technologies or blockchain.[22] In fact, these may not only change the way we do payments but also the whole trading and settlement world. According to the Bank of England, the technology could have far-reaching implications and its impact on the financial industry could be much wider than payments. "Many have come to believe that this technology can be adapted to record and verify financial transactions, from clearing securities to making cross-border payments."[23]

That said, will the risks and uncertainty related to virtual currencies (e.g. Anti-Money Laundering (AML), Know Your Client (KYC) issues) prevent a further adoption of crypto-technologies? If adopted, to what extent can these technologies trigger simplification of banking processes and cost structure? Finally, to what extent will "smart contracts", which are programs that contain conditionality and can automatically execute the terms of the contract if the conditions are met, be applied in the financial sector?

Adapt (to) Regulation

Finally, the future of FinTech will largely depend on its capacity to cope with the highly demanding regulatory framework of the financial sector. On the other hand, regulators will need to increase clarification and ensure a harmonized level playing field in order to protect customers and remove barriers to market developments. In closing, regulation may become either the catalyst for the development of FinTech or its main inhibitor.

FinTech firms have already managed to successfully penetrate the financial services industry by leveraging innovation to deliver better service to customers. FinTech now has the potential to bring a more radical change within this industry and become a core constituent of its infrastructure and processes, thereby boosting the speed and agility of financial services.

---

[20] Jamie Dimon, CEO of JPMorgan, Annual Letter to Shareholders, 2014.

[21] PwC, *Capitalizing on the promise of Big Data*, 2013.

[22] A public and unbreakable ledger that serves as a record of transactions that was first brought by bitcoin.

[23] *The Wall Street Journal*, "UBS to Open Blockchain Research Lab in London", April 2015.

The Future of Financial Services

By Axel Apfelbacher

FinTech Thought Leader

The following dialogue between *Artus*, a digital financial adviser of the future, and a *User* of a very specific banking service (mortgage financing) outlines the major concepts of the (retail) finance industry of the future. After each sequence, the relevant concepts are described with respect to their impact on the interaction between users of financial services and the future ecosystem of providers. These impacts will not be limited to the chosen example but apply to any type of financial transaction.

The Future of Financing

"Artus, please organize the mortgage for our future home we picked an hour ago."

"… Mortgage processed … I have contracted with Crowdlending-Pool Europe III for a 20-year contract. You can move house on Monday, the MoveBots will be there at 7 am."

Financing the purchase of a new home will become a very smooth, very rapid process, outpacing current processing speeds by more than 99%. Following the order book logic of stock exchanges, mortgages will be made visible to multiple parties interested in taking a lending position in a specific (real estate) market. All criteria that an interested borrower requires to close a transaction are captured by Digital Financial Assistants (DFAs) who compare various offers available on the lending exchange against these parameters which have been defined by the users of these services. Available cash flows for repaying the mortgage, the existing income and wealth structure, and overall financial goals for the investor are known to the DFA who can then compare all available offers and execute a (smart) contract on the basis of all available data.

Crowdlending will become a significant additional channel for accumulating and allocating cash flows that individual investors are awarding to crowdlending pools which will be organized by platforms and insured through credit default swap arrangements against loan losses. Despite the drag on gross margins

as a consequence of insurance, crowdlending will be very competitive due to lower technology costs for cash flow matching and analysis of borrowers' credit qualities. After reaching the trough of disillusionment in 2017, crowdlending will develop into a standard financing structure along more traditional ways of capital accumulation.

The Future of Identity

"Wonderful. Any additional input required?"

"No, all parameters are available. Your avatar ID will be entered into the global asset database as owner of your new home in Madrid on Monday. Please validate the transaction within 24 hours at the global ID centre on Lombard Street (former Bank of England)."

Blockchain technology will change the nature of financial transactions as it leads to fundamental changes in the global financial architecture. Where current financial data management is driven by discreet databases inside financial institutions that communicate with one another through secured communications channels, the future of financial transaction processing will be a world of one or multiple global asset data bases. These databases will store all financial data of financial market participants that choose to use these cheaper and easier to use transaction engines. Following the blockchain logic, these databases will be distributed around the globe and transactions will require validation from all or at least a qualified majority of these databases to be executed.

This distributed ledger system is designed to reduce the likelihood of hacking as the amount of computing power necessary to break the system is vast. However, it comes at the price of having all financial data distributed across a global network of databases that are owned by potentially untrustworthy market participants. Therefore, a blockchain world will require either an intermediary or the use of pseudonyms in financial transactions to avoid full financial disclosure to the outside world. Given the need of regulators for that kind of transparency, a global blockchain implementation mandates either intermediaries to step in and comply with KYC rules (similar to today's practice) or a translation engine that allows the regulators to interpret the pseudonymic blockchain ledger entries through the use of an ID database to maintain AML processes. Both concepts are extant today, and may continue to be so in the future, although there may be a slight preference for the intermediary model.

Furthermore, users of financial services will have the option to determine a transactional threshold as well as specific types of transactions for which a separate validation process will be required. This may take place in outlets that used to be bank branches which have now turned into ID validation centres. Here, the identity of individual market participants will be checked through a comparison of digital and non-digital features and tokens that are designed to generate proof of one's identity. Re-entry of such an analogue element for (at least) large transactions will decrease the likelihood of system-wide security breaches and exploits that threaten the validity of the overall financial system.

The Future of Money

"Artus, please display our financial status."

"The total processing fees of 1.4% of transaction value will be transferred with the purchase price on Monday. Your monthly mortgage charge of 1,957 ePounds will be debited on the 1st of every month. You are committing 27% of your net income. Including your normalised level of expenses, you'll have saved an adequate amount of money to cover the tuition fees for your children by 2021."

The issuance of electronic currency by the national banks around the world is a consequence of the technological capabilities derived from blockchain technology. National governments and supranational financial market committees will push for an implementation of fully transparent global asset databases that enable real-time tracking of financial flows. Cash will probably remain for a very long time a parallel and anonymous transaction mechanism, however most transactions will become available on these online networks due to the ease of use and transaction speed of globally organized asset databases. Therefore, the issuance of electronic currency (e.g. "ePounds"), controlled by the central banks of participating countries, will become a standard way of managing the monetary base of a currency.

When asked why they implemented such an all-encompassing digital currency regime, central banks, regulators, and tax agencies will refer to the auditability and traceability of financial flows as well as the lower transactional costs associated with the use of official e-currencies. Such transparency will require new governance mechanisms to balance transparency and freedom in a world of ubiquitous surveillance.

The Future of Saving and Consumption

"Artus, is there any room to manoeuvre? I'd like to take my family on an extended holiday in Africa."

"Your savings rate is 10% of net income. The rate to achieve your net wealth target by the age of 57 is an annualized 8.2%. May I recommend a wonderful resort in Portugal instead who are looking for new customers and are offering 4 weeks for your family at a bargain price?"

The question of whether to use available cash resources for saving or consumption will be increasingly answered by DFAs, relying on the one hand on inputs we have given them which reflect our consumption versus saving preferences and the importance of reaching our financial goals. On the other hand, these assistants will tap all available resources, mainly through product information that is available online, to suggest the most fitting price/product mix that matches as closely as possible our financial position as well as our willingness to spend money.

There will be an ecosystem of independent vs. dependent DFAs, reflecting the charging model of the providers that will live off usage fees or referral fees/advertising revenues from providers of the products and services that are being channelled through the DFAs' analysis engine. Some DFAs will offer their users the choice of whether they are willing to pay for their services with money or the (restricted or unrestricted) use of anonymized transactional and other data for advertising purposes. New property rights for personal data will finally enable the owner of such data to determine the degree to which such data can and shall be disclosed to outside parties and will finally put a price on the use of such data by external parties.

The trade-off between the immediate use of cash resources and saving such resources for future uses will turn to a more long-term perspective for those users with longer-term financial goals that they enable the DFA to compare against immediate spending desires. The individual user will still be able to overrule the Digital Assistant (DA) but the nagging voice talking about the validity of the longer-term goals will at least put the next purchase into a wider context, potentially delaying such purchase for another day. Thus, the saving vs. consumption decision will be based on a more sophisticated financial outlook provided by an unbiased DA.

The Future of Financial Literacy

"Artus, the resort looks fabulous. Can you please inform my boss about my intention to take an extended holiday and arrange accommodation and transport after approval?"

"… Holiday request processed … and approved. Enjoy your trip. Your flight details are available on your Watchlet. Please remember to take your annual financial education test next month as your license will expire on 17 May."

As intermediaries are squeezed out of the financial value chain, replaced by Digital Assistants who base their decision making on inputs from individual market participants, the current approach of financial regulation that focuses on regulating intermediaries will be challenged. Therefore, regulation will be increasingly asking for proofs of financial literacy and will make the nature of financial transactions dependent upon the results of obligatory tests designed to display the level of understanding of an individual with respect to financial knowledge. Without such testing, financial regulation will struggle to capture all relevant aspects of future financial transactions, whilst providers of Digital Assistants will design their business models to avoid a position of financial risk taking in the decision-making process. Thus, the individual will become the focus of regulatory action and knowledge of financial flows and the impact of specific decisions on financial well-being will become increasingly important to avoid disastrous holes in the (retail) financial architecture.

The nature of financial services and the global financial architecture will evolve substantially within the next decade and will move towards a technology-enabled, highly automated advisory service that takes into account all available sources and uses of money that are still existing in the markets, making them available to every participant and in language that can be understood by everyone. These DFAs will be highly personalized, potentially issuer-independent, and highly interconnected to generate the best available financial results for their users and execute transactions automatically to reduce processing time and effort. The issuance of money by central banks will be transformed through the use of blockchain technology and will turn the transfer of money and all other types of financial instruments into real-time experience. Such automation and smart contracting available through the use of DFAs, based on electronic currency databases and transparent financial markets will help individuals make better decisions leading to a more positive financial future for users of these systems.

Banking on Innovation Through Data

By Dr Marc Torrens
CIO, Strands Labs

232

THE FUTURE OF FINTECH

Technology innovation has been vital to the online banking industry since Stanford Federal Credit Union offered the world's first internet banking portal in 1994.[1] The last few decades have seen the financial industry slowly incorporate internet-based technologies to open up new distribution and operational channels. However, most of that innovation has been around the operational aspects of the bank by incorporating different new digital channels.

Today, the vast majority of banks offer their products and services through internet channels such as web platforms or mobile applications. Digital banking allows customers to access almost all financial services from anywhere, at any time.

Banks, however, are still offering essentially the same products and services as they did in the 1990s. Compared to other industries such as entertainment, travel, or retail, banks are not yet using these channels to actually change their business model or propose new and more relevant products or services. A few bells and whistles aside, the banking industry has yet to be truly disrupted.

From Financial Product Vendors to Solution Providers

The transactional data banks are collecting from millions of customers and the new data revolution are the necessary ingredients to disrupt the products and services banks are currently offering. This disruption will shift banks from their current position of vendors of financial products to providers of financial solutions.

For example, a customer that wants to buy his dream car has thousands of products available to help him save or borrow money to attain that specific goal.

But, the customer would probably like to have a plan to achieve the goal with the right products. So, instead of offering customers a large catalogue of financial products to choose from, banks could offer personalized plans to meet the customer's specific needs. Financial products should serve as tools that facilitate everyday financial situations. Banks will start offering solutions to life events and situations instead of just the financial tools to overcome them.

Banks are actually very well positioned to do precisely this; they can develop technologies that offer financial solutions instead of a catalogue of products by learning from the data they have been collecting for decades. The challenge is to extract meaning from that data and use it to offer the right products at the right time to the right customer. This new knowledge should encode preferences and tastes from customers in a very precise way. These actionable insights can then be used to propose personalized financial solutions to specific customer challenges.

The Data Revolution is Here

So far we have seen how banks are in a uniquely privileged position to take the financial industry where it has never been. However, the outlook is not all sunshine and roses – banks are under a lot of pressure to do this before the giant internet companies beat them to it. Moreover, banks are facing a wave of unprecedented competition from an emerging set of pure FinTech players. Large internet companies and FinTech firms which have been leading the data revolution in other sectors are starting to enter the financial world. Big banks are very well aware of this threat and are starting to take the data revolution seriously. A notable example comes from Francisco Gonzalez, chief executive of BBVA, who stated in an opinion article entitled "Banks need to take on Amazon and Google or die" published in the *Financial Times* in 2013:[2]

> Some bankers and analysts think that Google, Facebook, Amazon or the like will not fully enter a highly regulated, low-margin business such as banking. I disagree. What is more, I think banks that are not prepared for such new competitors face certain death.

---

[1] See http://www.thefreelibrary.com/_/print/PrintArticle.aspx?id=17104850.

[2] "Banks need to take on Amazon and Google or Die", *Financial Times*, 2 December 2013, http://www.ft.com/cms/s/0/bc70c9fe-4e1d-11e3-8fa5-00144feabdc0.html#axzz3ojXmfGVg.

So, what is the unique competitive advantage financial institutions have to continue leading the innovation in the financial sector? How can they innovate to win the new battle against the Amazon, Apple, Google, and the FinTech start-ups?

What banks have in spades is reliable, quantifiable, and best of all, monetizable data. Unfortunately, banks largely lack a culture of internet innovation and the agile, quick-to-market IT organization that forms the DNA of FinTech start-ups and internet giants. The challenge of entering the data revolution from a bank's perspective is not negligible because core banking systems have been patched for decades and bank organizations have not been designed to rapidly innovate in this space. Internet and data innovation need a very specific type of organization that is a far cry from the way financial institutions operate. Specifically, banks have difficulties to innovate in the data and internet sectors for several reasons:

- A corporate organization and culture that is not designed for rapid innovation. Banks have been operating their IT development teams, using what is known in project management as "the waterfall approach" in which requirements are very well defined at the beginning of the project, and the final results must be seen at the end. This way of working is not the most appropriate to promote innovation. Internet companies and start-ups use agile methodologies to quickly iterate and implement new ideas, even though it is riskier as outcomes are often unknown and failure is part of the process.

- A lack of specialized talent from software engineering and data science. Engineers often prefer to devote their talent to smaller companies where they feel that their contribution has a larger impact, and where the company culture is innovation-based from the outset.

- A cumbersome, heterogeneous core IT infrastructure. Core banking infrastructures are very often composed of legacy and heterogeneous systems that incur huge costs to keep operational and secure. Building new systems is therefore seen in some scenarios as a second priority but not part of the bank's core business.

Banks are indeed starting to realize their situation and adapt their way of working to the innovative technology sector, but this may not be enough to compete against the new players.

So, How Can Banks Best Leverage Their Data Advantage?

The question that arises is then: how exactly can banks innovate to compete with these new players (e.g. internet giants and FinTech start-ups) by exploiting their unique data advantage?

Living in a world of interconnected systems in which real value comes more and more from data itself, banks must open up and offer well-structured and secure APIs[3] on top of which third-party innovators can develop the next generation of financial solutions. This is not a new approach in the technology sector; it has been widely used by the largest technology companies. For example, Apple through their Apple Store ecosystem opened their platform to allow third-party companies to innovate on top of their operating systems and devices. This approach makes Apple platforms much stronger and more powerful even though some of the innovation does not come directly from Apple but from other companies and start-ups. Google is also innovating by opening up services and APIs to other companies.

Banks should follow suit and start offering well-structured and secure APIs to open up their data and services to innovative developers. This approach requires middleware applications to interact with the core banking systems to enable developers to access the bank's services and data through robust APIs. This middleware layer would also involve a simplification of some of the IT infrastructure that currently hinders innovation within banks. With this approach, third-party companies could innovate new financial services while allowing banks to maintain their core business.

The FinTech application development community is endlessly creative and agile. Data APIs have the potential to enable tech companies, banks, and their customers to benefit from an increasingly valuable ecosystem of innovative solutions. This new approach not only has great potential to generate new revenue streams, but more importantly enables banks to actually lead the imminent disruption of their industry.

---

[3] See the chapter entitled "Embracing the Connected API Economy" for further details.

The Future of FinTech: A Tripartite Innovation Ecosystem

Data science applied to financial transactional data that banks hold opens up new avenues for innovation and will form the basis of the future of FinTech. The key to realizing this innovation is extracting knowledge from data that can be used in new applications, having basically encoded customer needs and preferences to generate actionable insights. Based on this new knowledge, machine learning technologies such as collaborative filtering will be able to offer customers precisely what they need at the moment they need it. Moreover, this new financial ecosystem will be able to offer more personalized solutions based on products already offered by banks. These solutions will enable consumers to achieve their specific goals with financial plans tailored to their precise needs and behaviours.

This proposed new ecosystem in which banks focus on their core business and allow technology companies to develop new financial services on top of bank data and services will undoubtedly lead to new business models involving the three parties: banks, tech companies, and customers. Although this scenario does not consider banks driving innovation on their own, they will still hold the fuel that powers this innovation ecosystem: data and services.

Why FinTech Banks Will Rule the World

By Philippe Gelis
CEO, Kantox

The financial industry is one of the last large industries that has not been completely disrupted by the digital revolution. Nevertheless, it seems that bankers do not have a very different approach to the people who ran the press, hospitality, and airline industries some years ago. Every industry will be "uberized", but it seems that most bankers still think it will be different in their case, probably because they consider that heavy regulation will protect them and limit the growth, or at least the impact, of FinTech. Bankers simply do not understand that tech companies are agile enough to take advantage of any piece of regulation.

They also continue to believe that customers still trust banks; however, since the 2008 financial crisis and due to the never-ending financial scandals (Libor-gate, the foreign exchange (FX) fixing scandal, etc.) customers (both individuals and businesses) have a huge appetite for alternative finance. Banks are no longer seen as partners, but rather as pure providers looking after their own interests and short-term profits.

It is a first step for banks to open incubators or to create venture capital (VC) funds to invest in start-ups, some of them FinTech, but it is definitely not enough. Most banks look to fund FinTech start-ups that create products to be added on top of their own products, which will make the user experience better, but they almost never invest in products that directly compete with them and therefore could cannibalize their customers or profits. Let me explain why this approach is completely wrong. We are now experimenting with the first wave of FinTech, which sees companies competing with banks on specific products, including, among many more:

- Loans and credit
- Payments
- Foreign exchange and remittance
- Wealth management

Lending Club is by far the global flagship FinTech company. The success of its IPO has been a game changer for the entire FinTech sector. So, banks are being pressured by newcomers but – and the "but" is really important – these disrupters are relying on old-school banks for banking services and banking infrastructure (bank accounts, payments, compliance, brokerage, etc.). In other words, they are re-inventing the user experience, the user interface, or the business model but not "the whole thing" (to steal a quote from Marc Andreessen). And by relying on banks to do business, FinTech companies are clients and so generate revenue for the bank. That is a co-optition (co-operative competition) model in which FinTech stays at the mercy of banks – they disrupt banks on one side but they bring them business on the other side. In the end, the banks still win.

It is important to note that many FinTech businesses have evolved from pure "P2P models" to "marketplace models" where the liquidity can come from peers or from financial institutions. Lending Club is known for getting up to 80% of its liquidity from financial institutions and not from peers. Here we have a clear example of banks considering it to be more efficient and therefore more profitable for them to lend money through Lending Club than through their outdated branches. In any event, the challenge is more in having deep liquidity than in locating the liquidity.

The second wave of FinTech, to come in the next three years, will be "marketplace banking" (or "FinTech banks"). This will be a type of bank based on five simple elements:

1. A core banking platform built from scratch.

2. An API[1] layer to connect to third parties.

3. A compliance/KYC infrastructure and processes.

4. A banking licence, to be independent from other banks and the ability to hold client funds without restrictions.

5. A customer base/CRM, meaning that the FinTech bank will have the customers and a customer support team.

---

[1] See the chapter entitled "Embracing the Connected API Economy" for further details.

The products directly offered by the FinTech bank will be limited to "funds holding", comprised of:

1. Bank accounts (multi-currency)

2. Credit and debit cards (multi-currency)

3. eWallet (multi-currency).

All other services (investing, trading, and brokerage; wealth management; loans, credit, and mortgages; crowdfunding (equity and social); insurance; crypto-currencies; payments; remittances and FX … this list is not exhaustive) will be provided by third parties through the API, including old-school banks, financial institutions, and FinTech companies.

Imagine that you are a client of this "marketplace bank" and that you need a loan. You do not really care if the loan is provided to you by Lending Club or Bank of America, what you look for is a quick and frictionless process to get your loan, and the lowest interest rate possible. So, through the API, the "marketplace bank" will consult all its third parties and offer you the loan that best suits you. We can imagine a process in which conditions offered by third parties are non-negotiable but we can also imagine a competitive bidding process to get the best offer for each client at any point in time.

In a recent informal chat with the manager of a global bank's venture capital arm, I finally understood that what banks fear most are technology companies (GAFA and FinTech) owning the customer relationship in the future, and that they become the mere white labels at the back end of the process. In such a scenario, banks do not own the client relationship and merely compete on price, creating significant pressure on their margins and profitability. It is a bit like when a company provides white-labelled products to retailers such as Carrefour or Tesco.

I have been asked several times about this business model and I think it's a no-brainer. It is a simple mix between an access fee to the "marketplace bank" and a revenue-sharing model with the third parties providing additional services. Here we have a completely different approach regarding the relationship with incumbents. FinTech banks, thanks to their banking licence, will no longer rely on any bank to be – and stay – in business, and so will not be at the mercy of incumbents. And what is even more powerful, through the marketplace,

incumbents will become "clients" of FinTech banks, so the system will be completely reversed.

We will see banks pay a commission to FinTech banks to serve their customers! The beauty of "marketplace banking" is that it competes directly with banks on core banking services without the need to build all the products. Now the question is, what is really needed to launch a "marketplace bank"?

1. Technology/API/Compliance/KYC: building the technology is a complex element but many people have the skills to do so. So it is definitely not the main barrier.

2. Banking licence: in Europe, the budget to get a banking licence is estimated to be approximately €20 million, though it could cost less or more, depending on the country. But it is not only about money. To be in business you need strong and experienced board members; without them regulators will probably not give you the green light. So you need to be able to convince investors and board members to trust you, based on a PowerPoint presentation, and to bet big on you. I think that we need the first wave of FinTech to be successful, with some exits and big returns, to have people betting a lot of money on "marketplace banking". As an entrepreneur you need to have demonstrated that you are able to execute and scale a FinTech business to lead that kind of new venture.

3. Customer base/CRM: This is the most complex part. How do you attract a critical mass of customers based on a simple offering (accounts + cards + eWallet) that relies on third parties for additional services? You cannot only rely on marketing and having a cool brand to attract hundreds of thousands of new customers if you have nothing really different to offer.

You also need focus: will you target individuals or businesses? Lower end or high net worth individuals? Small, medium, or large businesses? Will you focus on one single country or several? As always, it is all about customers and revenues, so you need a clear sales and marketing plan to quickly scale the customer base. I have been asked several times if the first "marketplace bank" will be launched by an old-school bank (an incumbent) or a FinTech start-up? I definitely think the latter. It is too disruptive and the risk of cannibalization is too high to see a bank assuming the risk.

Since 2010, new banks have been started, mainly in the UK, claiming they are "new generation digital banks". My view is that most of them have no clear differentiator. Being online only or opening 24 hours a day 7 days a week is not appealing enough to massively attract new customers. Others banks are looking to offer the "best" current account ever ... personally I do not see the point here. The first FinTech bank is still to be invented.

Anyway, most bankers are not worried enough by FinTech to react to its coming second wave. This creates a fantastic "window" for us FinTech entrepreneurs to build it. FinTech banks are inevitable! This is just a blueprint. To pull it off requires a lot of hard work. But given that the elements are already available, it is not a question of if but rather when the first pure FinTech banks appear. They will be lean, flexible, and unhindered by legacy systems and will not have the tarnished reputations of the incumbents. They will eat the lunch of the current banking dinosaurs and could well eventually rule the banking world.

The FinTech Supermarket – The Bank is Dead, Long Live the Bank!

By Spiros Margaris

Advisor, FinTech Forum; CEO, Margaris Advisory

"It is not the strongest of the species that survives, nor the most intelligent that survives. It is the one that is the most adaptable to change."

Charles Darwin, *The Origin of Species*

The financial institutions of the future will have to be very different from today's structures if they want to remain competitive while satisfying the ever-changing and increasing demands of customers. They will consist of a construct of primarily innovative and independent financial technology (FinTech) companies. These types of institutions provide lower fees in addition to improved performance and user experience. Most importantly, they represent a future that we can and want to believe in.

The new proposed financial institution is called best-in-class FinTech Supermarket, and its business model differentiates it from existing financial institutions such as banks, including those that already have partnerships with FinTech firms.

The FinTech Supermarket

The FinTech Supermarket proposal refers to an almost single-minded pursuit of primarily using FinTech firms as financial service providers. It is figuratively a logical development of well-known open fund architecture but with the important distinction that the best FinTech companies are offered in place of the best fund products. It is about the possibility of combining an open selection of the best FinTech partners and the best packages of financial services under one roof. Leading independent and innovative FinTech companies will provide the majority of all financial services.

At the same time, the FinTech Supermarket will always be open to cooperation with banks, insurance companies, or technology giants to ensure the best price-performance ratios and services. It is most likely that it will ultimately benefit more from using best-in-class FinTechs, which are more agile and nimble due to their size and more innovative due to their entrepreneurial spirit.

However, a key difference of this new financial institution is that it is not the financial industry incumbents which will allow FinTechs to participate in the overall services and business; rather, it will be the other way around. As for the general lack of branches, banks and maybe some FinTechs will eventually only offer them to the privileged clients. Other clients do not need them or simply cannot afford them. Banks that nevertheless retain branches will do so at a high cost to cover the client segment that is still uncomfortable with digital banking, among others. For a good example showing that service partners can work successfully within and for a larger structure, one needs to look no further than large websites that use Google, Bing, or Yahoo! Search as their default search engines. Both the search engine providers and the websites benefit from the partnership, and they both remain independent, strong, and successful in their own right.

Client benefits

- Access to "open FinTech architecture", which provides better financial services, better price/performance ratios, greater transparency, and subsequently a new and improved customer experience.
- Pre-selection of service providers, consolidation of services, assets, and ad hoc reports.
- Lower fees and therefore higher overall returns and savings.

FinTech benefits

- Access to more customers, allowing critical mass to be reached more quickly, and the creation of a solid foundation for expansion and growth.
- Maintenance of core competencies and independence: a partnership with or sale to a third party is not precluded.

FinTech supermarket benefits

- Reduction of costs and the ability to provide customers with independent best-in-class services.

- Continuous growth and acquisition of up-to-date know-how through financial services partnerships.
- Attractiveness, branding, and competitive advantage will strengthen through higher total returns, greater transparency, and faster adjustments to customer needs.

The business strategy of the FinTech Supermarket will be a "game changer" for financial services. In the insurance industry, it is already common for insurance brokers to compare suitable offers for clients and then put together an optimum package. Moreover, there are already FinTechs which negotiate better bank and insurance fees for their clients. In contrast, the FinTech Supermarket will analyse all matching FinTech services and prices on the market as well as the services of eligible banks, evaluate the findings, and then offer the best possible deal to the client. The FinTech Supermarket will thus create a whole new marketplace. It will increase the range of services for all parties – customers, FinTechs, banks, and insurance companies – which will lead to better services, price-performance ratios, and competitiveness.

The advance of new financial industry competitors and business models such as the FinTech Supermarket will bring about disruptive changes that could also be very painful for many participants. It will also naturally stabilize the income of the financial industry at a lower level through greater competition and associated pressure on profit margins.

To survive this trend, financial institutions must provide clear added value and unique customer experiences to keep their margins high. The approach taken by Apple can be considered a good future business model for the financial industry since it operates in an extremely competitive industry and has, so far, been very successful in maintaining its high profit margins.

Financial Regulation

Many, if not all, banks and financial institutions harbour the hope that regulation will kill off smaller banking competitors and FinTechs and hold back the technology giants. The remainder think they can reinvent themselves out of the innovation gap problem, but this is not likely to happen. If financial institutions rely on financial regulation to stop their competition, they will be dead in the water.

Nevertheless, FinTechs must prepare for the moment when new regulations will strengthen rules and oversight. They would be well advised to comply with regulations from the beginning and consider them to be critical to their prospects of success. They should therefore adapt and act accordingly. We should not forget that regulators and governments know or should know that FinTechs could serve them on many levels, such as improving overall banking customer experiences and banking services. International financial centres that do not understand the importance of FinTechs as one of the key components to determine their futures and to stay relevant will quickly lose their importance as such. Nurturing the FinTech industry, which represents the future, is part of nurturing their own futures.

Millennials

Clients, particularly millennials, want different things out of banking and also expect regulators and politicians to allow FinTechs and any competition to the status quo to prosper. Millennials – also known as Generation Y – are the generation born approximately between 1980 and 2000 and are considered to be one of the most important client segments for financial institutions. Therefore, there is an enormous need for financial institutions to become a viable destination for them, especially as their buying and investment power naturally increases and their business becomes essential to ensuring success.

Many solutions to the needs of millennials will be transferable to other generations in some form since we all want improvements in services that fulfil our current or future needs, as well as those that are as yet unknown. The famous quote by Henry Ford, founder of the Ford Motor Company, brings the point home: "If I had asked people what they wanted, they would have said faster horses." People will adapt easily to the improved services and customer experience that FinTechs will offer them and even to those services which customers did not know they wanted.

The traditional embossed structures, legacy systems, and ways of thinking of banks make it very difficult for them to solve the FinTech Equation (Innovation + Customer Experience + 24/7 = FinTech). However, it is absolutely essential for them to solve it to become a viable destination for millennials and the rest of us.

Coming Soon to a Town Near You!

To most people, the growing strength of FinTechs and technology giants as competitors to traditional banking comes as no surprise. The real news is how quickly they are becoming successful in the financial industry. This financial sector trend cannot be undone. However, the disruptive innovation of FinTech services and technology giants provides better opportunities to satisfy the customer needs of today and, more importantly, tomorrow.

The human and advisory factor in banking will never disappear; indeed, it will gain in importance. FinTechs must factor this into their strategies regardless of their technological power in order not to lose sight of their ultimate goal of providing clients with the best possible experience and value. FinTechs are specialized and focused on adapting to the dreams and desires of customers; they are therefore more flexible and adaptable than big financial companies. In addition, their justification and future are always closely linked with the satisfaction of customer needs and wants.

Technology giants and FinTechs will play an important role not only in the retail banking space but also in the B2B segment. Corporations can benefit from the technology and user experience advances that will initially be conceived and developed for the retail client segment. At the end, there will be no difference in the ways people or corporations use technology. One has only to look at how the iPhone and Apple's other technologies are used by both segments to see the huge potential.

The tremendous interest and investments of global venture capitalists in FinTech companies are reminiscent of the dot-com era. Although many dot-coms no longer exist, the survivors are here to stay and have changed our lives forever. FinTechs will change the future of today's financial institutions, and many will not survive or will be integrated within large institutions. However, what is certain is that they will change our understanding of and expectations for financial services forever and create new markets. This is just the beginning, and it is unstoppable.

Banks must beware that the technology giants are coming and that some FinTechs will become much bigger and more powerful than most banks would like. Furthermore, the technology-heavy business model of FinTechs is closer to the heart of technology giants. That fact makes the likelihood of many FinTechs being acquired by the technology giants a realistic one, since they see them as a perfect entry ticket into the financial industry.

Financial institutions would be well advised to try to evaluate the business model of the best-in-class FinTech Supermarket as quickly as possible. It should be kept in mind that new competitors do not need to adapt to old business models. They only need to implement their new business models, without the structural hurdles of old corporate power structures. Furthermore, legacy systems will kill many banks since many top programmers do not want to build their cutting-edge developments on them or work for such institutions in the first place.

If in doubt, bank management should remember that new competitors can and will move and seize opportunities much faster than them. Moreover, FinTechs, which often lack the money that incumbents have, benefit from a great advantage: it leaves them with few options but to innovate. The likely outcome of the financial competition war will be the fusion of primarily best-in-class FinTechs, technology giants, and banks. Whoever wants to play a leading role in the future has to understand that technology and customer experience will determine the outcome. The proposed best-in-class FinTech Supermarket structure provides all parties with a win-win situation and, above all, a business model that can quickly adapt to customer needs and, not least, to the future. The king is dead, long live the king!

Banks Partnering with FinTech Start-ups to Create an Integrated Customer Experience

By Bernard Lunn

Founding Partner, Daily FinTech Advisers

People sometimes assume that "entrepreneur" means "young dude in a garage" (cue iconic image of suburban garage in Silicon Valley). That image is out of date because today's entrepreneur could be a woman in Africa. It is also out of date because the entrepreneur could be working for a bank. (I use the term bank as short-hand for any financial institution which could be a bank, broker, or insurance company).

The venture capital (VC) funded start-up is only one framework for innovation.

Indeed, one may consider how banks can create the future by partnering with start-ups. Partner implies a relationship of equals. Historically the idea of partnering made little sense. FinTech meant being a vendor, selling technology to the banks. For the last few years the banks might have felt the water heating up, but it was still comfortable. The boiling point transition has not yet happened in Financial Services. The impact today on the bottom line is small. The VC money pouring into FinTech is betting that it will not be small for long. VCs are so confident because they have seen the speed with which incumbents have been impacted by digitization in other markets (such as media, travel, and retail).

Banks should feel urgency.

However that does not mean taking wild and ill-considered risks based on breathless media hype. The strategy has to be right. It is important to create win-win partnerships between banks and FinTech start-ups.

Partnering, a Core Competency in the Digital Age, is all about Data

Banks cannot think clearly about this until they accept that almost all of the valuable data is outside their IT firewall – it is out on the open internet. This "programmable web" is a giant resource that FinTech start-ups use to win in terms of shorter time to market and lower cost value propositions.

To leverage this power, bank business leaders need to become familiar with a bit of technical jargon called an API.[1] API stands for Application Programming Interface; it simply means how to get resources (data and algorithms) from an external system and send resources back to that external system. Most of the resources that banks need do *not* sit behind their IT firewall. Most of those resources are on the open internet and belong to the FinTech start-ups that banks need to partner with.

The good news is that this is a win-win partnership – as long as established players choose the right start-ups to partner with. Some start-ups do want to "eat your lunch". They provide a service today to *part* of the banks' market. They might not sell to banks' customers *just yet* (because they are starting with a segment of the market that has been ignored by incumbents), but when they get to scale they *will* be going after the bank's core customers. The threat from some start-ups is very real.

Other FinTech start-ups want to partner with banks. These are the marketplaces, such as Lending Club and Angel List that win network effects by enticing other firms to add value to their data. They want banks to use their data. That is how they win the network effects game. Some banks may choose to ride the rapid value creation of these marketplaces by investing in them through accelerators and corporate VC funds – but investing is not the same as partnering. These transactional models fall within a bank's organizational comfort zone and can be very profitable. If you invested early in say Lending Club or Angel List, you would have done well. However, that is very different from using resources from these network marketplaces to move the bank's revenue/profit needle. A minority

---

[1] See the chapter entitled "Embracing the Connected API Economy" for further details.

investment does not confer proprietary advantage in digital businesses. If a network marketplace offers a proprietary advantage to somebody who owns some shares, they will not win the network effects game (and then your shares won't be worth much). The APIs have to be open in order to win. Banks win by adding value on top of open data, not by controlling the data.

These win-win partnerships are all about data.

All the "hot spaces" that one reads about in the tech media are about data. Think of the Internet of Things (devices creating data), wearables (our clothes and fashion accessories creating data about what our body is doing that is transforming health care and insurance), or in-car devices and sensors creating data that is transforming transportation and insurance.

Think of network marketplaces in the wealth management market such as Lending Club and Angel List. These marketplaces create a lot of data – which they are happy to make available to partners who will add value to that data and by doing so add to the network effects for the marketplace.

Add Value at the Customer Experience Level

Data needs context and that means clever algorithms and user experience designs that delight customers and anticipate their needs. That is where banks can create value. Networked marketplaces are not new. For example, stock exchanges are networked marketplaces that spew out data feeds. To win the network effect game, these networked marketplaces have to empower an ecosystem, even if the players in that ecosystem (the service businesses that add value to the data) become more valuable than them. So, they are motivated to work with banks that will add value on top of their API.

Banks are service businesses – not marketplaces – and should not suffer from marketplace envy. Consider NYSE and NASDAQ. These are dominant marketplaces in massive markets, yet NYSE was acquired for $8.2 billion[2] and Charles Schwab (SCHW) is valued at over $40 billion. If you do not add value on top of these marketplace APIs, the FinTech start-ups that do want to eat your lunch will do so. This is a race and the prize goes to the swift.

By using external APIs, banks can escape the legacy system rust and compete at start-up speed. Banks can then deploy a huge advantage when they launch using these APIs – a well-known brand.

Big Brand plus Start-up Agility is a Winning Combination

To seize that advantage, banks need to put themselves in their customers' shoes and to address the pain-points that early adopters of these marketplaces have discovered. The early adopters of these marketplaces see the potential value, but they also see past the hype and understand that they do not offer any silver bullet. Banks that get this kind of feedback from focus groups can react in one of two ways:

- "Phew, I am pleased that it is all over and we can ignore it." This is like hearing that consumers were having problems buying stuff online around 1996.

- This is clearly the future and these early adopters are giving us our "to do list". This is the smart reaction and should drive the Customer Experience design.

The Great Rebundling

Networked marketplaces win by unbundling, by doing one thing well. To get network effects, the user friction has to be very low. It has to be "click here to transact". Banks are service businesses that can survive and thrive through the FinTech storm by serving the complex needs of two types of customers through rebundling these atomized experiences into an integrated user experience for:

- Wealthy people, and

- Small and medium-sized businesses.

---

[2] http://www.bloomberg.com/news/articles/2012-12-20/intercontinentalexchange-said-in-merger-talks-with-nyse-euronext.

To serve those customers, banks need to first figure out where the trend is heading and then do something harder – forget about what customers are asking for today and figure out what they would be asking for if they knew it was possible. The disruptive technologies – mobile, blockchain, Internet of Things, wearables – enable so many new services that we really are only constrained by imagination and by real customer need; there are plenty of real customer needs, so the important factor is imagination and the will to act on it.

Rebundling in Wealth Management

Moore's Law will remorselessly drive down price – eventually to free – of commodity services such as asset allocation. This is what robo advisers are doing today – asset allocation for 25 basis points.

Do not try to compete at this commodity layer with a high cost structure. The consolidation at this layer will be brutal and somebody like Vanguard with existing scale has the advantage.

There is plenty of room for innovation at the higher layers of data science, personalization, and reporting. This is the rebundling opportunity. Some robo advisers will try to avoid the consolidation phase by moving up the value stack into the world of wealth managers, focusing on the rebundling of complementary services. This is a race.

The key to the rebundling opportunity is a new breed of "micro asset managers" that are emerging as the early adopters of marketplaces such as Lending Club and Angel List. They are typically focused on one asset class. For example, micro asset managers are tapping into P2P lending marketplaces (such as Lending Club but also specialist ones for small businesses, auto loans, and education) and applying their knowledge and some algorithms to search for better risk-adjusted returns. In Angel List, these micro asset managers are angel investors who are becoming micro VC funds through syndicates that bring them what we used to call "limited partners".

Lending Club and Angel List are already mature and are disrupting these markets. On Daily FINTECH[3] we also profile ventures at an earlier stage that are doing this across other asset classes such as public equity, public debt, FX, and

private equity. These emerging micro asset managers charge a fraction of the incumbent asset managers because their costs are far lower – they trade and the marketplaces do the rest (back office admin and access to investors). These micro asset managers are low cost and agile because they think about one thing and one thing only – profitable trades.

Wealth managers can win during the rebundling phase by creating simplified, delightful user experiences that enable risk diversification across asset classes, industries, and geographies and that can grab the low hanging fruit (alpha) that these micro asset managers are spotting. Gross revenue will decline during the unbundling phase due to digital competition. During the rebundling phase, net revenue will increase because the marketplace-enabled micro asset managers will charge less than the traditional fund managers and because the alpha from being early in these marketplaces will attract new assets. These network marketplaces also offer total transparency down to individual assets, enabling wealth managers to get one step ahead of regulatory drivers such as the Markets in Financial Instruments Directive (MIFID) II.

Rebundling in Small and Medium Enterprise (SME) Banking

The rebundling opportunity in small and medium business banking sits at the intersection of corporate financial software (accounts payable, accounts receivable, purchase to pay, e-invoicing, treasury management, supply chain management) and finance. As the corporate financial software moves to the Cloud, it creates an inter-company network for exchanging data. In other words, it becomes a marketplace that offers data that can be leveraged to provide financial services. This is already working in supply chain finance, but we are only at the very early stages of this transition, which will affect all forms of business lending.

Banks deserted small business lending because it was not as scalable as consumer lending or corporate lending. The exit of the banks enabled networked

---

[3] "Daily FINTECH" is the company the author has set up and where he provides daily updates on the global FinTech sector: http://dailyfintech.com/.

marketplaces to unbundle lending by offering low cost solutions. During the rebundling phase, banks have the opportunity to create integrated financing services using a mix of term loans, cash flow lending, and asset lending. The CFO of a small business does not have the time or expertise to use all these marketplaces directly. Like the wealthy investors, they need help with complexity. This is the rebundling service opportunity for banks.

The Rebundling Phase Has to be Driven from the Top

Finance has not faced this level of disruption before, so there are no role models during this wave of disruption. However tech companies have faced this level of disruption on regular occasions, so banks can get inspiration from:

- Lou Gerstner's turnaround of IBM after it was nearly wiped out by the PC wave of disruption.
- Steve Jobs' turnaround of Apple after it too was nearly wiped out by the PC wave of disruption.
- Google's early intervention by buying Android and how that saved Google from being disrupted by mobile.
- Facebook's late intervention by buying Instagram and WhatsApp to avoid being disrupted by mobile.

Common threads in all these transformation programmes:

- Customer Focus

  The tech giants did not ask customers "what do you want?" via traditional focus groups. They figured out where the trend was heading (what new technology was coming) and created products that met real needs but which customers were not asking for because customers did not know what was technically possible.

- Culture

  Lou Gerstner summed it up in his classic book (*Who Says Elephants Can't Dance*[4]). Gerstner writes that he knew before he started that a big challenge would be changing the culture. At the end he writes that changing culture was not one of many challenges, it was *the* challenge.

- CEO

  Real transformational innovation cannot be delegated. This has to be driven from the top. All the above examples illustrate this.

In summary, banks need to partner with FinTech start-ups to create an integrated customer experience and should learn the lessons from those tech giants who have transformed their global organizations over the last 20 years threatened by the internet boom and managed to succeed by reinventing themselves.

---

[4] Published in October 2009, https://books.google.co.uk/books/about/Who_Says_Elephants_Can_t_Dance.html?id=WyDMM6bz8SMC&source=kp_cover&hl=en.

The Rise of BankTech – The Beauty of a Hybrid Model for Banks

By Frank Schwab

Co-Founder, FinTech Forum; Former CEO, Fidor TecS AG

and Sophie Guibaud

Vice President European Expansion, Fidor Group

Today customers expect more innovative, faster, and efficient financial services in terms of money and speed. International transfer commissions of up to 8% and several days of waiting for one's own money are not acceptable in a world of real-time communication.

However, traditional banks have failed to provide these services because of overly stringent regulatory requirements and inflexible, slow-to-adapt legacy core banking systems. On one side, repeated financial crises in the last century (several of them caused directly by the banking industry) have led governments to issue more stringent banking regulation. Banks have had to implement these internally, reorganizing all processes around them and thus leaving little time to focus on innovation.

On the other side, legacy core banking systems dating from the 1960s–70s are lacking the necessary agility to allow for the development of innovative services which customers have been longing for and are now coming to expect from any service provider. Banks have been trapped into coping with high operating costs, functional gaps, low agility of their systems, immature IT infrastructures, expensive IT projects due to redundancies, inconsistencies and unintended dependencies across product lines and access channels, as well as a variety of different technologies used.

While some institutions have been looking into rebuilding their core and middleware banking system from scratch, high costs and long lead times have prevented them from doing it so far. It has led banks to provide clients with what they are capable of and not with what customers wanted.

Today, consumers spend more and more time online and have gained the ability to compare and choose the financial services best suited to their needs in a few clicks. They want better, faster, and cheaper services. In this context, a new category of start-ups has emerged aiming to fulfil users' needs in terms of financial services, not only by providing them with a more customer-centric experience but also by adopting new business models more suited to the customers' lifestyle. For example, some international money transfer companies now charge a low flat fee to make a transfer worldwide, no matter how high the amount transferred while others have decided to charge a low variable fee depending on the amount.

A Viacom Media Survey from 2014[1] states that 53% of customers do not think their bank offers anything different from other banks, resulting in low switching rates from one bank to another. So far, consumers have mainly switched bank accounts driven by life changes such as starting university, getting married, or signing up for a mortgage. However, this might change in the near future with the arrival of new financial services and neo-banks with more innovative and differentiated offerings than traditional banks.

While governments are working on making it easier for consumers to switch bank accounts, banks should focus on providing their clients with the customer-centric services they are longing for and will ultimately seek at other banks. But which are the areas banks should focus on? Smooth onboarding, fast and seamless payments, 24/7 banking, mobile banking, sharing economy, alternative investment opportunities, or digital currencies are some options. The higher the perceived pain for the customer, the more successful the offer solving it.

The frictionless integration of financial services into the digital lifestyle of a customer's life is the technical challenge a bank has to face in order to cope with future challenges. It is necessary that banks act and think as FinTech companies and not only as enablers of FinTech by adopting an open cultural approach.

FinTech start-ups have been challenging and reinventing all aspects of the banking sector over the past few years. Is banking under attack? Most banks think so. However, while the banking industry is preparing for the atomization of financial services, we, at Fidor, have been thinking a bit differently. We do not believe that in a world where customer-centric experience is key, clients should have to go from one app to another to use the financial services they need or spend several hours a month to reconcile their money flows from various apps and offerings.

---

[1] http://www.millennialdisruptionindex.com/wp-content/uploads/2014/02/MDI_Final.pdf.

Over the past few years, we have been working on establishing a hybrid banking model, where we focus on what we do best and partner with FinTech companies for the rest with the goal of offering the best financial services to our clients from a single platform, irrespective of who the provider is.

We have also positioned ourselves as a FinTech enabler through an open API[2] architecture, fidorOS, a new banking platform that seamlessly bridges traditional (accounts, deposits, transfers, loans etc.) and new banking services (peer-to-peer, crowdfunding, crypto-currencies etc.). Through this banking platform, we allow FinTech companies to develop their own financial services offering. While fidorOS performs the functions of a core banking system, it is actually built so that it runs on top of an existing legacy core banking system.

This effectively gives any user, be it a bank, a telecom, or a FinTech firm, the ability to launch new financial services quickly without the burden of maintaining and investing into highly expensive legacy systems in multiple countries. This hybrid model allows banks to fulfil two goals. First, it provides a better customer-centric experience to our clients and reaches out to new audiences, acting as an enabler for FinTech companies targeting these audiences. Since it is faster to implement than to change their legacy core banking systems, FinTech could be the opportunity for banks to serve their clients better through white-label solutions or referral agreements.

Imagine a one-stop banking marketplace where clients are able to use the best, fastest, and cheapest banking services, irrespective of the provider. Banks will keep on offering their best services and rely on FinTech for the rest. For example, Fidor's platform offers three different layers of lending:

- The first layer is comprised of a traditional overdraft provided by Fidor on which Fidor generates revenues through interest paid by customers.

- The second layer is comprised of peer-to-peer loans where Fidor leverages its community allowing Fidor customers to borrow and lend money from and to other Fidor customers negotiating interest rates directly with them and paying a commission to Fidor for using the service.

- The third and last layer is the integration of other P2P lending platforms, such as SMAVA, the biggest German P2P lending platform, allowing Fidor customers to borrow larger sums of money from several SMAVA users at the same time. Fidor earns a commission for sending its clients to SMAVA.

The main idea behind this is to create and offer a number of options including proprietary and third-party offers (open architecture banking) instead of constraining a client to make a formal application for one bank product offering with no alternative to it. Fidor has been positioning itself as an aggregator of these financial services – rebundling the "unbundled financial services".

In the meantime, banks could also conquer new customer segments, serving as the backbone to FinTech companies addressing markets underserved by banks (unbanked, kids, start-ups, digital natives etc.).

Let us illustrate this model with the example of the relationships between MVNOs (mobile virtual network operators) and traditional telecom companies. MVNOs are telecom operators using traditional telecommunications companies' infrastructures to operate. They have emerged in the late 1990s for two reasons, depending on countries' market environment. On one side, some governments wanted to increase competition in the telecom industry and forced telecom companies to open their infrastructure to them. In other countries, telecom companies themselves encouraged their arrival as they had spare wholesale minutes they wanted to sell. Telecom companies have lent their infrastructure to MVNOs at close to no additional costs for them. A large number of MVNOs have been focusing on niche market segments with specific needs like expat communities, SMEs, and/or low cost or prepaid model-oriented people.

If we apply this model to banking, banks would lend their core and middleware banking infrastructure and sometimes banking licence to FinTech companies for them to operate while indirectly reaching new audiences they have not been able to serve in the past. A very important point to raise is that while FinTech firms have been reinventing financial services towards a more customer-centric experience, some of the FinTech companies would not have been able to do so without the support of a bank. In particular we can think of money transfer companies and digital front-end banking offerings such as Simple or Moven in the US.

These FinTech companies have been successful in either addressing a particular pain-point experienced by clients around a given financial service or addressing

---

[2] See the chapter entitled "Embracing the Connected API Economy" for further details.

a specific target market or both. In particular, some of them have been targeting audiences that have been historically underserved by banks such as young people, the unbanked, SMEs or digital natives. Banks have been underserving them for a variety of reasons – these audiences were deemed too risky, not strategic, or banks simply did not know how to address them. Lending their infrastructure to FinTech companies is a good way for banks to reach out to these audiences indirectly.

A new era of a symbiotic bank–FinTech relationship is about to emerge, where banks will not only provide FinTech firms with their backbone infrastructure to operate but also rely on them to serve their clients better. According to JP Morgan's CEO, Jamie Dimon: "We are going to work hard to make our services as seamless and competitive as theirs. And we are also completely comfortable with partnering where it makes sense." It seems some banks have already realized the potential of this hybrid model.

FinTech Impact on Retail Banking – From a Universal Banking Model to Banking Verticalization

By Roberto Ferrari

General Manager, CheBanca; Board Member, Mediobanca Innovation Services

The digital disruption tide has arrived to hit the banking and financial services industry. This is not just a major technological change, or an addition of new channels, this is a profound overhaul of the whole retail banking model as the entire market structure will change. Pricing and revenues, customer experience, product and distribution models on which the universal banking model has been conceived in the last century are being challenged as never before. In 2015, the former Barclays' CEO Antony Jenkins claimed that the "universal bank model is dead" and JPMorgan Chase's CEO Jamie Dimon warned the financial community that "Silicon Valley is coming"… so what is happening?

The point is that traditional banks have not yet been capable of facing two major disruptive external forces simultaneously:

1. Change in regulation

2. Change in consumer habits (and technology).

Those two factors are intimately correlated, working together to make the picture even worse.

Firstly, since the financial crisis regulation on banking has become tougher. New capital and liquidity requirements have been imposed. Banking assets have been heavily scrutinized through stress tests. Many large banks have been fined for uncompetitive and unfair behaviour. This has had two major impacts:

- Banks have been focusing on heavy regulatory issues rather than on facing new market challenges.

- Cost of compliance and regulation has flown high – Accenture's FinTech Innovation Lab has estimated that most large banks have been spending 70 cents on the dollar on compliance and regulation.

Secondly, in the meantime, the exponential growth of the digital economy has changed consumer habits and technological platforms. The proliferation of digital channels is not only raising customer expectations, "spoiled" by Amazon, Apple, PayPal, and Google user experience standards, but has significantly changed the way customers see and use banking channels and products. This has further raised IT costs on one hand and is making the traditional core distribution channel – branches – oversized by a factor of 2:1.

The same regulatory and digital factors together are playing a significant role in squeezing retail banking revenues, on the basis of greater accessibility and transparency demand. As a net result there has been a significant structural increase in operating costs and a squeeze in profits. For instance the average administrative cost per employee of large European banks has risen by 68% in the ten years from 2003 to 2013, despite attempted cost reduction plans. Over 250,000 people have been laid off by the sector in Europe over the last seven years but it might not be enough.

The retail banking industry is still struggling to change its operating models and distribution footprint. Digital channels are built on top of inflexible, legacy IT frameworks resulting in increasing costs and complexity, and this ultimately creates additional legacy. Banks rely on old-fashioned IT systems and architecture with very complex product offerings. As a result it is estimated that IT represents 14% of banking costs, estimated at $461 billion in 2014, but at the same time 75% of this is just for maintenance.

Moreover, banks tend to keep a branch-focused approach, rather than moving full speed to a new digital omni-channel architecture. The top 25 global banks are spending on their branch network more than the top 25 global tech companies on R&D by a ratio of 2:1. Thus although banks have enough money to change their business model they do not go down this route. Scared of cannibalizing their own proprietary channels, of the complexity of their service and product portfolios, and significant organizational and IT challenges, they prefer to innovate in small steps instead of giant leaps.

However, the truth is that the full service model is no longer a viable answer to market demands – more radical thinking and planning are needed. In order to cross the widening chasm in front of banks, small steps will not be sufficient.

FinTech: The Rise of New Generation Banking?

New digital competition has developed, under the label of "FinTech". Digital competition and non-traditional new competitors are trying to exploit all this, starting to take away business opportunities from incumbent banks, targeting specific business lines, unbundling them, bypassing traditional players, and creating new marketplaces. It has been estimated that in 2014 the new FinTech sector has received investments of $12 billion (+300% vs. 2013).[1] In the US alone, FinTech investment jumped to $9.9 billion in 2014 and in 2015 it is continuing to grow. AngelList has listed 3,800 FinTech start-ups alone, trying to get business from traditional financial service players. While incumbent universal banks seem to retrench from global expansion plans (see recent announcements by HSBC, Barclays, and Deutsche Bank) digital newcomers can successfully challenge the status quo creating new streamlined business models focused on specific areas of banking. They can unbundle and break up the retail banking sector into different service and product segments.

For example, in Europe you do not need a bank to manage your transactions. You can open up a payment/e-money account with a prepaid/debit card with a Payment Institution[2] or with an Electronic Money Institute.[3] In the US players like Simple or Moven offer mobile banking accounts without the need to have a banking charter. Moreover, "Shadow Banking" (defined as the financial intermediaries involved in facilitating the creation of credit across the global financial system, but whose members are not subject to regulatory oversight – the shadow banking system also refers to unregulated activities by regulated institutions) is growing, and is estimated to be worth $71tn. Pension funds and asset management companies are

replacing traditional banks in corporate capital market financing. New, even hybrid, versions of funding and lending alternatives are blossoming almost everywhere. Universal banks, with stringent capital and RWA (risk weighted assets) regulatory requirements and high NPL (non-performing loan) stocks, are losing ground to new players in providing financing and capital.

The unbundling of the full service universal banking model is already happening. All retail banking components are at risk here. From payments and transactions to investing and trading, from lending to risk assessment, from small business banking services to funding and capital gathering. McKinsey estimated that a stunning 52% of retail banking revenues are at risk, being attacked by FinTech start-ups. The segments most at risk as identified by McKinsey are the macro-vertical sectors such as payment transactions (Transactional), Investing, and Financing.

Each of the verticals is a large cluster containing several sub-segments and in every single vertical segment there are FinTech challengers well positioned to take business from traditional, incumbent retail banks. Each segment has got its own challengers, from Lending Club to Kickstarter, from Wealthfront to Dwolla, from TransferWise to Kabbage. The Lending Club IPO made history at the end of 2014 representing the first of a new wave of FinTech "unicorns" ready to materialize.

In order to enter the market, these B2C vertical players successfully roll out new added value services. To do so, they may themselves collaborate with new FinTech B2B solution providers that can help provide a new digital fronting user experience (UX) and middleware/back end stack (i.e. providers of cross-platforms), that can be used by different B2C FinTech players. As a result, the whole retail banking value chain is being digitalized by new entrants. This is meant by the above Verticalization scheme.

Vertical Segment #1: Transactional Services

This cluster includes a large range of payment services and according to McKinsey can account for up to 15% of global retail banking revenues which are being attacked by FinTech firms. New players include banking/transactional service providers such as Moven to send-money and cross-border remittance services

---

[1] Source: Accenture Study March 2015.

[2] http://www.fca.org.uk/firms/firm-types/payment-services-institutions/.

[3] http://www.fca.org.uk/firms/firm-types/emoney-institutions.

such as TransferWise, POS payment firms like i-Zettle to e-commerce digital payment platforms like Stripe, to name only a few. TransferWise, Square, Stripe, and i-Zettle all belong to the so-called "unicorns" with a valuation of at least $1 billion in May 2015 according to Finovate.

Transactional services have been one of the first segments to be unbundled. Looking at credit card schemes or at PayPal (probably the first FinTech company) one realizes that banks have already lost ground. New players are growing, for example Venmo, a payment app, transferred $1.3 billion in the 1st quarter of 2015. However, this is still small if compared to PayPal's $230 billion transactions value during 2014.

Another component of the transactional business vertical is digital currencies such as bitcoin. It is clear that real-time cross-border payments are a key need brought about by the digitization of commerce and consumer habits that banks have not been able to satisfy well. The leading tech giants have focused on this segment to provide financial services without becoming a bank. Facebook has launched its own platform of P2P payments. We will witness in the next few years a process of "Whatsappization" of sending money and remittances frictionlessly, as simply as sending a text. In Europe the introduction of the Payment Services Directive 2 (PSD2) legislation and third-party payment providers will further open the market, letting non-banking players have access to customers' bank accounts. Sofort, a German company acquired by Klarna, is already developing new services in this sector.

A stack of new value-added services is provided in combination with payments: account aggregators, portfolio management services (PMS) and budgeting software, and digital currencies exchange platforms, to name but a few. They can be targeted to improve the UX or to facilitate exchanges and will be further enhanced as the market opens up.

Vertical Segment #2: Investing

Robo-advisory (digital investment) platforms are becoming more visible. Wealthfront and Betterment are the most famous in the US, with about $4 billion of assets under management, and Nutmeg in the UK. In this cluster there are many players. None of them has reached the level of a "unicorn" but there are some already close to

the $1 billion threshold led by Wealthfront and Betterment. This is a segment that is expected to explode as it has been estimated by AT Kearney that robo advisers will run $2 trillion assets under management by 2020,[4] boosted also by initiatives of large traditional players such as Charles Schwab with its launch of the "Intelligent Portfolios" platform, the launch of Vanguard's online advice, Fidelity's acquisition of E-Money and so on. Moreover, incumbents' online trading platforms are being challenged by new digital players such as the online brokerage Robinhood in the US and eToro in Europe, among many others. New ways of cost-cutting/best performance and socially and community empowered trading solutions are emerging and will challenge big incumbents.

The overall objective here is accessibility of investment guidance to a broader audience. Getting an independent financial advisor is not easy (you need to have a minimum capital to invest) and it is costly, often represented by an annual 1% management fee based on your total assets. Online trading can be costly as well and has been built for heavy traders who often would be considered expert investors/traders. The new digital platforms promise democratization, significantly lowering asset management and trading costs and helping customers with easy-to-use solutions and social behavioural-based software tools.

The business at stake here is potentially huge. The evolution of social welfare policies and its impact on pensions and retirement will further boost market potential, opening up additional possibilities, as is happening in the UK with the recent pension scheme reform. There are two main questions:

- Will this vertical be able to expand internationally, as asset management and investment advisory legislation may differ geographically?
- Will digital-only platforms be replaced or challenged themselves by hybrid digital and human interfaces (such as Personal Capital in the US)?

This is a vertical where incumbent players seem to react faster, at least in the US, to the threat from FinTech start-ups and the whole market, especially consumers, could benefit tremendously from such a competitive battle. Also this vertical is triggering the growth of additional value-added software tools, from personal

---

[4] http://www.bloomberg.com/news/articles/2015-06-18/robo-advisers-to-run-2-trillion-by-2020-if-this-model-is-right.

financial planning to tax optimization, from e-learning/gaming to big data analytics. Here as well the whole stack is being revolutionized by additional frictionless user experience-led interfaces and customer-driven analytics and engines.

Vertical Segment #3: Financing

The third macro-cluster is about financing and capital raising. Traditional incumbent banks are struggling to provide the needed capital and financing options to small businesses and consumers. Changed capital demands, risk measurement frameworks, and new regulatory requirements are making this much more difficult.

On the other side FinTech start-ups are successfully making their inroads, with the rise of crowdfunding, alternative finance, and marketplace-P2P lending platforms. This is the only segment where two start-ups have already gone public, with Lending Club and OnDeck in the US, and it already accounts for 10 "unicorns". Alternative finance solutions are fast growing – in the US Lending Club's new loans in 2014 reached $3 billion with a +265% growth rate vs. 2013. An E&Y and University of Cambridge report confirmed that this was about the same growth rate alternative finance players experienced in Europe between 2012 and 2014.

Although the original business model of a peer-to-peer (P2P) lending platform has been focused on the disintermediation of banks in order to offer higher returns to investors while offering more attractive interest rates to borrowers, financial institutions have reentered the P2P market. For instance, about 80% of Lending Club's funding no longer comes from peers/consumers but from institutional investors and even venture capital in search for higher yield. So it looks more like an alternative lending to institutions than a person-to-person/peer-to-peer (P2P) business. At the same time crowdfunding platforms like Kickstarter and Indigogo are providing alternative capital to small businesses financed by individual investors. Moreover, we can see the rise of additional B2B hybrid platforms like restricted business angel syndicates such as OurCrowd or AngelList. This is likely to be the vertical with the highest form of disintermediation of traditional banking. We are also starting to see what is likely to be "FinTech 2.0", i.e. the second phase of FinTech where banks and challenger start-ups work together to build a combined offer.

This trend has started already, often referred to as co-option, a necessary combination of competition and collaboration for the benefit of both partners. In the UK, for instance, Santander and RBS have signed a commercial alliance with Funding Circle, a P2P lending platform. Their small business clients in search of financing will be offered access to Funding Circle's investor platform. Another example is the London-based InvestUp crowdfunding FinTech start-up, which is currently running pilots with two of the top six banks in the UK.

Vertical Segment #4: Cross-software Platforms

The last horizontal stack of the proposed Verticalization scheme is composed of cross-software platforms that will be needed across segments. Know Your Customer (KYC) and identity management will be key in the future of banking to make sure that the frictionless design of on-boarding and user experience is backed by solid antifraud and ID authentication systems. API[5] middleware platforms will be key to efficiently open up, develop, and enrich online services. New core banking systems, often cloud-based, are being developed and these could open up new competitive scenarios such as FinTech firms applying for a banking licence or banks digitalizing their core business. Cross-border trade finance, payments tools, and networks need to be developed to enable the digitization of financial services. Big data and new analytics capabilities are needed to extract value and personalize the customer segmentation and service in all unbundled segments. This is creating an extraordinary development of new software capabilities across the board that will impact the whole financial sector.

Will FinTech Succeed? How Should Banks Respond?

Banks need to react. Some will respond appropriately – many established financial services players are already investing heavily into the FinTech sector – some will not and it will be too late. Will FinTech start-ups replace banks? Will all service offerings

---

[5] See the chapter entitled "Embracing the Connected API Economy" for further details.

be focused on verticals only, removing the need for universal banks? Nope – at least not in the next 15–20 years.

There is a reason why there is not yet a Facebook of banking or a fully global retail bank. Capital requirements are very tough and regulation is complex. This is not an excuse not to digitalize the business. Banks must become "FinTech banks" in 5–10 years if they want to survive, but turning a global financial business into a digital player is not easy. There will be a high level of M&A activity among traditional banks and a very strong natural selection among the FinTech start-ups as well, as in every post-Schumpeterian creative destruction phase. And there will be a lot of disintermediation, collaboration, and co-option among banks, between banks and FinTech firms, and among FinTech businesses as well. As a result, there will be different business models co-existing in the marketplace. Banks should move from just incubating or financing start-ups to acquiring some of them, letting them lead and digitally transform the vertical segment they are focused on for the whole bank. Bear in mind that banks are in essence IT companies, handling money and data. Will they remember this?

At the same time banks have to choose what to give up in order to simplify operations and their product range. There is no other way – either you change and streamline or you die long term. Going down this path banks could simply outsource some of their product factories, optimizing their value chain and

focusing more on integrated KYC checks, omni-channel delivery, and real personalized customer relationships and service offerings. As is happening in the P2P lending arena, banks can create their own marketplaces, collaborating with FinTech firms; they can connect investors with borrowers, connecting supply with demand. FinTech firms, on the other hand, will have to decide if they want to collaborate with banks or go it alone. They could focus on both a direct B2C but also an indirect B2B2C market entry strategy by offering a white-labelled solution of their service to the bank and its customer base. This has to be carefully managed in order not to distract the FinTech firm from its own consumers and its direct route to market strategy if desired. On the other hand if the FinTech firms want to reach real scale and experience, they might need some key partnerships with established players. Banks own clients. FinTech firms own new technology and the right mindset. Will they work together for a win-win outcome? Why not?

If they do so, we could see faster international expansions in the sector, with smarter FinTech companies cherry-picking their local banking partners. Banks and big tech giants may decide to expand internationally not via a universal bank model but by selecting the most efficient and streamlined vertical services. In summary, there is enough space for a large variety of business models and players. One thing is certain: financial services will change forever and for the better.

Embracing the Connected API Economy

By Richard Peers

Director, Financial Services Industry, Microsoft

and Shashi Rana

Enterprise and Strategy Architect, Microsoft

Previous chapters articulated the importance of connecting established financial services players and FinTech firms via Application Programming Interfaces, known as APIs. This chapter will provide details to fully understand the API economy. The connected economy is changing the way businesses innovate. Find out what it means for you and how to join the revolution.

The API Economy: Helping Financial Services Companies to Build Better Products

Markets and industries are changing faster than ever. Disruption takes many forms and businesses must grapple with the "innovator's dilemma": how to set the pace of change without stumbling over the legacy of the past. They need to embrace new technologies wisely to innovate fast at low cost and low risk. Application Program Interfaces (APIs) offer a powerful way to do this.

The Business Value of APIs

An increasing number of companies are using APIs externally to change how they interact with customers and their supply chain. Internally they are using APIs to change how the IT department works with the rest of the business. The key point is that an API platform can change the way IT delivers and the business innovates. But it does not require wholesale changes or five-year transformation programmes. Instead, take the first few easy steps on the journey using the API approach and continue in an agile, iterative way.

The API economy is based around four building blocks: social, mobile, analytics, and cloud. Apps and services can be linked rapidly and cost-effectively to create an extended value proposition. For example, buyers and sellers could be connected via an exchange, where all parts of the value chain come from separate parties and are linked via APIs to facilitate an end-to-end transaction.

The Rise and Rise of APIs

There are already more than 11,000 public APIs and perhaps ten times as many private ones.[1] They make it possible for developers to share services and data easily and to build applications that link to other people's services and data. This is creating new business models and new sources of value for companies. The Internet of Things (IoT), social media, changes in IT delivery, and the desire for multi-channel customer experiences will drive further growth in the API economy.

Everything is Connected to Everything Else

In order to participate in the new digital world, think about your business as one of many neurons that interact with each other in a wider value chain. You cannot expect to own the entirety of a consumer's experience or to participate in all their digital interactions. So the API approach lets you focus on what you do best and connect with others to do the rest.

Getting Started

In the past, if companies spotted a niche or an inefficiency in the market they would need to build all of the technology to create a new product offering. However, using APIs enables them to take their pre-existing intellectual property

---

[1] http://www.slideshare.net/3scale/progress-in-the-api-economy-april-2014.

and link it to new services, saving time and money and allowing business to create new or extend existing value propositions. Although APIs have been available for many years, it is only the modern APIs that have been designed for today's "plug and play" world.

Simply put, at a very basic level, by simply enabling business to do more rapid prototyping, with low cost and overhead, is a benefit in itself. Traditionally on-boarding developers, creative agencies, or even working with existing partners to do experiments was a long, costly affair leaving businesses frustrated with the lack of agility. Making small changes to the way you partner, design, execute, and orchestrate has big impacts on cost savings and agility. Embracing the API economy is not all about exposing your APIs externally. There are benefits for using the model internally and also clearly applying it with partners. Being ready for when the business model is right and mature enough for your business is part of the winning strategy.

An API platform helps you connect your business processes, services, content, and data to partners, internal teams, and independent developers in an easy and secure way.

In brief, we recommend:

- Introducing the API model in small steps;

- Rapid, agile prototyping, development, and testing using APIs;

- Exploring new approaches to development;

- Renting and using an off-the-shelf API management platform.

This approach maximizes flexibility and innovation while reducing risk and minimizing costs.

Understanding APIs

API stands for application programming interface. It is a way for developers to access services and resources from other pieces of software that they did not write. For example, it is common for web applications to have APIs that let other

applications integrate with them. But it is more than mere middleware or just a service gateway.

A company releases its API specifications to the public or chosen third parties so that other developers can design products that work with it. It connects devices, processes, services, and software in a digital ecosystem (see the following Figure).

Figure: APIs everywhere

The Business Value of APIs for the Financial Services Industry

Open or public APIs are the tip of the iceberg; there are many more private APIs than public ones. Fuelled by mobile, cloud, social, big data, and the IoT, the number has grown enormously over the last decade.

APIs offer new ways to differentiate yourself and build a competitive advantage by, for example:

- Integrating content from partners to create opportunities to cross-sell and upsell;

- Creating new lines of business;

- Extending product offerings by using corporate data in new ways;

- Strengthening the brand by providing a consistent, personalized experience across multiple customer touch points;

- Enabling reusability, so new partner integrations are faster;

- Delivering services internally in a more efficient way.

API Business Models

APIs can also make money directly or indirectly. There are various business models to choose from:

- Free. Companies can open up their API to generate new revenue or share information widely. For example, Transport for London's journey planner API or Amazon's Product Advertising API which lets people advertise Amazon products on their own site.

- The API is the product. Companies like Twilio and Stripe sell their services to other app developers exclusively, via an API: internet telephony and instant messaging as a service in the case of Twilio and internet payments for Stripe.

- Developer pays. Some companies sell access to their information via an API, either on a pay-as-you-go model, with transaction fees, or with a monthly or annual fee.

- Developer gets paid. Some companies share revenue with developers. For example, The Guardian shares advertising revenue with developers and Walgreens' QuickPrints API pays a percentage of revenue to app developers who use the company's photo printing service via the API.

- Content acquisition. The content acquisition model gathers valuable data for business use such as feedback, opinion, or content. For example, the Flickr API lets people upload images to the site.

- Content syndication. This makes content available to be published by third parties such as the TripAdvisor API which lets travel websites share user reviews.

Drivers of the API Economy

Over the past 15 years, APIs have flourished everywhere but we do not think that is the end of the story. In fact, we are still in the early days of the API economy. Four things are going to drive its future growth: the IoT, social media, the need to deliver amazing, consistent experiences across multiple customer touch points, and the ambition of progressive IT departments to contribute more directly to the business growth.

- Gartner projects that the total economic value-add from the IoT will be $1.9 trillion by 2020 across many – almost all – industries. Endpoints of the IoT will grow at a 35.2% CAGR from 2013 through 2020, reaching an installed base of 25.0 billion units. In 2020, 8.3 billion "things" will ship, with more than half of them consumer applications. The IoT will support total services spending of about $263 billion in 2020.

- It is a huge opportunity (see the following Figure) and APIs are critical for getting the most out of internet-connected devices and tapping this market opportunity.

- Social media. "Over the next eight years we may recognize that social media is not just another piece of technology that changes the world," but, according to Social3, "a new era very similar to the industrial revolution. While the industrial revolution changed the way we produce (the first half of a business), the social revolution is changing the way we sell, market, service and deliver our solutions

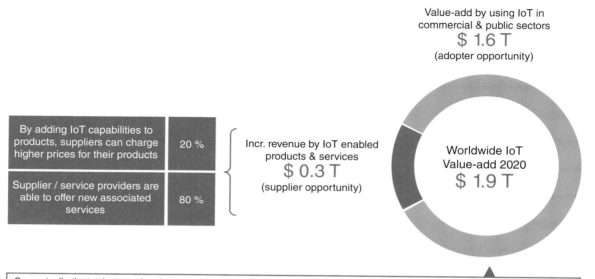

Value-add by using IoT in commercial & public sectors
$ 1.6 T
(adopter opportunity)

By adding IoT capabilities to products, suppliers can charge higher prices for their products — 20 %

Supplier / service providers are able to offer new associated services — 80 %

Incr. revenue by IoT enabled products & services
$ 0.3 T
(supplier opportunity)

Worldwide IoT Value-add 2020
$ 1.9 T

Conceptually, the total economic value-add across all sectors is a measure of GDP, so the values in this diagram represent incremental global GDP. Value-add can be derived within an industry sector by either increasing sales, or decreasing input costs, or both. **The value-add represents the aggregate benefits that businesses derive through the sale and usage of IoT technology.**

Figure: The graph was created from Gartner's research as quoted above

(the second half of a business)." As this trend continues to grow, companies will use APIs to engage with social media, understand the opportunities, and explore ways to make money from it without damaging their brands.

- Multi-channel customer experiences. Businesses are constantly seeking new ways to engage with customers. For example, retailers already embrace multi- or omni-channel strategies that integrate web, physical stores, and mobile. But with proliferating channels – including internet, mobile, kiosk, stores, branches, digital walls, in-car, games, TV, and more – companies need the agility to exploit new channels quickly and cost-effectively. Imagine being able to deliver a consistent customer and brand experience on a new channel in less than a month.

- The proactive IT department. Consider an IT department that stays in the back room, only doing desktop and server stuff, constantly saying "no" and focusing purely on "keeping the lights on". On the other hand, imagine an IT department

that proactively gives business decision-makers new ways to attract, retain, and engage customers or improve business efficiency and agility or reach new customers, markets, and supply chain partners. Which department would you rather lead? If you were CEO, which one would you rather have in your business? APIs are an important tool for transforming IT departments.

How to Join the API Economy: Start Small, Start Now

Companies should embrace APIs in stages over time. If the process is well-orchestrated, every step will create value, thus making the process self-sustaining, manageable, and cost-effective. You do not need a fully-developed strategy for social, apps, or channels. Nor do you need a completely new business model. Take an iterative approach to innovation by experimenting and learning with small, incremental projects. For example:

- Get creative apps and web front-ends built quickly and cheaply.

- Rent and use the platform without fully integrating it.

- Start by exposing a handful of functions for developers to use.

- Leave stubs for future development.

- Try "rent-before-buy-before-build" and "configure-before-customize" approaches.

- Do not invest heavily in infrastructure and in-house resources for this prototyping and rapid development stage.

Do not start with a pre-conceived set of rules or limit your creativity worrying about security, risk, or other constraints. Instead brainstorm all the possibilities and then pick a few low-risk, quick-win possibilities to start with.

Existing Middleware is not the Answer

Most middleware systems do not have the necessary functions to deliver a true API. For example, they often lack a process to on-board developers, an app store, key management, and monitoring tools to report on consumer behaviour and usage.

Dedicated API platforms are designed to get developers up and running quickly, making it easy to:

- Expose data services through well-crafted APIs which are robust and easy to scale;

- Register and on-board developers;

- Submit, review, and approve apps;

- Provide accessibility while protecting the business from threats, back-end overload, and service issues;

- Monitor how people are using the APIs with detailed reporting;

- Get insight into customer behaviours;

- Add features such as news feeds, geo-location, search engine integration;

- Investigate errors and performance problems to improve responsiveness.

The big question is whether you want to rent, build, buy, configure, or customize. The platform which allows you to rent and configure is by far the cheapest and our recommended approach to leverage the API economy in financial services.

Banking Like Water

By Frank Sonder
CEO & Co-Founder, foresee

Let us move from the technical aspects of application interfaces (APIs)[1] to the customer. Customers are at the centre of the FinTech revolution, so what do they expect from financial services in the future? In his famous *New York Times* interview[2] David Bowie described the future of the music industry as "music like water". Thirteen years later we listen to songs on Spotify or Apple Music and gain mobile access to an almost infinite music library. As a result, we are witnessing diminishing intellectual property, the extinction of copyrights on a large scale, and an almost entirely new business model for the music industry. Similar scenarios apply to movies, transportation, and overall to the way we consume media.

Banking is next. Digitalization and intelligent algorithms put the financial services industry under extensive pressure. Their products and services are not even original or unique and today are largely the same wherever you bank. Financial services will transform in the same way as music towards becoming completely digital and ubiquitous. In addition, clients are losing trust, new competition is arising, and the regulatory pressure is stronger than ever before. A business model that was supposed to be safe is continuously eroding. What if banking becomes a simple infrastructure component too? What about new currencies that are not backed by governments and political unions but by communities? Might it be bitcoin or paying with mobile phone minutes as in Kenya?

Nowadays almost all business models, products, and banking services are challenged by FinTech start-ups or peer-to-peer networks. We increasingly pay via mobile and digital, finance our ventures via crowdfunding, and increasingly invest based on algorithms and cognitive computing.

It is time to rethink banking radically – if we need it at all.

---

[1] See the chapter entitled "Embracing the Connected Economy" for further detail about APIs.

[2] http://www.nytimes.com/2002/06/09/arts/david-bowie-21st-century-entrepreneur.html.

The futurist Gerd Leonhard suggests asking a very generic question: "Is my business dispensable?" For the banking business the answer is as simple as the question: Hell, yeah! If we have a look at the general business functions in banks, this becomes even more evident. There is a lending business, a deposit business, an investment business, and services such as money transfer, providing cash, and a banking infrastructure in general. And today each of these business activities is threatened fundamentally by FinTech start-ups, tech corporations, or peer-to-peer networks.

The single most important reason for this is the digitalization of our entire society that increasingly removes intermediaries from business transactions.

The Middleman Problem

Peer-to-peer network solutions have already made many business models for intermediaries across multiple industries obsolete, connecting buyer and seller directly and cutting out the middleman. Airbnb is connecting hosts with guests, myTaxi and Uber find drivers for passengers, "prosumers" (a person who consumes and produces content, derived from "prosumption", a dot-com era business term meaning "production by consumers") and customers meet on many different online platforms. Banking is a classic intermediary intending to reduce market uncertainty and information asymmetry in an imperfect market. But what if digitalization provides the foundation for a nearly perfect market in which buyers and sellers can conduct frictionless transactions – a market that does not need intermediaries like banks?

The End of Money

It is money that most clearly symbolizes our personal relationship with banks. One of our first lessons in economics is that there was a barter economy before the invention of currencies. Until then trading goods and services for goods or services was limited to a small community and direct relationships. As trade increased money filled the emerging gap and made it possible to exchange services for money and money for services. But the power of money exceeded that simple mechanism and became what empowered capitalism and particularly the finance capitalism of today. Money became the language of global "turbo-capitalism" and developed far beyond a market economy, linked to products and services – it can be just about investment.

But there might soon be a world without money as we know it. As money is such an integral part of our everyday life, that might be hard to imagine. We have to face it: we are already in that phase. There are more unredeemed air miles around than US dollars,[3] making it the biggest currency worldwide. Approximately 30% of the Starbucks revenue in coffee shops is made up of Starbucks Stars, their internal reward system. In Africa, Vodafone supported the development of an infrastructure where people pay with airtime, be it at the hairdresser or the newsstand. Using your Nike running gear in Mexico lets you earn credit points and use them to buy additional equipment. All this is a currency by definition but without calling it money. And so far we have not even mentioned digital crypto-currencies like bitcoin, a decentralized system not backed by governments or the financial industry but by a technological system.

The End of Capitalism?

We should stay within the economic context for now and have a closer look at what fundamentally underlies our economic system. Jeremy Rifkin[4] predicts that capitalism will be replaced or at least widely accompanied by a sharing economy by 2050. This new system might look more like Neolithic society rather than a new form of the capitalism that has only existed over the last 150 years or so. In the future, this time span might even be considered a relatively short episode compared to the existence of the human race.

Robots Take Over

Let us go ahead and tear down a few more banking business areas. Crowd lending and micro credits have been with us for quite some time, and this questions the lending business of every bank. Crowdfunding seems to be the peer-to-

peer approach to modern investment business. Taking artificial intelligence (AI) into account we might already have found the successor to today's portfolio management and investment banking: IBM Watson, the Jeopardy-winning supercomputer (which might be a misleading name after all) is already able to process a range of tasks formerly accomplished by humans. Intelligent algorithms are already able to predict the strategic intent of corporations based on every single piece of information they can find and understand. While a portfolio manager might be able to follow a certain number of companies closely to propose future investments, a cognitive computer system can far exceed that in terms of number and pace. Trust and credibility, clearly human domains, could be the last remaining advantages for a human advisor over a cognitive computer. Trust in financial institutions, however, was fundamentally damaged during the recent financial crisis.

No Apple Bank Around

A survey shows that digital strategy became the number one topic for banks in 2015, climbing three places from 2014. Although this seems to be an obvious priority, it is hard to imagine that the impact of digitalization has only been recognized now with such enormous and fundamental challenges ahead. There is serious competition from large tech corporations. For them, financial services are just another brick in the wall they build around their far-reaching ecosystem. However, it is not recommended to wait for the first appearance of a Google or an Apple Bank considering the vast amount of payment transactions and credit cards on file. They are already banks and there is no need for them to enter the banking business officially. It is much smarter to keep out of it due to the extensive regulations they would face.

The Digital Natives Challenge

The so-called digital natives are another challenge. Surely banks are addressing this upcoming target audience and acknowledge the fact that they have to take their needs and lifestyle into account. However nobody is embracing the full impact of this change. Digital natives need to become the core of every future banking business model. Instead, institutions raise the question of how to get customers back into the branch. While branches are still considered their most valuable asset, the question is completely off topic for digital natives. Most of them have never had

---

[3] http://www.theguardian.com/money/2005/jan/08/business.theairlineindustry.

[4] Rifkin is the bestselling author of 20 books on the impact of scientific and technological changes on the economy, the workforce, society, and the environment.

a relationship with a bank or an experience related to retail banking. Another wrong question is the one about customers' expectations, not only, but especially, those of digital natives. Instead, banks should face the fact that their potential clients have no expectations at all, just as they do not expect a lot more than a regular and silent service from their water or power supplier.

Banking as a Service

For European banks, a silent revolution is scheduled for 2016 – silent but incredibly powerful. European legislation has already forced the public railway and telecommunication monopolies to open up their infrastructure to competition. Following the inconspicuously named Payment Services Directive[5] banks need to offer an API (application programming interface) for third parties to show revenue and account balances but most of all to initiate a money transfer. The term usually used for this is "banking as a service".

Confronted with these and other challenges and with a realistic analysis of the status quo we ask the final question: is there a chance at all for established financial players to defend themselves successfully against an eroding business model and the extremely powerful competition? It might sound cynical that the only reason to believe in the success of traditional financial institutions is the pure fact of their existence. In quantity, not quality.

To end on a positive note let us consider two prospective outlooks for banks of the future:

- Capital exchange

  The first relates to social capital. Philosopher Pierre Bourdieu defined three different forms of capital a person might acquire and trade: economic, cultural, and social capital. Today the core of our individual activities is focused on obtaining economic capital and successfully marketing education as our cultural capital. Economic capital is essential to acquire and, in particular, to trade. Social capital has been very limited so far but with the rise of social networks that changes rapidly. As technology evolves, every individual becomes better able to exchange the different forms of capital. Would that not be an exciting new business field for future banking?

  In that context, David Birch makes an interesting point in his book *Identity is the New Money*.[6] Money, he states, is only a simple form of memory. He refers to the stone currency of an island in the Pacific Ocean. As the stones were too heavy to move, it was enough just to remember which stone belonged to whom. He states that today there are more elaborate forms of memory which might make money obsolete.

- Security as unique selling point

  Another interesting business area for banks might be security. If there is one experience even digital natives have with a bank, then this is it. Everybody knows the lockbox with top secret documents in it. Or the heavy steel doors of the bank safe that gets robbed in almost every James Bond movie. If data is the currency of the 21st century why is my bank not taking care of that? Why are banks not helping consumers to monetize their own data and capital instead of Facebook, Google, and Co.? When banks pilot their new future branches, they entirely forget that there might also be a security experience valued by their customers.

What is Wrong with Water?

Finally, providing infrastructural services is not the worst option of all. If banking like water is a reality, we need somebody to deliver this service securely in time and place. And if future currencies become as sophisticated and promising as it seems today, we are even more in need of a competent supplier for these trendsetting identity services.

---

[5] http://eur-lex.europa.eu/legal-content/EN/TXT/PDF/?uri=CELEX:32007L0064&from=EN.

[6] David Birch, *Identity is the New Money* (London Publishing Partnership, 2014).

Eliminating Friction in Customers' Financial Lives

By Travers Clarke-Walker

Chief Marketing Officer, Fiserv

Stanley Kubrick's *2001: A Space Odyssey*, released in 1968, famously and accurately predicted a future with gadgets like video phones and tablet computers. A less discussed prediction in the film was the emergence of a universal currency of "credits" – gone were dollars, yen, and pounds.

Then there is Douglas Adams' *Hitchhikers Guide to the Galaxy* published in 1979, which heralded the Babel Fish – affording its user the ability to understand all languages.

There is often unnecessary complication for the casual user in multiple versions of the same thing, be it currency or language. Once those complications are solved – as they were in these science fiction examples – the particular innovation becomes a seamless and expected part of life. Anything less would be viewed as a nuisance at best.

With almost unlimited processing power and data storage in the hands of over half the world's population, unnecessary, restrictive, and cumbersome differences can be overcome. That is why the rise of the "best single version" of a product or service is now happening: Facebook for personal connections, LinkedIn for business connections, Spotify for music, aggregator services to demystify choice, and so on. The rise of single proposition offerings around peer-to-peer (P2P) lending and investment, international remittances, and payments is precisely because it can be done better once and well than it can be done by thousands of institutions that are part of a seemingly ancient matrix of companies and offerings.

What these successful new companies have figured out, and what mainstream financial institutions continue to wrestle with, is that the balance of power has shifted from the company to the customer. This is more than a placating mantra that proclaims "the customer is always right". The best FinTech disrupters understand the information customers have access to and the ways customers influence each other. In a world where customers (and employees) publicly discuss their experiences, companies can no longer inflate claims about the quality of their offering. At least not in a way that anyone trusts.

This contributes to a growing sense that the new vanguard of single proposition financial services offerings will replace traditional banking. In fact, one study found that nearly half of millennials in the United States expect tech start-ups to disrupt traditional banking operations and nearly three-quarters would be more excited about financial services offerings from big tech companies (Google, Amazon, and so forth) than they would from their bank.[1]

This tells us that customers' expectations are changing. They expect simplicity, ease, and seamlessness. They expect transparency and reliability. Some company, somewhere, will deliver it. Some company, somewhere, will deliver financial services when and where the customer demands it.

This is not a signal that all hope is lost for the banks. Financial institutions have delivered innovations that drastically improve the customer experience and address major pain-points. Mobile banking has addressed a serious point of friction that online banking created – the need to be at your computer to log on. This point could easily be belaboured with statistics, but it is easier to observe what the Royal Bank of Scotland already has: that their "busiest branch" is the 7:01 train from Reading to Paddington. This is the norm.

Mobile banking is a step in the right direction. Its rate of adoption and the value of transactions being moved are projected to double in the UK by 2020.[2] Globally, mobile banking is transforming low-income people's access to financial services (though in many cases mobile operators have been the disrupters). Mobile banking demonstrates what is possible when financial institutions deliver products and services that place the customer's experience at the centre.

Catching Up to the Future

There is exactly one constant when it comes to technological innovation: if you do not do it, someone else will. Those looking to be at the forefront will need to rethink traditional models and approach innovation like a start-up.

---

[1] http://www.millennialdisruptionindex.com/.

[2] http://newsroom.fiserv.com/releasedetail.cfm?ReleaseID=907511.

Change the Prism: Solve the Friction First

The quantity of possible innovations and their seemingly constant rate of change make it difficult to know where to go next. Traditionally, financial institutions have started from a place of cost savings and risk mitigation, both areas of friction for the bank, but not necessarily for the customer. The solution with the best cost-benefit ratio is the solution that is taken on. Realizing those benefits, however, depends entirely on the rate of customer adoption.

And that is the thing of it. Customer adoption is in no way impacted by whether or how the bank benefits.

Every start-up entrepreneur knows the pitch deck starts with a slide outlining the problem being solved. This is often referred to as the pain-point or friction. The deck does not outline the start-up's problem or the investor's problem. It seeks to address the customer's problem.

There are arguably few places consumers experience more friction than in managing their financial lives. Financial institutions that thrive in the future will focus first on the customer's experience. This is what the competition is doing and what all of the single proposition offerings have figured out.

If we look through the lens of the customer's needs, wants, and frustrations, it becomes much easier to prioritize product and service development. What frustrates the customer most? What keeps him or her from using a particular product? The latter point may be as much a matter of marketing and education as it is of product development. For example, more than half of people who are not using mobile banking in the US say it is because of security concerns.[3] The irony is that mobile banking is roundly considered more secure than online banking, so it seems awareness and trust-building may be an antidote to friction in that case.

Financial services companies that are able to adapt to the changing pace of consumer demand will start with a synopsis of what they are solving, and then maintain laser-sharp focus until the customer's friction has been removed. The result will be a product or service that meets the needs of the customer in an entirely new way. And with it, increased adoption, satisfaction, retention, and cost savings.

Rethink Product/Service Development Cycles

Going back to the temple-based money lenders of ancient Greece, banking's traditional branch model remained largely unchanged for thousands of years. Business model innovations typically amounted to little more than changes to fee structures or incentives. Even through modern times, the rate of change has not been characterized by a sense of urgency.

In theory, everyone knows times have changed, but this is not always expressed in practice. In fact, in 2014 McKinsey reported that banks in Europe had digitized only 20–40% of their processes, and allocated less than 1% of total spending to digital.[4] Financial institutions have a difficult time making major technology investments only to dispose of them a few years later. For banks to compete, this mind-set must change. The speed with which technology and information evolve compels financial services providers to implement systems that allow for agile decision-making and more rapid deployment. Metrics should aim to be near-term and technology should be in a constant state of beta testing.

This is what the history of banking has taught us: do not build another complex, difficult-to-upgrade system. FinTech is changing fast and it will continue to do so.

Let Someone Else Build It

Financial services tech providers are already developing cutting-edge products and services. This is what they do best, creating everything from products that ease the process of loan underwriting to biometric solutions that take advantage of things like mobile fingerprint readers and – maybe soon – brain wave detectors that allow a person to access his account simply by thinking his password. These partners can bring in the accelerators and innovators banks would not typically know about.

[3] Fiserv 2014 Consumer Trends Survey.

[4] http://www.mckinsey.com/insights/business_technology/the_rise_of_the_digital_bank.

They know how to layer on existing technology (and they also know when not to).

What financial institutions uniquely have to offer is a cultivated selection of offerings that are relevant to the communities in which they operate. These institutions have the potential to offer a level of education, support, and service that single product providers will have difficulty replicating. This is a significant competitive advantage and it is where financial institutions are smart to focus, all the while leveraging tech providers' IP and resources.

Anticipate When the Customer Will Need You, and be There

From the customer's perspective, financial services is not a sector or a business relationship. Financial services are a part of life, something people experience and interact with all day, every day. The opportunity for financial institutions is to participate in the customer's experience. This is about being in the right place at the right time, every time.

Financial institutions have access to extraordinary amounts of unused processing power that can be unleashed to improve the customer's experience. For example, if geolocation services place a mobile banking customer in a car dealership, alerts can immediately be sent to extend a loan offer. This allows the customer to know which offer (the bank's or the dealer's) is more competitive without having to do the research. Mobile banking apps can even incorporate features, such as car model and make searches or used vehicle book values. These are services that deliver value to the customer at exactly the moment they need it.

In physics, friction is the enemy of speed; in financial services technology, activity or transactional friction are the end users' nemeses. Financial institutions and technology providers around the world would do well to recognize that the future will be owned by those who make the complexity of life as simple as one currency and one language. This is what the consumer wants and needs. It is where business and services will have to go. It really is that simple.

The future of FinTech is already here. It is enabling financial services that move at the speed of life. The only question now: who will be participating in it?

FinTech is the Future Itself

By David Gyori

CEO, Banking Reports

Humanity is looking forward to a uniquely exciting period in the long history of financial services. One that is turbulent, but unusually transformative. One that is full of unexpected ideas, creative disruptors, loud successes, and threatening failures. So buckle up, my reader, and come along with me for this beautiful, but bumpy ride and keep your eyes open because you will see things that are revolutionary in the 4,000-year history of financial services.

Let's begin our journey into 2030! Take a seat next to me in this self-driving car!

1st Stop: The Survivors

Do you see these skyscrapers? This is the traditional financial district. Some companies have survived and some have not, but the basic traditional institutional forms had to remain with us from the past.

Banks remained because institutions taking household deposits on a large scale have to be heavily regulated, monitored, overseen, and controlled by financial authorities.

Insurers and re-insurers survived because taking on risk collectively and sharing costs of a negative event within a community creates a structural form that is inevitable.

Asset managers are still here because it makes sense that specialized professionals create and meticulously manage sizeable units of investments.

2nd Stop: The Cashless Beggar

You wanted to stop here. That guy with the old iPhone 10 in front of him on the street is a beggar. Why does he have the iPhone there? Well, he receives money through the "iBeg-app". You see, people passing by on the street just swing their smart-watch in front of that old iPhone 10 and punch a button. That button is the sum they want to pay. We are in a de facto cashless society. Some states have banned cash but it is hard for some old people get rid of the nostalgia of carrying a physical wallet.

For those few still using cash, old ATMs have been substituted by cash-drones and human ATMs. You can order cash from your bank and a drone delivers it to you. Peer-to-peer ATMs (aka human ATMs) are apps on your phone. You punch in how much cash you need and choose a person nearby offering that cash for a tiny commission. Money flows from your account through an escrow to the other person's account. Just like in an Uber-app you see the profile and the rating of the other person.

3rd Stop: The Self-Pay Store

Let's pop into this supermarket and buy some things. I have opened the self-pay application on my smartphone. You can see it very well: there is no cashier. That is past. People check in the items through their phone and pay by pushing a button. This way we buy more because we don't have to stand in line and we monitor real-time how much we are spending in our basket. So seamless! I have heard this story of my parents standing in line. I mean what a strange thing: you want to buy stuff and in return the shop makes you stand in line? Absurd. Shoplifters? Each basket of goods has a distinct total weight. Shoplifting is way down.

4th Stop: The Metropolitan Museum of Plastic Cards

The Metropolitan has the largest collection of plastic cards. This is so much fun! People used to have wallets with stuff like their driver's licence and these strange plastic credit cards in them. I can understand why people carried a driver's licence: imagine that cars don't drive themselves but people have to drive them! It is understandable that a licence was needed for that. But these plastics must have been totally ridiculous. Did you know that people had to swipe these through machines and often punch in numbers, and those little machines even printed a paper slip? Totally crazy! Banks issued these cards. They often paid artists to design the colors, patterns, and pictures on these small plastic cards. At some stage people used plastic cards and mobile wallets in parallel. They punched in the data from their card into their smartphone and so they used the phone to pay but they still used their plastic, too.

I am glad that you like the exhibition! There is now a really nice temporary gallery of cheques. Cheques were these written orders of payment. You are right, they did not make any sense to begin with. But it was actually quite hard to get rid of them. In the transition period people used smartphone cheque-deposit apps. They took pictures of the front and the back sides of this paper slip with their smartphone camera, sent the picture to their bank via an app, and their bank deposited the sum from the cheque onto their account. Can you imagine that?

Cruising in Office Mode

In "Office Mode" your phone's screen is appearing on these built-in laptops. This is what we call phoneputer. Your phone provides the software and the hardware and you link it to a laptop screen and keyboard so you physically work on a laptop, but it is all happening hardware- and software-wise on your smartphone. So while the car takes us to the other part of the city we will work a little bit.

We will report a data loss incident to our cloud-insurer. The insurer operates a robo call-centre. There is no complicated call-centre menu system. The artificial intelligence driven robot picks the phone up immediately. It conducts emotional recognition and senses that we are angry. A biometric fraud-protection system analyses our voice along 140 vectors and concludes that we are telling the truth, this is not a fraudulent claim.

Charity donations also have become so much easier. We will use a direct and immediate charity site. You push a button and your money immediately arrives at a random, pre-screened person's phone in a developing country.

We will visit our bank's virtual branch. Since our society eliminated cash and cheques the relevance of a branch is decreasing. A very thorough ID check can be conducted remotely, so accounts can be opened up and operated digitally in a client-not-present way. There are several kinds of virtual branches:

- A totally virtual branch that we can access via internet – advisors are AI propelled.

- A totally virtual branch, where advisors are avatars backed by humans. This is also called a drone branch.

- A virtual branch, surrounding real advisors, projected online by video.

- A video advisor with either one- or two-way video access.

- Augmented branch: a real branch that we can access via internet and get loads of digital info besides being able to video-chat to advisors.

Since I am a client at GAFA Bank I can choose which type of virtual branch to use. GAFA Bank was established by Google, Apple, Facebook, and Amazon in 2020. After the famous PayPal IPO in 2015, when eBay spun off the payment company these four giants teamed up to form something new that challenged incumbent banks. GAFA Bank's philosophy is to enable FinTech companies to sell their products through them. So they are serving as an "aggregator" for FinTechs. They aggregate the most suitable solutions for your financial need and help you choose the best alternative, which is usually a FinTech company's offer. It proved to be such a powerful strategy that traditional incumbent banks also tried it but they were less successful. This is why GAFA Bank is now the largest bank in terms of total assets globally.

We will also purchase some food for you online. We will pay with a 100% asset-backed, distributed-ledger-type digital currency called Inter-Coin. Well, you are coming from 2016 so you already know about bitcoin. Inter-Coin people have learned the necessary lessons from the story of bitcoin. They have kept the good things and made up for the missing ones. Inter-Coin obviously works in distributed-ledger logic. It is backed by Gold, Silver, Platinum, and Palladium (10%), USD (35%), EUR (10%), JPY (5%), GBP (5%), CHF (5%), and RMB (30%). You can transact with Inter-Coins globally almost real-time for free. People love it all around the globe and large economies back it happily since it creates demand for their currencies, unlike bitcoin which posed competition to them.

5th Stop: The Password Memorial

People used passwords for decades. They struggled with combinations of numbers and letters. Biometric identification alternatives have taken over. Fingerprints, retinas, irises, blinking, voice and facial recognition, hand movements, heartbeat-analysis, and typing speeds are among the exciting and innovative solutions we use nowadays. Biometrics provide more user convenience, reduction of fraud, greater consumer satisfaction, and more cost efficiency. This memorial monument has been erected in remembrance of the password, that strange phenomenon that so many people and machines spent their scarce resources on.

6th Stop: The Global Financial Regulatory Council Headquarters

In the first two decades of the 21st century globalization was already dominant, but financial services regulators were operating at national levels. Regulation itself posed a great barrier to internationalization for FinTech companies. The regulatory patchwork was complicated and impossible to fully comply with. GFRC, the Global Financial Regulatory Council, was established in 2025 and it has been doing incredible work ever since.

7th Stop: The FinTech City

This 30-storey building is home to thousands of FinTech start-ups and FinTech investors. Each floor is occupied by different FinTech companies: data analytics, personal finance, wealth management, mobile wallets, P2P payments, remittance services, challenger banks, neo-banks, API[1] providers, treasury solutions, insurance-tech, crypto-currencies, crowdfunding, P2P lending, invoice trading and cash-flow services, user interface (UI), user experience (UX) and customer experience (CX) specialists, biometrics and identification, wearables, information security, alternative risk management and scoring, artificial intelligence (AI) and robo advisors, emotional banking experts, funds, investment bankers, venture capitalists, angel investors, accelerators, incubators, labs, and co-working spaces. This is a huge building. In 2014, there were approximately 5,000 FinTech companies and 25,000 full licence banks globally. By 2016, the number of banks remained unchanged but the number of FinTech companies grew to 25,000, so it quintupled in two years. By 2030 the number of banks fell to 12,000 and the number of FinTechs grew to 50,000. FinTechs are smaller than banks, but all together they represent a huge force.

But wait a minute! I just looked at my smartwatch and now I see, my dear reader, that it is time for you to depart. Please swipe your watch here and take this shuttle! Have a safe journey back! Back to the past, back to 2016. I hope to see you again in the future, in the future of FinTech, in the future of "The Future".

---

[1] See the chapter entitled "Embracing the Connected API Economy" for further details.

A Future Without Money

By Chris Gledhill

CEO & Co-Founder, Secco Bank

Most sci-fi films have one element in common: they are set in some utopian future where they do not need money. There is no poverty, no greed, and no war. Instead the pursuit of happiness and self-betterment is the order of the day. Sounds awesome, right? It is probably too good to be true but assuming it is, in part, correct and sometime in the near future money becomes redundant, how do we get there? This section explores a roadmap from 21st-century money-obsessed cultures to a future without money.

They say to predict the future one must look to the past and there is certainly a rich history in financial services and the concept of money. It is true there have been significant changes in how money operates over the millennia but the really exciting developments have been in the last century with the advent of modern computing. There is one niggling problem though – the innovations in the field of money have been largely about convenience of form rather than the concept itself, e.g. the movement from coins to paper was great because it solved a weight problem. What we are lacking is a fundamental re-invention of the concept of money.

Take banking for example – when the internet came along banks looked at their paper forms and processes and translated them into websites. Then when smartphones emerged they squashed the same pages into smaller screens. What we have ended up with is a digital version of centuries-old constructs – few have asked whether, given today's digital technology, we would have designed financial services in the same way. The same is true for money – some of the problems money was invented to solve some 3,000 years ago have gone away, others have changed. In fact, most of the core requirements for money have gone yet we still use money. So what is the alternative? Here we look at three emerging challenger economic models and associated technologies with real potential to become the next evolutionary phase of money.

Challenger Economic Model #1: Power is Money

The energy utility market is facing disruption in the form of battery technology. When the balance tips towards it being cheaper to store than generate electricity we will see localized power management. Leaders in this space are companies like Tesla with their line of in-home battery products. These would allow households to disconnect from electricity suppliers, generate, and store their own electricity. Why stop there though? What if a household can generate more power than it uses – how does it sell that power back to households/industry with more power-hungry requirements – enter the Energy Economy (EE).

For an EE to work we need all homes wired into some sort of national grid (already present in most developed nations!) and we need individuals to replace their wallets with batteries (we already carry batteries in our pockets, wrapped up in a smartphone!). How might this work in practice? There is something interesting happening in the West African nation of Ghana. In Ghana it is not unusual to have power blackouts for 2–3 days at a time. This poses a problem for businesses reliant on mobile phone communications. Enter the Power Bank Phone, a phone popular in Ghana that is unremarkable except for a giant 10,000mAh (measure commonly used to describe the energy charge that a battery will hold) concealed within and a USB port for charging other devices. The owners of a Power Bank Phone can offer to charge other people's phones and devices in exchange for products and services – essentially turning kilowatt-hours into a currency! A comparison can be drawn with schemes like M-Pesa in Sub-Saharan Africa where phone credits are used as currency, however in an EE the currency is also a commodity. An EE would be an economic sink model where energy is generated then consumed, with our need to consume forever exceeding our ability to generate, the delta being the inherent "value". What makes this even more exciting are developments in 3D printing and so-called "replicator" technologies, named after a fictional device in Star Trek that can turn energy into matter to create tangible items. Einstein's famous equation

$$E = MC^2$$

states that energy (E) in a system (an atom, a person, the universe) is equal to its total mass (M) multiplied by the square of the speed of light (C, equal to 186,000 miles per second). When used in the context of an energy economy we have a currency that is also a commodity that can take the form of a consumable giving us a potential financial equation of …

$$£ = MC^2$$

Unlike bitcoin, a crypto-graphic proof of wasted energy or carbon trading, the byproduct of generating energy, an EE uses the energy itself as the currency.

Challenger Economic Model #2: Hyper Frugality

What happens if we mess with the supply/demand balance, if we create a massive abundance of supply that far exceeds our demand as consumers. The logical outcome would be that the "cost" of consumables continues to drop to near negligible levels – basically everything becomes free making money redundant. The same outcome would present itself if our demand for goods and services dropped to the point where we became so frugal that we had negligible consumption, again negating the need for money – this is Hyper Frugality.

To get to this state at least one of two things need to happen.

We automate our work (increase supply) – a trend we have witnessed since the industrial revolution and one that continues to accelerate is the automation of work. This has driven down the cost of extracting raw materials, the manufacturing and the distribution of goods. Coupled with robotics and artificial intelligence (AI) we might get to a state whereby the entire supply underpinning our existence becomes automated and self-maintaining to the point where all material demands are provided for. Whilst the vision is a way off, the practice is being trialled via experiments in Universal Basic Income (UBI). UBI gives citizens a basic salary they can live comfortably by, without requiring work in return. For participants the concept of money loses its weight to the point that it has negligible importance in their mind-set providing they live within reasonable means.

We change our existence model (decrease demand) – another way to disrupt supply/demand is to change our way of living to reduce our demand on resources or become part of a self-sustaining ecosystem. This model can be witnessed today in remote Amazonian tribes that form part of their ecosystem and live within the means of their habitat. Some abstract models of existence have been proposed, particularly out of the transhumanist movement. Through transhumanism we could have the ability to change our plane of existence and essentially our species to a place where money becomes irrelevant. For example, with the advent of virtual reality (VR) technologies we would spend an increasing amount of time in VR rather than real worlds. In VR worlds our consumption model need not to be dependent on physical supply and so the economic model swings towards that of negligible demand, thus money becomes redundant. Taking transhumanism to the extreme we might be able to evolve as a species beyond biological into a digital existence where central processing unit (CPU) petaflops (defined as the measure of a computer's processing speed and which can be expressed as a thousand trillion floating point operations per second) might become our commodity of choice. Either way, it is difficult to see how money in its current form would survive such a journey.

Challenger Economic Model #3: Reputational Currency

The third challenger economic model is reputation. The reputation of an individual, rather than her bank balance, is more akin to how we naturally measure someone's value outside of economics. Consider people like Mahatma Gandhi and Anjezë Gonxhe Bojaxhiu (aka Mother Teresa) who famously did not have monetary wealth but their reputational wealth was immense. On the contrary, some that we have despised most throughout history have been the richest or the most obsessed with the accumulation of monetary wealth. So if reputation is a more efficient currency mechanism how do we use reputation to gain access to products and services – the answer is that we kind of already are!

Banks and other financial services have always looked towards data points beyond someone's basic bank balance when assessing their credibility, or more importantly creditability! Companies like credit reference agencies do exactly that – they look at an individual's history of managing credit and boil it down to a credit reputational score. Outside of banking we see reputational scoring taking off with the Sharing Economy and other trust-based business models. Things like eBay buyer/seller ratings and Uber driver/passenger or AirBnB guest/host ratings are exactly that. All these scores are accumulated within silos and become effective ways to assess members by their respective communities. What we are now seeing is a cross-pollination of reputational scoring between silos and industries, e.g. someone's social media records can now be used to assess credit worthiness.

Followed through to its natural aggregated conclusion we would end up with one centralized reputational score that is an amalgamation of all walks of life. It would be your education, credit reference, social media, employment history, transactional records, connections, memberships etc. all rolled into a single score. This would be an extremely rounded way of assessing someone's trust and integrity but how do we convert this into a currency capable of dethroning money in its cold hard numeric form? Introducing reputational currencies.

Reputation Currency (RC) is akin to giving everyone his or her own individual share price and shares. With RC we would each have our own currency, the value of which is pegged to our reputation. In this RC world you would not go to a bank for a loan, you could "quantitative ease" your own currency – basically print your own cash. This would be logically the same as getting a loan as there would be more of your currency in circulation, thus devaluing your currency over a period of time – just like paying back a bank loan. An RC system opens up exciting concepts such as investing in other people's futures. You could, for example, purchase reputational currency in an undergraduate thus funding their tuition, and gain from the uplift in their reputation that comes with earning a degree. Collectively you might invest in say an Oxbridge 100 index (top 100 Oxford and Cambridge graduates) rather than a FTSE 100 index in the hope that the individual's reputation will continue to increase. Perhaps where this can benefit society most though is the charity sector. Consider someone who is homeless on the streets. Their reputational score would be very low, akin to penny stocks. You could invest in their currency then pick them up, give them training, put them in a suit, get them a job, and ultimately watch their reputational score explode and reap the benefits in owning part of their reputational stock. It would mean for the first time in human history that it becomes lucrative to help rather than exploit people.

With a reputational currency system we start to see retailers price things in an individual's currency and wrap into it things like loyalty, discounts, rewards, and offers to the point that we all get custom pricing. The concept of an item's value or worth would no longer be universal as pricing is now a very personal thing, just as reputational currencies become an inward-looking currency system. In an RC system, concepts such as relative rich and poor cease to become relevant to us and so ultimately money itself becomes irrelevant – it is like the last iteration of money before we no longer need it.

The three challenger economic models above are not exhaustive but a representative sample of what might be in store this century, triggered by the FinTech revolution. For the most part these challenger models have cultural challenges rather than technical ones. Not all would welcome the end of money, not least those that have accumulated an awful lot of the stuff! But with all the exponential technological changes it would be naive to believe our view of money will be the same as our children's or grandchildren's view.

Ethics in FinTech?

By Huy Nguyen Trieu

Managing Director, Citi; Author, *Disruptive Finance*

With no ethics, Finance 2.0 is doomed to repeat the mistakes of traditional finance. But there is an easy solution.

Finance is a strange industry. One day, it is Dr Jekyll, the other it is Mr. Hyde. On the bright side, finance plays an important social role, from helping consumers buy a house to supporting small and medium-sized enterprises (SMEs) in borrowing money. On the dark side, we all know those horror stories about predatory lenders and products that were mis-sold to bank clients.

Why is that? It is because finance is at the heart of society and the economy – try to find a dynamic economy without a strong financial sector – and therefore yields an enormous leverage. Any decisions in finance can therefore have significant impact – whether positive or negative. For example, it would be very difficult for a young graduate joining a consulting company to lose $1 million in one day – except perhaps by burning the building … The same graduate on a trading floor could lose that amount in 10 seconds. So leverage is very high – and therefore cutting corners can be a higher temptation for employees.

This brings me to ethics and values. It goes without saying that all industries and all companies need ethics and values. However, a local merchant without ethics might have less disastrous consequences for society than say a bank, or an insurance company – again, it is all about leverage. If you read this book, you might agree that some of today's start-ups will become tomorrow's financial giants – the next Googles in finance if you will. And in the same way as traditional finance can have a positive or negative impact on society, Finance 2.0 will face the same challenge – and potentially much more. Because not only could Finance 2.0 benefit from the same leverage as traditional finance, it might be much more impactful because of the use of technology.

First, is there any obvious reason why a FinTech start-up, once it becomes a $100bn company, would behave differently from today's financial conglomerates? I do not think so. I do not think that people working in a financial institution are fundamentally different – i.e. less ethical – than those working in other industries. But the higher leverage and the potential for quick gains make it much easier to succumb to temptation – if there are no proper barriers in place. Which means that today's FinTech start-ups could be exposed in the future to the same issues that banks and insurance companies have faced (e.g. mis-selling, price fixing, etc.) but also potentially other problems due to the augmented use of technology, for example:

- A better exploitation of data is already revolutionizing core pillars of finance, like lending. And there is definitely a rationale for lenders to better assess the credit risk of borrowers. It seems logical that your profession or your studies could have an impact on your ability to pay a loan. But with the billions of pieces of data that a lender could process, what if they found that having rich friends also impacted your credit score? Or if your employer announced a redundancy plan in your division, should your credit score based on big data suddenly plummet?

- Pushing the thought process further, are we certain that the more data we have, the better it will be for consumers? Let's take the example of insurance – which in essence is a mutualization of risk. Insurance works because we cannot be certain about various outcomes such as a car being stolen or health issues. But with the increasing amount of data coming from big data or wearables, we are witnessing an individualization of risks. At the moment, this translates into positive incentives ("go to the gym, get a discount"), so no one is worse off. But of course, the end game is a total individualization of each risk, and then what happens if you are overweight and never go to the gym? Would we be moving to a society where the best risks (which are usually also the most privileged part of society) would get the better conditions, and the worst ones would be significantly worst off?

These two examples show that the increasing use of technology, big data, and artificial intelligence will lead to a huge social impact from Finance 2.0. FinTech start-ups should therefore pay special attention to ethics and values; however it is not the case today. By looking at the homepages of 16 leading FinTech start-ups, what do we notice? Half of them have an "About us" category, a third have a "Help" section, many have a "News" or "What we do" link. But none of these 16 companies has a section called "Our values" or "Ethics". Obviously, we could argue that real estate on a homepage is very precious, and that "values" or "ethics" is not a differentiating factor for a start-up, and does not merit any place there.[1]

But then, this does not feel right either. Many FinTech start-ups are marketing themselves as a better, cheaper, but also more ethical alternative to traditional finance – in other words, as a choice for consumers who felt abused by the ethical lapses of banks or insurers. If this is so important, why are their values not on the front page? My feeling – from being involved with FinTech start-ups and bankers alike – is that most of this message is marketing more than anything else. And I am clearly not implying that FinTech start-ups are immoral, but rather that they are amoral.

In other words, it is not that FinTech start-ups have bad values or bad ethics, it is more that they have no values or ethics. And I do not mean it as a criticism, but as a fact – having been an entrepreneur myself. When you launch a start-up, thinking of values or ethics is usually not your first priority. Your first priorities are finding an idea, developing a product, hiring a team, raising money, finding clients, making sure you have enough money to pay your team, etc. The reality is that there is enough stress and pressure so that you rarely have the time to think of other things like ethics or values. To summarize, today's situation is not satisfactory:

- Finance 2.0 will need very strong values and ethics because of its impact on society.
- FinTech start-ups market themselves as being different from traditional finance – which suffered from lack of ethics – but do not really regard ethics as a priority either.
- This is because ethics and values do not have an immediate benefit for the survival and development of start-ups.

How do we solve that conundrum? One of the obvious answers is through regulation, which I think can be helpful but is not the answer. Regulation usually comes after something bad has happened, and is not an adequate solution. For example,

---

[1] Transferwise, eToro, Nutmeg, Ondeck, Osper, CurrencyCloud, Wealthfront, Calastone, Credit Benchmark, CrowdCube, Funding Circle, Gocardless, Invoiceable, Lending Club, Square, and Stripe. List chosen as the top 16 of 130 FinTech start-ups, http://www.disruptivefinance.co.uk/?p=354.

the banks have been subject to an intense amount of regulation since the 2008 crisis, but even in 2014 – six years later – there were still examples of clear ethical breaches by individuals that resulted in multi-billion fines. So if regulation is not sufficient to prevent individuals from acting unethically, what is? The answer in my opinion is to encourage ethical behaviour through values that have been ingrained in the culture of the start-up. For FinTech start-ups to build a culture that includes ethics and values there are three important requirements:

- Realize that values and ethics have a social and economic impact: for entrepreneurs who want to create very successful companies, understand that having strong values will not only have an impact on society, but also their own business.

- Understand that culture is developed from inception: start-up founders need to be aware that whatever values or ethics they have at the beginning of the start-up will have a huge impact down the line.

- Demand the scrutiny of stakeholders: get ethics and values on the agenda of venture capital, employees, clients, and journalists.

As I mentioned, most entrepreneurs do not focus on ethics, because ethics will not help them with the immediate survival of their start-ups. However, most entrepreneurs do want to change the world, and have big visions, and would therefore be very receptive to those ideas. Awareness will therefore already be a very big first step. If entrepreneurs understand that the culture of their future billion-dollar company is being built by all the small decisions that they take on a day-to-day basis, then that would be a very big step forward indeed. If in addition to asking their team "how will this new feature make money?" they also ask "should we be doing this?" then these are the roots of a strong culture that will permeate the whole organization. Will most entrepreneurs be willing to do that? I believe so. They just need to be aware.

I think that FinTech CEOs will also be very receptive to including ethics in their start-ups as they realize that a strong culture will not only impact society, but also the success of those start-ups. Just think of how many bank CEOs would today prefer to focus on their business, rather than spend their time changing the culture of their organizations? Or take the very telling example of Wonga, one of the first FinTech start-ups that was on its way to becoming a tremendous success story.

Wonga was launched in 2007 and used sophisticated credit scoring models to lend money to consumers, while achieving a very low default rate. Wonga was expected to be worth more than £10bn in 2015, but instead they were heavily fined by the UK regulator because "in an investigation begun by the Office of Fair Trading (OFT) and taken forward by the FCA, Wonga was found to have sent letters to customers in arrears from non-existent law firms, threatening legal action". Also, "330,000 customers who are currently in excess of 30 days in arrears, will have the balance of their loan written off and will owe Wonga nothing".[2]

Instead of becoming the next Google in finance, Wonga's future is now much more uncertain, and is subject to very heavy regulatory scrutiny. For a FinTech CEO, we are not talking about theoretical problems that could happen in 20 years' time; it is a very concrete example for a start-up pre-IPO. Of course, the reality of an entrepreneur is that it is a very hard journey, and anything not essential will be relegated to second priority. And it would be unfair only to put the onus on entrepreneurs, when society as a whole should care. The various stakeholders of a start-up should therefore also put ethics and values at the top of their priority list. For example:

- Investors and venture capitalists should demand that their start-ups communicate their values and should not tolerate unethical behaviour.

- Employees should know what the values of the founders are before they make the leap of faith and join a start-up.

- Clients should question the values of the start-up.

- Journalists should not focus solely on business models and valuations of start-ups, but also question their impacts on society.

Having myself been an entrepreneur, I am of course very wary of well-intentioned people who give general advice that is un-implementable. So here is a piece of actionable advice for FinTech entrepreneurs, start-up founders, and tech CEOs, who believe that their start-ups will change the world, and will have an impact on society, but also very selfishly want to make it a huge success.

On your homepage, next to the "About us", "Products", and "FAQ", why don't you add a link to a page called "Our values" and tell the world what you believe in? Spending time with your team to write this page will force start-up CEOs to reflect on what is important to them, what impact they can have on society, and say it to the world. This will in turn help them hire people who will share the same values, get money from investors who understand their principles, and build the right culture for a sound multi-billion-dollar company in the future of FinTech.

---

[2] http://www.fca.org.uk/news/wonga-major-changes-to-affordability-criteria, Announcement from the Financial Conduct Authority, 2 October 2014.

List of Contributors

All chapters are included in this book, all abstracts can be read online on www.TheFINTECHBook.com.

Bibhupriya Acharya
FinTech Thought Leader

www.linkedin.com/in/bibhupriya
www.twitter.com/acharyabi

See abstract:
How Your Mobile May Decide Your Next Car

Michael Adebisi
Director, NewTime Group

www.linkedin.com/pub/michael-adebisi/1/974/1a5

See abstract:
FinTech Future in Frontier Markets: Africa

George Anastasi
Chief Business Development Officer & Co-Founder, Funding Tree

www.linkedin.com/in/georgeanastasi
www.twitter.com/_GeorgeAnastasi

See abstract:
The Funding Tree Reality—A Place for Real Businesses, Funded by Real People, Started by Real Entrepreneurs

Hamish Anderson
CEO, Money Mover

www.linkedin.com/in/hamishjanderson
www.twitter.com/moneymovr

See abstract:
Peer-to-peer Solutions for UK's Growing Export Market

Nicole Anderson
CEO, FINTECH Circle Innovate

www.linkedin.com/in/nicolejmanderson
www.twitter.com/NicoleAnMo

See chapter:
Corporate Venture Capital – The New Power Broker in the FinTech Innovation Ecosystem

See abstract:
Where Have All the Pinstripes Gone?

Axel Apfelbacher
FinTech Thought Leader

https://www.linkedin.com/in/axel-apfelbacher-cfa-a13391

See chapter:
The Future of Financial Services

Anup Aryal
Senior Business Consultant at Forbes Accounting & Business Consultants

www.linkedin.com/in/aryalanup
www.twitter.com/anuparyal

See abstract:
The FinTech Revolution: Role of Regulation

Yoni Assia
CEO & Founder, eToro

www.linkedin.com/in/yassia
www.twitter.com/yoniassia

See chapter:
eToro – Building the World's Largest Social Investment Network

Dele Atanda
CEO, Digitteria

www.linkedin.com/in/deleatanda
www.twitter.com/DeleAtanda

See abstract:
Bitcoin: Crytpo-currency or Crypto-commodity?

Andrew Campbell
Data Analyst, Quantopian

www.linkedin.com/profile/view?id=375269646

www.twitter.com/TheAndyCamps

See chapter:

To Crowdsource a Hedge Fund

Collin Canright
Principal, Canright Communications

www.linkedin.com/in/collincanright

www.twitter.com/collincanright

See abstract:

The FinTech Field of Engagement

Richard Carter
Chief Executive, The Nostrum Group

www.linkedin.com/pub/richard-carter/12/b1b/9a3

www.twitter.com/richard_nostrum

See abstract:

The Advent of Digital Lending

Ruth Chamberlain
Co-Founder & Marketing, Investly

www.linkedin.com/pub/ruth-chamberlain/a/b10/b3b

www.twitter.com/Ruth_E_C

See abstract:

FinTech in Estonia

Toby Chambers
Director Strategic Planning, We Care Foundation

www.linkedin.com/pub/toby-chambers/2b/653/2bb

www.twitter.com/Ecalism

See abstract:

The Death of Financial Capitalism and the Birth of Ecalism

Susanne Chishti
CEO & Founder, FINTECH Circle; Chairwoman, FINTECH Circle Innovate

www.linkedin.com/in/susannechishti

www.twitter.com/SusanneChishti

See chapter:

Angel Investing – Access to "Smart Money" to Fund the Best FinTech Companies

See abstract:

What Are the Secrets to Creating a FINTECH Hub?

Travers Clarke-Walker
Chief Marketing Officer, Fiserv

www.linkedin.com/in/traverscw

www.twitter.com/Traverscw

See chapter:

Eliminating Friction in Customers' Financial Lives

Rael Cline
Co-Founder & CEO, MediaGamma

www.linkedin.com/in/raelcline

www.twitter.com/raelcline

See chapter:

FinTech Solutions Benefiting other Sectors

Alain Clot
CEO, Dexia Credit Local; President, France FinTech

www.linkedin.com/in/alainclot

www.twitter.com/alaintheassets

See chapter:

La (French) FinTech Connection

Claire Cockerton
CEO & Chairwoman, ENTIQ

www.linkedin.com/pub/claire-cockerton/16/23/a79

www.twitter.com/clairecockerton

See chapter:

Nurturing New FinTech Communities

See abstract:

Beyond Bitcoin: The Future of the Blockchain

Juan Colon
Co-Founder, Darwinex

www.linkedin.com/in/juancolonbolea

www.twitter.com/Darwinexchange

See abstract:

Long Tail—Returns Beyond the Efficient Frontier

Derek Corcoran
Chief Experience Officer, Avoka Technologies

www.linkedin.com/in/derekcorcoran

www.twitter.com/cxofficer

See chapter:

Avoka – An Overnight Success, 13 Years in the Making

Terry Cordeiro
FinTech Thought Leader

www.linkedin.com/pub/terry-cordeiro/10/869/874

www.twitter.com/terryc_uk

See chapter:

Design is No Longer an Option – User Experience (UX) in FinTech

Neil Costigan
CEO, BehavioSec

www.linkedin.com/in/neilcostigan

www.twitter.com/BehavioSec

See chapter:

Behavioural Biometrics – A New Era of Security

John Coulter
Managing Director, Trendrating

www.linkedin.com/pub/john-coulter/0/b95/8b6

www.twitter.com/jjcoulter44

See abstract:

Momentum Investing Gains Momentum

Felipe Daguila
Head of APAC, gTech Ads GS, Google

www.linkedin.com/in/felipedaguila

www.twitter.com/felipedaguila

See abstract:

FinTech Influence on Today's Generation

Sushankar Daspal
Digital Strategist

www.linkedin.com/in/sushankardaspal

www.twitter.com/sushankar

See abstracts:

FinTech Impact on Society—The Rise of the "Convenience Seeker" and "Optimizer"
Impact of FinTech in Emerging Economies like India

Akber Datoo
Partner, D2 Legal Technology LLP

www.linkedin.com/pub/akber-datoo/1/591/110

www.twitter.com/akber_datoo

See chapter:

FinTech Solutions in Complex Contracts Optimization

David Desharnais
Former CMO, Traxpay; SVP and GM of Digital and Commercial Platforms, American Express

www.linkedin.com/in/davdesh

www.twitter.com/davedesharnais

See chapter:

Rewiring the Deal – The Path Forward for B2B Supply Chains

Romain Dreyfus
Consultant, ADNco

www.linkedin.com/pub/romain-dreyfus/20/490/687/en

www.twitter.com/romaindreyfus?lang=fr

See abstract:

Financial Inclusion, the Main FinTech Revolution

Daniel Drummer
Management Consultant, McKinsey & Company

www.linkedin.com/pub/daniel-drummer-ll-m/12/8b6/9a/en

See abstract:

*After the Dust of Revolution Has Settled—The Long-Term View
on FinTech*

Thierry Duchamp
Founder & COO, Scaled Risk

www.linkedin.com/profile/view?id=7501456

www.twitter.com/DuchampThierry

See chapter:

Big Data is the Cornerstone of Regulatory Compliance Systems

Christine Duhaime
*Lawyer, Think Tank Founder, Digital Finance Institute
and Duhaime Law*

www.linkedin.com/pub/christine-duhaime/2/953/6a3

www.twitter.com/cduhaime

See abstract:

*How Emerging Markets Will Explode in FinTech and Solve Financial Inclusion
Problems*

Manie Eagar
President/CEO, DigitalFutures; Director, Bitcoin Alliance of Canada

www.linkedin.com/in/manieeagar

www.twitter.com/manieeagar

See chapter:

FinTech + Digital Currency – Convergence or Collision?

Jessica Ellerm
Partner Development Manager, TyroPayments

www.linkedin.com/in/jessicaellerm

www.twitter.com/JessicaEllerm

See abstracts:

Moral Hazard in Banking—Fintech's Elephant in the Room
Why Darwin Would Have Predicted FinTech

Jakob Etzel
Co-Founder, predictR and 25th-floor

https://at.linkedin.com/in/jakobetzel/en

www.twitter.com/jakobetzel

See chapter:

Predictive Algorithms – Building Innovative Online Banking Solutions

Tim Evans
Strategy, Innovation & Brand Director, Verus360

www.linkedin.com/in/timevans24

www.twitter.com/Verus_Tim

See abstract:

The FinTech Long Tail and the Rise of the Quantified Business

Sanford Ewing
President, SPAN - Financial Technology Advisory

www.linkedin.com/in/sfewing

www.twitter.com/wingofsand

See abstract:

Gaps Need To Be Closed in the FinTech Space

Nazim Faid
Corporate, Banking and Finance Lawyer, Kaufhold & Reveillaud

www.linkedin.com/profile/view?id=387856644

www.twitter.com/nazimfaid

See chapter:

Luxembourg, a Future FinTech Hub?

LIST OF CONTRIBUTORS

Markus Gnirck
Co-Founder, Startupbootcamp FinTech

www.linkedin.com/in/mgnirck/en

www.twitter.com/mgnirck

See chapter:

Singapore, the FinTech Hub for South East Asia

Mark Goldspink
CEO, The AI Corporation

https://uk.linkedin.com/in/mark-goldspink-1249881a

See abstract:

Managing a "Point of Sale" Revolution

Rodolfo Gonzalez
Partner, Foundation Capital

www.linkedin.com/in/gonzalezrodolfo

www.twitter.com/fifaifofo

See chapter:

Lending (Capital) in the 21st Century

Richard Goold
Head of Tech Law, EY (UK & Ireland)

www.linkedin.com/in/richardgoold

www.twitter.com/GooldRichard

See chapter:

Investment and Capital – Back to Basics

Daniel Gradenegger
CBDO & Co-Founder, MUUME AG

www.linkedin.com/pub/daniel-gradenegger/27/95b/b19/en

See abstract:

Effortless Shopping

Peta Grewal
Sales & Marketing, Kontainers UK

www.linkedin.com/in/petagrewal

See abstract:

The Disconnects of the Connected World: Welcome to the Great Digital Divide

Julia Groves
Founding Chair, UK Crowdfunding Association

www.linkedin.com/in/juliasgroves

www.twitter.com/juliasgroves

See abstract:

Seven Forces for Financial Innovation

Sophie Guibaud
Vice President European Expansion, Fidor Group

www.linkedin.com/in/sophieguibaud

www.twitter.com/SophieGuibaud

See chapter:

The Rise of BankTech – The Beauty of a Hybrid Model for Banks

David Gyori
CEO, Banking Reports

www.linkedin.com/in/davidgyoribankingreports

www.twitter.com/Banking_Reports

See chapter:

FinTech is the Future Itself

Sebastian Haas
Co-Founder & Managing Partner, MEP Mobile Equity Partner

www.linkedin.com/in/sebastianoskarhaas

www.twitter.com/SebOskarHaas

See chapter:

Vienna as the No.1 FinTech Hub in Mobile Payments?

Luke Hally
CEO & Founder, DragonBill

www.linkedin.com/in/lukehally

www.twitter.com/digitalGeek_au

See chapter:

FinTech Solutions for Small Businesses

Georgia Hanias
Head of Global Communications, Innovate Finance
www.linkedin.com/pub/georgia-hanias/22/836/282
www.twitter.com/GeorgiaHanias

See abstract:
Why London is the Epicentre of FinTech

Alessandro Hatami
Founder, The Pacemakers
www.linkedin.com/in/aehatami
www.twitter.com/ahatami

See chapter:
Can Banks Innovate?

Adam Hayes
Co-Founder & CEO, ChainLink
www.linkedin.com/in/ahayes4?

See chapter:
Blockchain and Crypto-currencies

George Heiler
Co-Founder, predictR
www.linkedin.com/in/georg-heiler-019b3767?

See chapter:
Predictive Algorithms – Building Innovative Online Banking Solutions

Karin Hodnigg
Product Manager, Econob
www.linkedin.com/in/karinhodnigg
www.twitter.com/hodnigg

See chapter:
Ultra-Fast Text Analytics in Trading Strategies

Damian Horton
CEO & Co-Founder, Huffle
www.linkedin.com/in/damianhorton
www.twitter.com/AussieHuffle

See abstract:
From Dynamic Growth to Dynamic Capital

Rube Huljev
Former Sales Director, CardMobili
www.linkedin.com/in/telcosales
www.twitter.com/getkingdon

See chapter:
Payments and Point of Sales (POS) Innovation

Edwin Jacobs
IT and FinTech Lawyer (Partner), time.lex
www.linkedin.com/in/jacobsedwin
www.twitter.com/FinTechLawyers

See abstract:
Creative Innovation and FinTech Laws & Regulations

Tanay Jaipuria
Business Analyst, McKinsey & Company
www.linkedin.com/in/tanayjaipuria
www.twitter.com/tanayj

See abstract:
The State of Consumer FinTech

Curt Jensen
CEO, Connexxs
https://www.linkedin.com/in/curt-jensen-11732450

See abstract:
Financing Mobile Phones

Vinesh Jha
CEO, ExtractAlpha
www.linkedin.com/pub/vinesh-jha/0/441/503

See chapter:
Crowdsourced Alpha

Oscar A. Jofre
Founder & CEO, KoreConX
www.linkedin.com/in/oscarjofre/
www.twitter.com/oscarjofre

See chapter:
Regulated Crowdfunding Eco-Systems

Susan Joseph
Founder, Leverige LLC

www.linkedin.com/in/susangjoseph

www.twitter.com/SusanJoseph1786

See chapter:

FinTech: The Not So Little Engine That Can

Bjoern Erik Juengerkes
Head of Business Development, biw AG

www.linkedin.com/in/juengerkes/en

www.twitter.com/juengerkes

See chapter:

FinTechs and Banks – Collaboration is Key

Sukhi Jutla
FinTech Thought Leader

www.linkedin.com/pub/suki-jutla/68/1ab/44b

https://twitter.com/SukhiJutla

See chapter:

India's FinTech Ecosystem

See abstracts:

How Can FinTech be Utilised to Prevent Market Manipulation Activities and Help Banks to Become More Compliant?
Will Wearable Technology Revolutionise People's Financial Health?

Manoj K. Kashyap
Assurance Partner, Banking and Capital Markets, Global FinTech Leader, PwC

www.linkedin.com/in/manoj-kashyap-69070695

See chapter:

How Emerging Technologies Will Change Financial Services

Husayn Kassai
CEO & Co-Founder, Onfido Background Checks

www.linkedin.com/in/husaynkassai

www.twitter.com/HusaynKassai

See abstract:

Background Checking: The Silent Engine Driving FinTech Forward

Robert J. Kauffman
Professor, Singapore Management University

www.twitter.com/rob7585/

See abstract:

Faster Clearing and Settlement of Payments: A Freakonomics View of a "Hidden Side" of the Future of Money

Scott Kerr
Corporate Partner, Harper Macleod LLP

www.linkedin.com/in/scotttrkerr

www.twitter.com/ScottKerr_MN

See abstract:

FinTech Hubs—Spokes or Cogs?

Sudhir Kesavan
Head of Product Management, FinTech & Digital Solutions

www.linkedin.com/pub/sudhir-kesavan/0/a74/627

www.twitter.com/Sudkes

See abstract:

FinTech and the Promise of Prosperity

Faisal Khan
Banking & Payments Consultant, Faisal Khan & Company

www.linkedin.com/in/faisalkhan99

www.twitter.com/babushka99

See abstract:

The Difficulty Facing the Payment Industry in Pakistan

Max Kortrakul
CEO, StockRadars

www.linkedin.com/in/teerachart

www.twitter.com/maxxam

See abstract:

Why Simplicity Can Make Stock Investment a Lot Sexier?

Benedikt Kramer
Founder & CEO, BCB Biometric Credit Bureau

www.linkedin.com/in/benediktkramer

See abstract:

Technology Changed Micro-Finance in Africa

Arunkumar Krishnakumar
Senior Manager, FS Data, FinTech & Blockchain, PwC

www.linkedin.com/in/arunkumarkrishnakumar

www.twitter.com/Karunk

See abstract:

Data—Fuel of the FinTech Customer Journey

Sachin Kumar
FinTech Enabler

www.linkedin.com/pub/sachin-kumar/6/733/a43

www.twitter.com/SachinLKumar

See abstract:

Bank Orchestrated Auto Purchase of Tomorrow

Stuart Lacey
Founder & CEO, Trunomi

www.linkedin.com/pub/stuart-lacey/29/b46/585

www.twitter.com/trunomi

See abstract:

Why Business-led Data Monetisation is a Mere Stepping-stone to the Consent to Share End Game

Daniel Liebau
Founder, Lightbulb Capital

www.linkedin.com/pub/dan-liebau/3/692/b13

www.twitter.com/liebauda

See abstract:

Let's Value FinTech

Marc Lien
Director of Innovation & Digital Development, Lloyds Banking Group

www.linkedin.com/in/marclien

www.twitter.com/marclien

See chapter:

Partnerships Are the Key to Addressing Financial and Digital Exclusion

Bernard Lunn
Founding Partner, Daily FinTech Advisers

www.linkedin.com/in/bernardlunn

www.twitter.com/bernardlunn

See chapter:

Banks Partnering with FinTech Start-ups to Create an Integrated Customer Experience

Antonios Manessis
Co-Founder & CEO, BETCAFE.com

www.linkedin.com/in/manessis

www.twitter.com/Tonemanessis

See abstract:

Betting with Cryptocurrencies

Spiros Margaris
Advisor, FinTech Forum; CEO, Margaris Advisory

www.linkedin.com/pub/spiros-margaris/b/735/57b

www.twitter.com/SpirosMargaris

See chapter:

The FinTech Supermarket – The Bank is Dead, Long Live the Bank!

See abstract:

The FinTech Agent Who Came in from the Cold

Nako Mbelle
Founder & CEO, FinTech Recruiters Inc

www.linkedin.com/in/fintechrecruiters

www.twitter.com/NakoMbelle

See abstract:

9 Hiring Strategies to Win the FinTech Talent War

Warren Mead
Partner, Head of Challenger Banks and Global Co-Lead FinTech, KPMG

www.linkedin.com/in/warrenmeadkpmguk

www.twitter.com/mrfintech

See chapter:

Banking and the E-Book Moment

Anshuman Mehta
Founder & CEO, Casteller, Inc.

www.linkedin.com/in/connectanshuman

www.twitter.com/anshumanmehta

See abstracts:

Disrupting the Disruptors—In Defense of the Freelancer

Towards B2B Marketplace Innovation

Michael Mellinghoff
Managing Director, TechFluence

www.linkedin.com/pub/michael-mellinghoff/0/372/646

www.twitter.com/Mellinghoff

See chapter:

The Digital Investment Space – Spanning from Social Trading to Digital Private Banking – A FinTech Sector Made for Disruption?

Rébecca Menat
Director of Communications, The Assets

www.linkedin.com/profile/view?id=306963402

www.twitter.com/RebMelMen

See chapter:

Why We're so Excited About FinTech

Devie Mohan
Marketing of Services, Thomson Reuters

www.linkedin.com/in/deviemohan

www.twitter.com/devie_mohan

See abstract:

A Trend Analysis: Which Path Will FinTech Choose?

Eric Mouilleron
Founder & CEO, Bankable

www.linkedin.com/pub/eric-mouilleron/12/391/390

www.twitter.com/wearebankable

See chapter:

Bankable – Banking as a Service

Neringa Murauskiene
Export Manager, Flokati

www.linkedin.com/pub/neringa-murauskiene/77/552/848

www.twitter.com/FOBISS_BV

See abstract:

Would You Employ Artificial Intelligence to Manage the Cash at Your Bank?

Sam Murrant
Consumer Payments Analyst, DataMonitor

www.linkedin.com/pub/sam-murrant/55/97a/461

www.twitter.com/SamMurrant

See abstract:

The Big Payments Question: Why Should I Use This?

Kunal Nandwani
Founder & CEO, uTrade Solutions

www.linkedin.com/in/kunalnandwani

www.twitter.com/kunalnandwani

See abstract:

Future of FinTech

Indrek Neivelt
CEO, Pocopay

www.linkedin.com/pub/indrek-neivelt/23/b68/271

See abstract:

FinTech Alliances to Compete with Banks

Wah Chun Ng
Graduate Analyst, Credit Suisse

www.linkedin.com/in/wahchun

www.twitter.com/wahchun927

See abstract:

Why You Should Launch Your FinTech Startup in Singapore

Rachel Nienaber
VP Engineering, Currency Cloud

www.linkedin.com/in/rachelswailes

www.twitter.com/currency_cloud

See chapter:

Banks Need to Think Collaboration Rather Than Competition

Yinka Opaneye
CEO, OKA Consulting

twitter.com/OKAConsulting

See abstracts:

Financial Inclusion/ FinTech Exclusion

In 'FinTech' We Trust

Péter Orlovácz
Former Head of Digital, AXA Bank Europe

www.linkedin.com/in/peteror

www.twitter.com/peteror_

See chapter:

The Insurance Opportunity

Carrie Osman
Chief Provocateur & Co-Founder, CRUXY&CO

www.linkedin.com/pub/carrie-osman/16/a2/757

www.twitter.com/carrie_loves_

See abstract:

The Future of FinTech: It's Time to Disrupt

Francisco Meré Palafox
CEO & Co-Founder, Bankaool, S.A. Institución de Banca Múltiple

www.linkedin.com/pub/francisco-mer%C3%A9-palafox/5/4b4/454

www.twitter.com/paco_mere

See chapter:

Why Am I Not Gonna Be Able to Enter a Bank?

Jean-Michel Pailhon
FinTech Thought Leader

www.linkedin.com/in/jeanmichelpailhon

See chapter:

La (French) FinTech Connection

Kitty Parry
Founder & CEO, Social Media Compliance Ltd

www.linkedin.com/in/kittyparry

www.twitter.com/KittyParry

See abstract:

When Innovation and Technology Are Global and Rapid, Can Financial Services Keep Up?

Jeff Paterson
Co-Founder, Fourex

See abstract:

A Common Cents Solution To Currency Exchange

Brandon Pazitka
Brand Provocateur & Consultant, CRUXY&CO and BJLP Ltd.

www.linkedin.com/in/bpazitka

www.twitter.com/CRUXY_CO

See abstract:

What it Takes to Create a Consumer-centric Solution?

Richard Peers
Director, Financial Services Industry, Microsoft

www.linkedin.com/in/microsofta2z

www.twitter.com/peerster

See chapter:

Embracing the Connected API Economy

Jesus Perez
CEO, Financialred.com

www.linkedin.com/in/jesusperezsanchez

www.twitter.com/especulacion

See abstract:

Media Role in FinTech

Sarah-Rose Perry
Risk & Compliance Manager, WestPac Institutional Bank

www.linkedin.com/in/srrogers

www.twitter.com/sarahroserogers

See abstract:

The Evolution of Banks in a Mobile Era: Internal Innovation, Unbundling, or Just Rolling the Dice

Patrick Pfeffer
CEO, Aescuvest

www.twitter.com/aescuvest

See abstract:

From FinTech to HealthCare

Dobromir Piekarski
CEO, Finanteq and eLeader

www.linkedin.com/in/dobromirpiekarski

www.twitter.com/dobry365

See abstract:

*How Superwallets Move Banks From the Background
to the Front of the Value Chain*

Loic Pitrou
APAC Director, Additiv and Solutions2Markets

www.linkedin.com/in/loicpitrou

www.twitter.com/FinTechSG

See abstracts:

APAC Digital Journey for Private Banking
Robo-Advisors in APAC

Martin Prebio
Co-Founder, predictR and 25th-floor

www.linkedin.com/in/martinprebio

www.twitter.com/bountin

See chapter:

*Predictive Algorithms – Building Innovative Online
Banking Solutions*

Frederique Prevost
Executive Coach, Aware Square Ltd

www.linkedin.com/in/fredprevost

www.twitter.com/AwareSquare

See abstract:

FinTech Evolution Needs Ethics Revolution

Andreas Pusch
CEO, finatris Financial Solutions

https://de.linkedin.com/in/andreas-pusch-191440

See abstract:

Private Banking 2020

Efi Pylarinou
Founding Partner, Daily FinTech Advisers

www.linkedin.com/in/efipylarinou

www.twitter.com/efipm

See abstract:

Mirror, Mirror on the Wall, Where is the Juiciest Part of This All?

Kayar Raghavan
Angel Investor and Non-Executive Director

www.linkedin.com/pub/kayar-raghavan/0/88/931

www.twitter.com/kayarraghavan

See chapter:

Providing Capital and Beyond

Shashi Rana
Enterprise and Strategy Architect, Microsoft

www.linkedin.com/in/srana

See chapter:

Embracing the Connected API Economy

Zahir Rana
Chairman, Spior

www.linkedin.com/in/zahirrana

www.twitter.com/zahirrana2

See abstract:

Financial ICT Infrastructure

Liliana Reasor
CEO & Founder, Novus Ordo Capital

www.linkedin.com/pub/liliana-reasor/7/b4/827

www.twitter.com/lreasor

See abstract:

Is Bitcoin Merely a Payment System and Who Might Want to Hold Bitcoins?

Cesar Jimenez Richardson
VP, Sales and Operations, Strands Americas

www.linkedin.com/in/jimenezcesar

www.twitter.com/alwayscesar

See chapter:

*Smartphones, FinTech, and Education – Helping the Unbanked
Reach Financial Inclusion*

Robert Ritacca
Co-Founder & CIO, GoVesting.com

www.linkedin.com/pub/robert-ritacca/49/139/561

See abstract:

The Future of Robo-Advisory and RIA's: Working Together to Provide Uber Like P2P Benefits

Jorge Ruiz
Global Head, Digital Acceleration, Citi

www.linkedin.com/in/jorgearuiz

www.twitter.com/jorge_a_ruiz

See chapter:

The Next Chapter in Citi's Story of Innovation

Valentin Saportas
CEO, MortgageHippo

www.linkedin.com/pub/valentin-saportas/7/132/348

www.twitter.com/vsaportas

See abstract:

The Changing Role of Loan Officers in Online Lending

Markus Schicho
CEO, Econob

www.linkedin.com/pub/markus-schicho/55/788/8a0/en

www.twitter.com/econob

See chapter:

Ultra-Fast Text Analytics in Trading Strategies

Frank Schwab
Co-Founder, FinTech Forum; Former CEO, Fidor TecS AG

www.linkedin.com/in/frankschwab

www.twitter.com/FrankJSchwab

See chapter:

The Rise of BankTech – The Beauty of a Hybrid Model for Banks

Mike Simcock
CEO, ClearMacro

www.linkedin.com/in/michael-simcock-49547786

See abstract:

Investment Communication and Technology, The New Frontier

Paolo Sironi
Thought Leader, Wealth Management Investment Analytics, IBM

www.linkedin.com/in/paolosironipso

www.twitter.com/thepsironi

See chapter:

My Robo Advisor was an iPod – Applying the Lessons from Other Sectors to FinTech Disruption

Karl M Sjogren
Blogger, FairShare Model

www.linkedin.com/in/karlsjogren

www.twitter.com/fairsharemodel

See abstract:

The Fairshare Model

Jan Skoyles
Marketing Manager, Coinsilium

www.linkedin.com/in/janskoyles

www.twitter.com/Skoylesy

See abstract:

FinTech: A Golden Opportunity

Christopher Smith
Former Content Editor, Syndicate Room

www.linkedin.com/in/smithcn

www.twitter.com/smithcn

See chapter:

Leading the Way with an Investor-led Approach to Crowdfunding

Vipul Somaiya
Co-Founder, Tax-Plus Accountants

www.linkedin.com/in/vipulsomaiya

See abstract:

Unleashing Emerging India

Frank Sonder
CEO & Co-Founder, foresee

www.linkedin.com/in/franksonder

See chapter:

Banking Like Water

Andra Sonea
FinTech Thought Leader

www.linkedin.com/in/andrasonea

www.twitter.com/andrasonea

See chapter:

So, You Think the Innovation Lab is the Answer?

See abstract:

Banking Architecture: A Framework for Assessing If and Where Your FinTech Concept Might Apply

Matthieu Soule
Senior Strategic Analyst, L' Atelier BNP Paribas US

www.linkedin.com/in/matthieusoule/en

www.twitter.com/matthieusoule

See abstract:

Future of Privacy for Financial Services: From Physical Vaults and Bank Secrecy to Data Leverage and Digital Literacy?

Bob Stark
VP Strategy, Kyriba Corporation

www.linkedin.com/pub/bob-stark/3/488/b61

www.twitter.com/kyribacorp

See abstract:

Why the CFO is the MVP of the Organization

Daniel Steeves
Consultant, Advisor, Architect and CEO at Beyond Solutions

www.linkedin.com/in/danielsteeves

www.twitter.com/DanielSteeves

See chapter:

The Social Impact of FinTech in Nigeria

Russell Stern
CEO, SolarFlare Communications

www.linkedin.com/pub/russell-stern/1/22/b71

www.twitter.com/stern10g

See abstract:

The Next Generation Cyber Defense—Distributed, Active Security

Narendiran Sundararajan
Manager – Research (ICT), Centre for Innovation Incubation and Entrepreneurship, IIM Ahmedabad

www.linkedin.com/in/naren2108

www.twitter.com/naren2108

See chapter:

India's FinTech Ecosystem

Shankar Sundarrajan
Digital Strategist

www.linkedin.com/profile/view?id=6581740&trk=nav_responsive_tab_profile

www.twitter.com/Shankarsundar

See abstracts:

After Emotional Quotient and Intelligent Quotient, Make Way for "Financial Wellbeing Quotient"

We All Have Some Bytes of the Customer Data but Who Will Own the Customer Relationship and What Will Be the Distribution Model?

Avinash Swamy
Industry Marketing, Banking and Financial Markets, IBM

www.linkedin.com/in/avinashswamy

www.twitter.com/AvinashSwamy

See abstract:

How Are Banks Responding to FinTech?

Brian W. Tang
Managing Director, Asia Capital Markets Institute (ACMI)

www.linkedin.com/pub/brian-w-tang/3/129/713

www.twitter.com/CapMarketsProf

See chapter:

Crowdfunding and Marketplace (P2P) Lending – Online Capital Marketplaces as New Asset Classes to Access Funding

Paolo Tasca
Economist, Deutsche Bundesbank

www.linkedin.com/in/ptasca

www.twitter.com/PaoloTasca

See chapter:

Blockchain and Crypto-currencies

Denis Thomas
Management Consultant, KPMG

www.linkedin.com/in/tdenisk

www.twitter.com/tdenisk

See chapter:

Payment Solutions Including Apple Pay

Dr Marc Torrens
CIO, Strands Labs

www.linkedin.com/in/marctorrens

www.twitter.com/marctorrens

See chapter:

Banking on Innovation Through Data

Stefano L. Tresca
Managing Partner, iSeed; Author, Mentor and Investor

www.linkedin.com/in/stefanotresca

www.twitter.com/StartupAgora

See chapter:

The Rise of the Rest in FinTech

Huy Nguyen Trieu
Managing Director, Citi; Author, Disruptive Finance

www.linkedin.com/in/huynguyentrieu

www.twitter.com/Huynguyentrieu

See chapter:

Ethics in FinTech?

Marcin Truszel
CEO, Kontomatik

www.linkedin.com/in/marcintruszel

www.twitter.com/mtruszel

See chapter:

Current Trends in Financial Technology

Daniel Tyoschitz
Strategy Coach, 650 Labs

www.linkedin.com/in/danieltyoschitz/en

www.twitter.com/DanielTyoschitz

See abstract:

The Lens To The Future—Still Silicon Valley

Alan Underdown
Managing Director, UK/Europe at Satuit Technologies

www.linkedin.com/in/underdown

www.twitter.com/underdown_alan

See abstract:

How Virtual Reality is Becoming Actuality in Financial Services

Teun van den Dries
Founder & CEO, GeoPhy

www.linkedin.com/in/teunvandendries

www.twitter.com/TeunvandenDries

See abstract:

Big Data Analytics—Opening Up the Opaque Market of Real Estate

Eric van der Kleij
Former Head of Level 39 Technology Accelerator; Managing Director, ENTIQ

www.linkedin.com/pub/eric-van-der-kleij/35/676/8a7

www.twitter.com/Ericvanderkleij

See chapter:

Tech Giants Becoming Non-Bank Banks

Fabian Vandenreydt
Global Head of Securities Markets, Innotribe & The SWIFT Institute, SWIFT

www.linkedin.com/in/fvandenreydt

www.twitter.com/fvandenreydt

See chapter:

FinTech Trends from the Frontline – Building Collaborative Opportunities for Start-ups, Market Infrastructures, and Wholesale Banks

Lea Veran
CMO, FinexKap

www.linkedin.com/pub/l%C3%A9a-veran/40/85/4/en

www.twitter.com/Leaveran

See abstract:

A Cry for Regulation

Fabrizio Villani
Group Manager, FinTech Italia

www.linkedin.com/in/fabriziovillani/en

www.twitter.com/FintechItalia

See abstracts:

*FinTech Global Tour Goes to Italy to Discover an Entrepreneurial
Renaissance
FinTech Global Tour Goes to Spain to Find Both Local & Global
Innovation*

Gerben Visser
Managing Partner, Incubasia Ventures

www.linkedin.com/in/vissergerben

www.twitter.com/gerbenvisser

See chapter:

Singapore, the FinTech Hub for Southeast Asia

Dirk Vonden
Senior Manager, ARKADIA Management Consultants GmbH

www.linkedin.com/in/dirkvonden

www.twitter.com/Dvonden

See abstract:

It's the End of the Bank As We Know It

Rich Wagner
CEO, Advanced Payment Solutions

www.linkedin.com/pub/rich-wagner/1/5aa/3b5

www.twitter.com/Rich_at_APS

See abstract:

Traditional Banking Systems Not Fit for Purpose: UK's Unwanted Borrowers

Benjamin Wakeham
Founder & CEO, Pollen

www.linkedin.com/in/benjiwakeham

www.twitter.com/BenjiWakeham

See chapter:

The Next Big Innovation in FinTech – Identity

Johannes Waldstein
Co-Founder & UK MD, Finalogic

www.linkedin.com/in/johanneswaldstein

www.twitter.com/waldsteinj

See abstract:

The Agile Stadium (FinTech in Sports)

Grégory Weber
Director and FinTech Leader, PwC Luxembourg

www.linkedin.com/pub/gr%C3%A9gory-weber/5/610/610

See chapter:

How Emerging Technologies Will Change Financial Services

Jan C. Wendenburg
Member, Executive Board, XCOMpetence AG

www.linkedin.com/in/wendenburg

www.twitter.com/JanWendenburg

See chapter:

Global Compliance is Key

Ivo Weevers
Co-Founder, Albert – Mobile Invoicing App

www.linkedin.com/in/ivoweevers

www.twitter.com/ivoweevers

See chapter:

Design is No Longer an Option – User Experience (UX) in FinTech

Claudio Wilhelmer
Co-Founder & CEO, Sweep GmbH

www.linkedin.com/pub/claudio-wilhelmer/66/5a0/982

See abstract:

Payment 2.0: The Race to Become Your Mobile Wallet Has Begun

Nick Williams
Consumer Digital Director, Lloyds Banking Group

www.linkedin.com/in/nick-williams-4a285710

www.twitter.com/nick_williams38

See chapter:

*Partnerships Are the Key to Addressing Financial
and Digital Exclusion*

Michael David Wolper
CMO, GlobeOne

www.linkedin.com/in/michaeldwolper

www.twitter.com/MichaelWolper

See chapter:

Remittances – International FX Payments at Low Cost

Roman Zrazhevskiy
SVP Product Strategy, ETNA

www.linkedin.com/in/romanzrazhevskiy

www.twitter.com/etnasoft

See abstract:

How to Build FinTech Without Going Broke

Nasir Zubairi
Venture Partner, FinLeap

www.linkedin.com/in/nasirzubairi

www.twitter.com/naszub

See abstract:

How To Get A FinTech Right

All chapters are included in this book, all abstracts can be read online on www.TheFINTECHBook.com.

Index

E

F

S